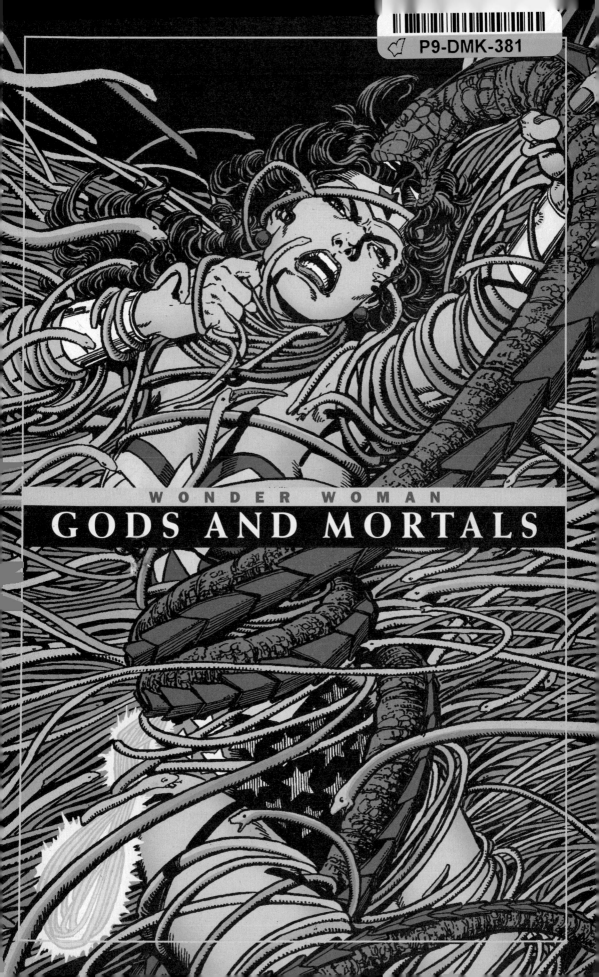

WONDER WOMAN

GODS AND MORTALS

WONDER WOMAN: GODS AND MORTALS

Published by DC Comics. Cover, introduction and compilation
copyright © 2004 DC Comics. All Rights Reserved.

Originally published in single magazine form in WONDER WOMAN #1-7.
Copyright © 1987 DC Comics. All Rights Reserved. All characters, names,
their distinctive likenesses and related elements are trademarks of
DC Comics. The stories, characters and incidents featured in this publication
are entirely fictional. DC Comics does not read or accept unsolicited
submissions of ideas, stories or artwork.

DC Comics, 1700 Broadway, New York, NY 10019
A Warner Bros. Entertainment Company
Printed in Canada. First Printing.
ISBN: 1-4012-0197-0

Cover art by George Pérez
Cover color by Tom Smith
*Inking reconstruction on pages 139-140, 142-148, 150-151, 153-154,
156-158, and 160 by Bob Wiacek
Special thanks to Phil Jimenez

WONDER WOMAN
GODS AND MORTALS

GEORGE PÉREZ LEN WEIN GREG POTTER Writers

GEORGE PÉREZ Penciller

BRUCE PATTERSON Inker

TATJANA WOOD Colorist

JOHN COSTANZA Letterer

GEORGE PÉREZ Original Series Covers

Bob Wiacek Inking reconstruction on Chapter Six*

Heroic Age Color reconstruction and enhancement

Wonder Woman created by William Moulton Marston

INTRODUCTION BY
GEORGE PÉREZ

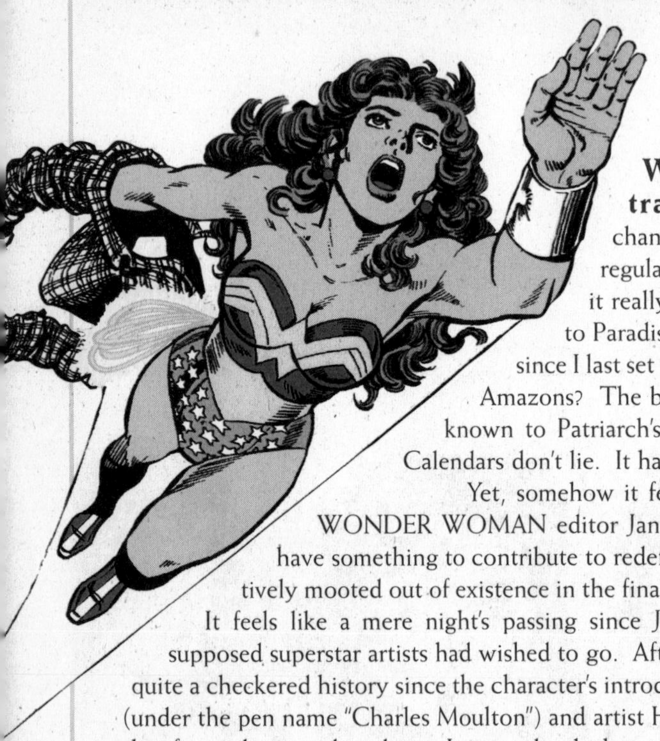

Wow — it sure feels strange traveling this road again. So many changes have dotted the landscape since I last regularly trekked these mythical pathways. Has it really been over 16 years since I first journeyed to Paradise Island? Has it been longer than a decade since I last set foot on Themyscira, the mythical isle of the Amazons? The birthplace of Princess Diana — the heroine known to Patriarch's World as Wonder Woman? Yes, it has. Calendars don't lie. It has indeed been a long time.

Yet, somehow it feels like only yesterday that I sat in then-WONDER WOMAN editor Janice Race's office and suggested that I may have something to contribute to redefining the Amazon Princess, who was effectively mooted out of existence in the final pages of CRISIS ON INFINITE EARTHS. It feels like a mere night's passing since Janice embraced me for going where few supposed superstar artists had wished to go. After all, the WONDER WOMAN series had quite a checkered history since the character's introduction by writer William Moulton Marston (under the pen name "Charles Moulton") and artist H.G. Peter in 1940 and had become a series that few volunteered to draw. It was a book that was assigned to whoever might be available, regardless of interest or compatibility. Despite some creative highpoints during its four decades of publication, there had been far too many lows along the way, and the character had been revamped so many times that its continuity had become a muddled mess.

Then came CRISIS ON INFINITE EARTHS, a series intended to simplify the DC Universe — and one of the prime candidates for a continuity cleanup was its first and best-known super-heroine. The problem was, however, that while the company wanted a new Wonder Woman, it wasn't quite set on what exactly "new" meant. Several creators had come in with concepts that retained little but the Wonder Woman name. Some of these were actually good ideas, worthy of treatment and development — but they just weren't Wonder Woman. DC may have wanted a new Wonder Woman, but it still wanted to keep its iconic character recognizable.

Enter Greg Potter. Greg's proposal stuck to the basic Wonder Woman origin with certain touchstones as Paradise Island, Steve Trevor and the contest to determine which Amazon would go to "Man's World" still in place, albeit in altered forms. It was Greg who conceived of the Amazons being reincarnations of women murdered through pre-history and that Ares would be the first major threat that prompted Diana to go to Man's World — specifically Greg's hometown of Boston, Massachusetts — to save it from the machinations of the God of War. However, beyond that there were several aspects to Greg's treatment that didn't sit right with the DC staffers, especially the female employees. Considering that Wonder Woman was DC's female icon, that didn't bode well for the reboot. Also problematic was the artist chosen for the new series, who wasn't an ideal choice either. But DC needed to get a WONDER WOMAN series on the stands, and it looked like they'd have to settle for what they had since no other options seemed available. That's when I walked into Janice Race's office, on what seems like only yesterday.

I had wanted to do a specific Wonder Woman story arc for years. I was inspired by a 2-part NEW TEEN TITANS story that Marv Wolfman wrote in which I got to draw Paradise Island for the first time and got my first taste of drawing Greek gods. Further inspired by Walt Simonson's take on Marvel's *Thor* and all the great fantasy films of Ray Harryhausen, I came up with the concept that would eventually become the "Challenge of the Gods" arc that appeared in issues #10-14 of my run. When CRISIS effectively cancelled the original WONDER WOMAN series I figured that that story would just be one of many ideas that never saw fruition. But, when I learned of the situation of the WONDER WOMAN relaunch — and knowing what wonders superstar creators like Frank Miller and, especially, John Byrne had done with rethinkings of Batman and Superman, respectively — I rather impulsively suggested that I might like to take a crack at WONDER WOMAN for at least the first 6 issues, allowing me to finally do that "Challenge of the Gods" story after all. Remember the embrace from Janice I mentioned earlier? Well, it happened that yesterday.

As comics history, and these collections, will attest, my run exceeded my initial 6-month commitment by nearly 5 years. Janice Race left DC to be replaced by the invaluable Karen Berger as editor of WONDER WOMAN. I cannot overstate Karen's contributions to the success of my run on the series. One of the most astute, intelligent and far-thinking individuals that has ever graced this industry, tough, but fair, knowing when to lean in and when to back off, Karen is the gold standard by which I judge all editors. I cannot thank her enough for helping me through my first attempts at writing.

And I cannot let another paragraph go by without acknowledging and thanking my other collaborators in crime, like Greg Potter, for starting the ball rolling. Greg may have left early when the series' direction veered my way, but he was there first and several of his concepts still stand as part of Wonder Woman's new history. And mere thanks seem woefully inadequate to express my gratitude for scripter Len Wein and inker Bruce Patterson's contributions in making me look better than I was. Len's words brought life and clarity to my ideas, while Bruce's brush added lushness and sparkle to my pencils. The series would have been a lot less without them.

I could go on about what it was like to actually plot and draw the stories collected here in this volume, but then this would be just about me, and not about the true star of this book, Princess Diana, my dear Wonder Woman. I am eternally grateful to all the creators and fans, past and present, who allowed me to walk the path to Themyscira, a journey begun only yesterday and which I travel again today.

I hope you enjoy the journey as much as I did — and do.

George Pérez
December 14, 2003

George Pérez is one of the most popular and influential artists working in the comics industry today, with a career spanning over three decades. In addition to his relaunch of WONDER WOMAN, his work highlights include JUSTICE LEAGUE OF AMERICA, THE NEW TEEN TITANS and CRISIS ON INFINITE EARTHS for DC Comics, Avengers *and* Fantastic Four *for Marvel Comics, and* Solus *for CrossGen Entertainment. He recently completed the highly anticipated AVENGERS/JLA crossover and is currently working on THE NEW TEEN TITANS: GAMES graphic novel.*

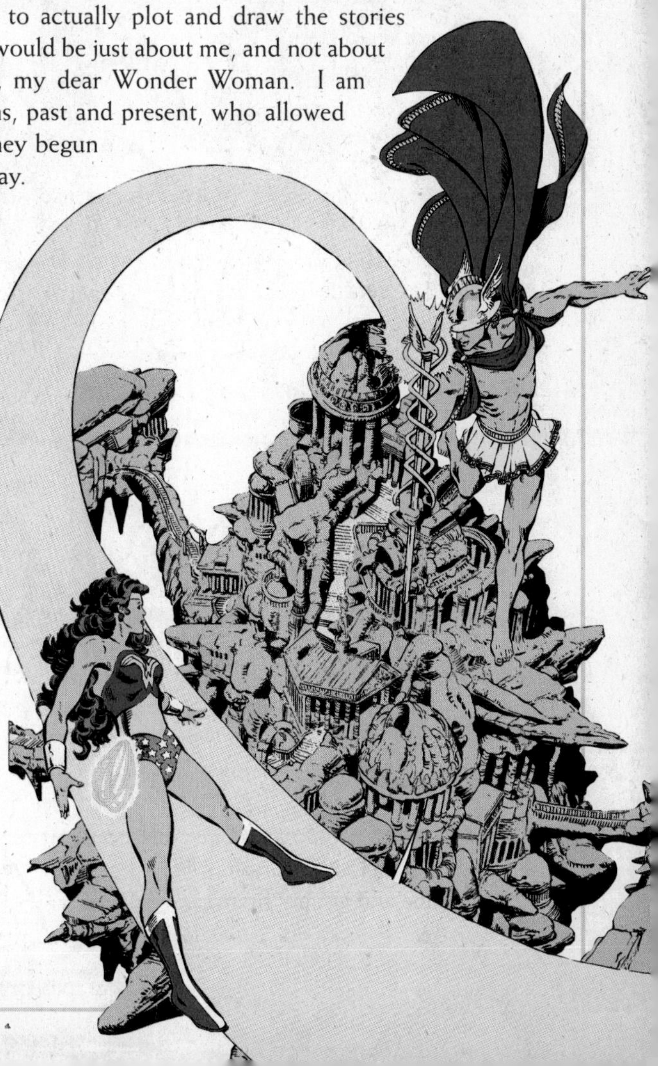

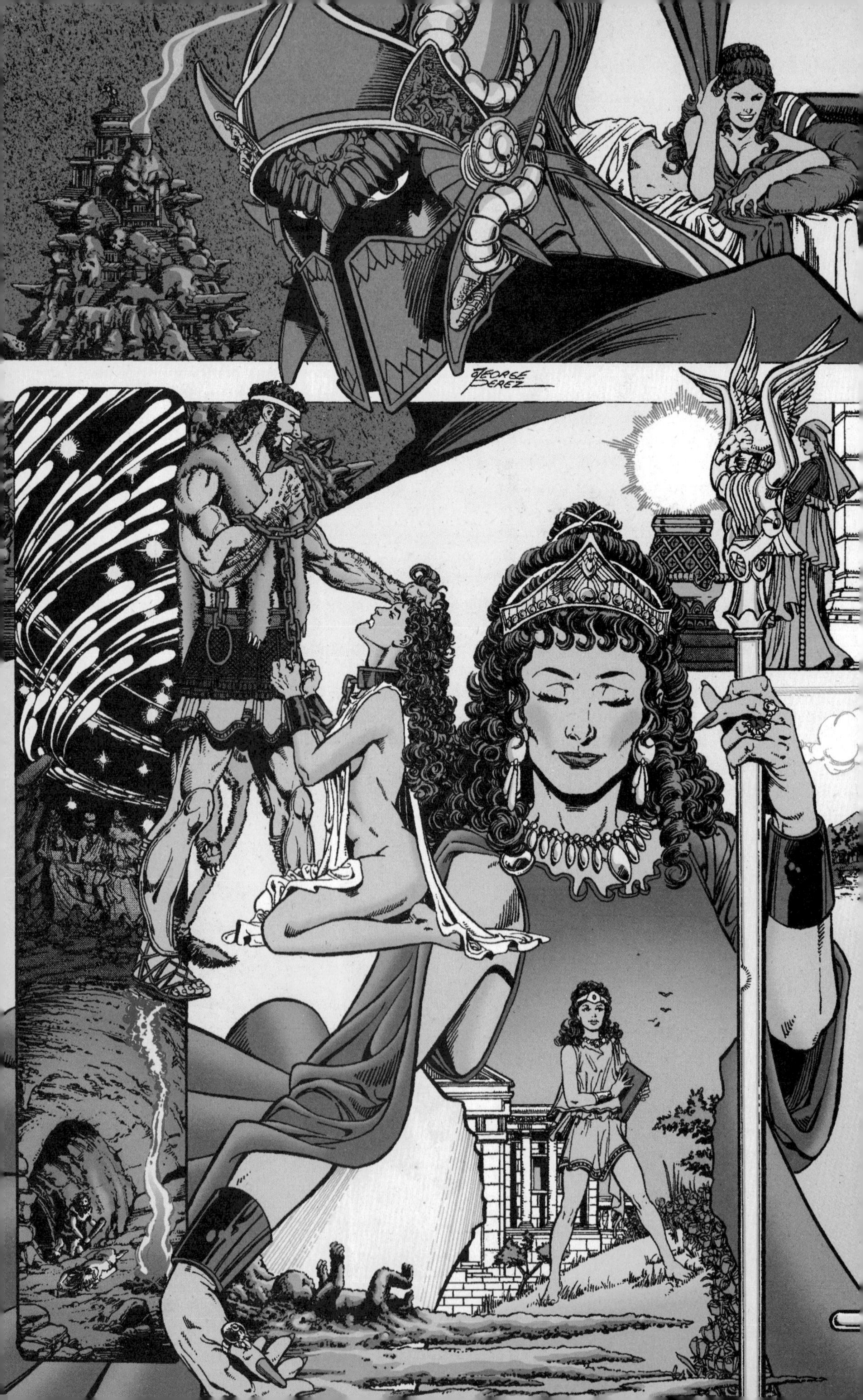
GEORGE PEREZ

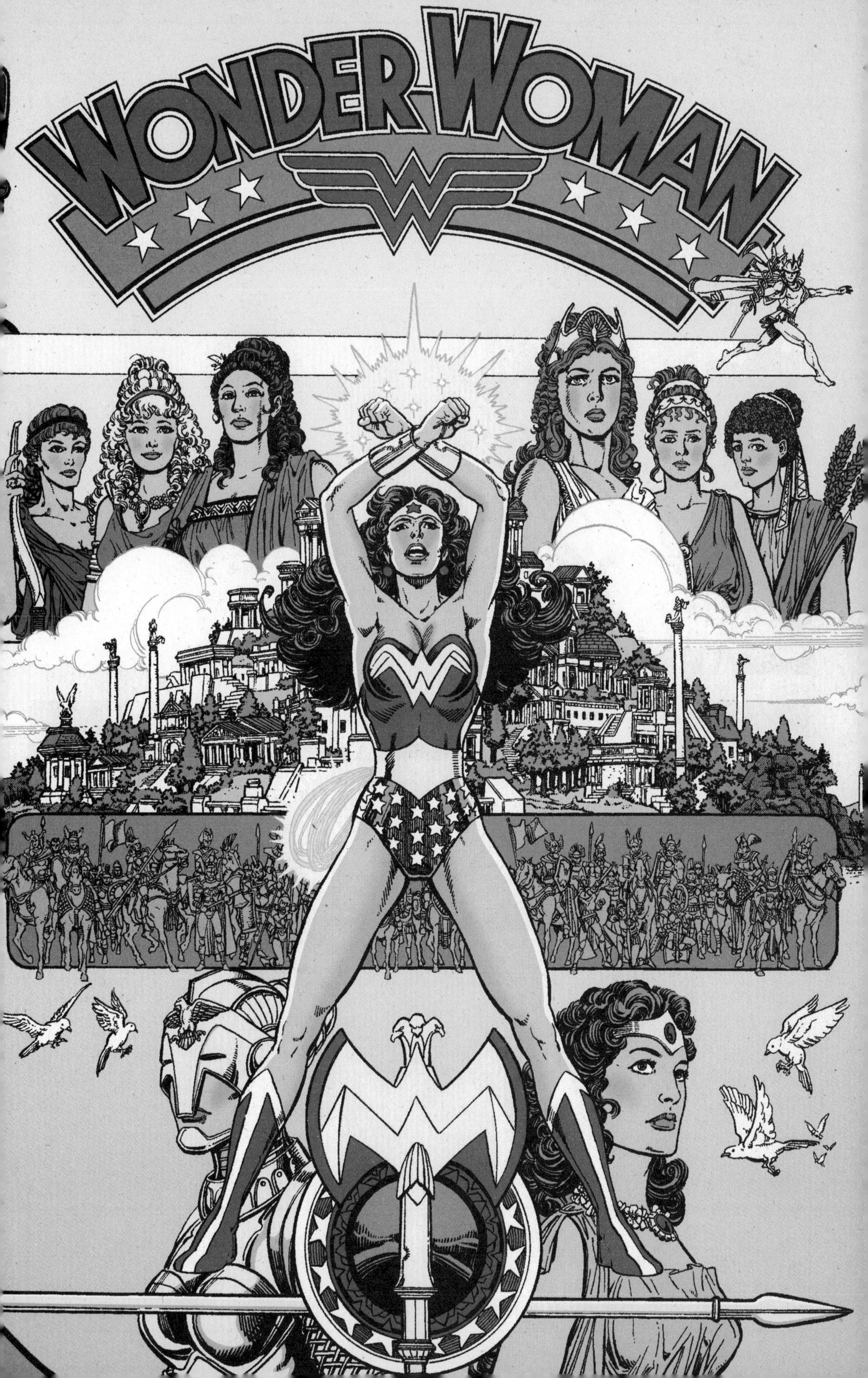
WONDER WOMAN

WONDER WOMAN

CHAPTER ONE

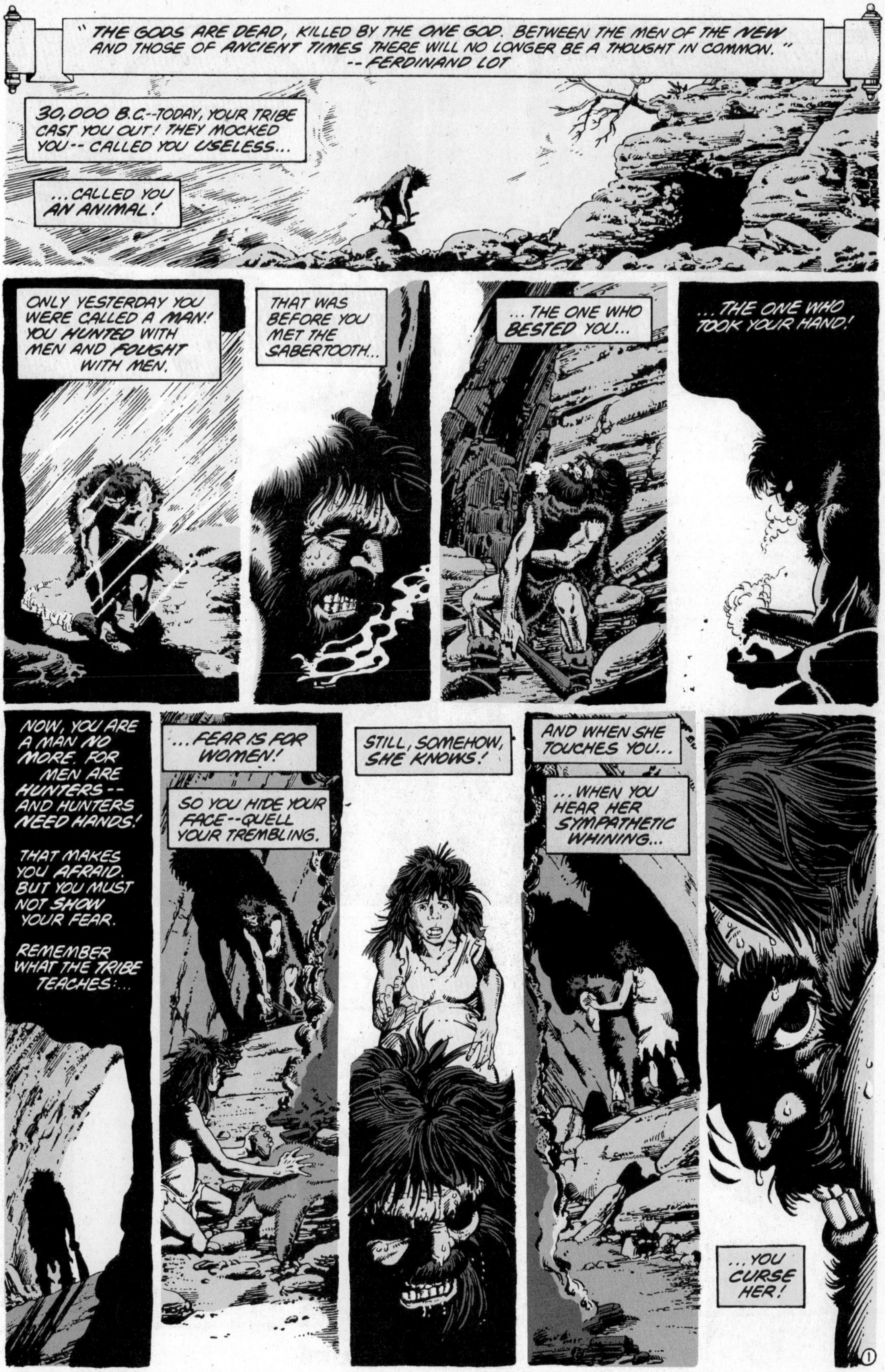
"THE GODS ARE DEAD, KILLED BY THE ONE GOD. BETWEEN THE MEN OF THE NEW AND THOSE OF ANCIENT TIMES THERE WILL NO LONGER BE A THOUGHT IN COMMON."
-- FERDINAND LOT
30,000 B.C.--TODAY, YOUR TRIBE CAST YOU OUT! THEY MOCKED YOU-- CALLED YOU USELESS...
...CALLED YOU AN ANIMAL!
ONLY YESTERDAY YOU WERE CALLED A MAN! YOU HUNTED WITH MEN AND FOUGHT WITH MEN.
THAT WAS BEFORE YOU MET THE SABERTOOTH...
...THE ONE WHO BESTED YOU...
...THE ONE WHO TOOK YOUR HAND!
NOW, YOU ARE A MAN NO MORE. FOR MEN ARE HUNTERS-- AND HUNTERS NEED HANDS!
THAT MAKES YOU AFRAID. BUT YOU MUST NOT SHOW YOUR FEAR.
REMEMBER WHAT THE TRIBE TEACHES:...
...FEAR IS FOR WOMEN!
SO YOU HIDE YOUR FACE--QUELL YOUR TREMBLING.
STILL, SOMEHOW, SHE KNOWS!
AND WHEN SHE TOUCHES YOU...
...WHEN YOU HEAR HER SYMPATHETIC WHINING...
...YOU CURSE HER!

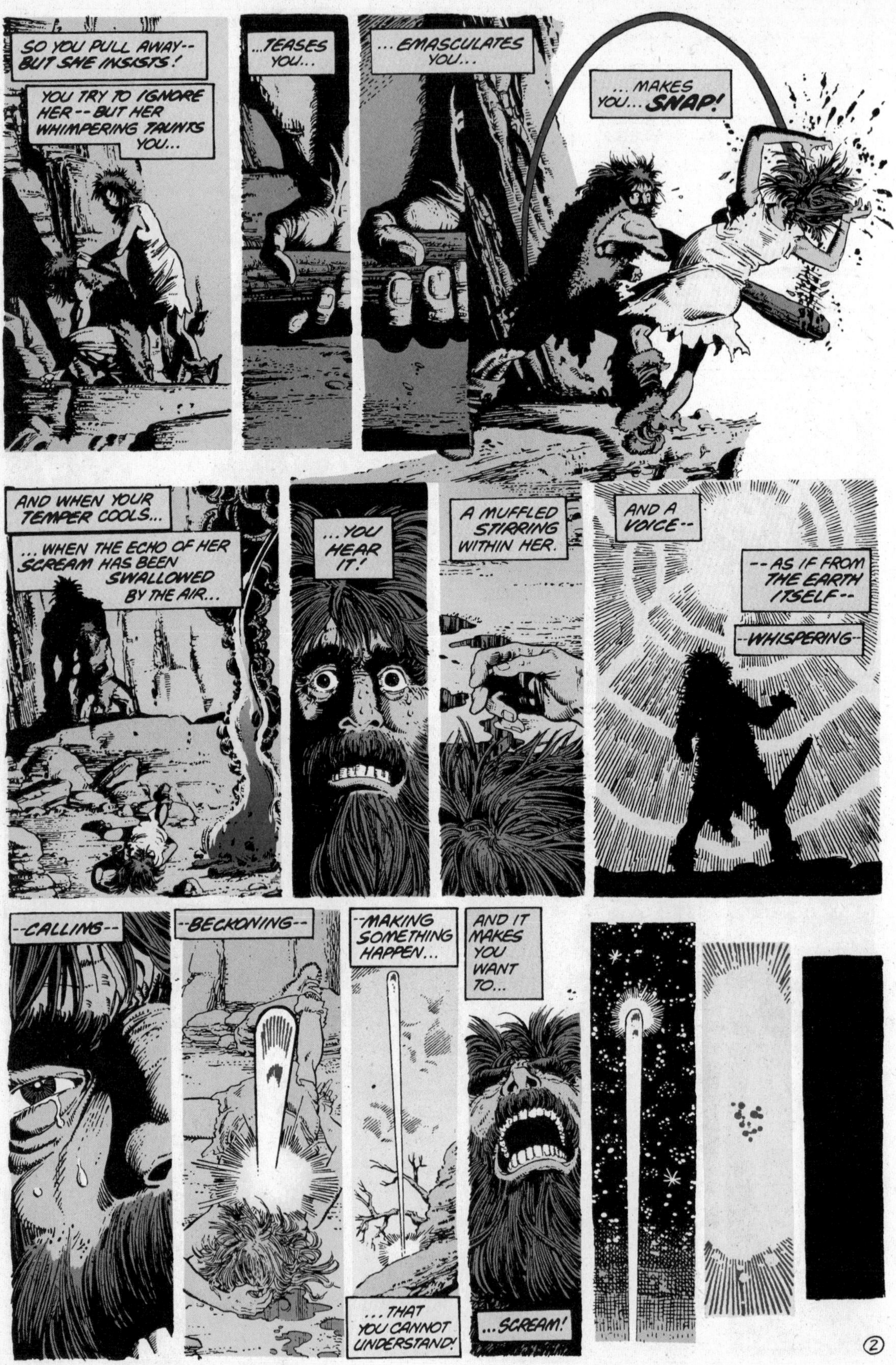
SO YOU PULL AWAY-- BUT SHE INSISTS!
YOU TRY TO IGNORE HER -- BUT HER WHIMPERING TAUNTS YOU...
...TEASES YOU...
...EMASCULATES YOU...
...MAKES YOU...SNAP!
AND WHEN YOUR TEMPER COOLS...
...WHEN THE ECHO OF HER SCREAM HAS BEEN SWALLOWED BY THE AIR...
...YOU HEAR IT!
A MUFFLED STIRRING WITHIN HER.
AND A VOICE--
--AS IF FROM THE EARTH ITSELF--
--WHISPERING--
--CALLING--
--BECKONING--
--MAKING SOMETHING HAPPEN...
...THAT YOU CANNOT UNDERSTAND!
AND IT MAKES YOU WANT TO...
...SCREAM!
2

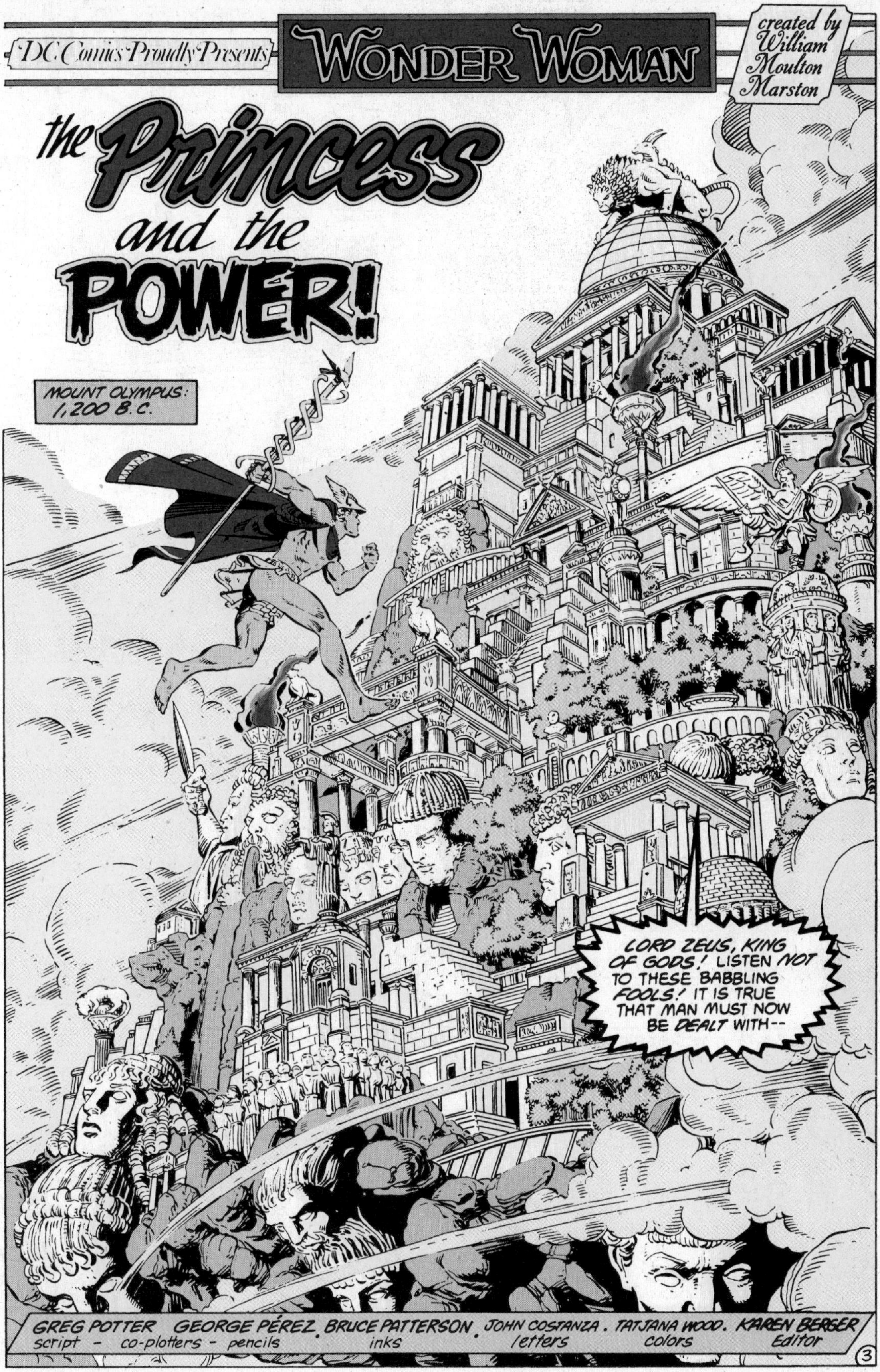
DC Comics Proudly Presents
WONDER WOMAN
created by William Moulton Marston
the Princess and the POWER!
MOUNT OLYMPUS: 1,200 B.C.
LORD ZEUS, KING OF GODS! LISTEN NOT TO THESE BABBLING FOOLS! IT IS TRUE THAT MAN MUST NOW BE DEALT WITH--
GREG POTTER script - GEORGE PÉREZ co-plotters - pencils . BRUCE PATTERSON inks . JOHN COSTANZA letters . TATJANA WOOD colors . KAREN BERGER Editor
3

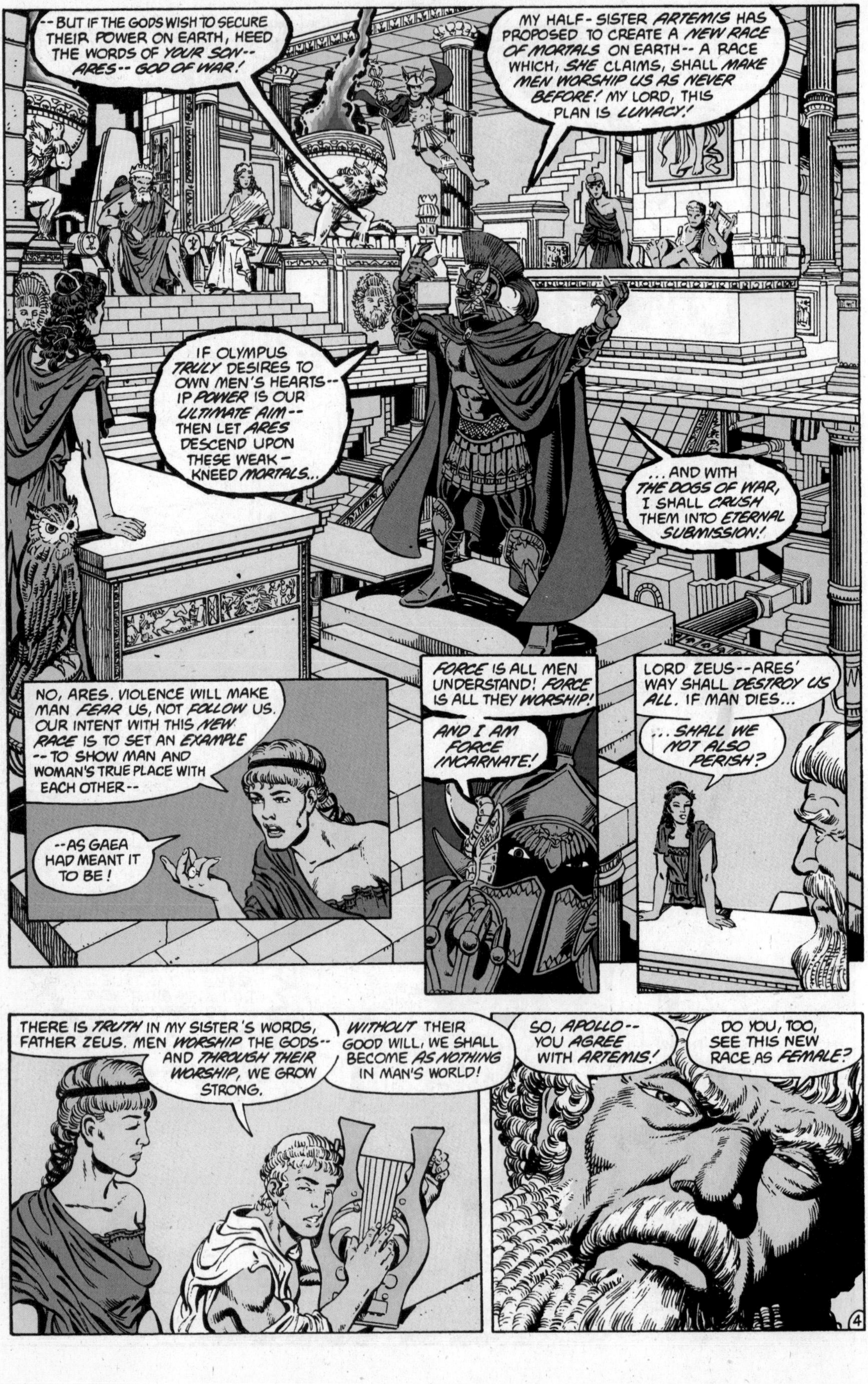
--BUT IF THE GODS WISH TO SECURE THEIR POWER ON EARTH, HEED THE WORDS OF YOUR SON-- ARES-- GOD OF WAR!
MY HALF-SISTER ARTEMIS HAS PROPOSED TO CREATE A NEW RACE OF MORTALS ON EARTH-- A RACE WHICH, SHE CLAIMS, SHALL MAKE MEN WORSHIP US AS NEVER BEFORE! MY LORD, THIS PLAN IS LUNACY!
IF OLYMPUS TRULY DESIRES TO OWN MEN'S HEARTS-- IF POWER IS OUR ULTIMATE AIM-- THEN LET ARES DESCEND UPON THESE WEAK-KNEED MORTALS...
...AND WITH THE DOGS OF WAR, I SHALL CRUSH THEM INTO ETERNAL SUBMISSION!
NO, ARES. VIOLENCE WILL MAKE MAN FEAR US, NOT FOLLOW US. OUR INTENT WITH THIS NEW RACE IS TO SET AN EXAMPLE --TO SHOW MAN AND WOMAN'S TRUE PLACE WITH EACH OTHER--
--AS GAEA HAD MEANT IT TO BE!
FORCE IS ALL MEN UNDERSTAND! FORCE IS ALL THEY WORSHIP!
AND I AM FORCE INCARNATE!
LORD ZEUS--ARES' WAY SHALL DESTROY US ALL. IF MAN DIES...
...SHALL WE NOT ALSO PERISH?
THERE IS TRUTH IN MY SISTER'S WORDS, FATHER ZEUS. MEN WORSHIP THE GODS-- AND THROUGH THEIR WORSHIP, WE GROW STRONG.
WITHOUT THEIR GOOD WILL, WE SHALL BECOME AS NOTHING IN MAN'S WORLD!
SO, APOLLO-- YOU AGREE WITH ARTEMIS!
DO YOU, TOO, SEE THIS NEW RACE AS FEMALE?
4

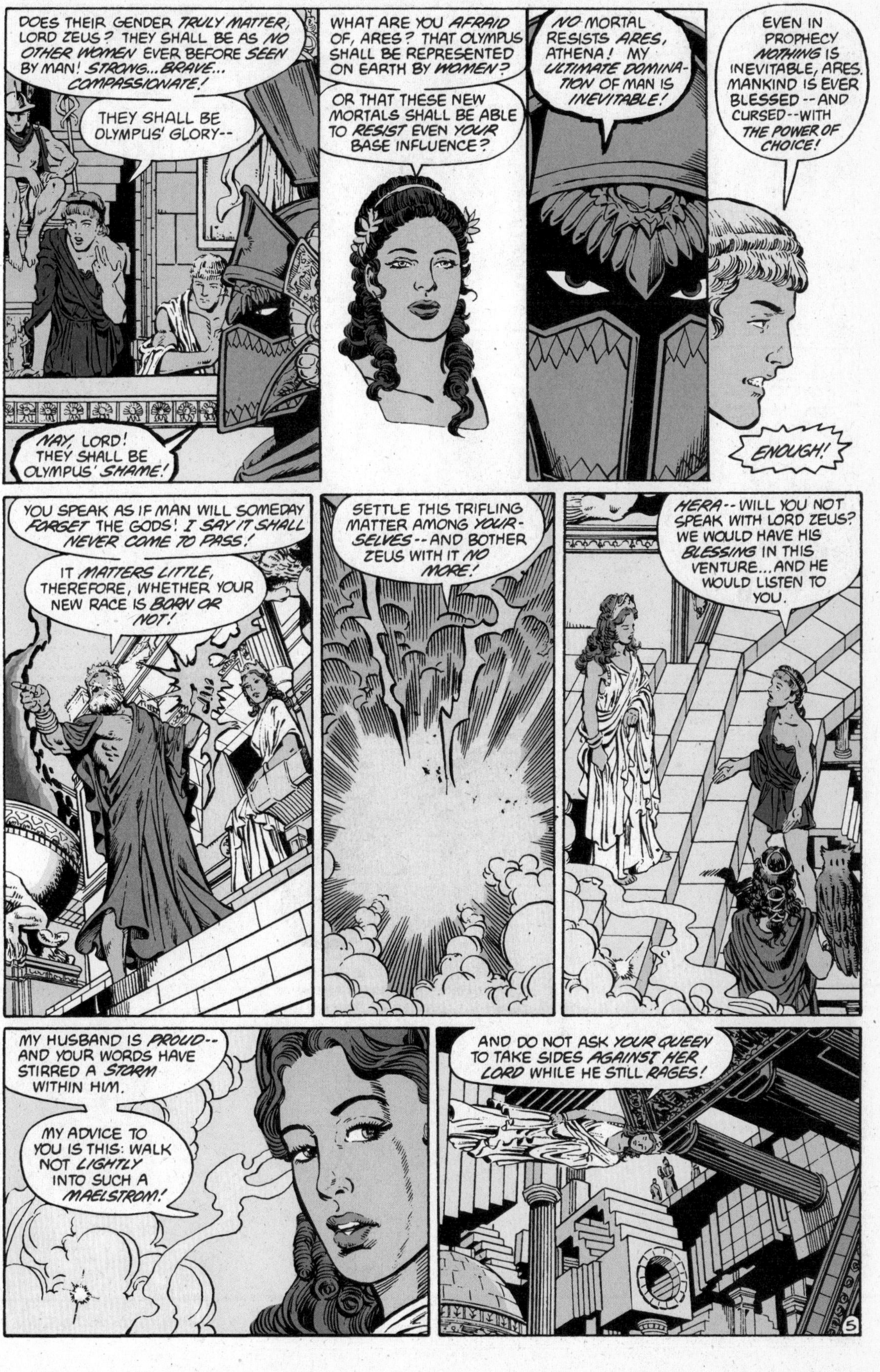
DOES THEIR GENDER TRULY MATTER, LORD ZEUS? THEY SHALL BE AS NO OTHER WOMEN EVER BEFORE SEEN BY MAN! STRONG...BRAVE... COMPASSIONATE!
THEY SHALL BE OLYMPUS' GLORY--
NAY, LORD! THEY SHALL BE OLYMPUS' SHAME!
WHAT ARE YOU AFRAID OF, ARES? THAT OLYMPUS SHALL BE REPRESENTED ON EARTH BY WOMEN?
OR THAT THESE NEW MORTALS SHALL BE ABLE TO RESIST EVEN YOUR BASE INFLUENCE?
NO MORTAL RESISTS ARES, ATHENA! MY ULTIMATE DOMINATION OF MAN IS INEVITABLE!
EVEN IN PROPHECY NOTHING IS INEVITABLE, ARES. MANKIND IS EVER BLESSED--AND CURSED--WITH THE POWER OF CHOICE!
ENOUGH!
YOU SPEAK AS IF MAN WILL SOMEDAY FORGET THE GODS! I SAY IT SHALL NEVER COME TO PASS!
IT MATTERS LITTLE, THEREFORE, WHETHER YOUR NEW RACE IS BORN OR NOT!
SETTLE THIS TRIFLING MATTER AMONG YOURSELVES--AND BOTHER ZEUS WITH IT NO MORE!
HERA--WILL YOU NOT SPEAK WITH LORD ZEUS? WE WOULD HAVE HIS BLESSING IN THIS VENTURE...AND HE WOULD LISTEN TO YOU.
MY HUSBAND IS PROUD--AND YOUR WORDS HAVE STIRRED A STORM WITHIN HIM.
MY ADVICE TO YOU IS THIS: WALK NOT LIGHTLY INTO SUCH A MAELSTROM!
AND DO NOT ASK YOUR QUEEN TO TAKE SIDES AGAINST HER LORD WHILE HE STILL RAGES!
5

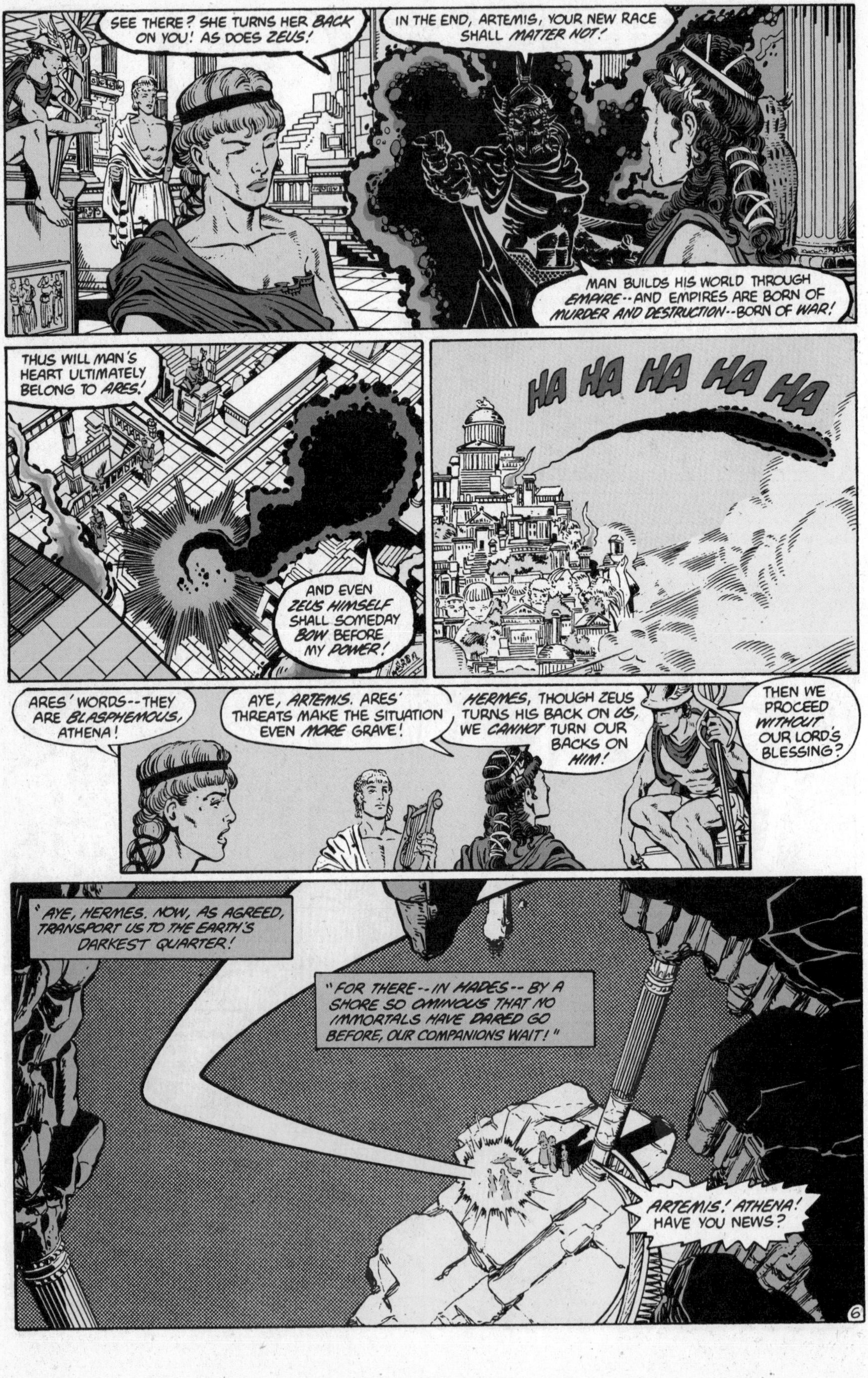
SEE THERE? SHE TURNS HER BACK ON YOU! AS DOES ZEUS!
IN THE END, ARTEMIS, YOUR NEW RACE SHALL MATTER NOT!
MAN BUILDS HIS WORLD THROUGH EMPIRE--AND EMPIRES ARE BORN OF MURDER AND DESTRUCTION--BORN OF WAR!
THUS WILL MAN'S HEART ULTIMATELY BELONG TO ARES!
AND EVEN ZEUS HIMSELF SHALL SOMEDAY BOW BEFORE MY POWER!
HA HA HA HA HA
ARES' WORDS--THEY ARE BLASPHEMOUS, ATHENA!
AYE, ARTEMIS. ARES' THREATS MAKE THE SITUATION EVEN MORE GRAVE!
HERMES, THOUGH ZEUS TURNS HIS BACK ON US, WE CANNOT TURN OUR BACKS ON HIM!
THEN WE PROCEED WITHOUT OUR LORD'S BLESSING?
"AYE, HERMES. NOW, AS AGREED, TRANSPORT US TO THE EARTH'S DARKEST QUARTER!
"FOR THERE--IN HADES--BY A SHORE SO OMINOUS THAT NO IMMORTALS HAVE DARED GO BEFORE, OUR COMPANIONS WAIT!"
ARTEMIS! ATHENA! HAVE YOU NEWS?
6

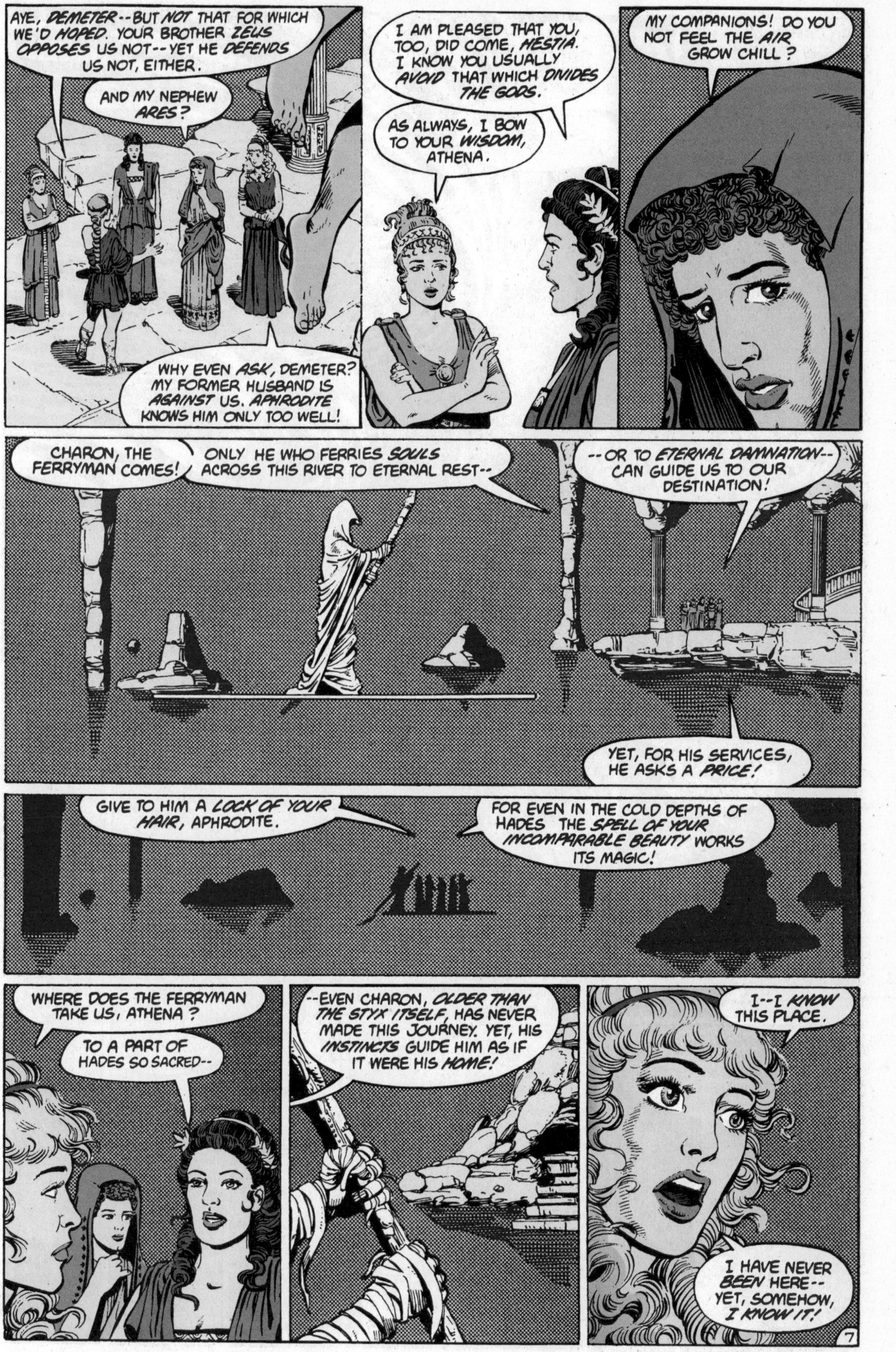
AYE, DEMETER--BUT NOT THAT FOR WHICH WE'D HOPED. YOUR BROTHER ZEUS OPPOSES US NOT--YET HE DEFENDS US NOT, EITHER.
AND MY NEPHEW ARES?
WHY EVEN ASK, DEMETER? MY FORMER HUSBAND IS AGAINST US. APHRODITE KNOWS HIM ONLY TOO WELL!
I AM PLEASED THAT YOU, TOO, DID COME, HESTIA. I KNOW YOU USUALLY AVOID THAT WHICH DIVIDES THE GODS.
AS ALWAYS, I BOW TO YOUR WISDOM, ATHENA.
MY COMPANIONS! DO YOU NOT FEEL THE AIR GROW CHILL?
CHARON, THE FERRYMAN COMES!
ONLY HE WHO FERRIES SOULS ACROSS THIS RIVER TO ETERNAL REST--
--OR TO ETERNAL DAMNATION--CAN GUIDE US TO OUR DESTINATION!
YET, FOR HIS SERVICES, HE ASKS A PRICE!
GIVE TO HIM A LOCK OF YOUR HAIR, APHRODITE.
FOR EVEN IN THE COLD DEPTHS OF HADES THE SPELL OF YOUR INCOMPARABLE BEAUTY WORKS ITS MAGIC!
WHERE DOES THE FERRYMAN TAKE US, ATHENA?
TO A PART OF HADES SO SACRED--
--EVEN CHARON, OLDER THAN THE STYX ITSELF, HAS NEVER MADE THIS JOURNEY. YET, HIS INSTINCTS GUIDE HIM AS IF IT WERE HIS HOME!
I--I KNOW THIS PLACE.
I HAVE NEVER BEEN HERE--YET, SOMEHOW, I KNOW IT!
7

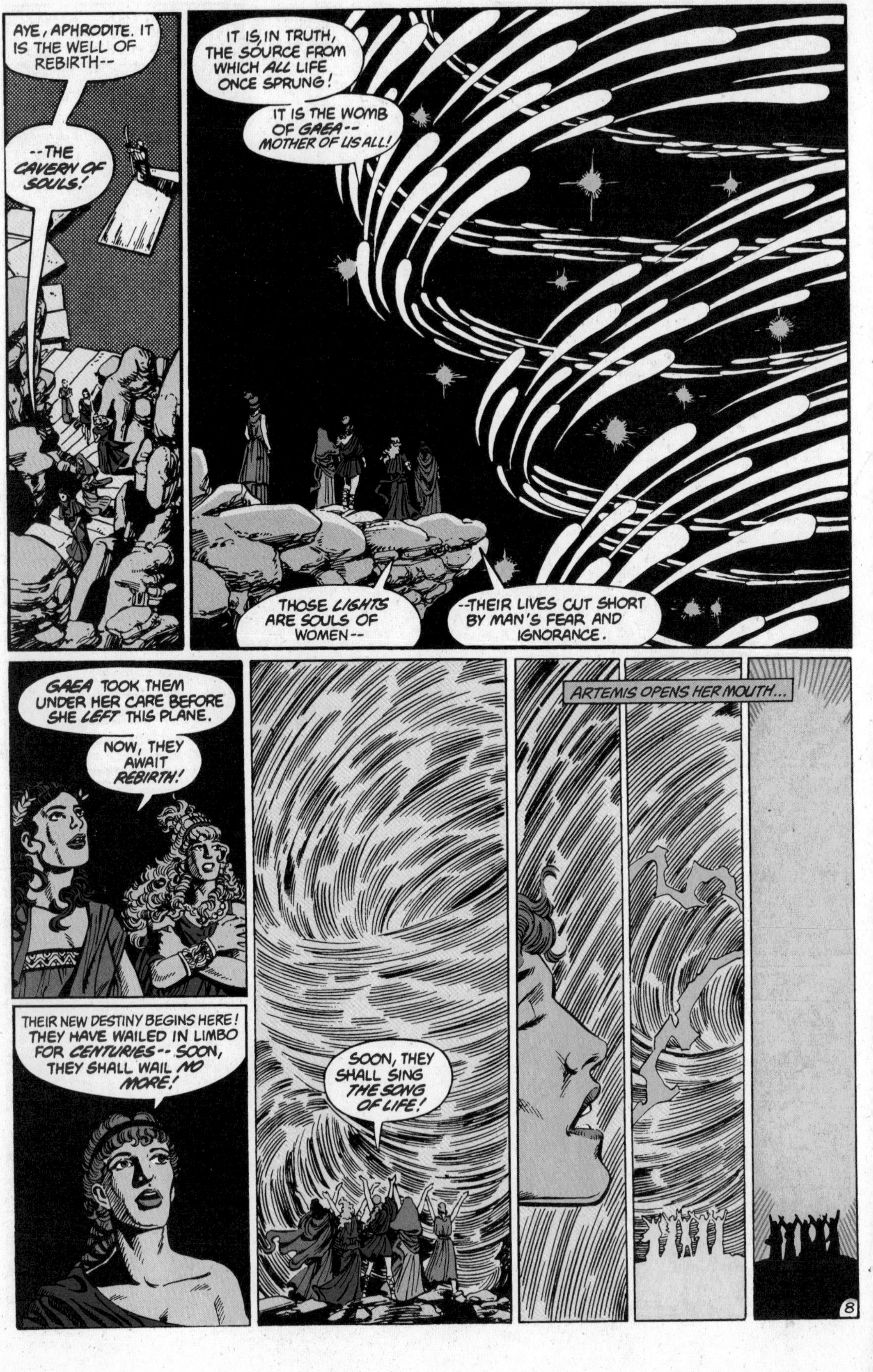
AYE, APHRODITE. IT IS THE WELL OF REBIRTH--
--THE CAVERN OF SOULS!
IT IS, IN TRUTH, THE SOURCE FROM WHICH ALL LIFE ONCE SPRUNG!
IT IS THE WOMB OF GAEA-- MOTHER OF US ALL!
THOSE LIGHTS ARE SOULS OF WOMEN--
--THEIR LIVES CUT SHORT BY MAN'S FEAR AND IGNORANCE.
GAEA TOOK THEM UNDER HER CARE BEFORE SHE LEFT THIS PLANE.
NOW, THEY AWAIT REBIRTH!
THEIR NEW DESTINY BEGINS HERE! THEY HAVE WAILED IN LIMBO FOR CENTURIES-- SOON, THEY SHALL WAIL NO MORE!
SOON, THEY SHALL SING THE SONG OF LIFE!
ARTEMIS OPENS HER MOUTH...
8

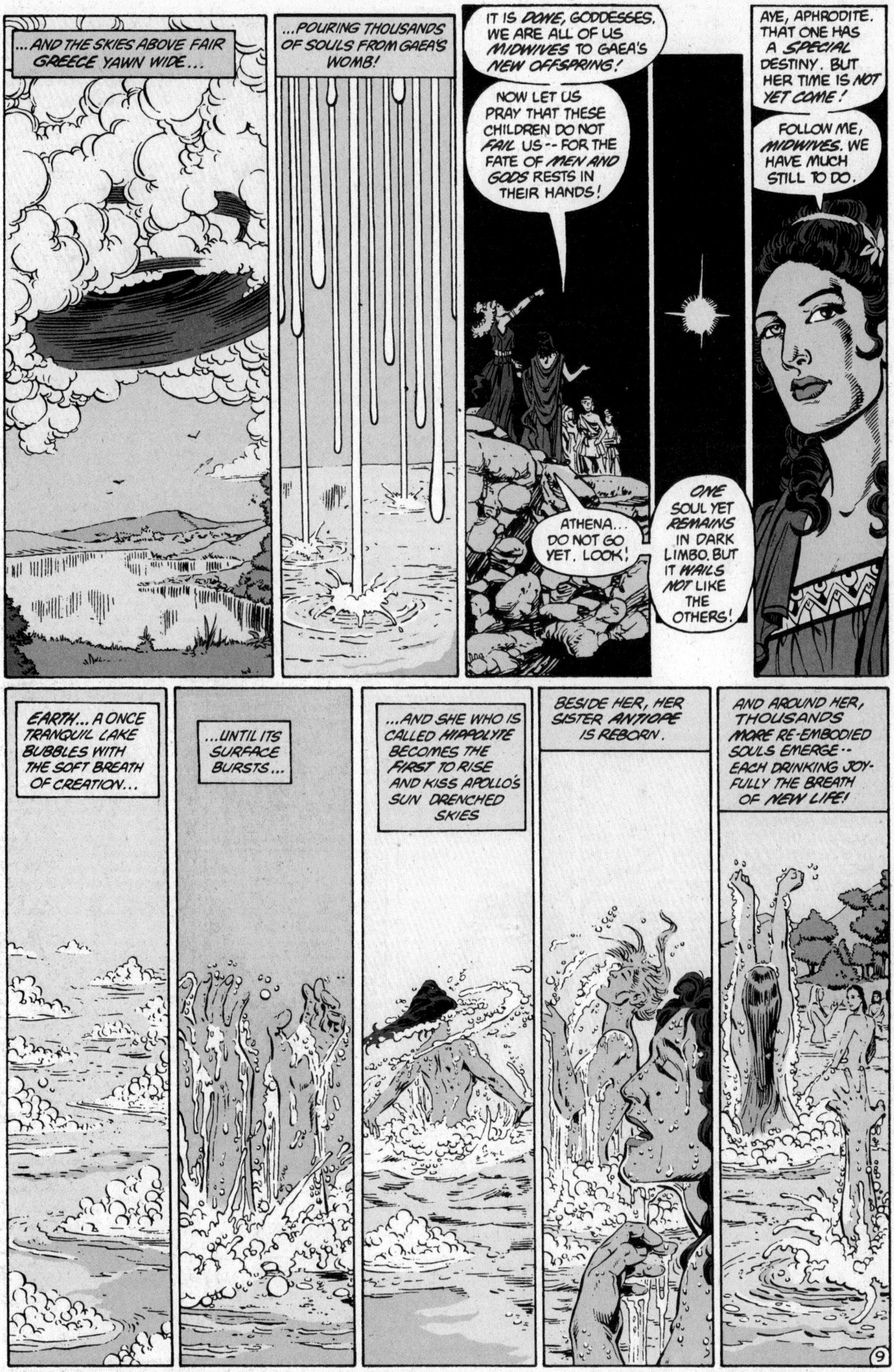
...AND THE SKIES ABOVE FAIR GREECE YAWN WIDE...
...POURING THOUSANDS OF SOULS FROM GAEA'S WOMB!
IT IS DONE, GODDESSES. WE ARE ALL OF US MIDWIVES TO GAEA'S NEW OFFSPRING!
NOW LET US PRAY THAT THESE CHILDREN DO NOT FAIL US-- FOR THE FATE OF MEN AND GODS RESTS IN THEIR HANDS!
ATHENA... DO NOT GO YET. LOOK!
ONE SOUL YET REMAINS IN DARK LIMBO. BUT IT WAILS NOT LIKE THE OTHERS!
AYE, APHRODITE. THAT ONE HAS A SPECIAL DESTINY. BUT HER TIME IS NOT YET COME!
FOLLOW ME, MIDWIVES. WE HAVE MUCH STILL TO DO.
EARTH... A ONCE TRANQUIL LAKE BUBBLES WITH THE SOFT BREATH OF CREATION...
...UNTIL ITS SURFACE BURSTS...
...AND SHE WHO IS CALLED HIPPOLYTE BECOMES THE FIRST TO RISE AND KISS APOLLO'S SUN DRENCHED SKIES
BESIDE HER, HER SISTER ANTIOPE IS REBORN.
AND AROUND HER, THOUSANDS MORE RE-EMBODIED SOULS EMERGE-- EACH DRINKING JOYFULLY THE BREATH OF NEW LIFE!
9

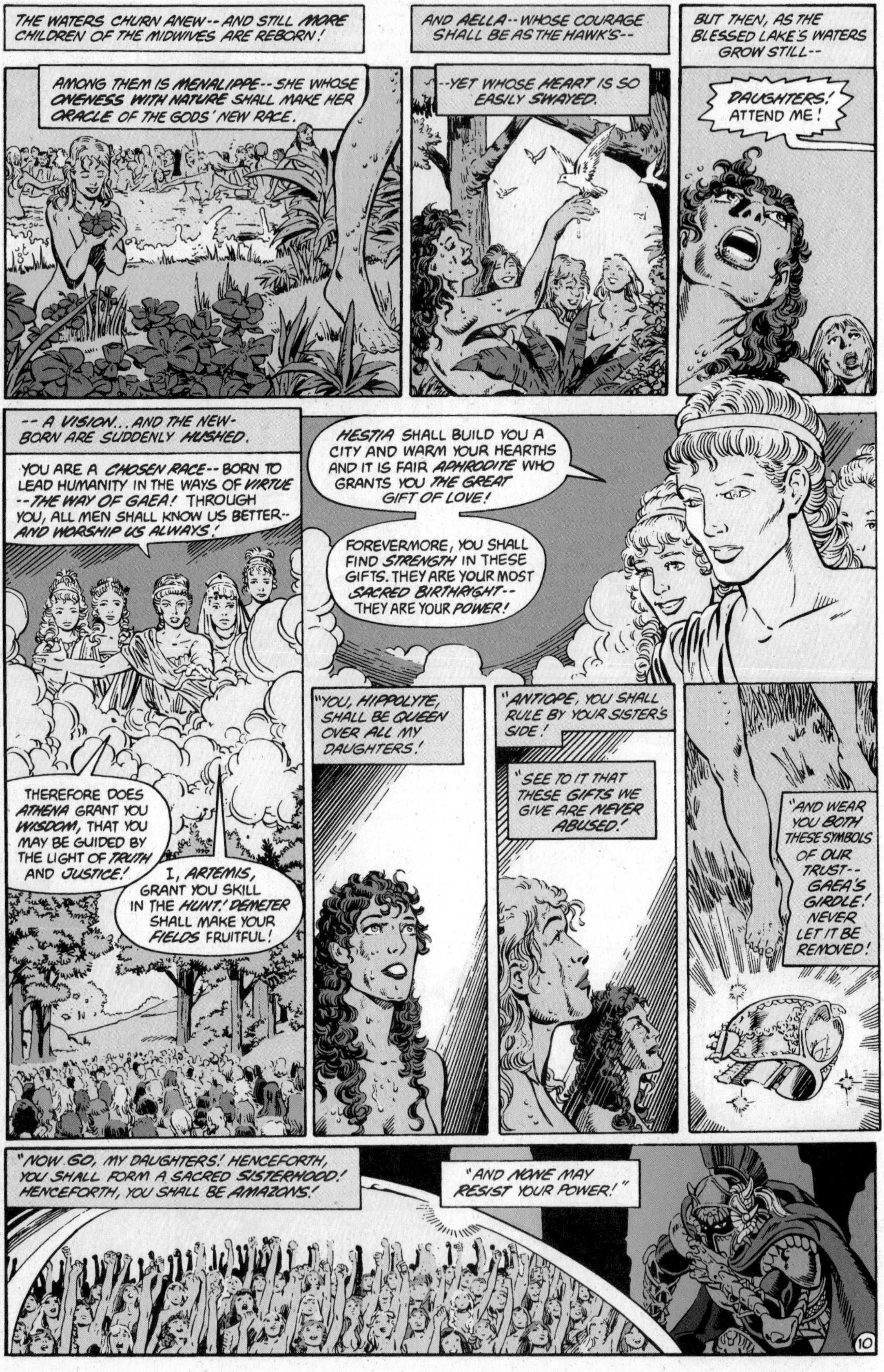
THE WATERS CHURN ANEW--AND STILL MORE CHILDREN OF THE MIDWIVES ARE REBORN!
AMONG THEM IS MENALIPPE--SHE WHOSE ONENESS WITH NATURE SHALL MAKE HER ORACLE OF THE GODS' NEW RACE.
AND AELLA--WHOSE COURAGE SHALL BE AS THE HAWK'S--
--YET WHOSE HEART IS SO EASILY SWAYED.
BUT THEN, AS THE BLESSED LAKE'S WATERS GROW STILL--
DAUGHTERS! ATTEND ME!
--A VISION...AND THE NEW-BORN ARE SUDDENLY HUSHED.
YOU ARE A CHOSEN RACE--BORN TO LEAD HUMANITY IN THE WAYS OF VIRTUE--THE WAY OF GAEA! THROUGH YOU, ALL MEN SHALL KNOW US BETTER--AND WORSHIP US ALWAYS!
THEREFORE DOES ATHENA GRANT YOU WISDOM, THAT YOU MAY BE GUIDED BY THE LIGHT OF TRUTH AND JUSTICE!
I, ARTEMIS, GRANT YOU SKILL IN THE HUNT! DEMETER SHALL MAKE YOUR FIELDS FRUITFUL!
HESTIA SHALL BUILD YOU A CITY AND WARM YOUR HEARTHS AND IT IS FAIR APHRODITE WHO GRANTS YOU THE GREAT GIFT OF LOVE!
FOREVERMORE, YOU SHALL FIND STRENGTH IN THESE GIFTS. THEY ARE YOUR MOST SACRED BIRTHRIGHT--THEY ARE YOUR POWER!
"YOU, HIPPOLYTE, SHALL BE QUEEN OVER ALL MY DAUGHTERS!
"ANTIOPE, YOU SHALL RULE BY YOUR SISTER'S SIDE!
"SEE TO IT THAT THESE GIFTS WE GIVE ARE NEVER ABUSED!
"AND WEAR YOU BOTH THESE SYMBOLS OF OUR TRUST--GAEA'S GIRDLE! NEVER LET IT BE REMOVED!
"NOW GO, MY DAUGHTERS! HENCEFORTH, YOU SHALL FORM A SACRED SISTERHOOD! HENCEFORTH, YOU SHALL BE AMAZONS!
"AND NONE MAY RESIST YOUR POWER!"
10

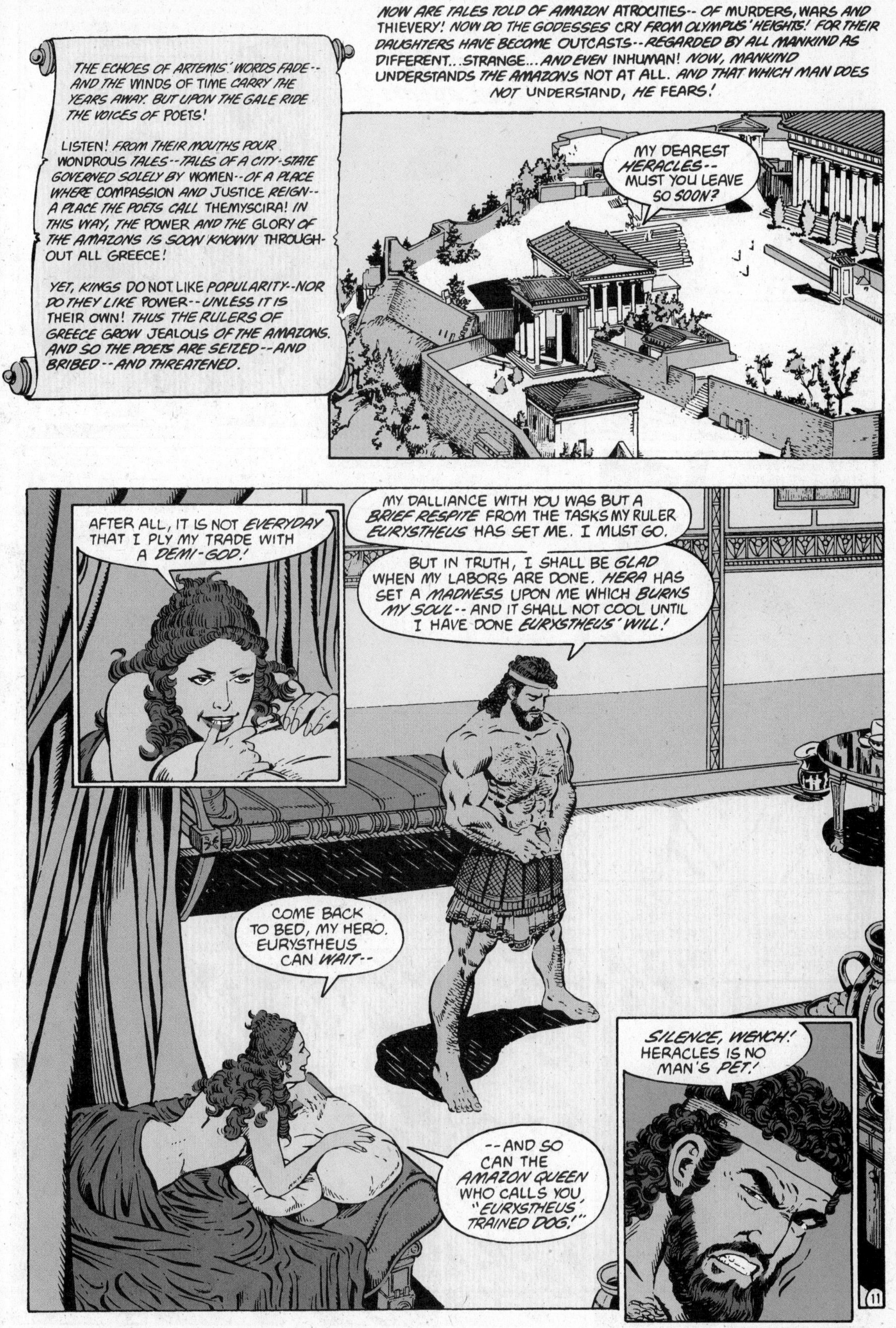

THE ECHOES OF ARTEMIS' WORDS FADE--AND THE WINDS OF TIME CARRY THE YEARS AWAY. BUT UPON THE GALE RIDE THE VOICES OF POETS!
LISTEN! FROM THEIR MOUTHS POUR WONDROUS TALES--TALES OF A CITY-STATE GOVERNED SOLELY BY WOMEN--OF A PLACE WHERE COMPASSION AND JUSTICE REIGN--A PLACE THE POETS CALL THEMYSCIRA! IN THIS WAY, THE POWER AND THE GLORY OF THE AMAZONS IS SOON KNOWN THROUGHOUT ALL GREECE!
YET, KINGS DO NOT LIKE POPULARITY--NOR DO THEY LIKE POWER--UNLESS IT IS THEIR OWN! THUS THE RULERS OF GREECE GROW JEALOUS OF THE AMAZONS. AND SO THE POETS ARE SEIZED--AND BRIBED--AND THREATENED.
NOW ARE TALES TOLD OF AMAZON ATROCITIES-- OF MURDERS, WARS AND THIEVERY! NOW DO THE GODESSES CRY FROM OLYMPUS' HEIGHTS! FOR THEIR DAUGHTERS HAVE BECOME OUTCASTS--REGARDED BY ALL MANKIND AS DIFFERENT...STRANGE...AND EVEN INHUMAN! NOW, MANKIND UNDERSTANDS THE AMAZONS NOT AT ALL. AND THAT WHICH MAN DOES NOT UNDERSTAND, HE FEARS!
MY DEAREST HERACLES--MUST YOU LEAVE SO SOON?
AFTER ALL, IT IS NOT EVERYDAY THAT I PLY MY TRADE WITH A DEMI-GOD!
MY DALLIANCE WITH YOU WAS BUT A BRIEF RESPITE FROM THE TASKS MY RULER EURYSTHEUS HAS SET ME. I MUST GO.
BUT IN TRUTH, I SHALL BE GLAD WHEN MY LABORS ARE DONE. HERA HAS SET A MADNESS UPON ME WHICH BURNS MY SOUL--AND IT SHALL NOT COOL UNTIL I HAVE DONE EURYSTHEUS' WILL!
COME BACK TO BED, MY HERO. EURYSTHEUS CAN WAIT--
--AND SO CAN THE AMAZON QUEEN WHO CALLS YOU, "EURYSTHEUS' TRAINED DOG!"
SILENCE, WENCH! HERACLES IS NO MAN'S PET!
11

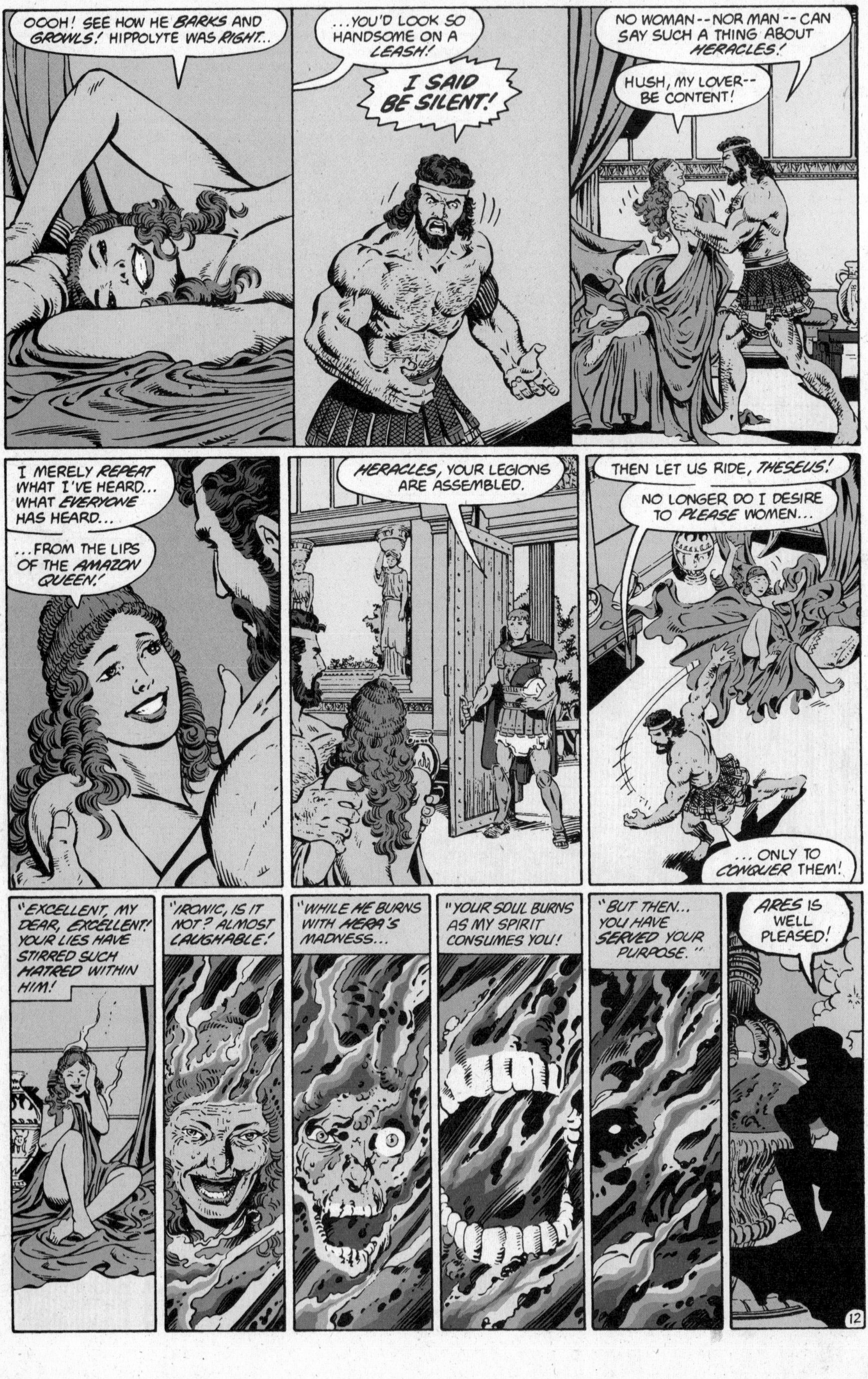
OOOH! SEE HOW HE BARKS AND GROWLS! HIPPOLYTE WAS RIGHT...
...YOU'D LOOK SO HANDSOME ON A LEASH!
I SAID BE SILENT!
NO WOMAN--NOR MAN--CAN SAY SUCH A THING ABOUT HERACLES!
HUSH, MY LOVER-- BE CONTENT!
I MERELY REPEAT WHAT I'VE HEARD... WHAT EVERYONE HAS HEARD...
...FROM THE LIPS OF THE AMAZON QUEEN!
HERACLES, YOUR LEGIONS ARE ASSEMBLED.
THEN LET US RIDE, THESEUS!
NO LONGER DO I DESIRE TO PLEASE WOMEN...
...ONLY TO CONQUER THEM!
"EXCELLENT, MY DEAR, EXCELLENT! YOUR LIES HAVE STIRRED SUCH HATRED WITHIN HIM!
"IRONIC, IS IT NOT? ALMOST LAUGHABLE!
"WHILE HE BURNS WITH HERA'S MADNESS...
"YOUR SOUL BURNS AS MY SPIRIT CONSUMES YOU!
"BUT THEN... YOU HAVE SERVED YOUR PURPOSE."
ARES IS WELL PLEASED!
12

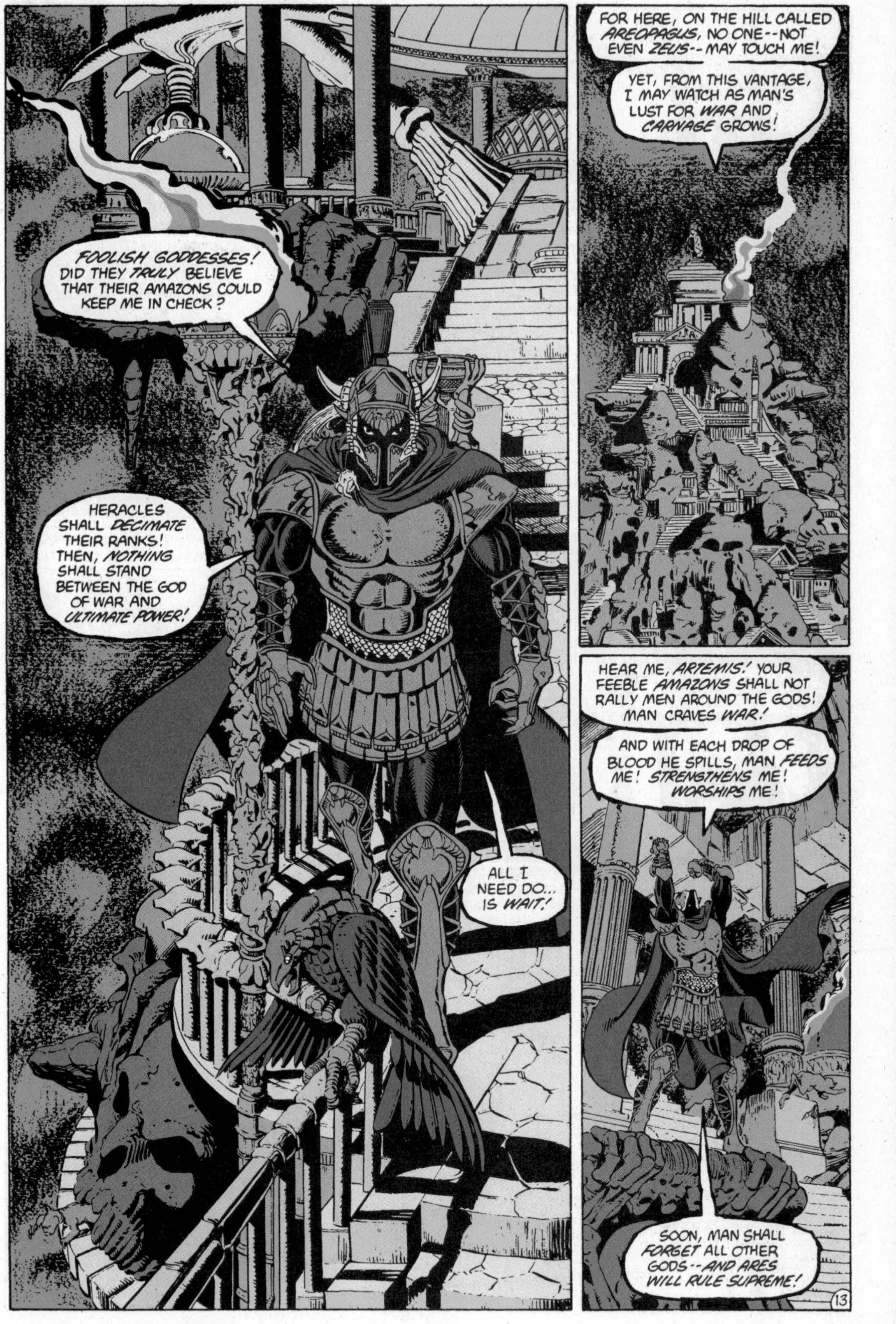
FOOLISH GODDESSES! DID THEY TRULY BELIEVE THAT THEIR AMAZONS COULD KEEP ME IN CHECK?
HERACLES SHALL DECIMATE THEIR RANKS! THEN, NOTHING SHALL STAND BETWEEN THE GOD OF WAR AND ULTIMATE POWER!
ALL I NEED DO... IS WAIT!
FOR HERE, ON THE HILL CALLED AREOPAGUS, NO ONE--NOT EVEN ZEUS--MAY TOUCH ME!
YET, FROM THIS VANTAGE, I MAY WATCH AS MAN'S LUST FOR WAR AND CARNAGE GROWS!
HEAR ME, ARTEMIS! YOUR FEEBLE AMAZONS SHALL NOT RALLY MEN AROUND THE GODS! MAN CRAVES WAR!
AND WITH EACH DROP OF BLOOD HE SPILLS, MAN FEEDS ME! STRENGTHENS ME! WORSHIPS ME!
SOON, MAN SHALL FORGET ALL OTHER GODS--AND ARES WILL RULE SUPREME!
13

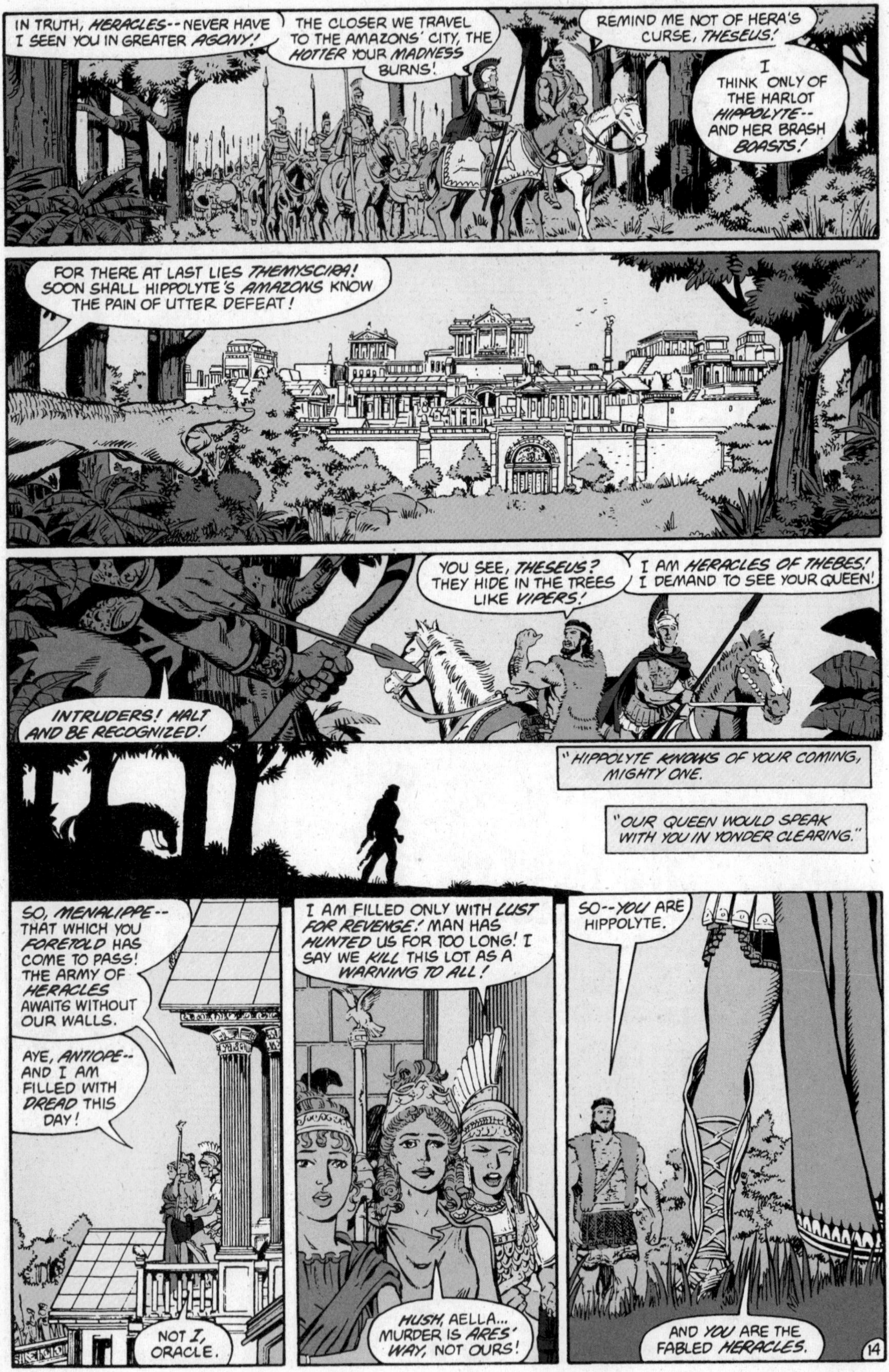

IN TRUTH, HERACLES-- NEVER HAVE I SEEN YOU IN GREATER AGONY!
THE CLOSER WE TRAVEL TO THE AMAZONS' CITY, THE HOTTER YOUR MADNESS BURNS!
REMIND ME NOT OF HERA'S CURSE, THESEUS!
I THINK ONLY OF THE HARLOT HIPPOLYTE-- AND HER BRASH BOASTS!
FOR THERE AT LAST LIES THEMYSCIRA! SOON SHALL HIPPOLYTE'S AMAZONS KNOW THE PAIN OF UTTER DEFEAT!
YOU SEE, THESEUS? THEY HIDE IN THE TREES LIKE VIPERS!
I AM HERACLES OF THEBES! I DEMAND TO SEE YOUR QUEEN!
INTRUDERS! HALT AND BE RECOGNIZED!
"HIPPOLYTE KNOWS OF YOUR COMING, MIGHTY ONE.
"OUR QUEEN WOULD SPEAK WITH YOU IN YONDER CLEARING."
SO, MENALIPPE-- THAT WHICH YOU FORETOLD HAS COME TO PASS! THE ARMY OF HERACLES AWAITS WITHOUT OUR WALLS.
AYE, ANTIOPE-- AND I AM FILLED WITH DREAD THIS DAY!
NOT I, ORACLE.
I AM FILLED ONLY WITH LUST FOR REVENGE! MAN HAS HUNTED US FOR TOO LONG! I SAY WE KILL THIS LOT AS A WARNING TO ALL!
HUSH, AELLA... MURDER IS ARES' WAY, NOT OURS!
SO--YOU ARE HIPPOLYTE.
AND YOU ARE THE FABLED HERACLES.
14

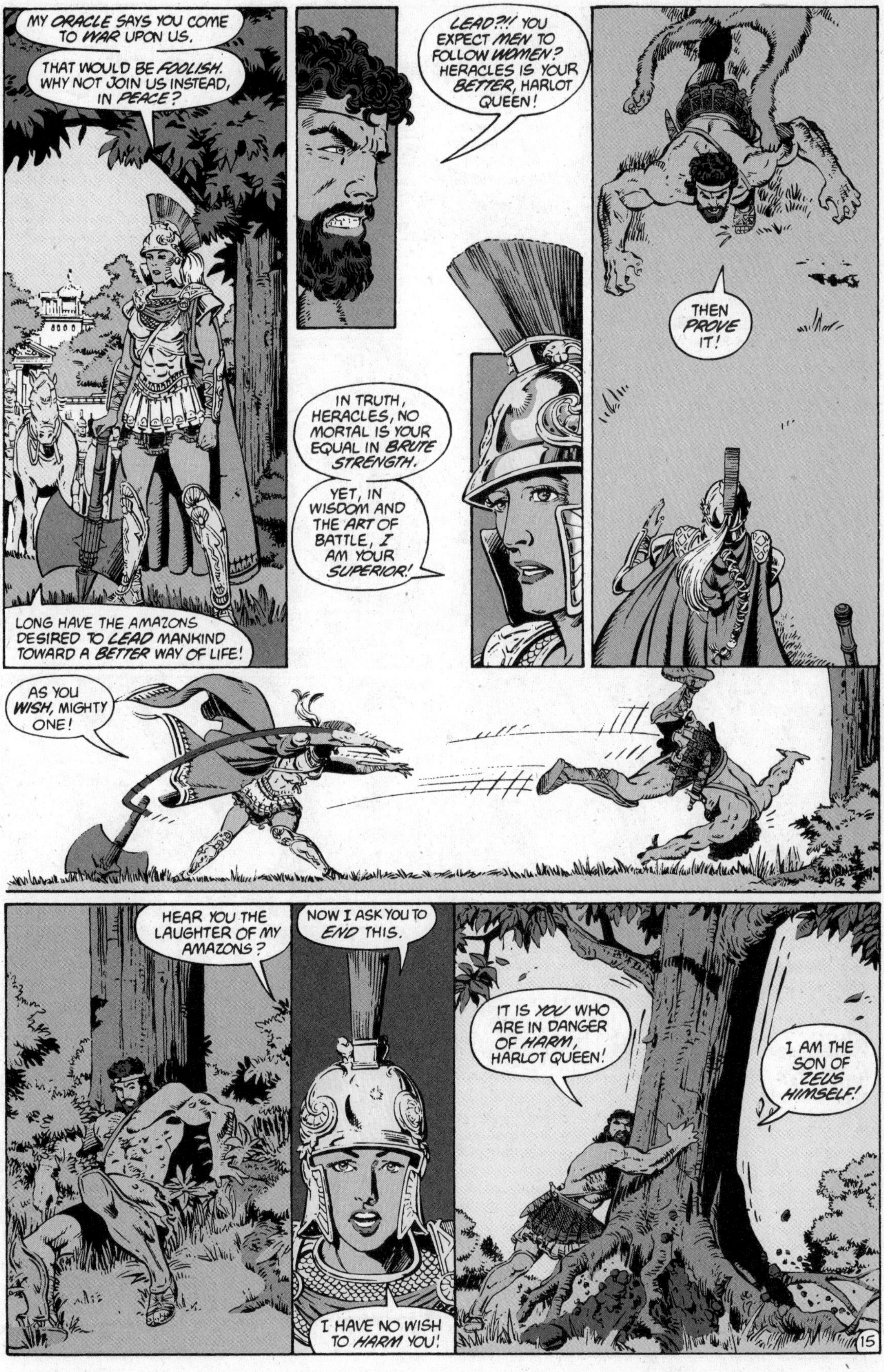
MY ORACLE SAYS YOU COME TO WAR UPON US.
THAT WOULD BE FOOLISH. WHY NOT JOIN US INSTEAD, IN PEACE?
LONG HAVE THE AMAZONS DESIRED TO LEAD MANKIND TOWARD A BETTER WAY OF LIFE!
LEAD?!! YOU EXPECT MEN TO FOLLOW WOMEN? HERACLES IS YOUR BETTER, HARLOT QUEEN!
IN TRUTH, HERACLES, NO MORTAL IS YOUR EQUAL IN BRUTE STRENGTH.
YET, IN WISDOM AND THE ART OF BATTLE, I AM YOUR SUPERIOR!
THEN PROVE IT!
AS YOU WISH, MIGHTY ONE!
HEAR YOU THE LAUGHTER OF MY AMAZONS?
NOW I ASK YOU TO END THIS.
I HAVE NO WISH TO HARM YOU!
IT IS YOU WHO ARE IN DANGER OF HARM, HARLOT QUEEN!
I AM THE SON OF ZEUS HIMSELF!
15

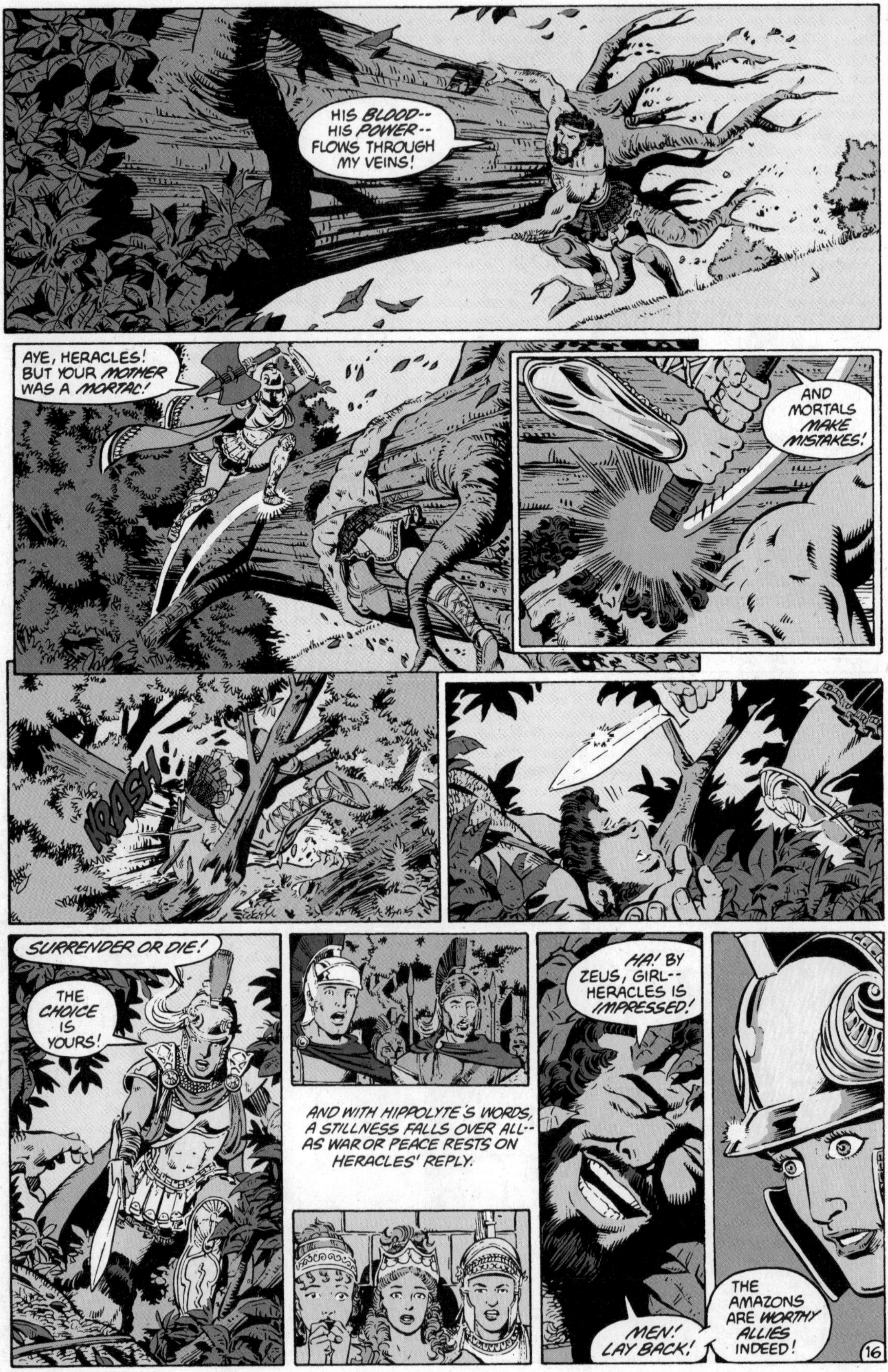
HIS BLOOD--
HIS POWER--
FLOWS THROUGH
MY VEINS!
AYE, HERACLES! BUT YOUR MOTHER WAS A MORTAL!
AND MORTALS MAKE MISTAKES!
KRASH
SURRENDER OR DIE!
THE CHOICE IS YOURS!
AND WITH HIPPOLYTE'S WORDS, A STILLNESS FALLS OVER ALL-- AS WAR OR PEACE RESTS ON HERACLES' REPLY.
HA! BY ZEUS, GIRL-- HERACLES IS IMPRESSED!
MEN! LAY BACK!
THE AMAZONS ARE WORTHY ALLIES INDEED!
16

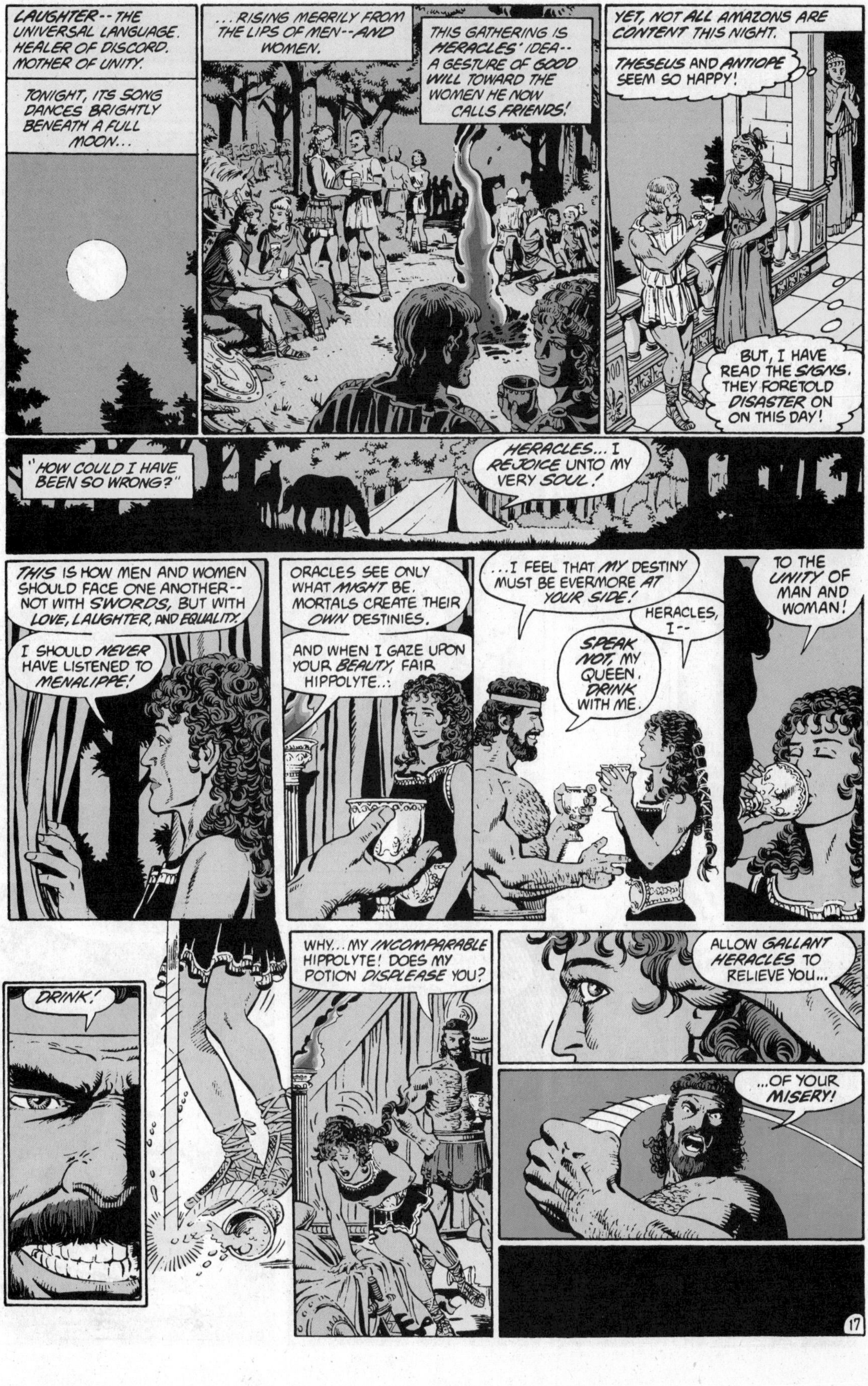
LAUGHTER--THE UNIVERSAL LANGUAGE. HEALER OF DISCORD. MOTHER OF UNITY.
TONIGHT, ITS SONG DANCES BRIGHTLY BENEATH A FULL MOON...
...RISING MERRILY FROM THE LIPS OF MEN--AND WOMEN.
THIS GATHERING IS HERACLES' IDEA-- A GESTURE OF GOOD WILL TOWARD THE WOMEN HE NOW CALLS FRIENDS!
YET, NOT ALL AMAZONS ARE CONTENT THIS NIGHT.
THESEUS AND ANTIOPE SEEM SO HAPPY!
BUT, I HAVE READ THE SIGNS. THEY FORETOLD DISASTER ON ON THIS DAY!
"HOW COULD I HAVE BEEN SO WRONG?"
HERACLES... I REJOICE UNTO MY VERY SOUL!
THIS IS HOW MEN AND WOMEN SHOULD FACE ONE ANOTHER-- NOT WITH SWORDS, BUT WITH LOVE, LAUGHTER, AND EQUALITY.
I SHOULD NEVER HAVE LISTENED TO MENALIPPE!
ORACLES SEE ONLY WHAT MIGHT BE. MORTALS CREATE THEIR OWN DESTINIES.
AND WHEN I GAZE UPON YOUR BEAUTY, FAIR HIPPOLYTE...
...I FEEL THAT MY DESTINY MUST BE EVERMORE AT YOUR SIDE!
HERACLES, I--
SPEAK NOT, MY QUEEN. DRINK WITH ME.
TO THE UNITY OF MAN AND WOMAN!
DRINK!
WHY... MY INCOMPARABLE HIPPOLYTE! DOES MY POTION DISPLEASE YOU?
ALLOW GALLANT HERACLES TO RELIEVE YOU...
...OF YOUR MISERY!
17

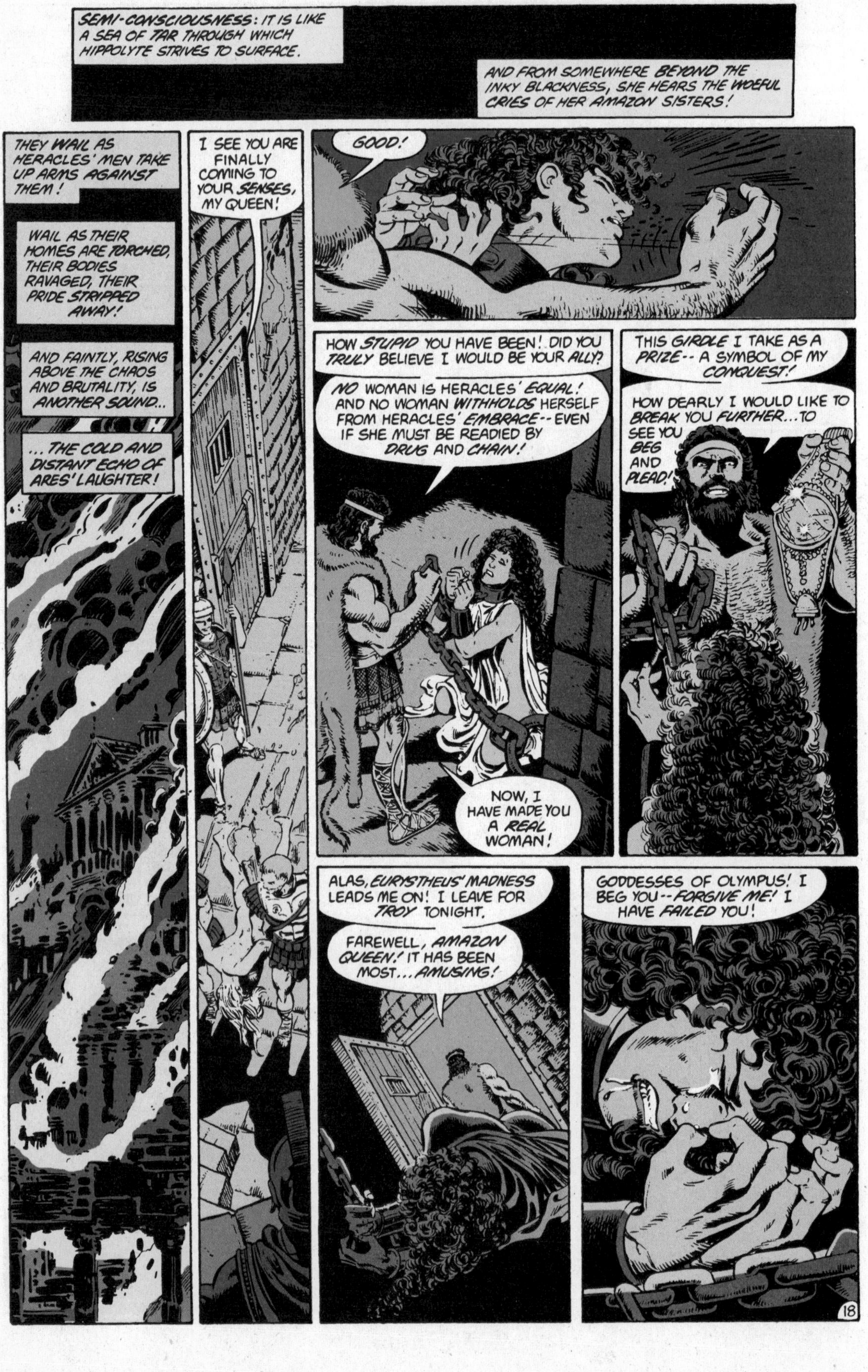
SEMI-CONSCIOUSNESS: IT IS LIKE A SEA OF TAR THROUGH WHICH HIPPOLYTE STRIVES TO SURFACE.
AND FROM SOMEWHERE BEYOND THE INKY BLACKNESS, SHE HEARS THE WOEFUL CRIES OF HER AMAZON SISTERS!
THEY WAIL AS HERACLES' MEN TAKE UP ARMS AGAINST THEM!
WAIL AS THEIR HOMES ARE TORCHED, THEIR BODIES RAVAGED, THEIR PRIDE STRIPPED AWAY!
AND FAINTLY, RISING ABOVE THE CHAOS AND BRUTALITY, IS ANOTHER SOUND...
...THE COLD AND DISTANT ECHO OF ARES' LAUGHTER!
I SEE YOU ARE FINALLY COMING TO YOUR SENSES, MY QUEEN!
GOOD!
HOW STUPID YOU HAVE BEEN! DID YOU TRULY BELIEVE I WOULD BE YOUR ALLY?
NO WOMAN IS HERACLES' EQUAL! AND NO WOMAN WITHHOLDS HERSELF FROM HERACLES' EMBRACE--EVEN IF SHE MUST BE READIED BY DRUG AND CHAIN!
NOW, I HAVE MADE YOU A REAL WOMAN!
THIS GIRDLE I TAKE AS A PRIZE--A SYMBOL OF MY CONQUEST!
HOW DEARLY I WOULD LIKE TO BREAK YOU FURTHER...TO SEE YOU BEG AND PLEAD!
ALAS, EURYSTHEUS' MADNESS LEADS ME ON! I LEAVE FOR TROY TONIGHT.
FAREWELL, AMAZON QUEEN! IT HAS BEEN MOST...AMUSING!
GODDESSES OF OLYMPUS! I BEG YOU--FORGIVE ME! I HAVE FAILED YOU!
18

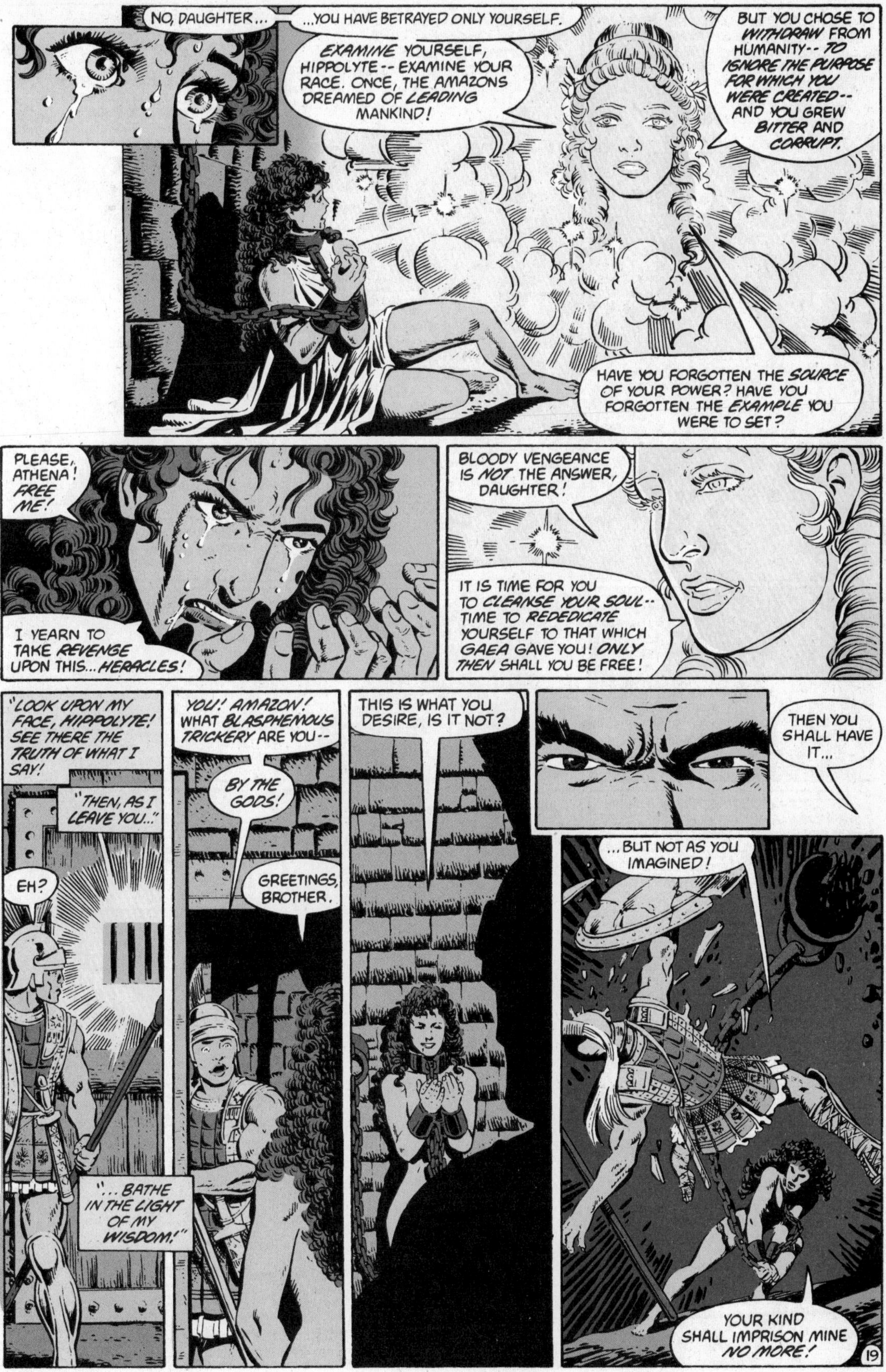
NO, DAUGHTER...
...YOU HAVE BETRAYED ONLY YOURSELF.
EXAMINE YOURSELF, HIPPOLYTE-- EXAMINE YOUR RACE. ONCE, THE AMAZONS DREAMED OF LEADING MANKIND!
BUT YOU CHOSE TO WITHDRAW FROM HUMANITY-- TO IGNORE THE PURPOSE FOR WHICH YOU WERE CREATED-- AND YOU GREW BITTER AND CORRUPT.
HAVE YOU FORGOTTEN THE SOURCE OF YOUR POWER? HAVE YOU FORGOTTEN THE EXAMPLE YOU WERE TO SET?
PLEASE, ATHENA! FREE ME!
I YEARN TO TAKE REVENGE UPON THIS... HERACLES!
BLOODY VENGEANCE IS NOT THE ANSWER, DAUGHTER!
IT IS TIME FOR YOU TO CLEANSE YOUR SOUL-- TIME TO REDEDICATE YOURSELF TO THAT WHICH GAEA GAVE YOU! ONLY THEN SHALL YOU BE FREE!
"LOOK UPON MY FACE, HIPPOLYTE! SEE THERE THE TRUTH OF WHAT I SAY!
"THEN, AS I LEAVE YOU..."
EH?
"... BATHE IN THE LIGHT OF MY WISDOM!"
YOU! AMAZON! WHAT BLASPHEMOUS TRICKERY ARE YOU--
BY THE GODS!
GREETINGS, BROTHER.
THIS IS WHAT YOU DESIRE, IS IT NOT?
THEN YOU SHALL HAVE IT...
...BUT NOT AS YOU IMAGINED!
YOUR KIND SHALL IMPRISON MINE NO MORE!
19

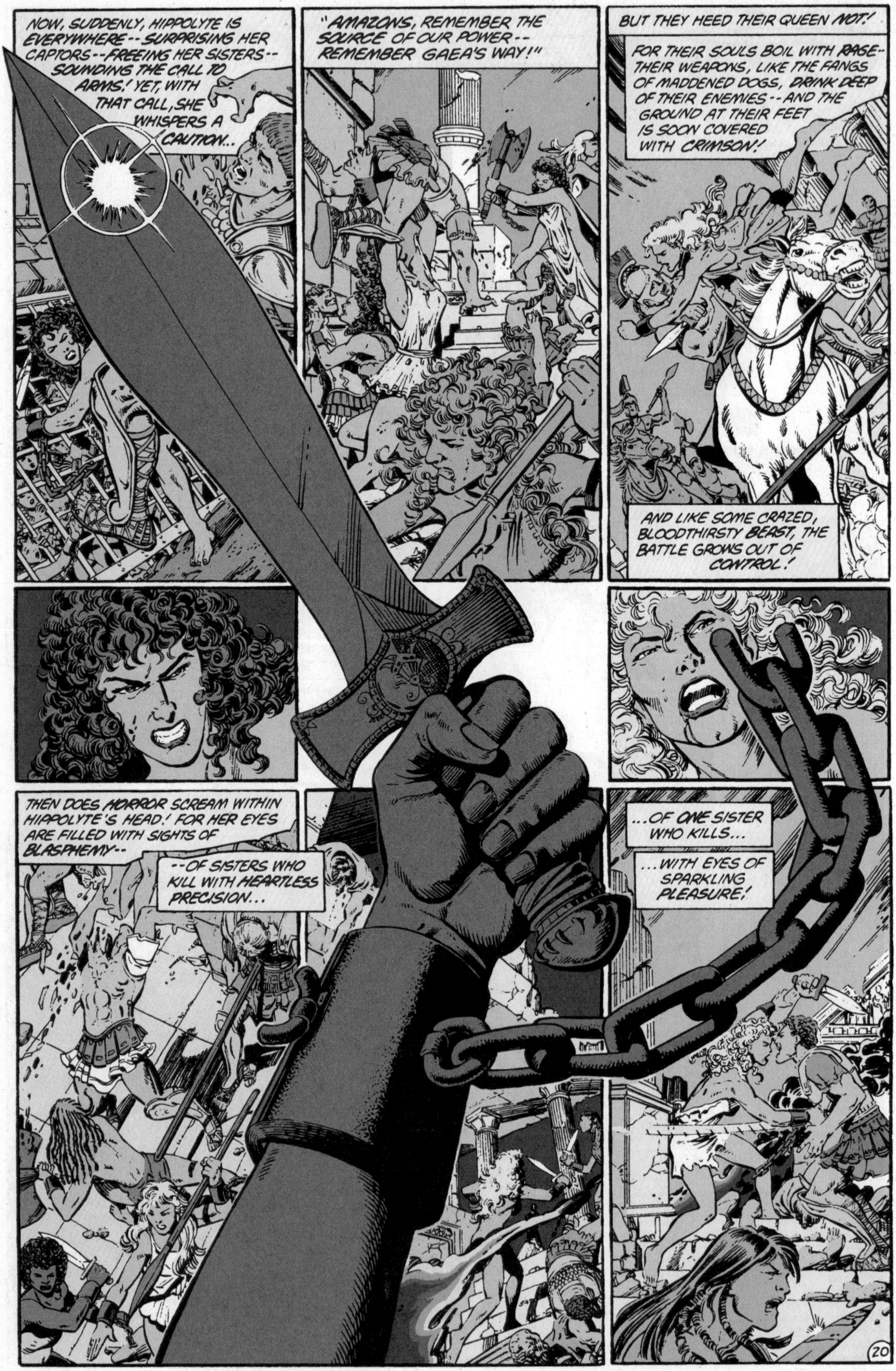
NOW, SUDDENLY, HIPPOLYTE IS EVERYWHERE -- SURPRISING HER CAPTORS -- FREEING HER SISTERS -- SOUNDING THE CALL TO ARMS! YET, WITH THAT CALL, SHE WHISPERS A CAUTION...
"AMAZONS, REMEMBER THE SOURCE OF OUR POWER -- REMEMBER GAEA'S WAY!"
BUT THEY HEED THEIR QUEEN NOT!
FOR THEIR SOULS BOIL WITH RAGE -- THEIR WEAPONS, LIKE THE FANGS OF MADDENED DOGS, DRINK DEEP OF THEIR ENEMIES -- AND THE GROUND AT THEIR FEET IS SOON COVERED WITH CRIMSON!
AND LIKE SOME CRAZED, BLOODTHIRSTY BEAST, THE BATTLE GROWS OUT OF CONTROL!
THEN DOES HORROR SCREAM WITHIN HIPPOLYTE'S HEAD! FOR HER EYES ARE FILLED WITH SIGHTS OF BLASPHEMY --
-- OF SISTERS WHO KILL WITH HEARTLESS PRECISION...
...OF ONE SISTER WHO KILLS...
...WITH EYES OF SPARKLING PLEASURE!
20

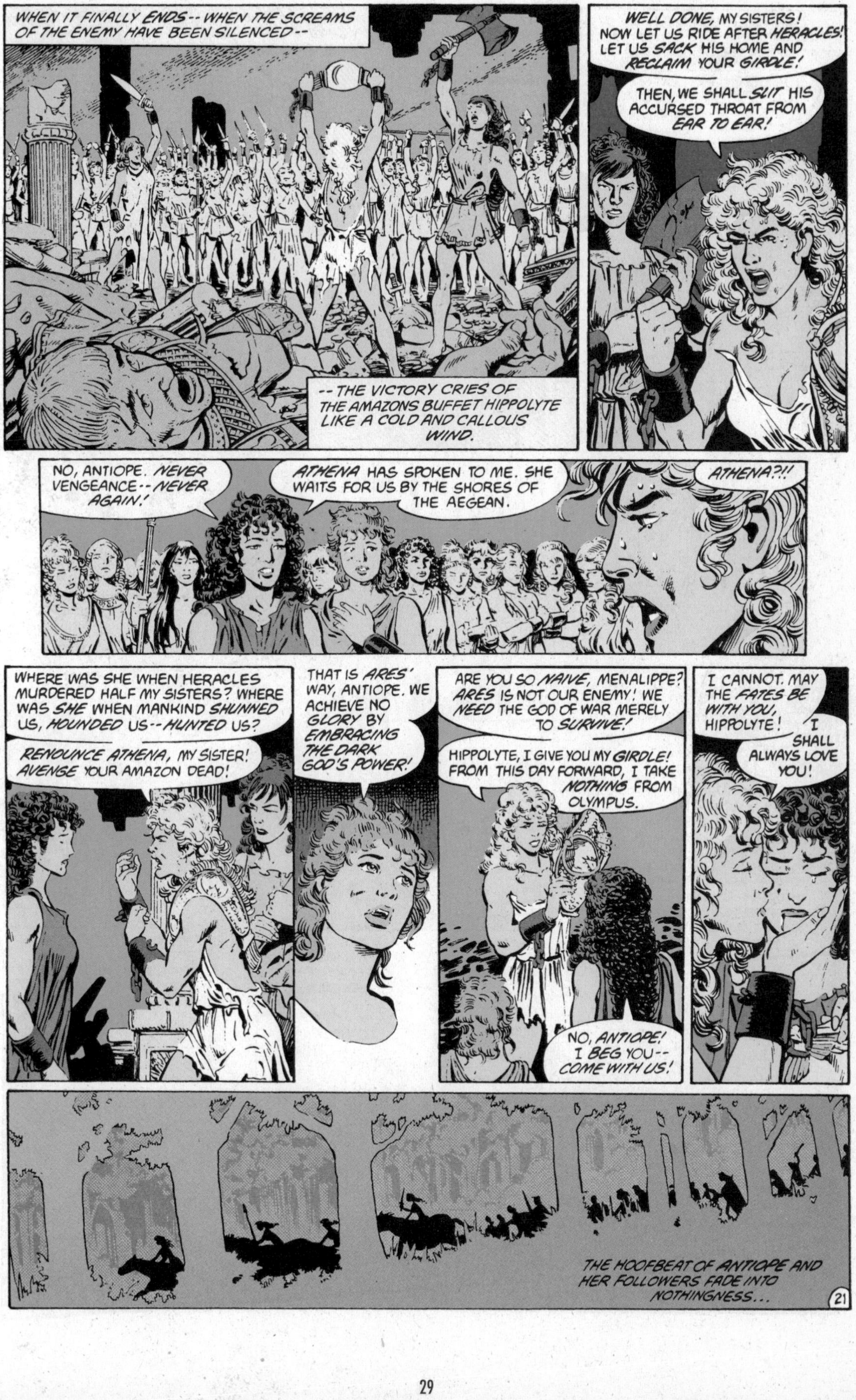
WHEN IT FINALLY ENDS-- WHEN THE SCREAMS OF THE ENEMY HAVE BEEN SILENCED--
--THE VICTORY CRIES OF THE AMAZONS BUFFET HIPPOLYTE LIKE A COLD AND CALLOUS WIND.
WELL DONE, MY SISTERS! NOW LET US RIDE AFTER HERACLES! LET US SACK HIS HOME AND RECLAIM YOUR GIRDLE!
THEN, WE SHALL SLIT HIS ACCURSED THROAT FROM EAR TO EAR!
NO, ANTIOPE. NEVER VENGEANCE-- NEVER AGAIN!
ATHENA HAS SPOKEN TO ME. SHE WAITS FOR US BY THE SHORES OF THE AEGEAN.
ATHENA?!!
WHERE WAS SHE WHEN HERACLES MURDERED HALF MY SISTERS? WHERE WAS SHE WHEN MANKIND SHUNNED US, HOUNDED US-- HUNTED US?
RENOUNCE ATHENA, MY SISTER! AVENGE YOUR AMAZON DEAD!
THAT IS ARES' WAY, ANTIOPE. WE ACHIEVE NO GLORY BY EMBRACING THE DARK GOD'S POWER!
ARE YOU SO NAIVE, MENALIPPE? ARES IS NOT OUR ENEMY! WE NEED THE GOD OF WAR MERELY TO SURVIVE!
HIPPOLYTE, I GIVE YOU MY GIRDLE! FROM THIS DAY FORWARD, I TAKE NOTHING FROM OLYMPUS.
NO, ANTIOPE! I BEG YOU-- COME WITH US!
I CANNOT. MAY THE FATES BE WITH YOU, HIPPOLYTE!
I SHALL ALWAYS LOVE YOU!
THE HOOFBEAT OF ANTIOPE AND HER FOLLOWERS FADE INTO NOTHINGNESS...
21

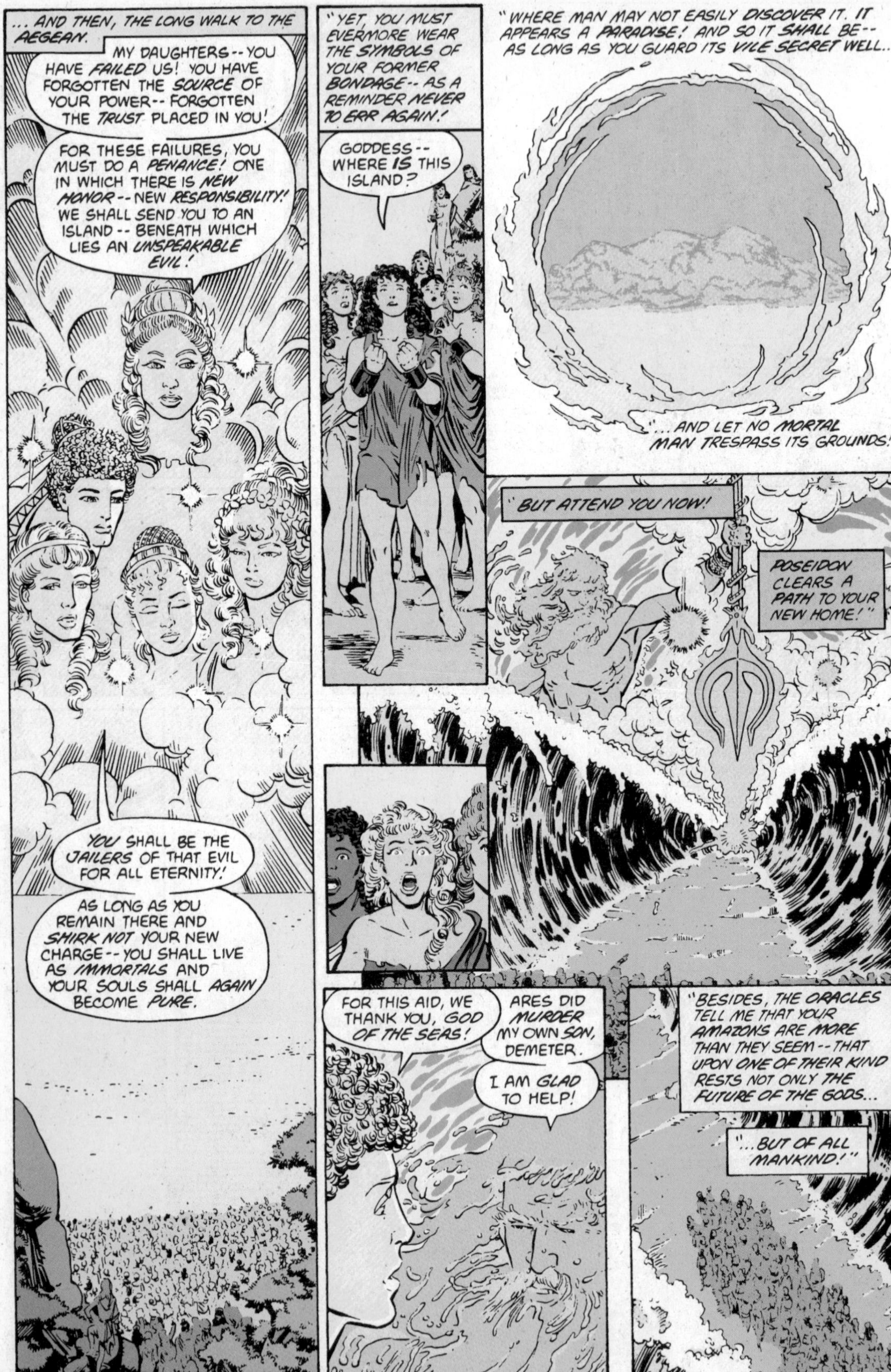
...AND THEN, THE LONG WALK TO THE AEGEAN.
MY DAUGHTERS--YOU HAVE FAILED US! YOU HAVE FORGOTTEN THE SOURCE OF YOUR POWER--FORGOTTEN THE TRUST PLACED IN YOU!
FOR THESE FAILURES, YOU MUST DO A PENANCE! ONE IN WHICH THERE IS NEW HONOR--NEW RESPONSIBILITY! WE SHALL SEND YOU TO AN ISLAND--BENEATH WHICH LIES AN UNSPEAKABLE EVIL!
YOU SHALL BE THE JAILERS OF THAT EVIL FOR ALL ETERNITY!
AS LONG AS YOU REMAIN THERE AND SHIRK NOT YOUR NEW CHARGE--YOU SHALL LIVE AS IMMORTALS AND YOUR SOULS SHALL AGAIN BECOME PURE.
22
"YET, YOU MUST EVERMORE WEAR THE SYMBOLS OF YOUR FORMER BONDAGE--AS A REMINDER NEVER TO ERR AGAIN!"
GODDESS--WHERE IS THIS ISLAND?
"WHERE MAN MAY NOT EASILY DISCOVER IT. IT APPEARS A PARADISE! AND SO IT SHALL BE--AS LONG AS YOU GUARD ITS VILE SECRET WELL...
"...AND LET NO MORTAL MAN TRESPASS ITS GROUNDS!
"BUT ATTEND YOU NOW!
POSEIDON CLEARS A PATH TO YOUR NEW HOME!"
FOR THIS AID, WE THANK YOU, GOD OF THE SEAS!
ARES DID MURDER MY OWN SON, DEMETER.
I AM GLAD TO HELP!
"BESIDES, THE ORACLES TELL ME THAT YOUR AMAZONS ARE MORE THAN THEY SEEM--THAT UPON ONE OF THEIR KIND RESTS NOT ONLY THE FUTURE OF THE GODS...
"...BUT OF ALL MANKIND!"

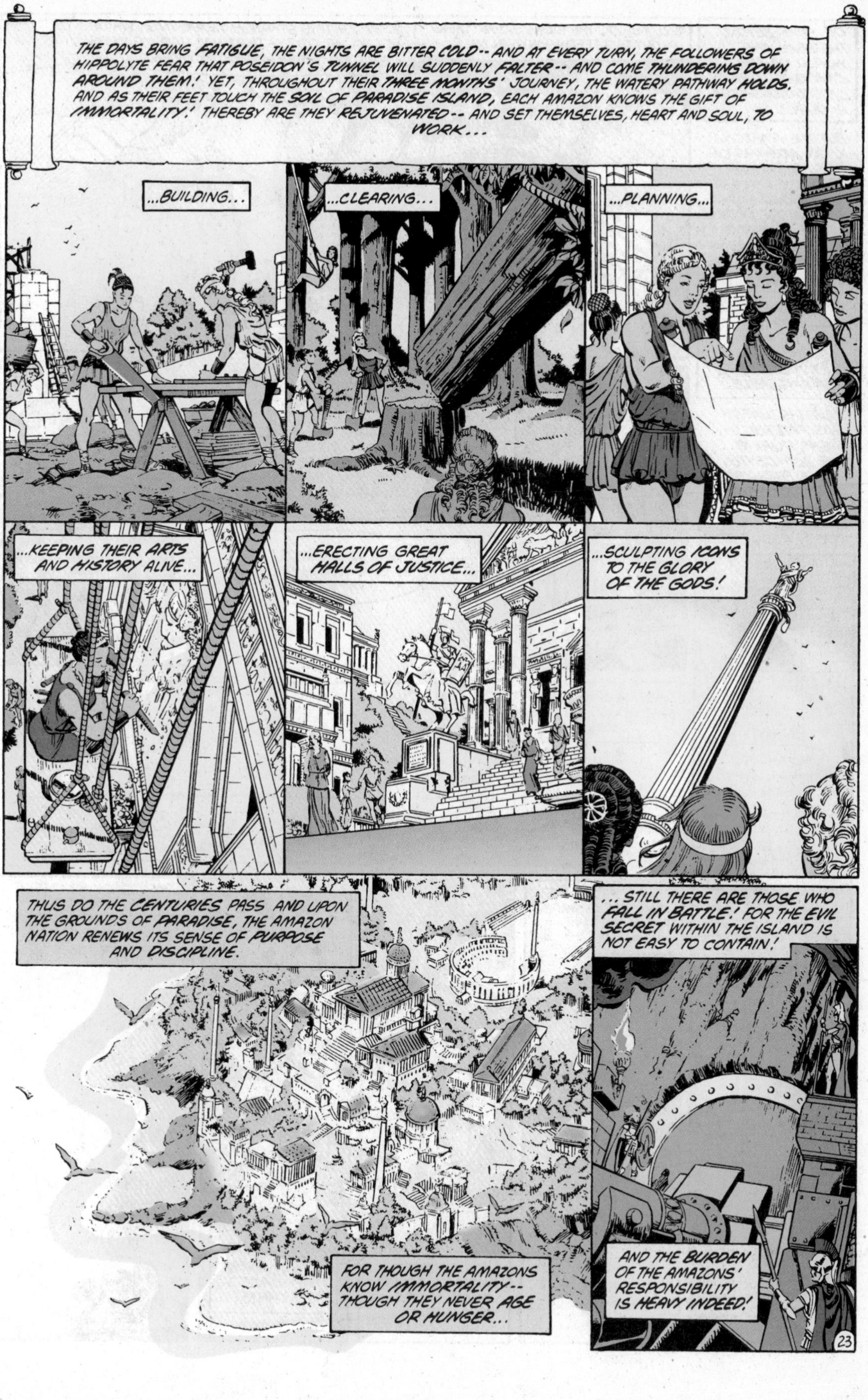
THE DAYS BRING FATIGUE, THE NIGHTS ARE BITTER COLD -- AND AT EVERY TURN, THE FOLLOWERS OF HIPPOLYTE FEAR THAT POSEIDON'S TUNNEL WILL SUDDENLY FALTER -- AND COME THUNDERING DOWN AROUND THEM! YET, THROUGHOUT THEIR THREE MONTHS' JOURNEY, THE WATERY PATHWAY HOLDS. AND AS THEIR FEET TOUCH THE SOIL OF PARADISE ISLAND, EACH AMAZON KNOWS THE GIFT OF IMMORTALITY! THEREBY ARE THEY REJUVENATED -- AND SET THEMSELVES, HEART AND SOUL, TO WORK...
...BUILDING...
...CLEARING...
...PLANNING...
...KEEPING THEIR ARTS AND HISTORY ALIVE...
...ERECTING GREAT HALLS OF JUSTICE...
...SCULPTING ICONS TO THE GLORY OF THE GODS!
THUS DO THE CENTURIES PASS AND UPON THE GROUNDS OF PARADISE, THE AMAZON NATION RENEWS ITS SENSE OF PURPOSE AND DISCIPLINE.
FOR THOUGH THE AMAZONS KNOW IMMORTALITY -- THOUGH THEY NEVER AGE OR HUNGER...
... STILL THERE ARE THOSE WHO FALL IN BATTLE! FOR THE EVIL SECRET WITHIN THE ISLAND IS NOT EASY TO CONTAIN!
AND THE BURDEN OF THE AMAZONS' RESPONSIBILITY IS HEAVY INDEED!
23

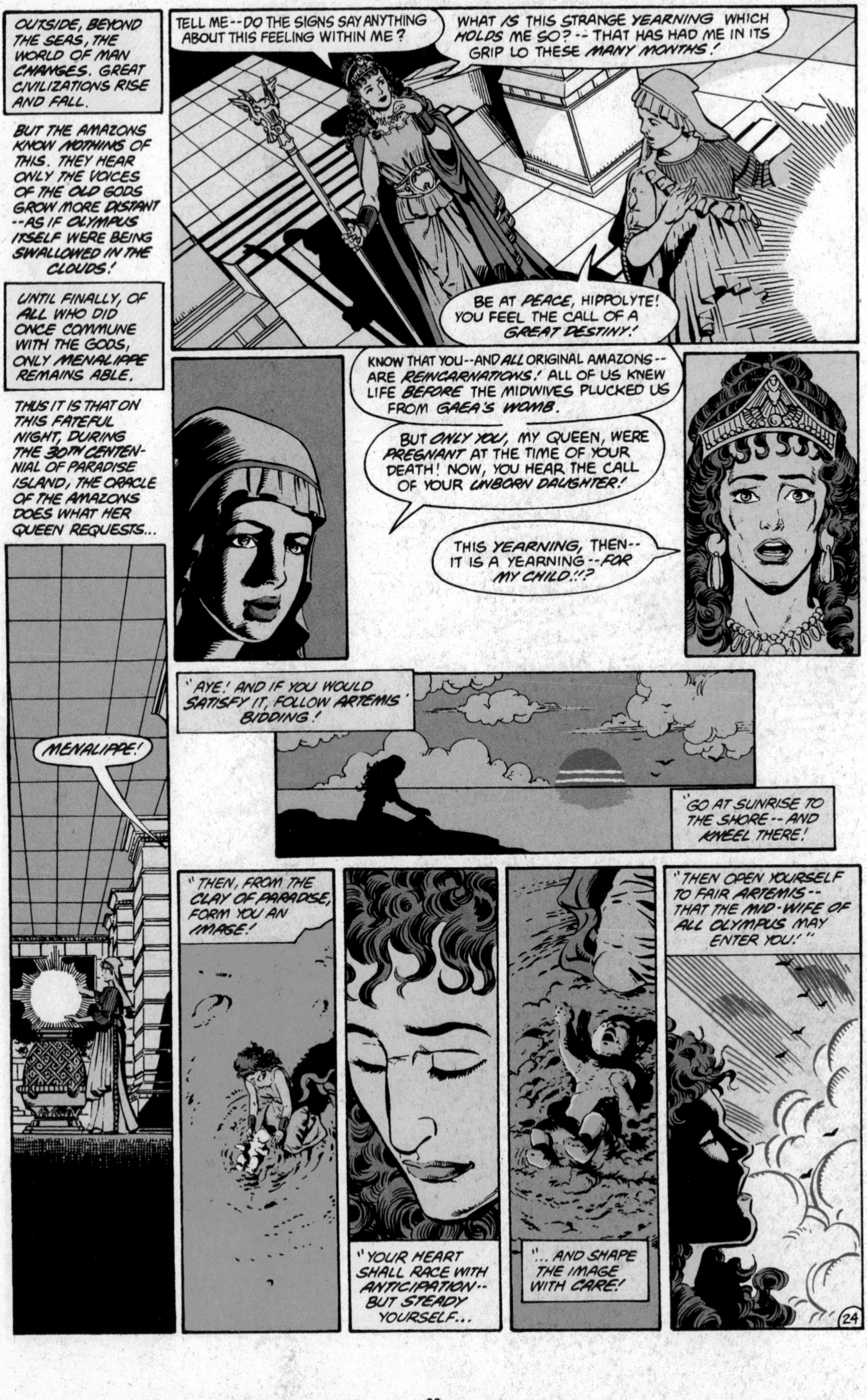

OUTSIDE, BEYOND THE SEAS, THE WORLD OF MAN CHANGES. GREAT CIVILIZATIONS RISE AND FALL.
BUT THE AMAZONS KNOW NOTHING OF THIS. THEY HEAR ONLY THE VOICES OF THE OLD GODS GROW MORE DISTANT --AS IF OLYMPUS ITSELF WERE BEING SWALLOWED IN THE CLOUDS!
UNTIL FINALLY, OF ALL WHO DID ONCE COMMUNE WITH THE GODS, ONLY MENALIPPE REMAINS ABLE.
THUS IT IS THAT ON THIS FATEFUL NIGHT, DURING THE 30TH CENTENNIAL OF PARADISE ISLAND, THE ORACLE OF THE AMAZONS DOES WHAT HER QUEEN REQUESTS...
MENALIPPE!
TELL ME--DO THE SIGNS SAY ANYTHING ABOUT THIS FEELING WITHIN ME?
WHAT IS THIS STRANGE YEARNING WHICH HOLDS ME SO? -- THAT HAS HAD ME IN ITS GRIP LO THESE MANY MONTHS!
BE AT PEACE, HIPPOLYTE! YOU FEEL THE CALL OF A GREAT DESTINY!
KNOW THAT YOU--AND ALL ORIGINAL AMAZONS--ARE REINCARNATIONS! ALL OF US KNEW LIFE BEFORE THE MIDWIVES PLUCKED US FROM GAEA'S WOMB.
BUT ONLY YOU, MY QUEEN, WERE PREGNANT AT THE TIME OF YOUR DEATH! NOW, YOU HEAR THE CALL OF YOUR UNBORN DAUGHTER!
THIS YEARNING, THEN--IT IS A YEARNING--FOR MY CHILD!!?
"AYE! AND IF YOU WOULD SATISFY IT, FOLLOW ARTEMIS' BIDDING!
"GO AT SUNRISE TO THE SHORE--AND KNEEL THERE!
"THEN, FROM THE CLAY OF PARADISE, FORM YOU AN IMAGE!
"YOUR HEART SHALL RACE WITH ANTICIPATION--BUT STEADY YOURSELF...
"...AND SHAPE THE IMAGE WITH CARE!
"THEN OPEN YOURSELF TO FAIR ARTEMIS--THAT THE MID-WIFE OF ALL OLYMPUS MAY ENTER YOU!"
24

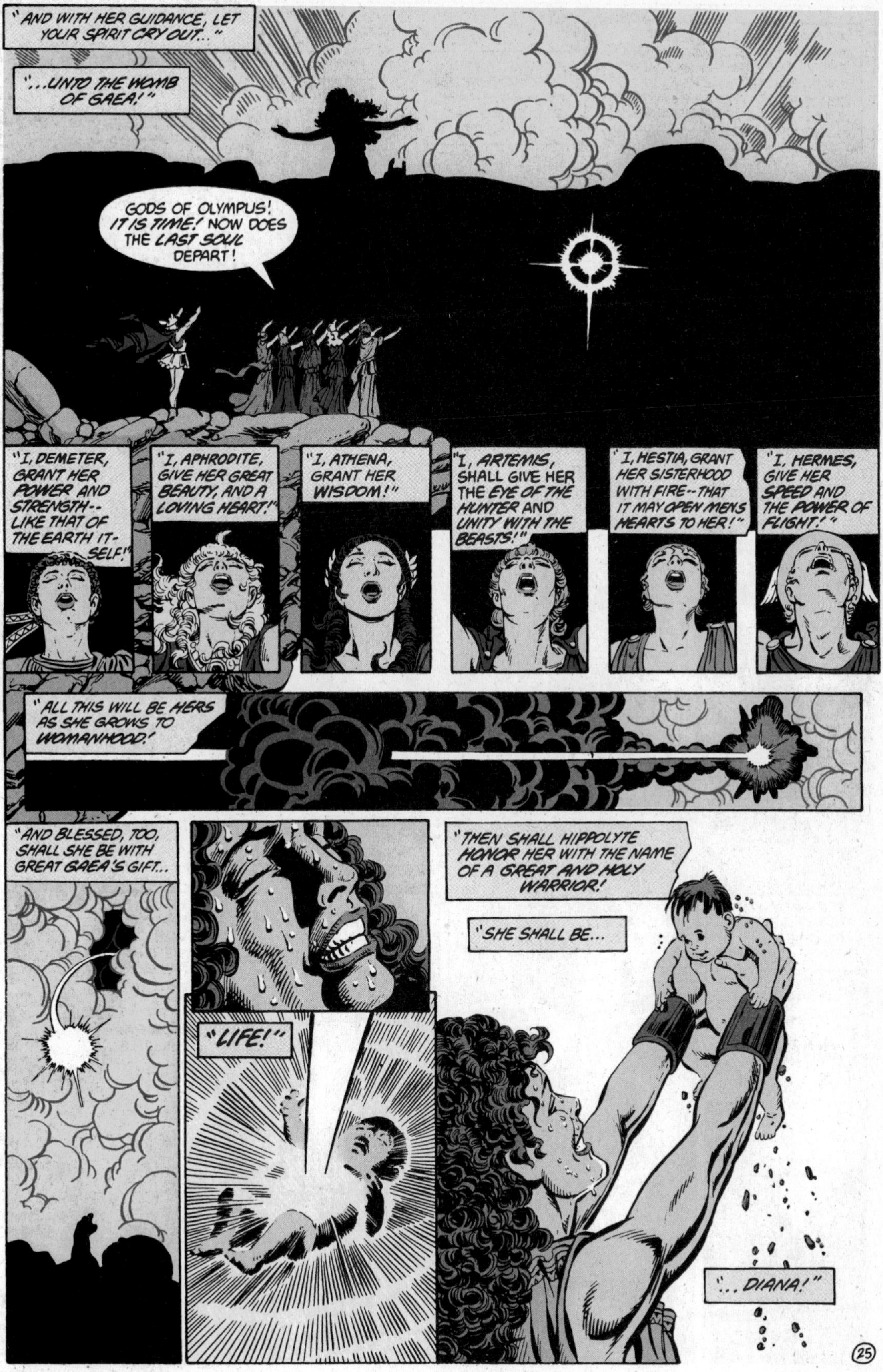
"AND WITH HER GUIDANCE, LET YOUR SPIRIT CRY OUT..."
"...UNTO THE WOMB OF GAEA!"
GODS OF OLYMPUS! IT IS TIME! NOW DOES THE LAST SOUL DEPART!
"I, DEMETER, GRANT HER POWER AND STRENGTH-- LIKE THAT OF THE EARTH IT-SELF!"
"I, APHRODITE, GIVE HER GREAT BEAUTY, AND A LOVING HEART!"
"I, ATHENA, GRANT HER WISDOM!"
"I, ARTEMIS, SHALL GIVE HER THE EYE OF THE HUNTER AND UNITY WITH THE BEASTS!"
"I, HESTIA, GRANT HER SISTERHOOD WITH FIRE--THAT IT MAY OPEN MENS HEARTS TO HER!"
"I, HERMES, GIVE HER SPEED AND THE POWER OF FLIGHT!"
"ALL THIS WILL BE HERS AS SHE GROWS TO WOMANHOOD!"
"AND BLESSED, TOO, SHALL SHE BE WITH GREAT GAEA'S GIFT...
"LIFE!"
"THEN SHALL HIPPOLYTE HONOR HER WITH THE NAME OF A GREAT AND HOLY WARRIOR!
"SHE SHALL BE...
"...DIANA!"
25

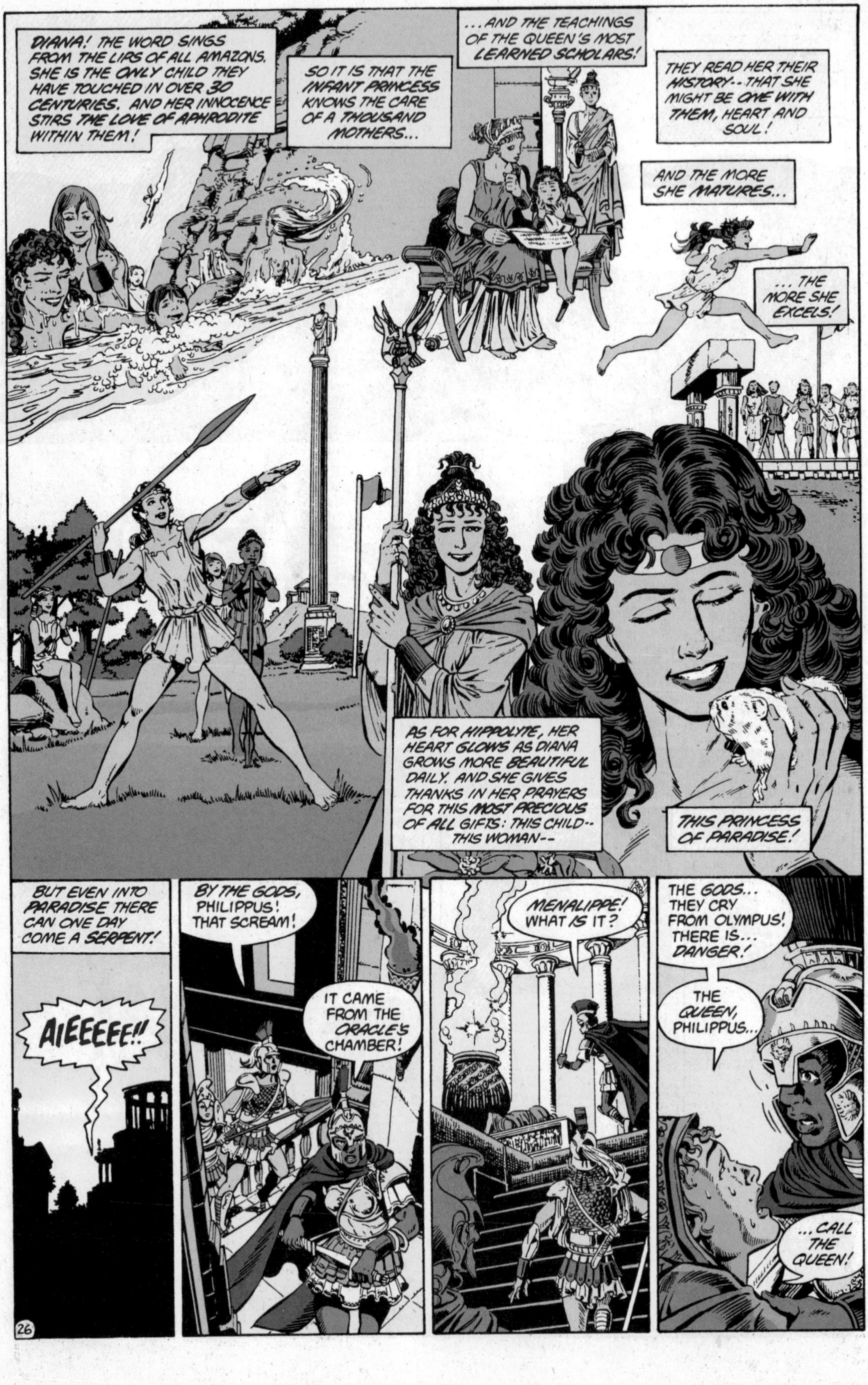
DIANA! THE WORD SINGS FROM THE LIPS OF ALL AMAZONS. SHE IS THE ONLY CHILD THEY HAVE TOUCHED IN OVER 30 CENTURIES. AND HER INNOCENCE STIRS THE LOVE OF APHRODITE WITHIN THEM!
SO IT IS THAT THE INFANT PRINCESS KNOWS THE CARE OF A THOUSAND MOTHERS...
...AND THE TEACHINGS OF THE QUEEN'S MOST LEARNED SCHOLARS!
THEY READ HER THEIR HISTORY--THAT SHE MIGHT BE ONE WITH THEM, HEART AND SOUL!
AND THE MORE SHE MATURES...
...THE MORE SHE EXCELS!
AS FOR HIPPOLYTE, HER HEART GLOWS AS DIANA GROWS MORE BEAUTIFUL DAILY. AND SHE GIVES THANKS IN HER PRAYERS FOR THIS MOST PRECIOUS OF ALL GIFTS: THIS CHILD-- THIS WOMAN--
THIS PRINCESS OF PARADISE!
BUT EVEN INTO PARADISE THERE CAN ONE DAY COME A SERPENT!
AIEEEEE!!
BY THE GODS, PHILIPPUS! THAT SCREAM!
IT CAME FROM THE ORACLE'S CHAMBER!
MENALIPPE! WHAT IS IT?
THE GODS... THEY CRY FROM OLYMPUS! THERE IS... DANGER!
THE QUEEN, PHILIPPUS...
...CALL THE QUEEN!
26

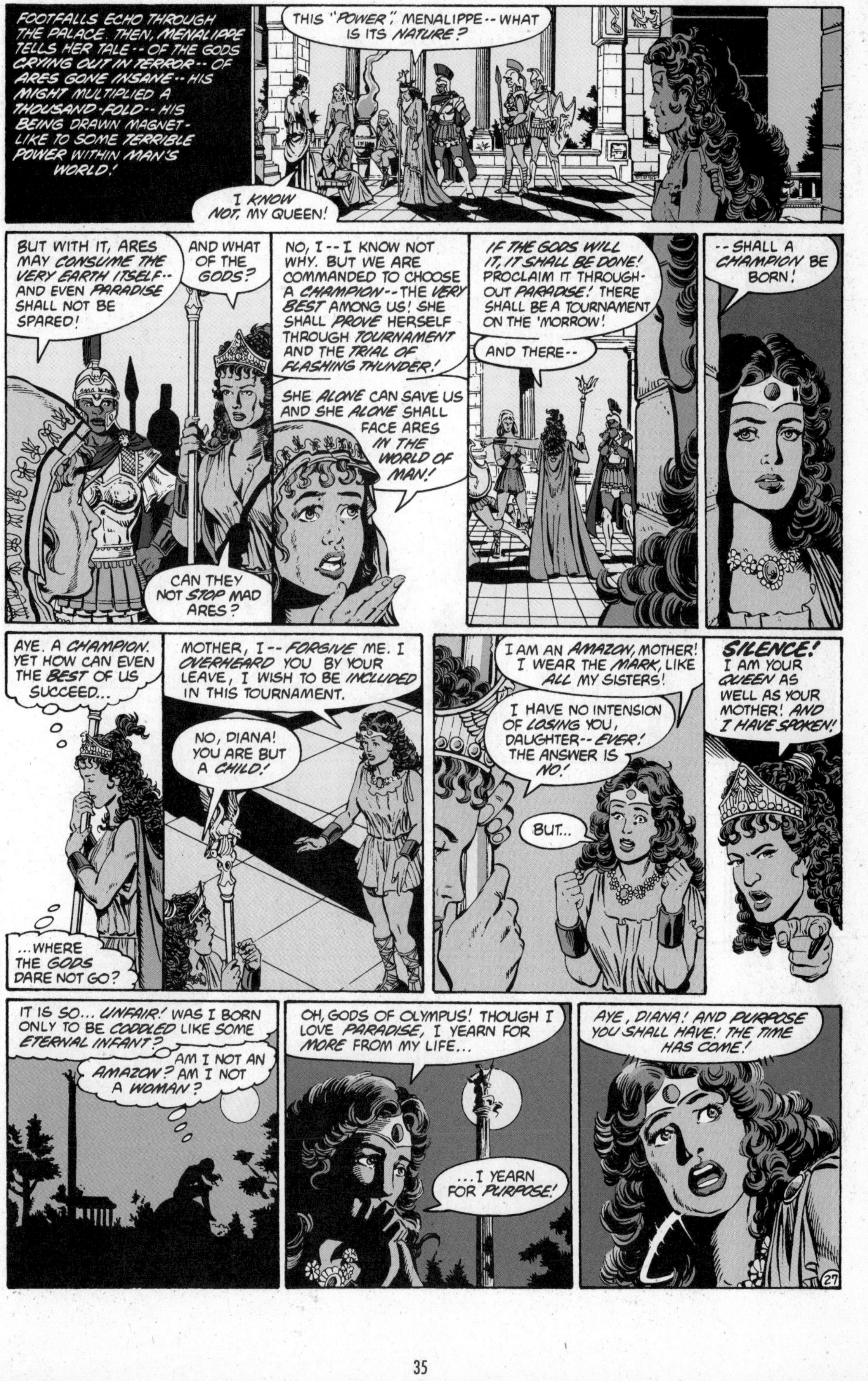
FOOTFALLS ECHO THROUGH THE PALACE. THEN, MENALIPPE TELLS HER TALE -- OF THE GODS CRYING OUT IN TERROR -- OF ARES GONE INSANE -- HIS MIGHT MULTIPLIED A THOUSAND-FOLD -- HIS BEING DRAWN MAGNET-LIKE TO SOME TERRIBLE POWER WITHIN MAN'S WORLD!
THIS "POWER", MENALIPPE -- WHAT IS ITS NATURE?
I KNOW NOT, MY QUEEN!
BUT WITH IT, ARES MAY CONSUME THE VERY EARTH ITSELF -- AND EVEN PARADISE SHALL NOT BE SPARED!
AND WHAT OF THE GODS?
CAN THEY NOT STOP MAD ARES?
NO, I -- I KNOW NOT WHY. BUT WE ARE COMMANDED TO CHOOSE A CHAMPION -- THE VERY BEST AMONG US! SHE SHALL PROVE HERSELF THROUGH TOURNAMENT AND THE TRIAL OF FLASHING THUNDER!
SHE ALONE CAN SAVE US AND SHE ALONE SHALL FACE ARES IN THE WORLD OF MAN!
IF THE GODS WILL IT, IT SHALL BE DONE! PROCLAIM IT THROUGHOUT PARADISE! THERE SHALL BE A TOURNAMENT ON THE 'MORROW!
AND THERE --
-- SHALL A CHAMPION BE BORN!
AYE. A CHAMPION. YET HOW CAN EVEN THE BEST OF US SUCCEED...
...WHERE THE GODS DARE NOT GO?
MOTHER, I -- FORGIVE ME. I OVERHEARD YOU BY YOUR LEAVE, I WISH TO BE INCLUDED IN THIS TOURNAMENT.
NO, DIANA! YOU ARE BUT A CHILD!
I AM AN AMAZON, MOTHER! I WEAR THE MARK, LIKE ALL MY SISTERS!
I HAVE NO INTENSION OF LOSING YOU, DAUGHTER -- EVER! THE ANSWER IS NO!
BUT...
SILENCE! I AM YOUR QUEEN AS WELL AS YOUR MOTHER! AND I HAVE SPOKEN!
IT IS SO... UNFAIR! WAS I BORN ONLY TO BE CODDLED LIKE SOME ETERNAL INFANT?
AM I NOT AN AMAZON? AM I NOT A WOMAN?
OH, GODS OF OLYMPUS! THOUGH I LOVE PARADISE, I YEARN FOR MORE FROM MY LIFE...
...I YEARN FOR PURPOSE!
AYE, DIANA! AND PURPOSE YOU SHALL HAVE! THE TIME HAS COME!
27

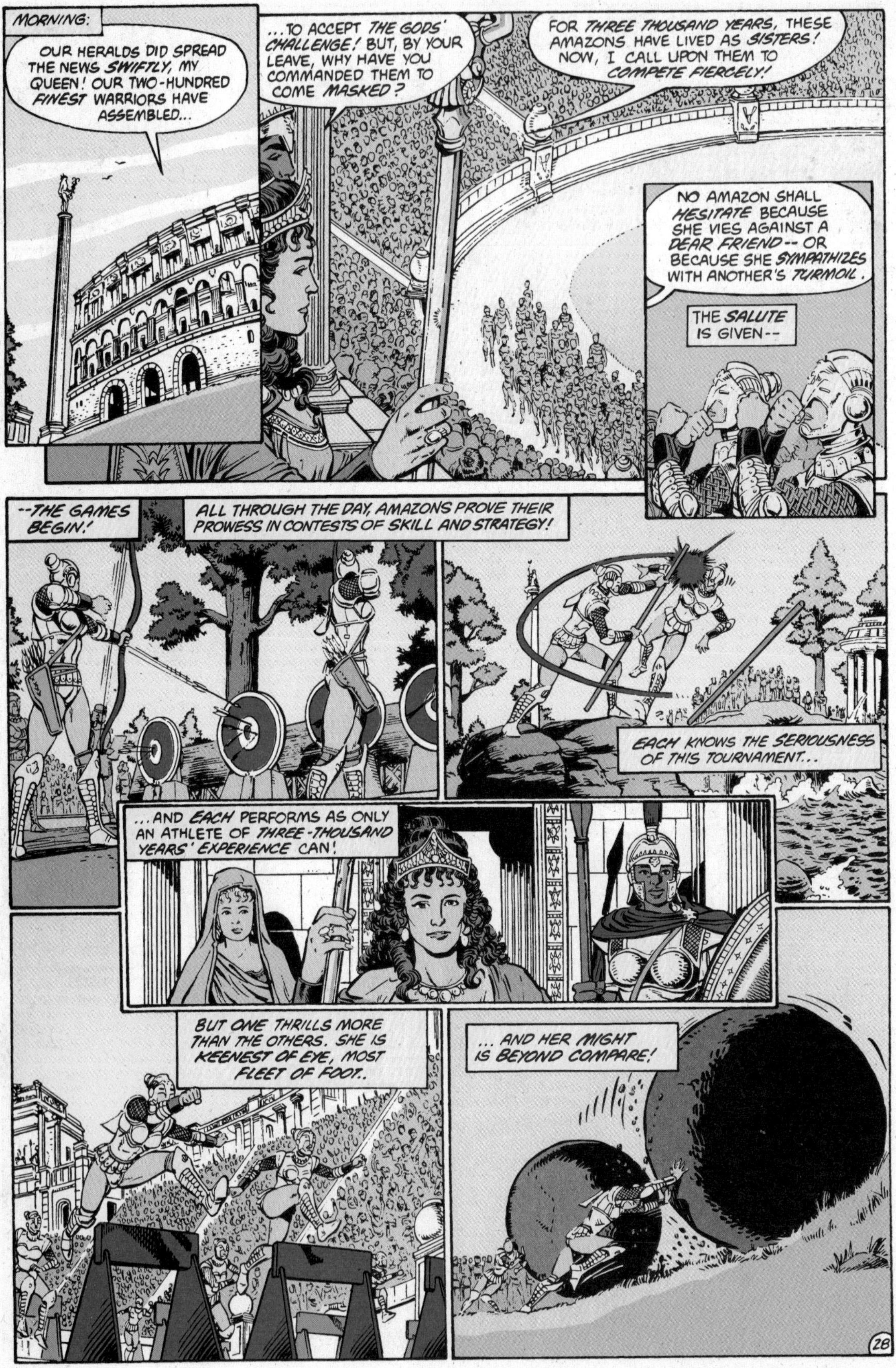
MORNING:
OUR HERALDS DID SPREAD THE NEWS SWIFTLY, MY QUEEN! OUR TWO-HUNDRED FINEST WARRIORS HAVE ASSEMBLED...
...TO ACCEPT THE GODS' CHALLENGE! BUT, BY YOUR LEAVE, WHY HAVE YOU COMMANDED THEM TO COME MASKED?
FOR THREE THOUSAND YEARS, THESE AMAZONS HAVE LIVED AS SISTERS! NOW, I CALL UPON THEM TO COMPETE FIERCELY!
NO AMAZON SHALL HESITATE BECAUSE SHE VIES AGAINST A DEAR FRIEND-- OR BECAUSE SHE SYMPATHIZES WITH ANOTHER'S TURMOIL.
THE SALUTE IS GIVEN--
--THE GAMES BEGIN!
ALL THROUGH THE DAY, AMAZONS PROVE THEIR PROWESS IN CONTESTS OF SKILL AND STRATEGY!
EACH KNOWS THE SERIOUSNESS OF THIS TOURNAMENT...
...AND EACH PERFORMS AS ONLY AN ATHLETE OF THREE-THOUSAND YEARS' EXPERIENCE CAN!
BUT ONE THRILLS MORE THAN THE OTHERS. SHE IS KEENEST OF EYE, MOST FLEET OF FOOT..
... AND HER MIGHT IS BEYOND COMPARE!
28

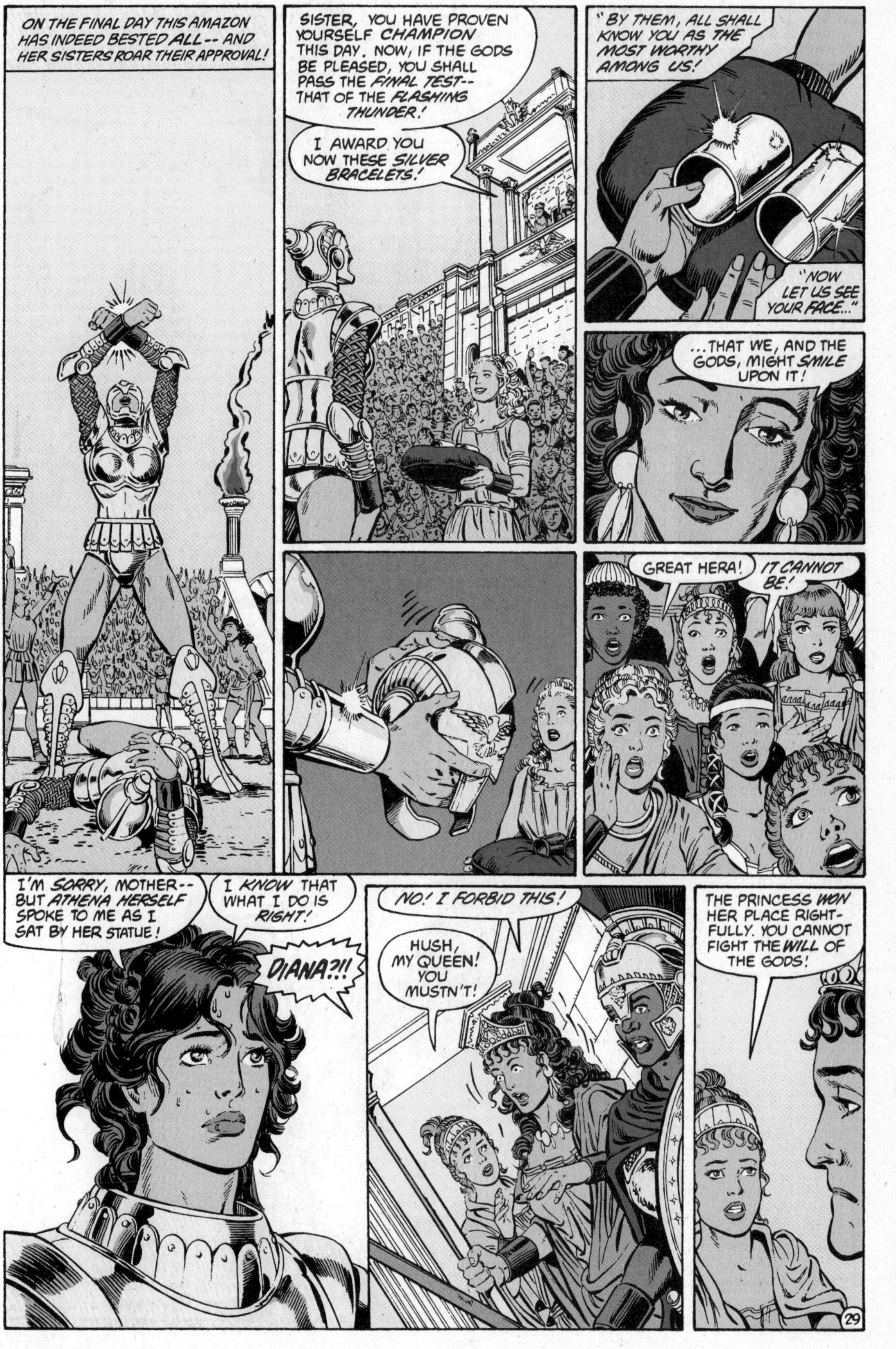

ON THE FINAL DAY THIS AMAZON HAS INDEED BESTED ALL -- AND HER SISTERS ROAR THEIR APPROVAL!
SISTER, YOU HAVE PROVEN YOURSELF CHAMPION THIS DAY. NOW, IF THE GODS BE PLEASED, YOU SHALL PASS THE FINAL TEST-- THAT OF THE FLASHING THUNDER!
I AWARD YOU NOW THESE SILVER BRACELETS!
"BY THEM, ALL SHALL KNOW YOU AS THE MOST WORTHY AMONG US!
"NOW LET US SEE YOUR FACE..."
...THAT WE, AND THE GODS, MIGHT SMILE UPON IT!
GREAT HERA!
IT CANNOT BE!
I'M SORRY, MOTHER-- BUT ATHENA HERSELF SPOKE TO ME AS I SAT BY HER STATUE!
I KNOW THAT WHAT I DO IS RIGHT!
DIANA?!!
NO! I FORBID THIS!
HUSH, MY QUEEN! YOU MUSTN'T!
THE PRINCESS WON HER PLACE RIGHT-FULLY. YOU CANNOT FIGHT THE WILL OF THE GODS!
29

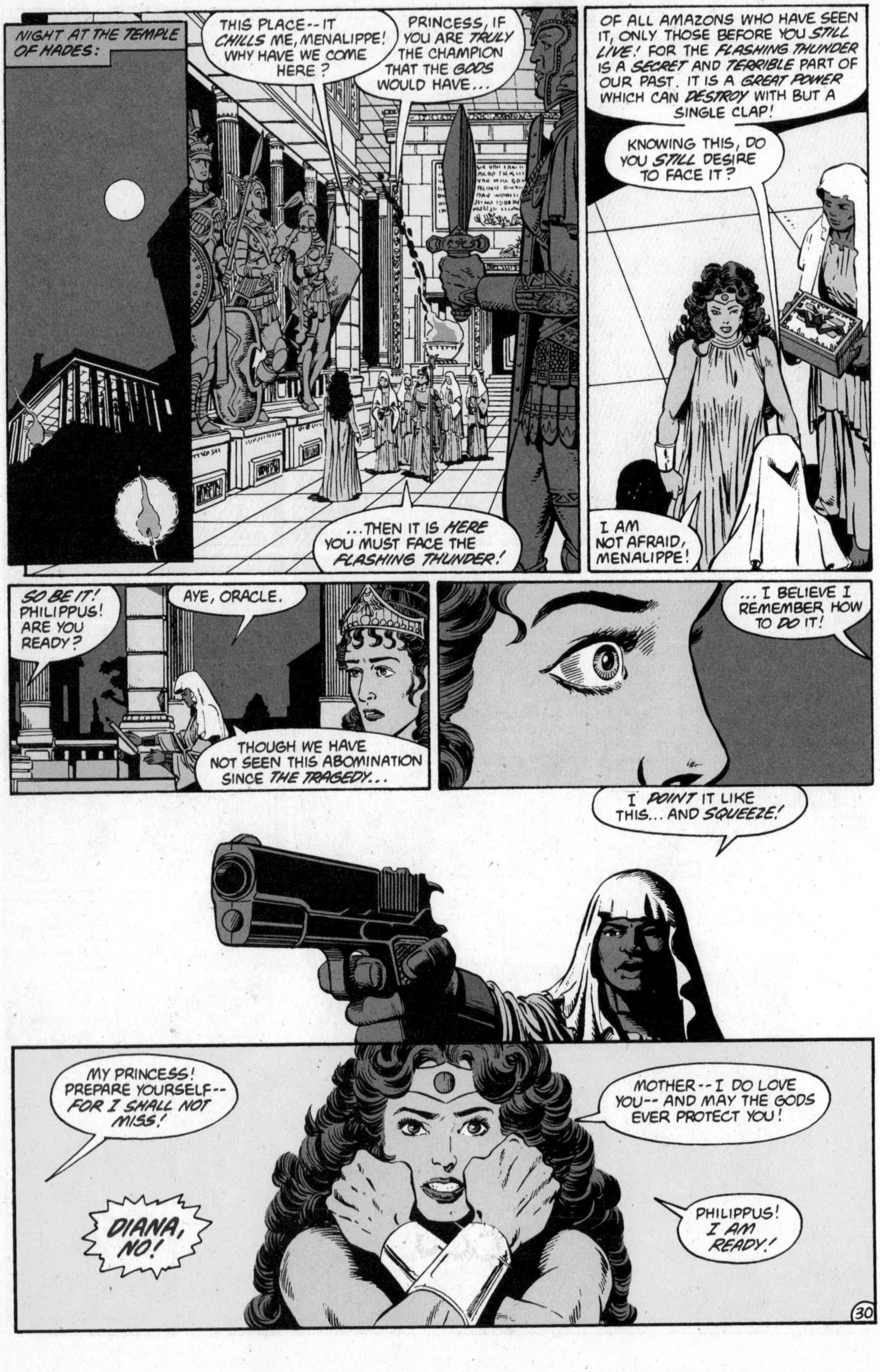
NIGHT AT THE TEMPLE OF HADES:
THIS PLACE--IT CHILLS ME, MENALIPPE! WHY HAVE WE COME HERE?
PRINCESS, IF YOU ARE TRULY THE CHAMPION THAT THE GODS WOULD HAVE...
...THEN IT IS HERE YOU MUST FACE THE FLASHING THUNDER!
OF ALL AMAZONS WHO HAVE SEEN IT, ONLY THOSE BEFORE YOU STILL LIVE! FOR THE FLASHING THUNDER IS A SECRET AND TERRIBLE PART OF OUR PAST. IT IS A GREAT POWER WHICH CAN DESTROY WITH BUT A SINGLE CLAP!
KNOWING THIS, DO YOU STILL DESIRE TO FACE IT?
I AM NOT AFRAID, MENALIPPE!
SO BE IT! PHILIPPUS! ARE YOU READY?
AYE, ORACLE.
THOUGH WE HAVE NOT SEEN THIS ABOMINATION SINCE THE TRAGEDY...
...I BELIEVE I REMEMBER HOW TO DO IT!
I POINT IT LIKE THIS... AND SQUEEZE!
MY PRINCESS! PREPARE YOURSELF--FOR I SHALL NOT MISS!
MOTHER--I DO LOVE YOU-- AND MAY THE GODS EVER PROTECT YOU!
DIANA, NO!
PHILIPPUS! I AM READY!
30

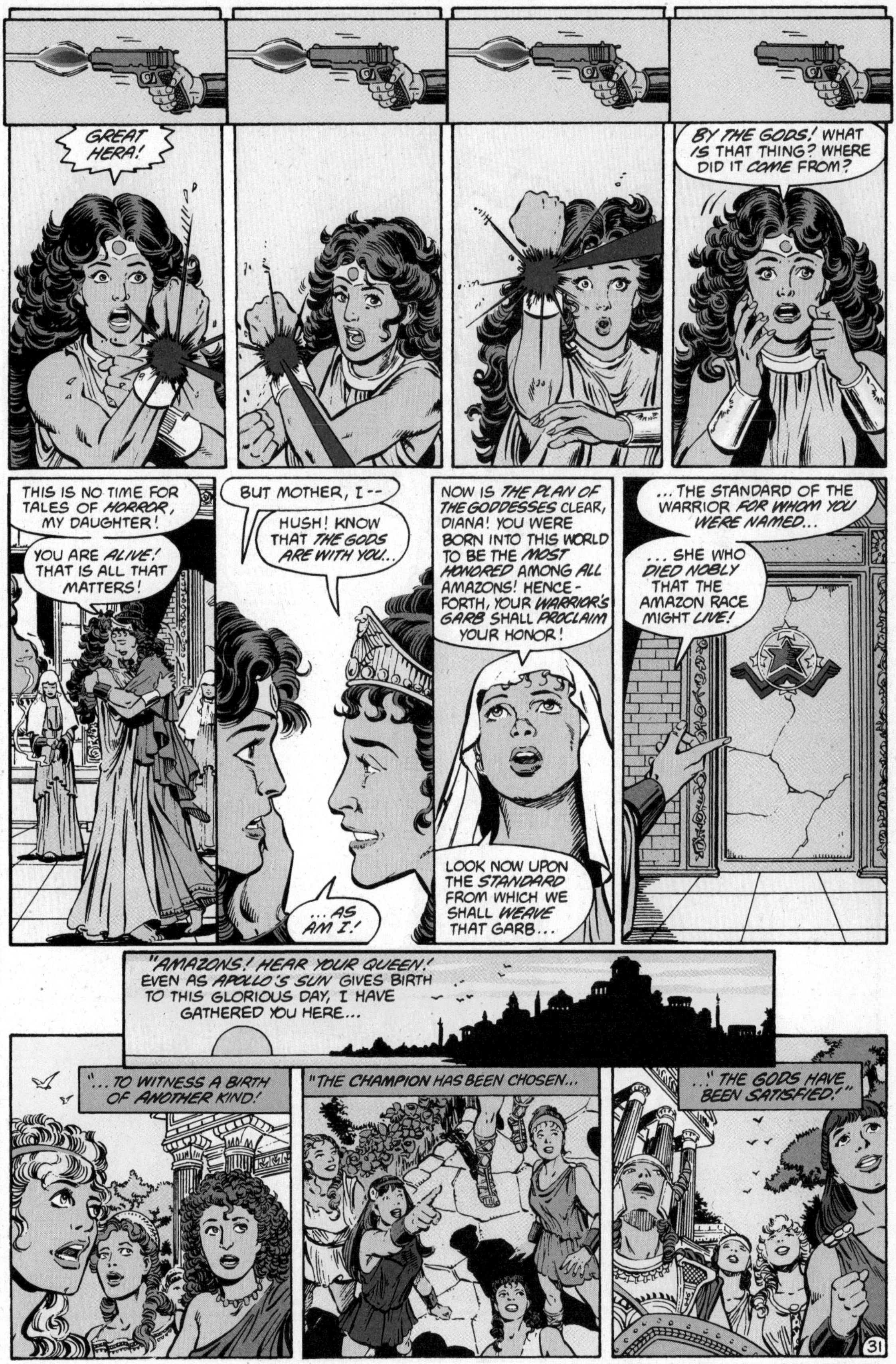
GREAT HERA!
BY THE GODS! WHAT IS THAT THING? WHERE DID IT COME FROM?
THIS IS NO TIME FOR TALES OF HORROR, MY DAUGHTER!
YOU ARE ALIVE! THAT IS ALL THAT MATTERS!
BUT MOTHER, I --
HUSH! KNOW THAT THE GODS ARE WITH YOU...
...AS AM I!
NOW IS THE PLAN OF THE GODDESSES CLEAR, DIANA! YOU WERE BORN INTO THIS WORLD TO BE THE MOST HONORED AMONG ALL AMAZONS! HENCEFORTH, YOUR WARRIOR'S GARB SHALL PROCLAIM YOUR HONOR!
LOOK NOW UPON THE STANDARD FROM WHICH WE SHALL WEAVE THAT GARB...
...THE STANDARD OF THE WARRIOR FOR WHOM YOU WERE NAMED...
...SHE WHO DIED NOBLY THAT THE AMAZON RACE MIGHT LIVE!
"AMAZONS! HEAR YOUR QUEEN! EVEN AS APOLLO'S SUN GIVES BIRTH TO THIS GLORIOUS DAY, I HAVE GATHERED YOU HERE...
"...TO WITNESS A BIRTH OF ANOTHER KIND!
"THE CHAMPION HAS BEEN CHOSEN...
..." THE GODS HAVE BEEN SATISFIED!"
31

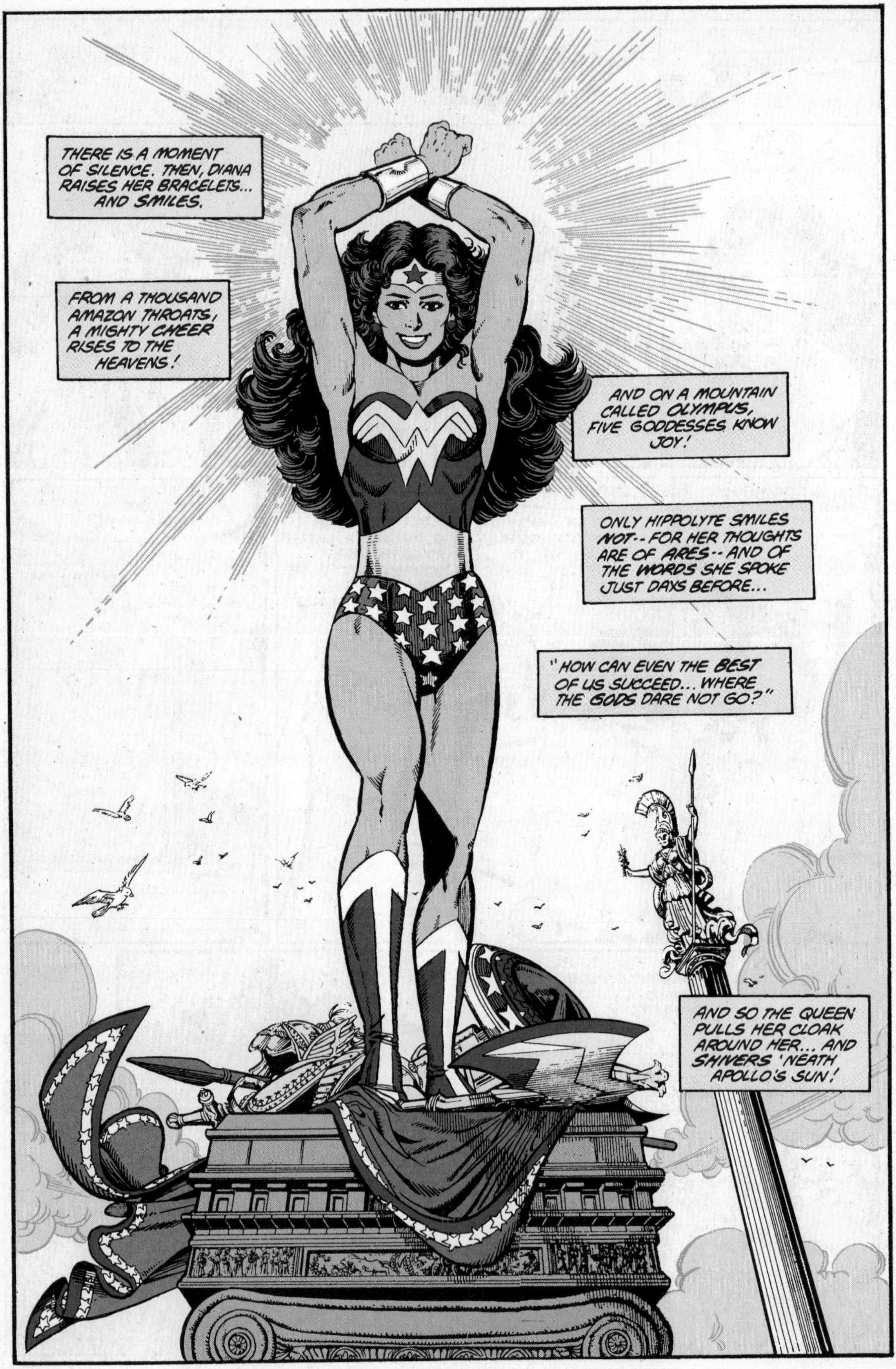
THERE IS A MOMENT OF SILENCE. THEN, DIANA RAISES HER BRACELETS... AND SMILES.
FROM A THOUSAND AMAZON THROATS, A MIGHTY CHEER RISES TO THE HEAVENS!
AND ON A MOUNTAIN CALLED OLYMPUS, FIVE GODDESSES KNOW JOY!
ONLY HIPPOLYTE SMILES NOT-- FOR HER THOUGHTS ARE OF ARES-- AND OF THE WORDS SHE SPOKE JUST DAYS BEFORE...
"HOW CAN EVEN THE BEST OF US SUCCEED... WHERE THE GODS DARE NOT GO?"
AND SO THE QUEEN PULLS HER CLOAK AROUND HER... AND SHIVERS 'NEATH APOLLO'S SUN!

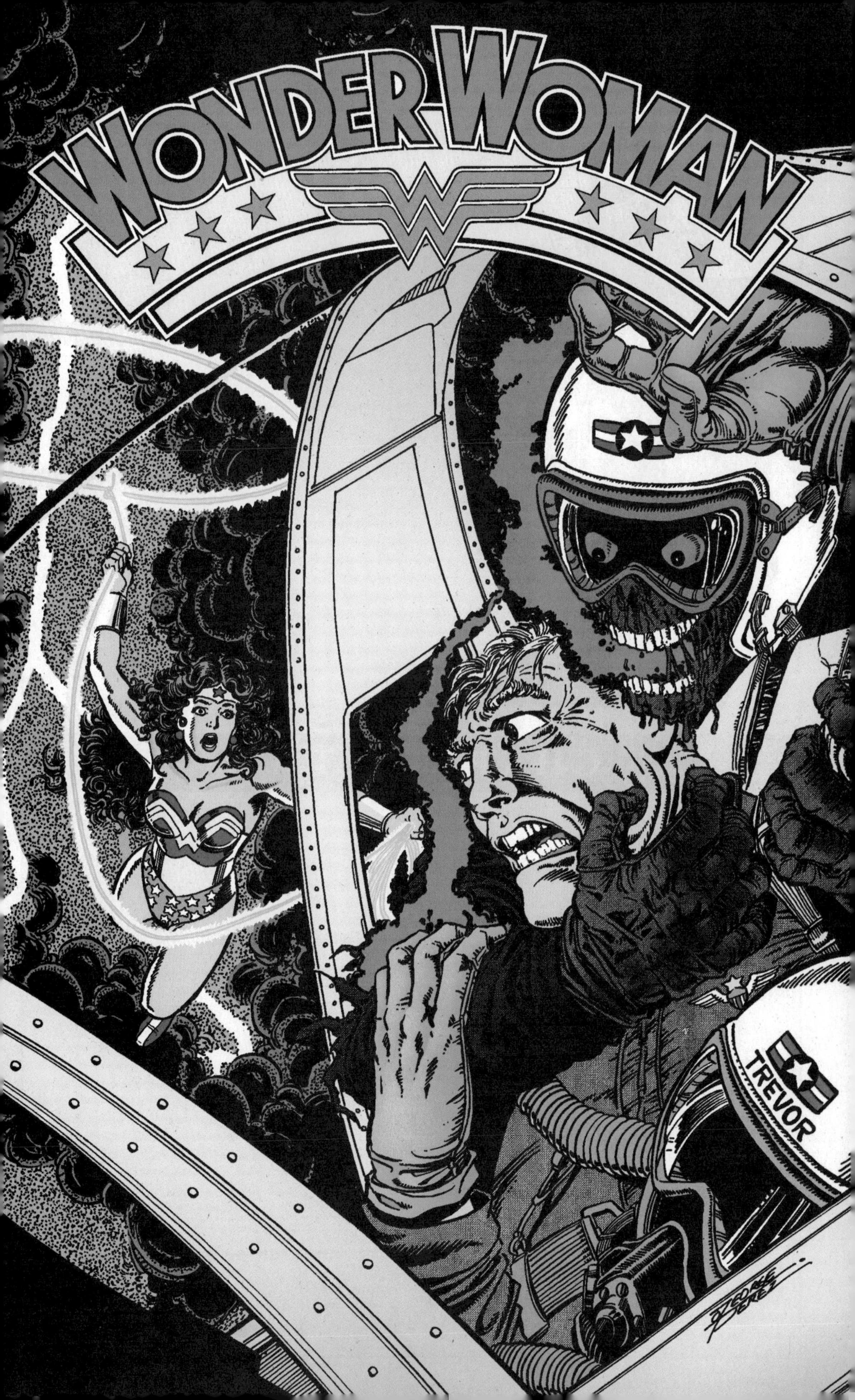
WONDER WOMAN
TREVOR

WONDER WOMAN

CHAPTER TWO

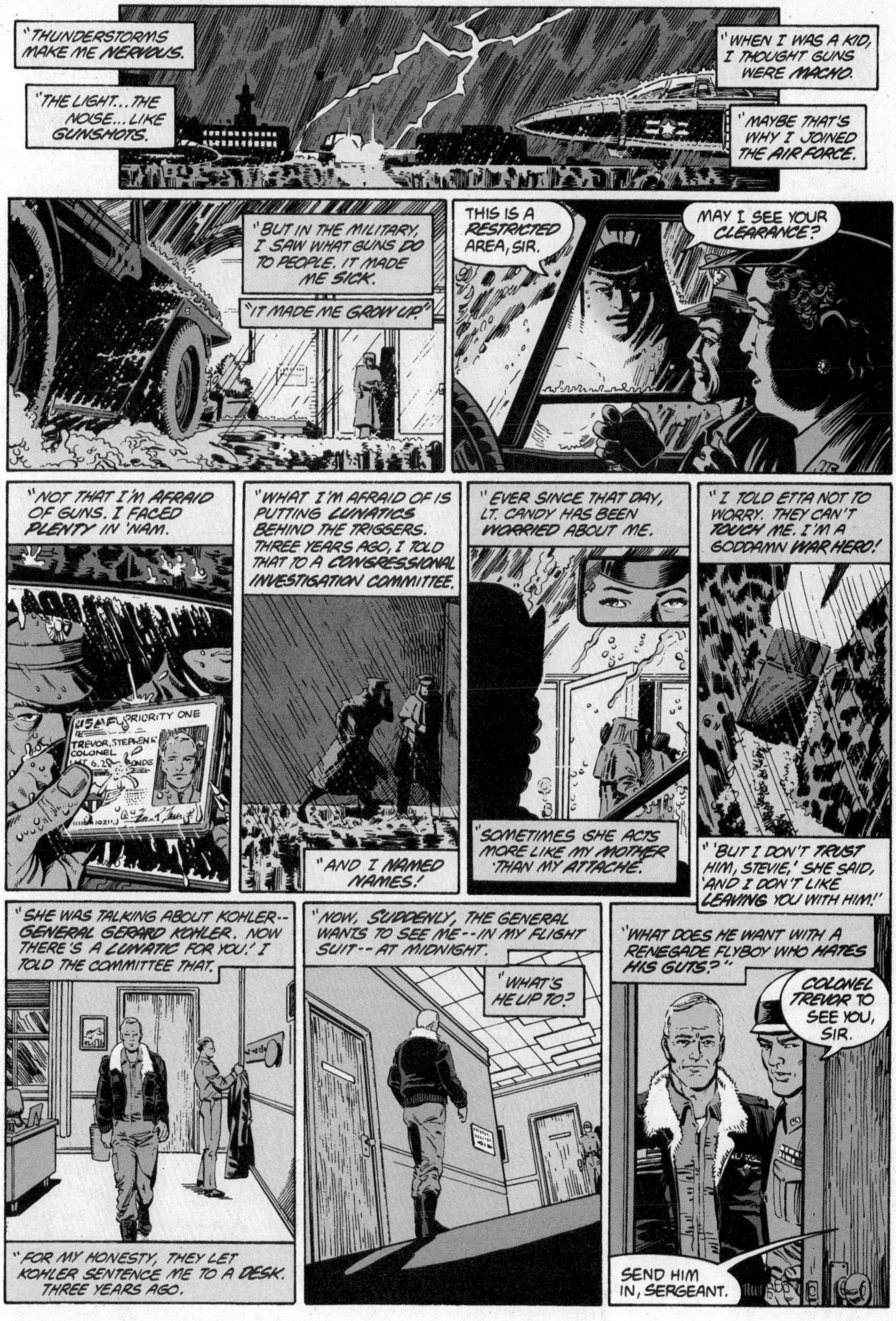

"THUNDERSTORMS MAKE ME NERVOUS.
"THE LIGHT... THE NOISE... LIKE GUNSHOTS.
"WHEN I WAS A KID, I THOUGHT GUNS WERE MACHO.
"MAYBE THAT'S WHY I JOINED THE AIR FORCE.
"BUT IN THE MILITARY, I SAW WHAT GUNS DO TO PEOPLE. IT MADE ME SICK.
"IT MADE ME GROW UP."
THIS IS A RESTRICTED AREA, SIR.
MAY I SEE YOUR CLEARANCE?
"NOT THAT I'M AFRAID OF GUNS. I FACED PLENTY IN 'NAM.
PRIORITY ONE
TREVOR, STEPHEN K
COLONEL
"WHAT I'M AFRAID OF IS PUTTING LUNATICS BEHIND THE TRIGGERS. THREE YEARS AGO, I TOLD THAT TO A CONGRESSIONAL INVESTIGATION COMMITTEE.
"AND I NAMED NAMES!
"EVER SINCE THAT DAY, LT. CANDY HAS BEEN WORRIED ABOUT ME.
"SOMETIMES SHE ACTS MORE LIKE MY MOTHER THAN MY ATTACHE.
"I TOLD ETTA NOT TO WORRY. THEY CAN'T TOUCH ME. I'M A GODDAMN WAR HERO!
"'BUT I DON'T TRUST HIM, STEVIE,' SHE SAID, 'AND I DON'T LIKE LEAVING YOU WITH HIM!'
"SHE WAS TALKING ABOUT KOHLER-- GENERAL GERARD KOHLER. NOW THERE'S A LUNATIC FOR YOU.' I TOLD THE COMMITTEE THAT.
"FOR MY HONESTY, THEY LET KOHLER SENTENCE ME TO A DESK. THREE YEARS AGO.
"NOW, SUDDENLY, THE GENERAL WANTS TO SEE ME-- IN MY FLIGHT SUIT-- AT MIDNIGHT.
"WHAT'S HE UP TO?
"WHAT DOES HE WANT WITH A RENEGADE FLYBOY WHO HATES HIS GUTS?"
COLONEL TREVOR TO SEE YOU, SIR.
SEND HIM IN, SERGEANT.

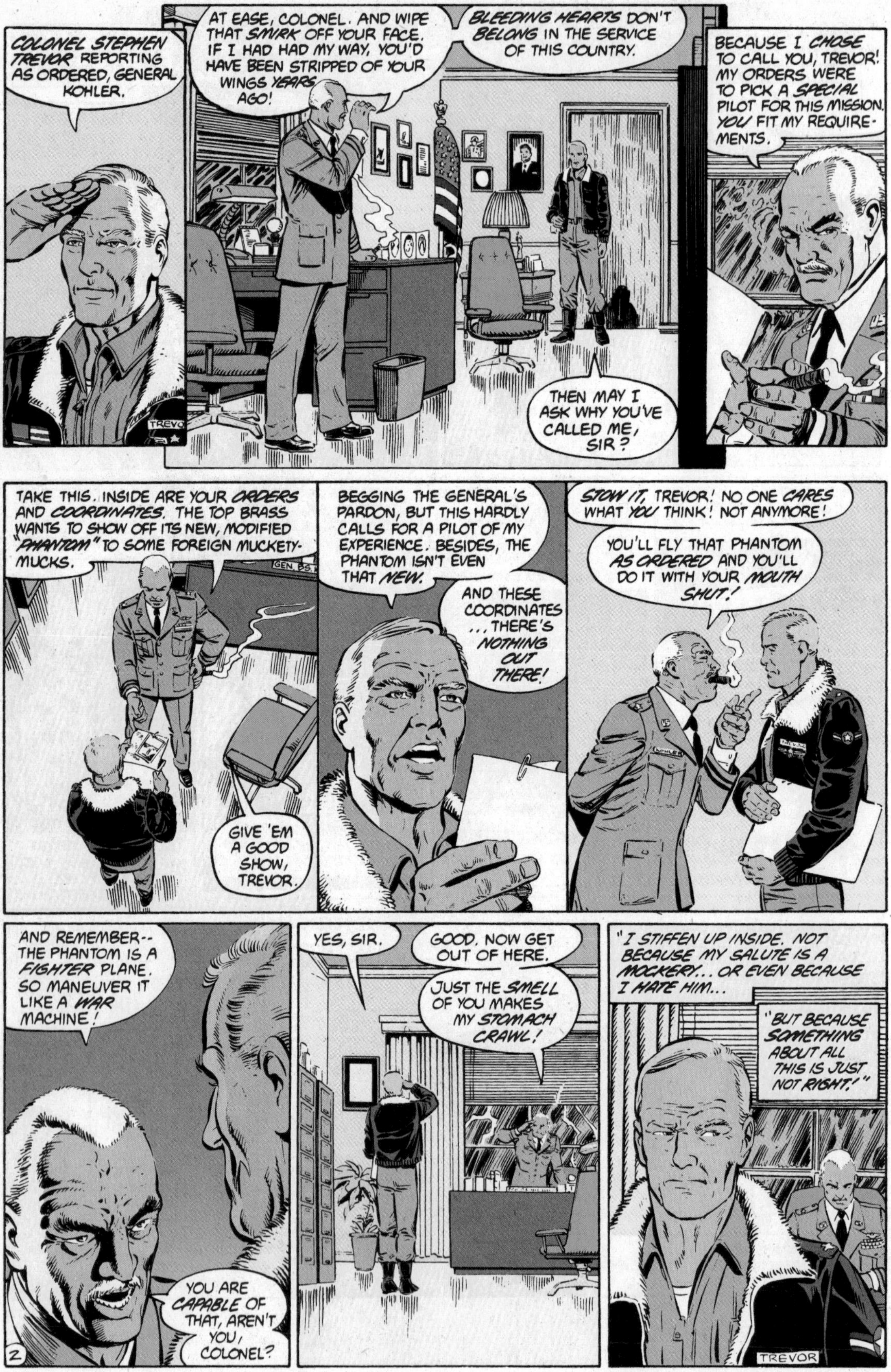
COLONEL STEPHEN TREVOR REPORTING AS ORDERED, GENERAL KOHLER.
TREVO
AT EASE, COLONEL. AND WIPE THAT SMIRK OFF YOUR FACE. IF I HAD HAD MY WAY, YOU'D HAVE BEEN STRIPPED OF YOUR WINGS YEARS AGO!
BLEEDING HEARTS DON'T BELONG IN THE SERVICE OF THIS COUNTRY.
THEN MAY I ASK WHY YOU'VE CALLED ME, SIR?
BECAUSE I CHOSE TO CALL YOU, TREVOR! MY ORDERS WERE TO PICK A SPECIAL PILOT FOR THIS MISSION. YOU FIT MY REQUIREMENTS.
TAKE THIS. INSIDE ARE YOUR ORDERS AND COORDINATES. THE TOP BRASS WANTS TO SHOW OFF ITS NEW, MODIFIED "PHANTOM" TO SOME FOREIGN MUCKETY-MUCKS.
GEN. BS.
GIVE 'EM A GOOD SHOW, TREVOR.
BEGGING THE GENERAL'S PARDON, BUT THIS HARDLY CALLS FOR A PILOT OF MY EXPERIENCE. BESIDES, THE PHANTOM ISN'T EVEN THAT NEW.
AND THESE COORDINATES ..., THERE'S NOTHING OUT THERE!
STOW IT, TREVOR! NO ONE CARES WHAT YOU THINK! NOT ANYMORE!
YOU'LL FLY THAT PHANTOM AS ORDERED AND YOU'LL DO IT WITH YOUR MOUTH SHUT!
KOHLER
AND REMEMBER-- THE PHANTOM IS A FIGHTER PLANE. SO MANEUVER IT LIKE A WAR MACHINE!
YOU ARE CAPABLE OF THAT, AREN'T YOU, COLONEL?
2
YES, SIR.
GOOD. NOW GET OUT OF HERE.
JUST THE SMELL OF YOU MAKES MY STOMACH CRAWL!
"I STIFFEN UP INSIDE. NOT BECAUSE MY SALUTE IS A MOCKERY... OR EVEN BECAUSE I HATE HIM...
"BUT BECAUSE SOMETHING ABOUT ALL THIS IS JUST NOT RIGHT!"
TREVOR

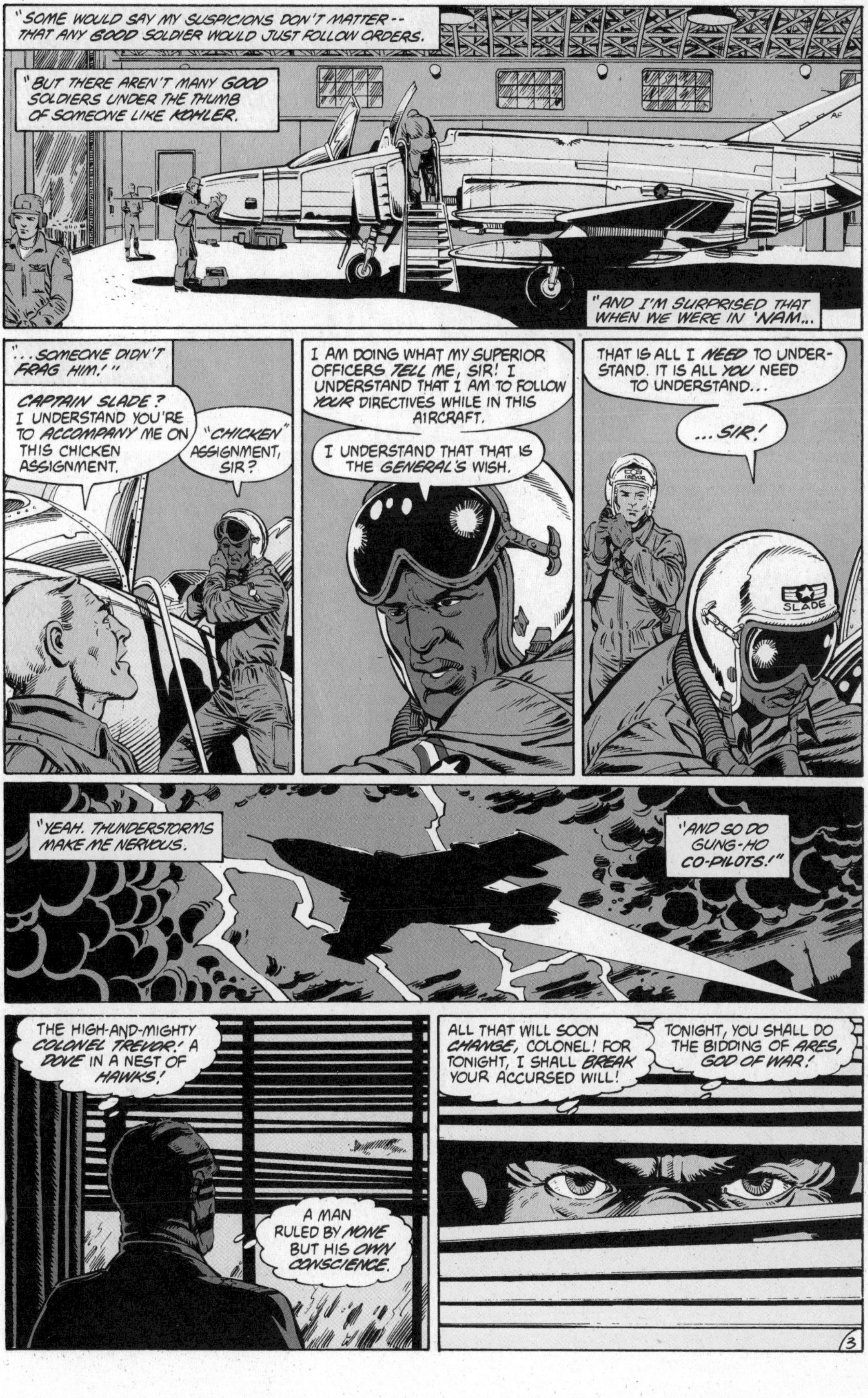
"SOME WOULD SAY MY SUSPICIONS DON'T MATTER-- THAT ANY GOOD SOLDIER WOULD JUST FOLLOW ORDERS.
"BUT THERE AREN'T MANY GOOD SOLDIERS UNDER THE THUMB OF SOMEONE LIKE KOHLER.
AF
"AND I'M SURPRISED THAT WHEN WE WERE IN 'NAM...
"...SOMEONE DIDN'T FRAG HIM!"
CAPTAIN SLADE? I UNDERSTAND YOU'RE TO ACCOMPANY ME ON THIS CHICKEN ASSIGNMENT.
"CHICKEN" ASSIGNMENT, SIR?
I AM DOING WHAT MY SUPERIOR OFFICERS TELL ME, SIR! I UNDERSTAND THAT I AM TO FOLLOW YOUR DIRECTIVES WHILE IN THIS AIRCRAFT.
I UNDERSTAND THAT THAT IS THE GENERAL'S WISH.
THAT IS ALL I NEED TO UNDERSTAND. IT IS ALL YOU NEED TO UNDERSTAND...
...SIR!
TREVOR
SLADE
"YEAH. THUNDERSTORMS MAKE ME NERVOUS.
"AND SO DO GUNG-HO CO-PILOTS!"
THE HIGH-AND-MIGHTY COLONEL TREVOR! A DOVE IN A NEST OF HAWKS!
A MAN RULED BY NONE BUT HIS OWN CONSCIENCE.
ALL THAT WILL SOON CHANGE, COLONEL! FOR TONIGHT, I SHALL BREAK YOUR ACCURSED WILL!
TONIGHT, YOU SHALL DO THE BIDDING OF ARES, GOD OF WAR!
3

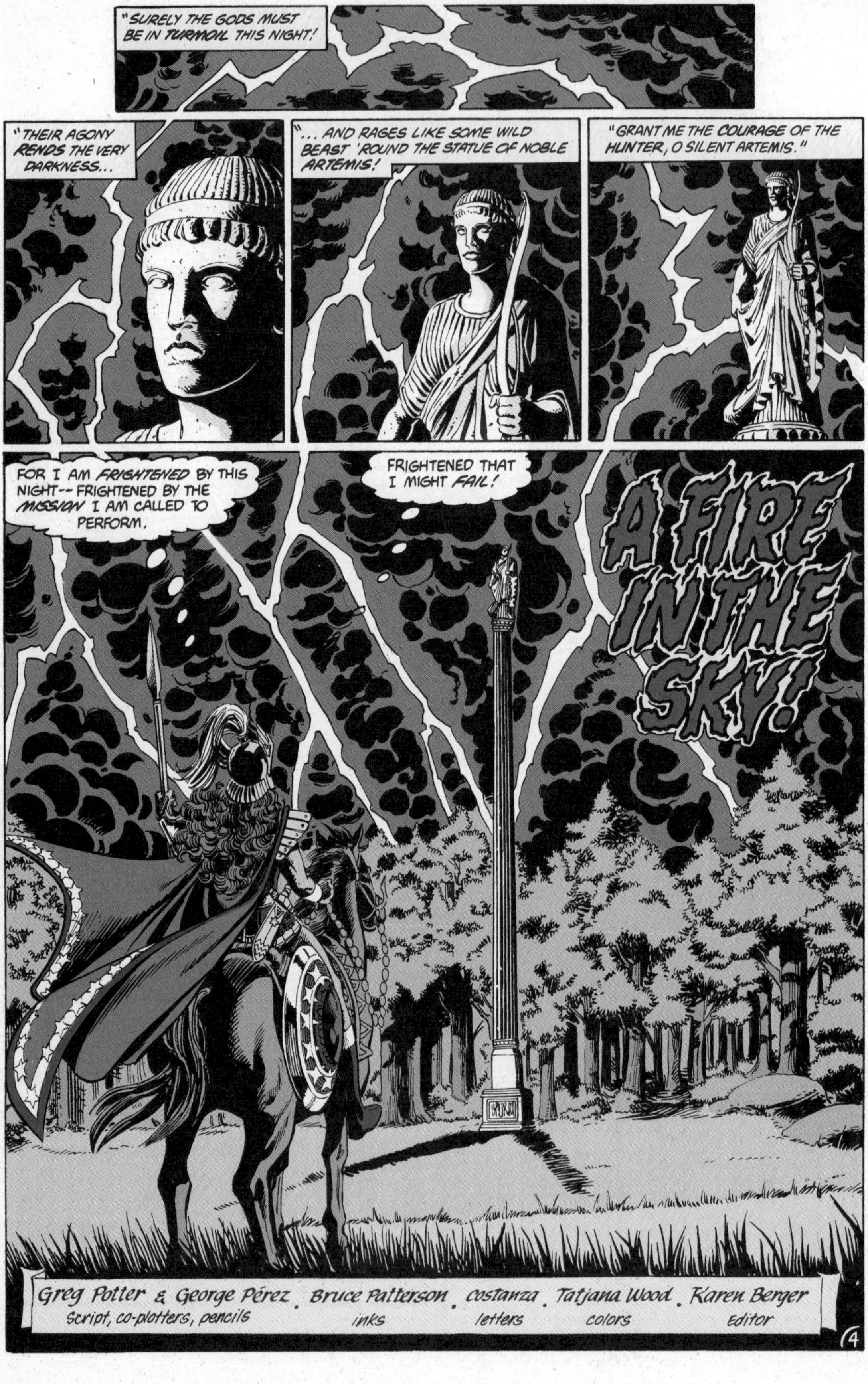
"SURELY THE GODS MUST BE IN TURMOIL THIS NIGHT!
"THEIR AGONY RENDS THE VERY DARKNESS...
"... AND RAGES LIKE SOME WILD BEAST 'ROUND THE STATUE OF NOBLE ARTEMIS!
"GRANT ME THE COURAGE OF THE HUNTER, O SILENT ARTEMIS."
FOR I AM FRIGHTENED BY THIS NIGHT-- FRIGHTENED BY THE MISSION I AM CALLED TO PERFORM.
FRIGHTENED THAT I MIGHT FAIL!
A FIRE IN THE SKY!
Greg Potter & George Pérez Script, co-plotters, pencils
Bruce Patterson inks
costanza letters
Tatjana Wood colors
Karen Berger Editor
4

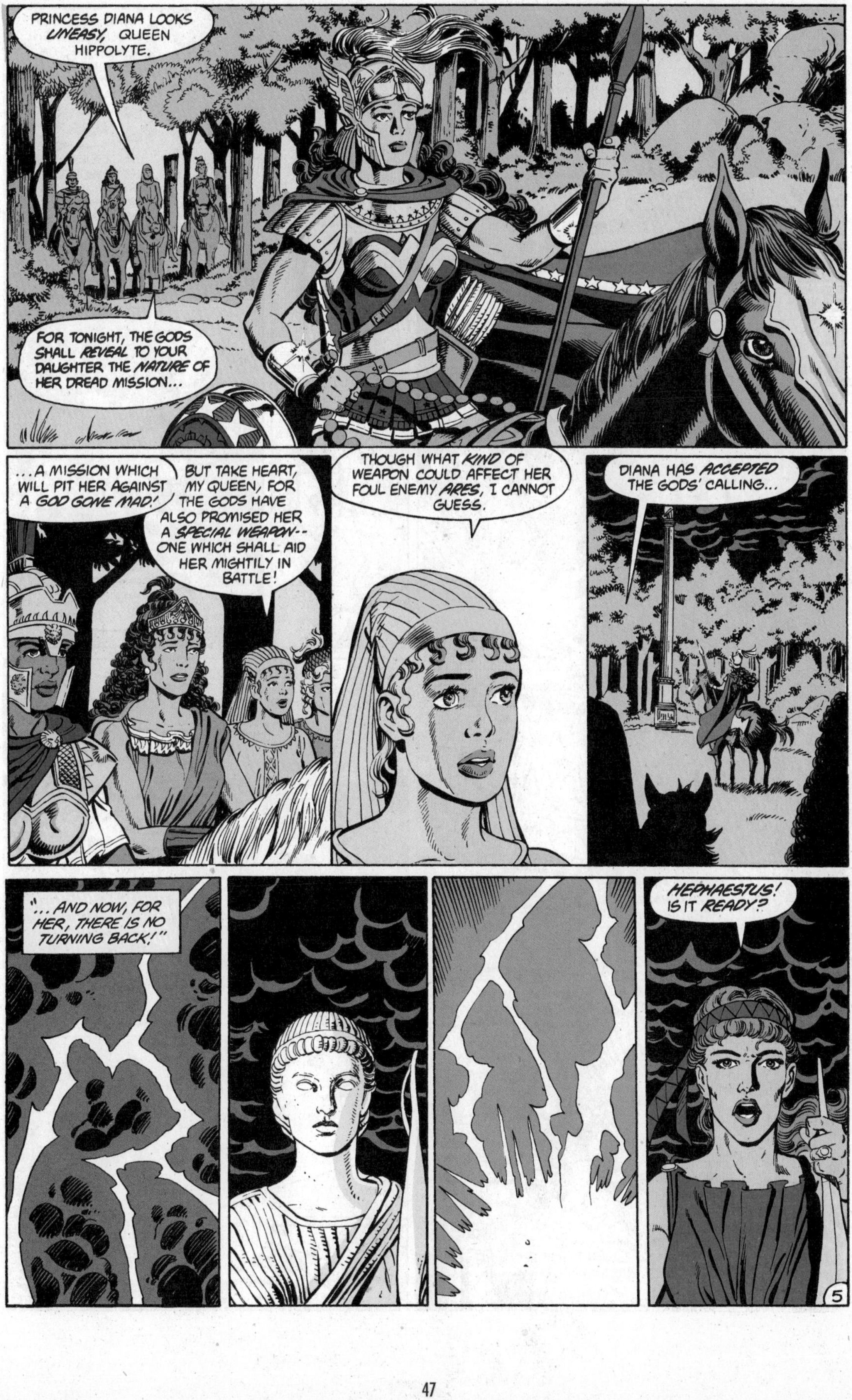
PRINCESS DIANA LOOKS UNEASY, QUEEN HIPPOLYTE.
FOR TONIGHT, THE GODS SHALL REVEAL TO YOUR DAUGHTER THE NATURE OF HER DREAD MISSION...
...A MISSION WHICH WILL PIT HER AGAINST A GOD GONE MAD!
BUT TAKE HEART, MY QUEEN, FOR THE GODS HAVE ALSO PROMISED HER A SPECIAL WEAPON-- ONE WHICH SHALL AID HER MIGHTILY IN BATTLE!
THOUGH WHAT KIND OF WEAPON COULD AFFECT HER FOUL ENEMY ARES, I CANNOT GUESS.
DIANA HAS ACCEPTED THE GODS' CALLING...
"...AND NOW, FOR HER, THERE IS NO TURNING BACK!"
HEPHAESTUS! IS IT READY?
5

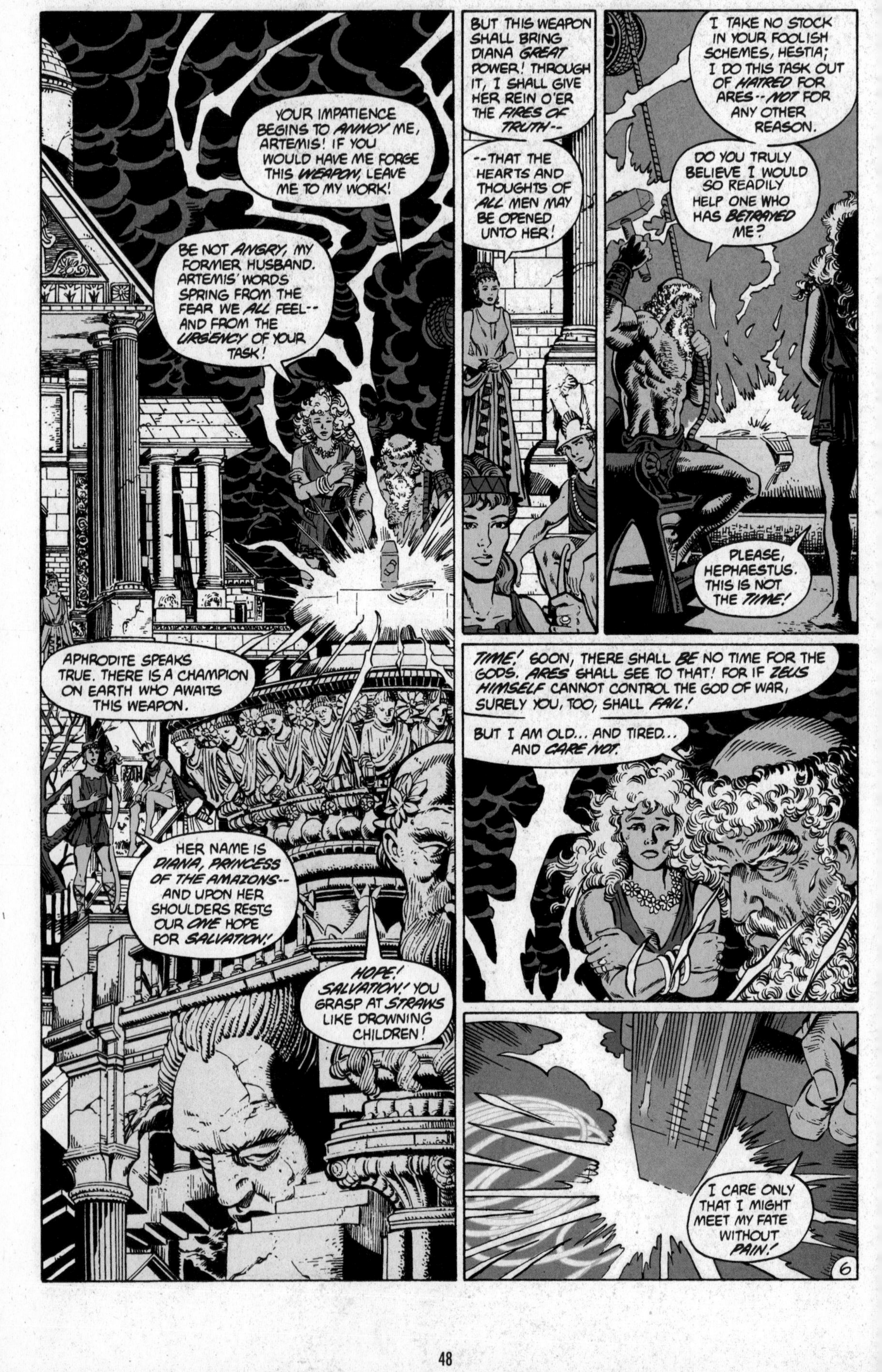
YOUR IMPATIENCE BEGINS TO ANNOY ME, ARTEMIS! IF YOU WOULD HAVE ME FORGE THIS WEAPON, LEAVE ME TO MY WORK!
BE NOT ANGRY, MY FORMER HUSBAND. ARTEMIS' WORDS SPRING FROM THE FEAR WE ALL FEEL-- AND FROM THE URGENCY OF YOUR TASK!
APHRODITE SPEAKS TRUE. THERE IS A CHAMPION ON EARTH WHO AWAITS THIS WEAPON.
HER NAME IS DIANA, PRINCESS OF THE AMAZONS-- AND UPON HER SHOULDERS RESTS OUR ONE HOPE FOR SALVATION!
HOPE! SALVATION! YOU GRASP AT STRAWS LIKE DROWNING CHILDREN!
BUT THIS WEAPON SHALL BRING DIANA GREAT POWER! THROUGH IT, I SHALL GIVE HER REIN O'ER THE FIRES OF TRUTH--
--THAT THE HEARTS AND THOUGHTS OF ALL MEN MAY BE OPENED UNTO HER!
I TAKE NO STOCK IN YOUR FOOLISH SCHEMES, HESTIA; I DO THIS TASK OUT OF HATRED FOR ARES--NOT FOR ANY OTHER REASON.
DO YOU TRULY BELIEVE I WOULD SO READILY HELP ONE WHO HAS BETRAYED ME?
PLEASE, HEPHAESTUS. THIS IS NOT THE TIME!
TIME! SOON, THERE SHALL BE NO TIME FOR THE GODS. ARES SHALL SEE TO THAT! FOR IF ZEUS HIMSELF CANNOT CONTROL THE GOD OF WAR, SURELY YOU, TOO, SHALL FAIL!
BUT I AM OLD... AND TIRED... AND CARE NOT.
I CARE ONLY THAT I MIGHT MEET MY FATE WITHOUT PAIN!
6

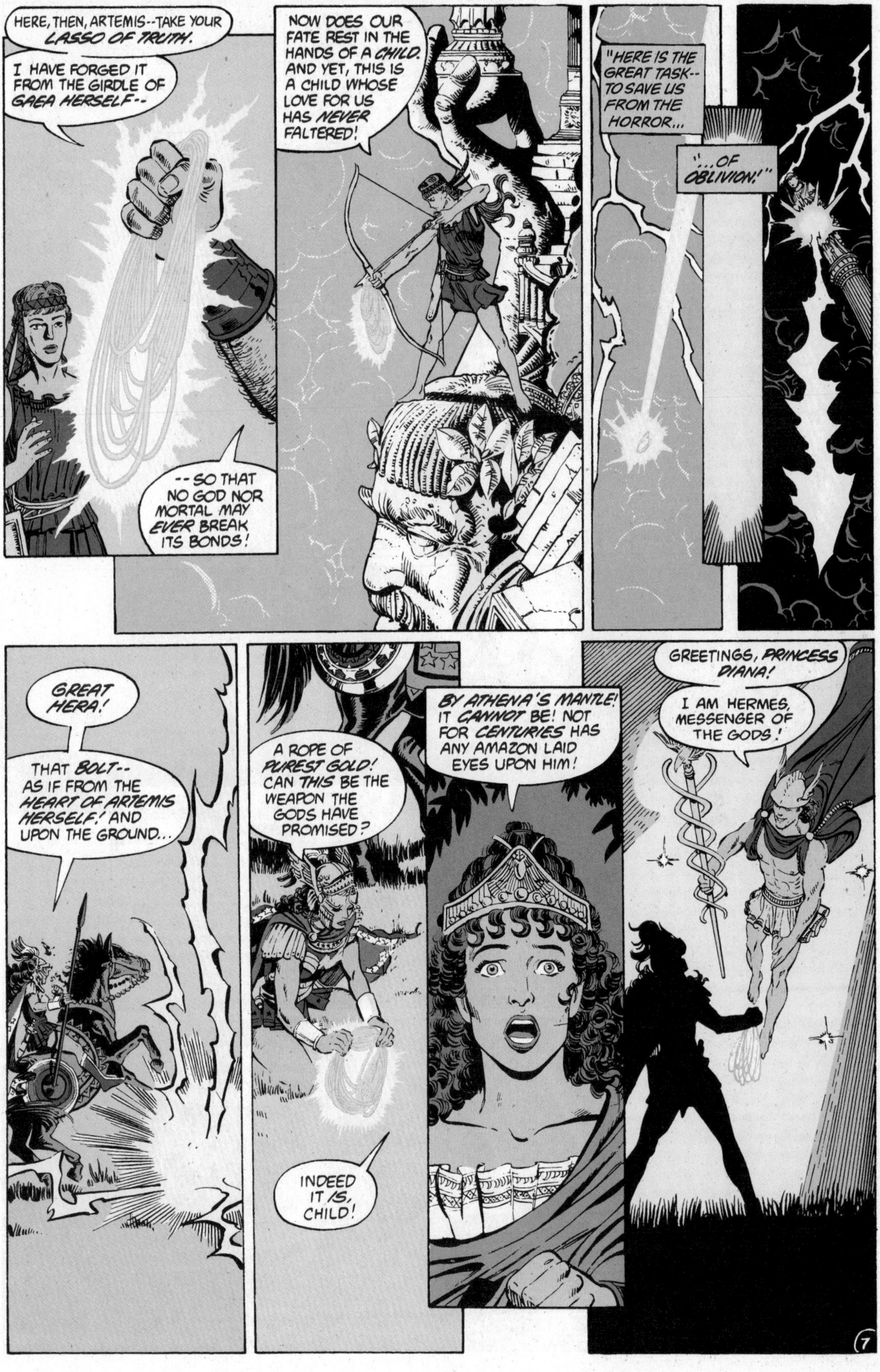
HERE, THEN, ARTEMIS--TAKE YOUR LASSO OF TRUTH.
I HAVE FORGED IT FROM THE GIRDLE OF GAEA HERSELF--
--SO THAT NO GOD NOR MORTAL MAY EVER BREAK ITS BONDS!
NOW DOES OUR FATE REST IN THE HANDS OF A CHILD. AND YET, THIS IS A CHILD WHOSE LOVE FOR US HAS NEVER FALTERED!
"HERE IS THE GREAT TASK-- TO SAVE US FROM THE HORROR...
"...OF OBLIVION!"
GREAT HERA!
THAT BOLT-- AS IF FROM THE HEART OF ARTEMIS HERSELF! AND UPON THE GROUND...
A ROPE OF PUREST GOLD! CAN THIS BE THE WEAPON THE GODS HAVE PROMISED?
INDEED IT IS, CHILD!
BY ATHENA'S MANTLE! IT CANNOT BE! NOT FOR CENTURIES HAS ANY AMAZON LAID EYES UPON HIM!
GREETINGS, PRINCESS DIANA!
I AM HERMES, MESSENGER OF THE GODS!
7

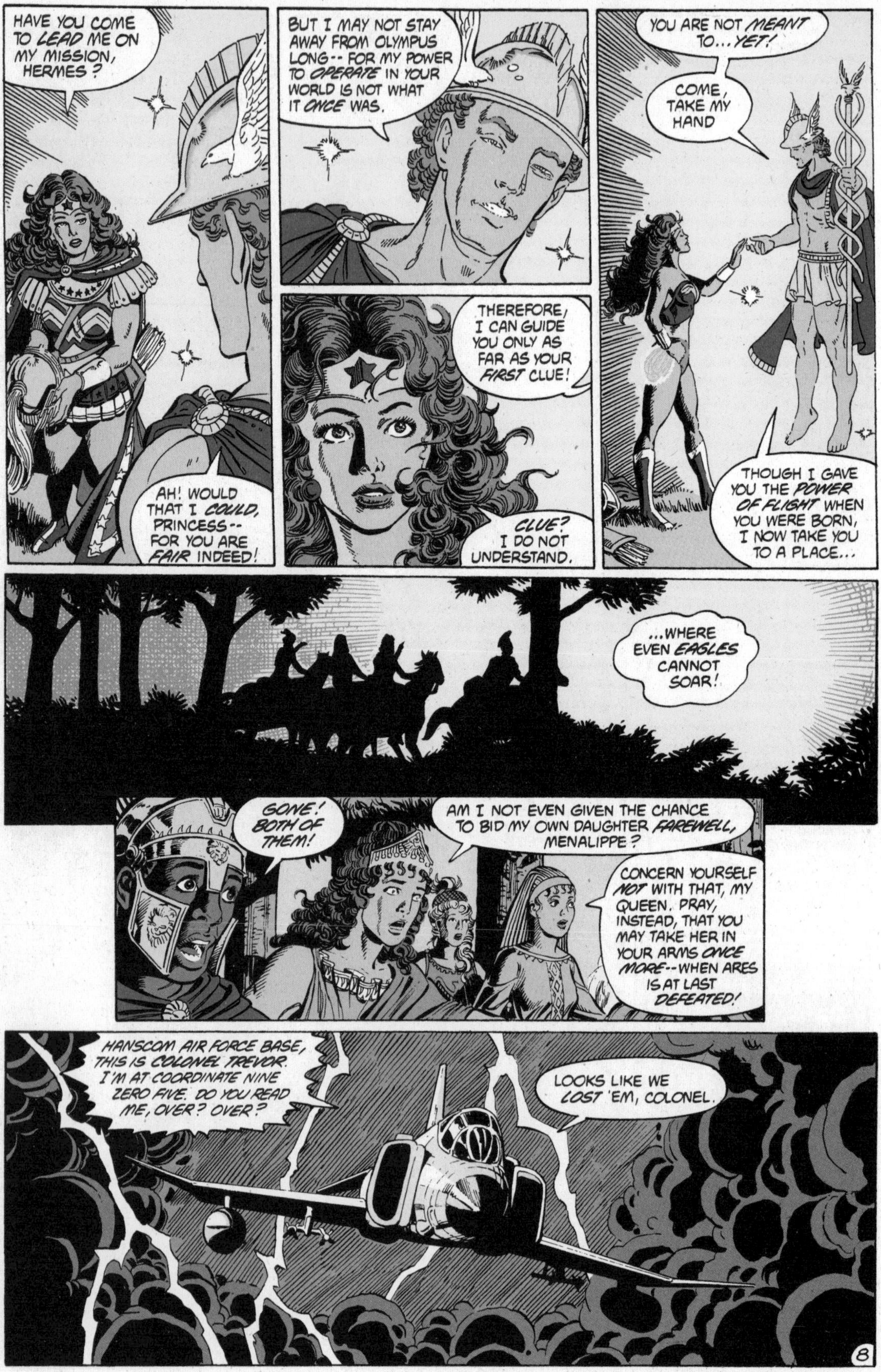
HAVE YOU COME TO LEAD ME ON MY MISSION, HERMES?
AH! WOULD THAT I COULD, PRINCESS-- FOR YOU ARE FAIR INDEED!
BUT I MAY NOT STAY AWAY FROM OLYMPUS LONG-- FOR MY POWER TO OPERATE IN YOUR WORLD IS NOT WHAT IT ONCE WAS.
THEREFORE, I CAN GUIDE YOU ONLY AS FAR AS YOUR FIRST CLUE!
CLUE? I DO NOT UNDERSTAND.
YOU ARE NOT MEANT TO... YET!
COME, TAKE MY HAND
THOUGH I GAVE YOU THE POWER OF FLIGHT WHEN YOU WERE BORN, I NOW TAKE YOU TO A PLACE...
...WHERE EVEN EAGLES CANNOT SOAR!
GONE! BOTH OF THEM!
AM I NOT EVEN GIVEN THE CHANCE TO BID MY OWN DAUGHTER FAREWELL, MENALIPPE?
CONCERN YOURSELF NOT WITH THAT, MY QUEEN. PRAY, INSTEAD, THAT YOU MAY TAKE HER IN YOUR ARMS ONCE MORE--WHEN ARES IS AT LAST DEFEATED!
HANSCOM AIR FORCE BASE, THIS IS COLONEL TREVOR. I'M AT COORDINATE NINE ZERO FIVE. DO YOU READ ME, OVER? OVER?
LOOKS LIKE WE LOST 'EM, COLONEL.
8

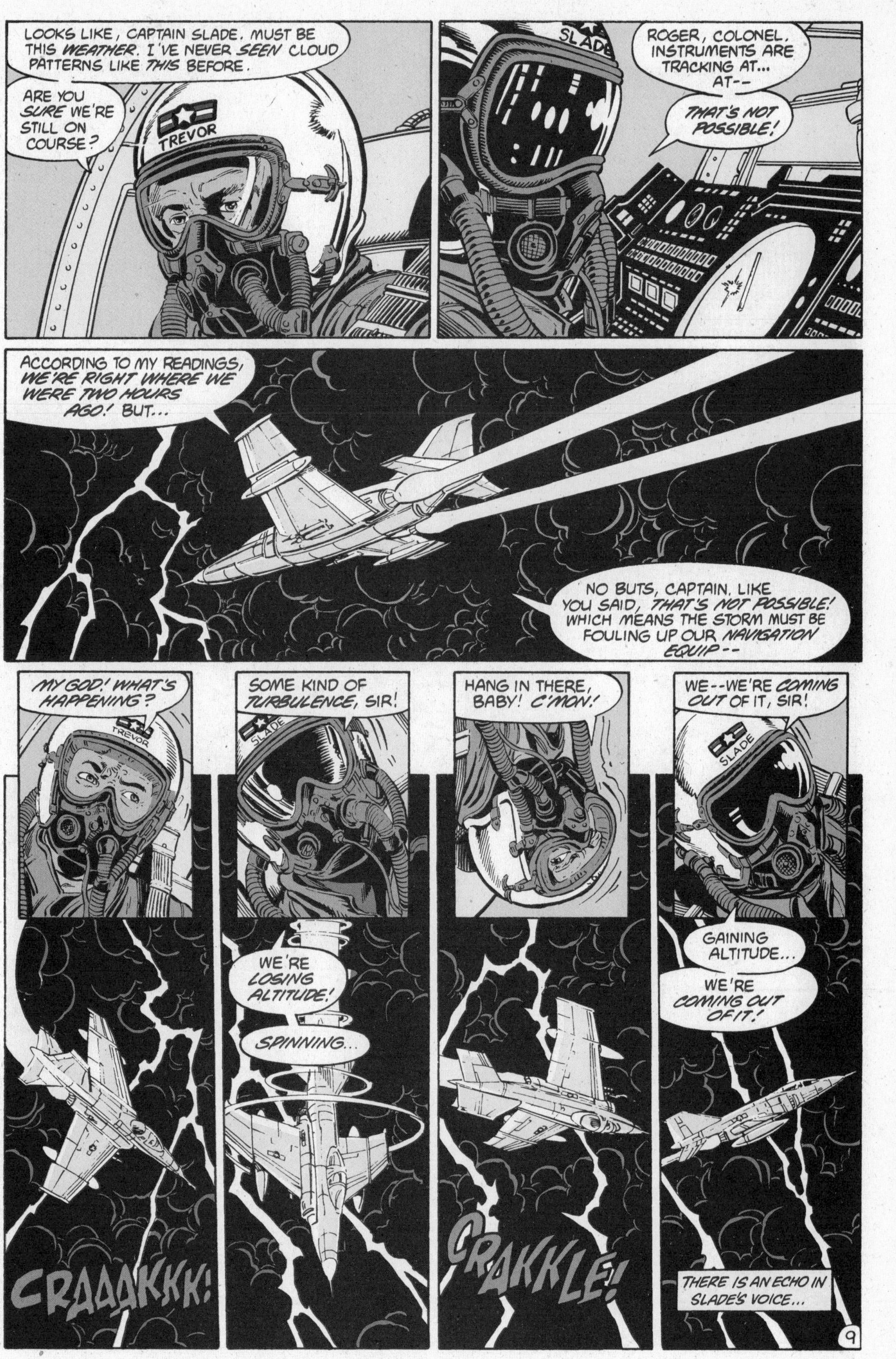
LOOKS LIKE, CAPTAIN SLADE. MUST BE THIS WEATHER. I'VE NEVER SEEN CLOUD PATTERNS LIKE THIS BEFORE.
ARE YOU SURE WE'RE STILL ON COURSE?
ROGER, COLONEL. INSTRUMENTS ARE TRACKING AT... AT--
THAT'S NOT POSSIBLE!
ACCORDING TO MY READINGS, WE'RE RIGHT WHERE WE WERE TWO HOURS AGO! BUT...
NO BUTS, CAPTAIN. LIKE YOU SAID, THAT'S NOT POSSIBLE! WHICH MEANS THE STORM MUST BE FOULING UP OUR NAVIGATION EQUIP--
MY GOD! WHAT'S HAPPENING?
CRAAAKKK!
SOME KIND OF TURBULENCE, SIR!
WE'RE LOSING ALTITUDE!
SPINNING...
HANG IN THERE, BABY! C'MON!
CRAKKLE!
WE--WE'RE COMING OUT OF IT, SIR!
GAINING ALTITUDE...
WE'RE COMING OUT OF IT!
THERE IS AN ECHO IN SLADE'S VOICE...
9

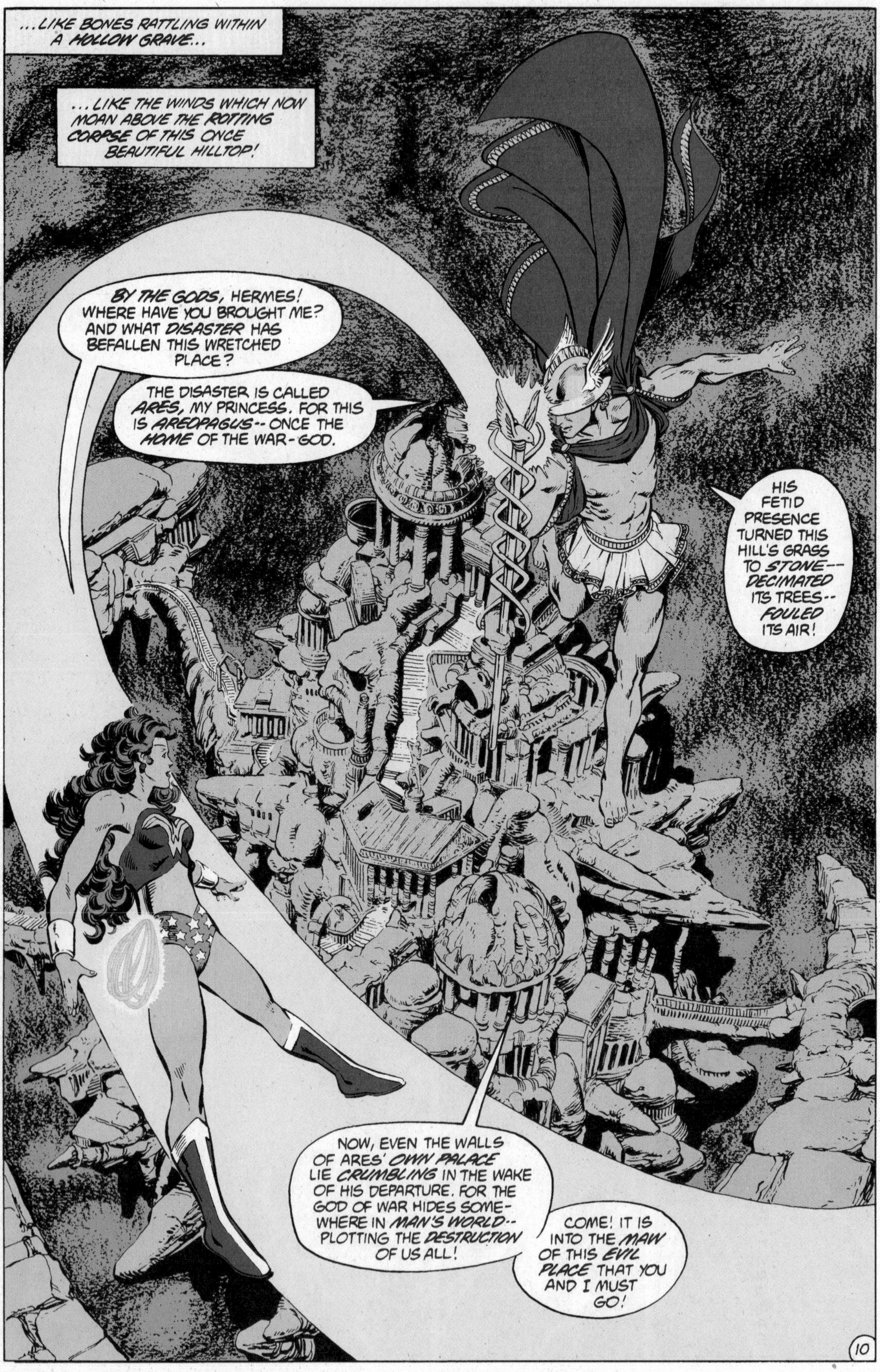

...LIKE BONES RATTLING WITHIN A HOLLOW GRAVE...
...LIKE THE WINDS WHICH NOW MOAN ABOVE THE ROTTING CORPSE OF THIS ONCE BEAUTIFUL HILLTOP!
BY THE GODS, HERMES! WHERE HAVE YOU BROUGHT ME? AND WHAT DISASTER HAS BEFALLEN THIS WRETCHED PLACE?
THE DISASTER IS CALLED ARES, MY PRINCESS. FOR THIS IS AREOPAGUS-- ONCE THE HOME OF THE WAR-GOD.
HIS FETID PRESENCE TURNED THIS HILL'S GRASS TO STONE-- DECIMATED ITS TREES-- FOULED ITS AIR!
NOW, EVEN THE WALLS OF ARES' OWN PALACE LIE CRUMBLING IN THE WAKE OF HIS DEPARTURE. FOR THE GOD OF WAR HIDES SOMEWHERE IN MAN'S WORLD-- PLOTTING THE DESTRUCTION OF US ALL!
COME! IT IS INTO THE MAW OF THIS EVIL PLACE THAT YOU AND I MUST GO!
10

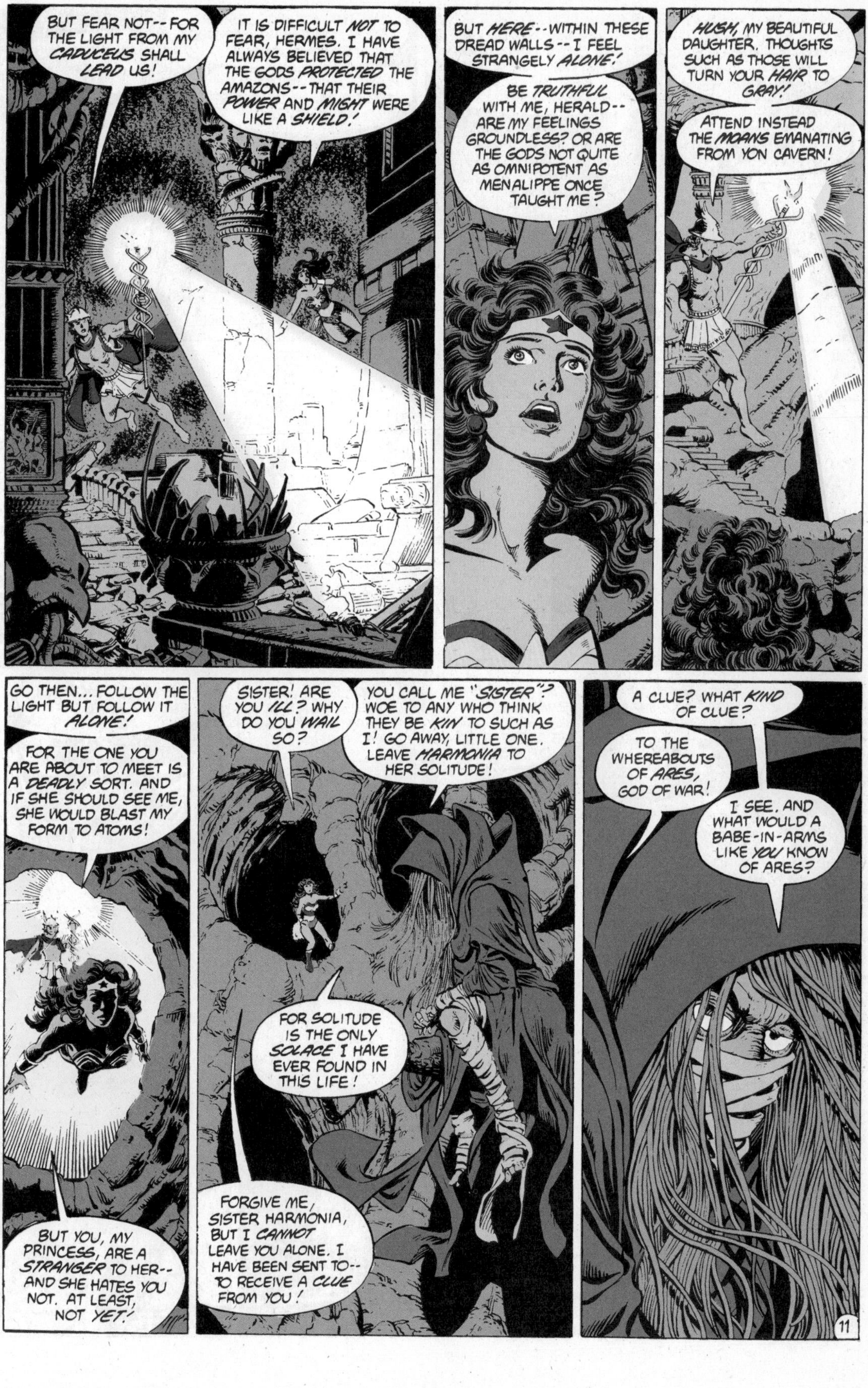
BUT FEAR NOT-- FOR THE LIGHT FROM MY CADUCEUS SHALL LEAD US!
IT IS DIFFICULT NOT TO FEAR, HERMES. I HAVE ALWAYS BELIEVED THAT THE GODS PROTECTED THE AMAZONS--THAT THEIR POWER AND MIGHT WERE LIKE A SHIELD!
BUT HERE--WITHIN THESE DREAD WALLS--I FEEL STRANGELY ALONE!
BE TRUTHFUL WITH ME, HERALD-- ARE MY FEELINGS GROUNDLESS? OR ARE THE GODS NOT QUITE AS OMNIPOTENT AS MENALIPPE ONCE TAUGHT ME?
HUSH, MY BEAUTIFUL DAUGHTER. THOUGHTS SUCH AS THOSE WILL TURN YOUR HAIR TO GRAY!
ATTEND INSTEAD THE MOANS EMANATING FROM YON CAVERN!
GO THEN... FOLLOW THE LIGHT BUT FOLLOW IT ALONE!
FOR THE ONE YOU ARE ABOUT TO MEET IS A DEADLY SORT. AND IF SHE SHOULD SEE ME, SHE WOULD BLAST MY FORM TO ATOMS!
BUT YOU, MY PRINCESS, ARE A STRANGER TO HER-- AND SHE HATES YOU NOT. AT LEAST, NOT YET!
SISTER! ARE YOU ILL? WHY DO YOU WAIL SO?
YOU CALL ME "SISTER"? WOE TO ANY WHO THINK THEY BE KIN TO SUCH AS I! GO AWAY, LITTLE ONE. LEAVE HARMONIA TO HER SOLITUDE!
FOR SOLITUDE IS THE ONLY SOLACE I HAVE EVER FOUND IN THIS LIFE!
FORGIVE ME, SISTER HARMONIA, BUT I CANNOT LEAVE YOU ALONE. I HAVE BEEN SENT TO-- TO RECEIVE A CLUE FROM YOU!
A CLUE? WHAT KIND OF CLUE?
TO THE WHEREABOUTS OF ARES, GOD OF WAR!
I SEE. AND WHAT WOULD A BABE-IN-ARMS LIKE YOU KNOW OF ARES?
11

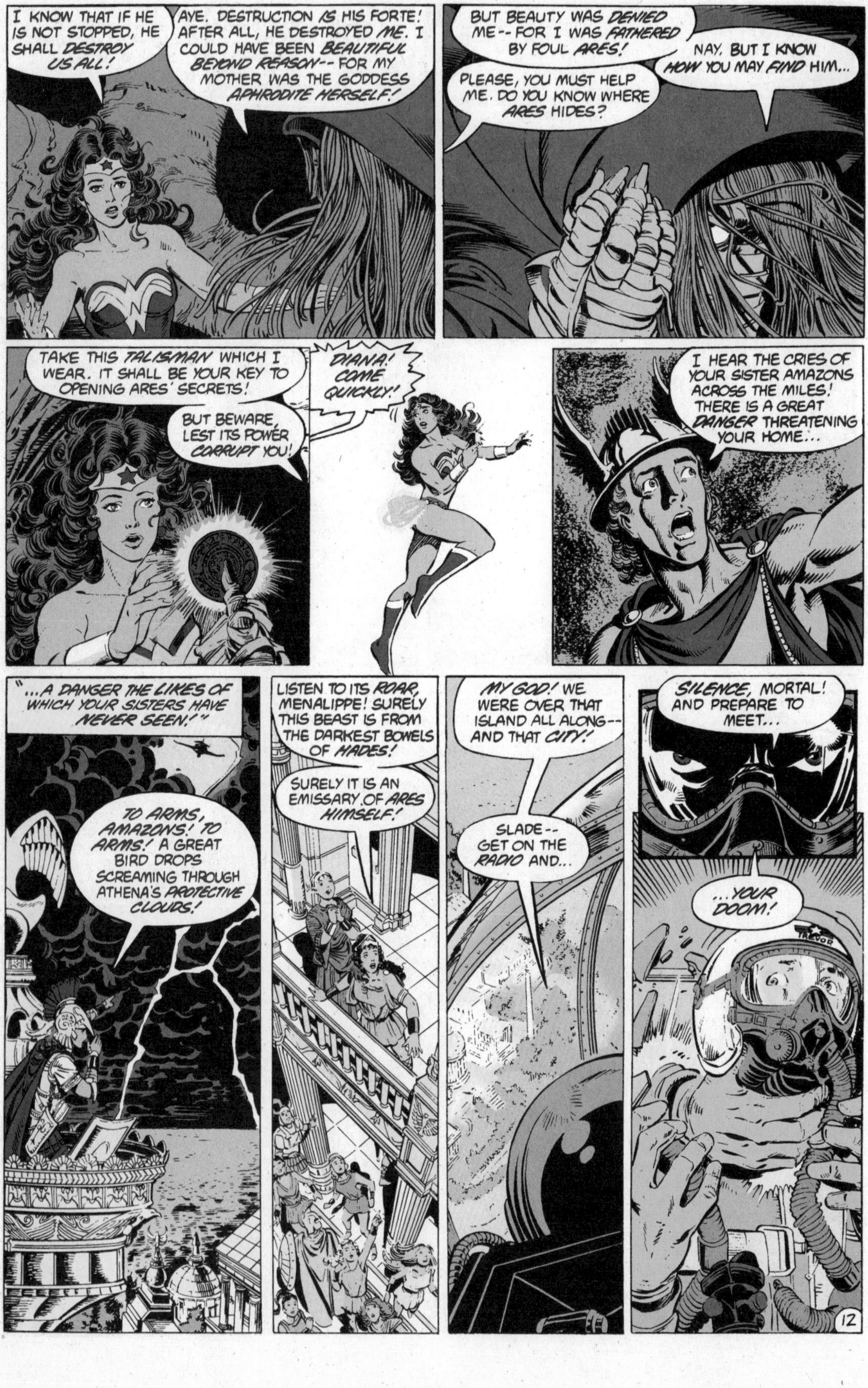

I KNOW THAT IF HE IS NOT STOPPED, HE SHALL DESTROY US ALL!
AYE. DESTRUCTION IS HIS FORTE! AFTER ALL, HE DESTROYED ME. I COULD HAVE BEEN BEAUTIFUL BEYOND REASON-- FOR MY MOTHER WAS THE GODDESS APHRODITE HERSELF!
BUT BEAUTY WAS DENIED ME-- FOR I WAS FATHERED BY FOUL ARES!
PLEASE, YOU MUST HELP ME. DO YOU KNOW WHERE ARES HIDES?
NAY, BUT I KNOW HOW YOU MAY FIND HIM...
TAKE THIS TALISMAN WHICH I WEAR. IT SHALL BE YOUR KEY TO OPENING ARES' SECRETS!
BUT BEWARE, LEST ITS POWER CORRUPT YOU!
DIANA! COME QUICKLY!
I HEAR THE CRIES OF YOUR SISTER AMAZONS ACROSS THE MILES! THERE IS A GREAT DANGER THREATENING YOUR HOME...
"...A DANGER THE LIKES OF WHICH YOUR SISTERS HAVE NEVER SEEN!"
TO ARMS, AMAZONS! TO ARMS! A GREAT BIRD DROPS SCREAMING THROUGH ATHENA'S PROTECTIVE CLOUDS!
LISTEN TO ITS ROAR, MENALIPPE! SURELY THIS BEAST IS FROM THE DARKEST BOWELS OF HADES!
SURELY IT IS AN EMISSARY OF ARES HIMSELF!
MY GOD! WE WERE OVER THAT ISLAND ALL ALONG-- AND THAT CITY!
SLADE-- GET ON THE RADIO AND...
SILENCE, MORTAL! AND PREPARE TO MEET...
...YOUR DOOM!
TREVOR
12

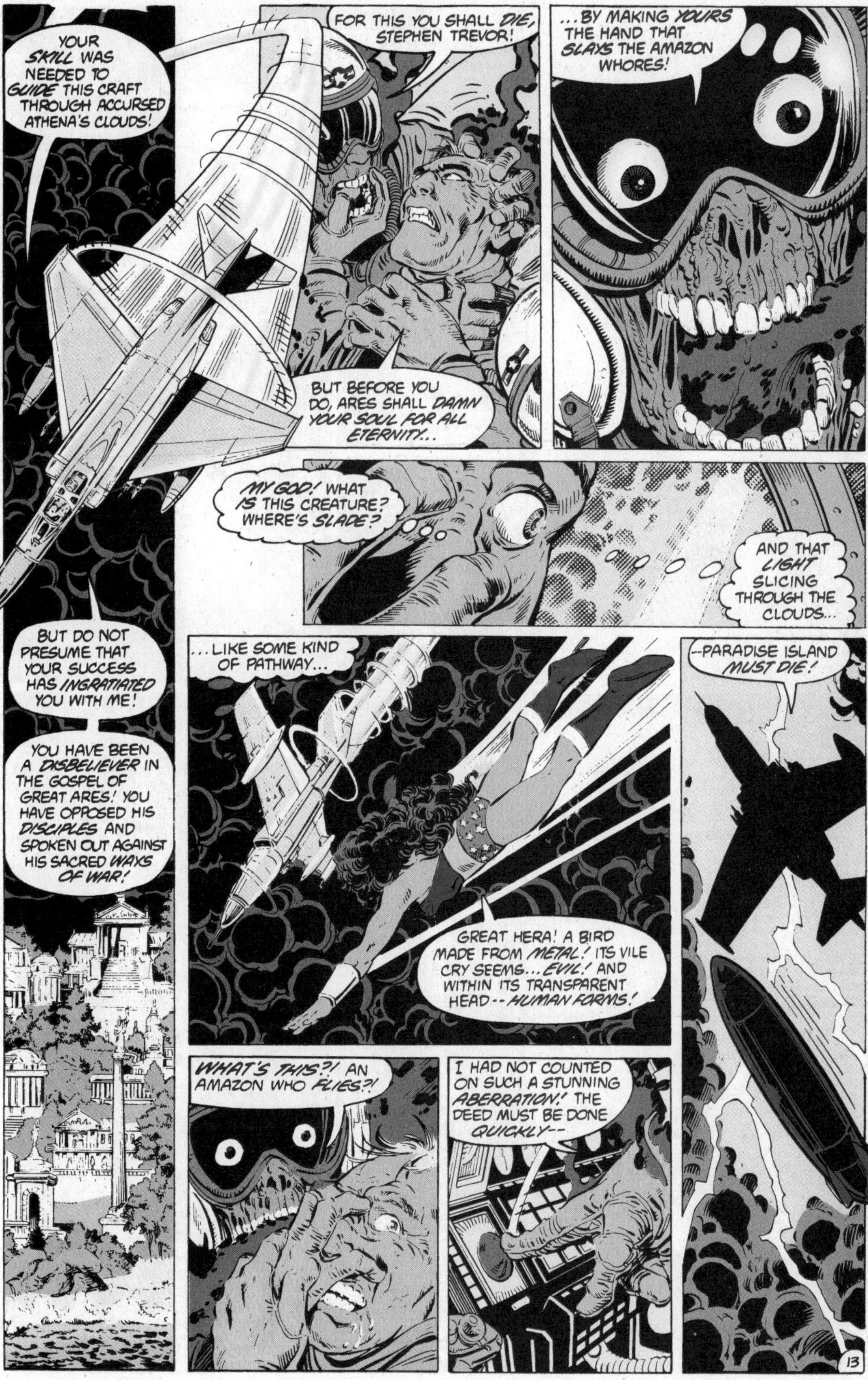
YOUR SKILL WAS NEEDED TO GUIDE THIS CRAFT THROUGH ACCURSED ATHENA'S CLOUDS!
FOR THIS YOU SHALL DIE, STEPHEN TREVOR!
BUT BEFORE YOU DO, ARES SHALL DAMN YOUR SOUL FOR ALL ETERNITY...
...BY MAKING YOURS THE HAND THAT SLAYS THE AMAZON WHORES!
MY GOD! WHAT IS THIS CREATURE? WHERE'S SLADE?
AND THAT LIGHT SLICING THROUGH THE CLOUDS...
BUT DO NOT PRESUME THAT YOUR SUCCESS HAS INGRATIATED YOU WITH ME!
YOU HAVE BEEN A DISBELIEVER IN THE GOSPEL OF GREAT ARES! YOU HAVE OPPOSED HIS DISCIPLES AND SPOKEN OUT AGAINST HIS SACRED WAYS OF WAR!
...LIKE SOME KIND OF PATHWAY...
GREAT HERA! A BIRD MADE FROM METAL! ITS VILE CRY SEEMS... EVIL! AND WITHIN ITS TRANSPARENT HEAD--HUMAN FORMS!
--PARADISE ISLAND MUST DIE!
WHAT'S THIS?! AN AMAZON WHO FLIES?!
I HAD NOT COUNTED ON SUCH A STUNNING ABERRATION! THE DEED MUST BE DONE QUICKLY--
13

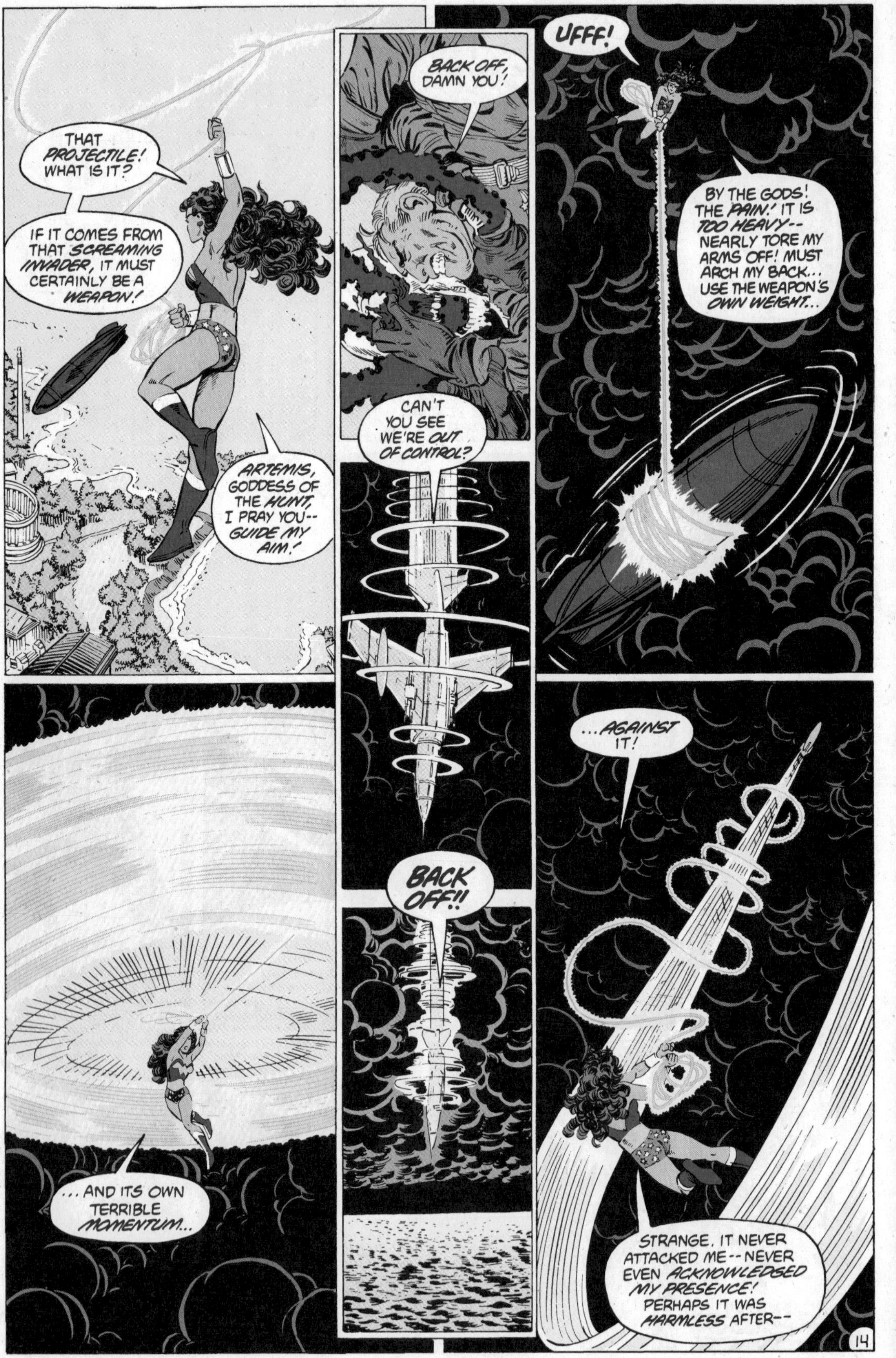
THAT PROJECTILE! WHAT IS IT?
IF IT COMES FROM THAT SCREAMING INVADER, IT MUST CERTAINLY BE A WEAPON!
ARTEMIS, GODDESS OF THE HUNT, I PRAY YOU-- GUIDE MY AIM!
BACK OFF, DAMN YOU!
CAN'T YOU SEE WE'RE OUT OF CONTROL?
UFFF!
BY THE GODS! THE PAIN! IT IS TOO HEAVY-- NEARLY TORE MY ARMS OFF! MUST ARCH MY BACK... USE THE WEAPON'S OWN WEIGHT...
...AND ITS OWN TERRIBLE MOMENTUM...
BACK OFF!!
...AGAINST IT!
STRANGE. IT NEVER ATTACKED ME--NEVER EVEN ACKNOWLEDGED MY PRESENCE! PERHAPS IT WAS HARMLESS AFTER--
14

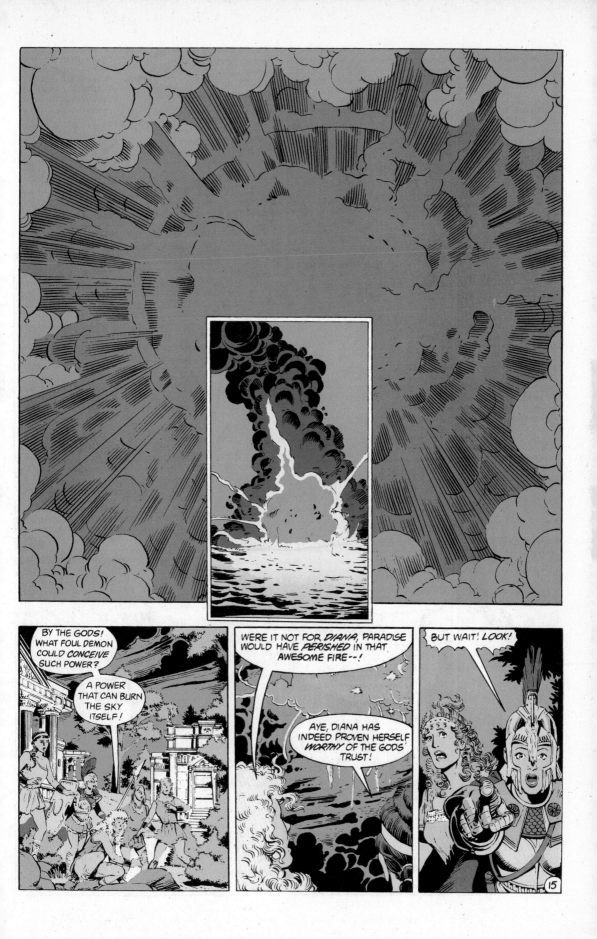

BY THE GODS! WHAT FOUL DEMON COULD *CONCEIVE* SUCH POWER?

A POWER THAT CAN BURN THE SKY ITSELF!

WERE IT NOT FOR *DIANA,* PARADISE WOULD HAVE *PERISHED* IN THAT AWESOME FIRE--!

AYE, DIANA HAS INDEED PROVEN HERSELF *WORTHY* OF THE GODS' TRUST!

BUT WAIT! *LOOK!*

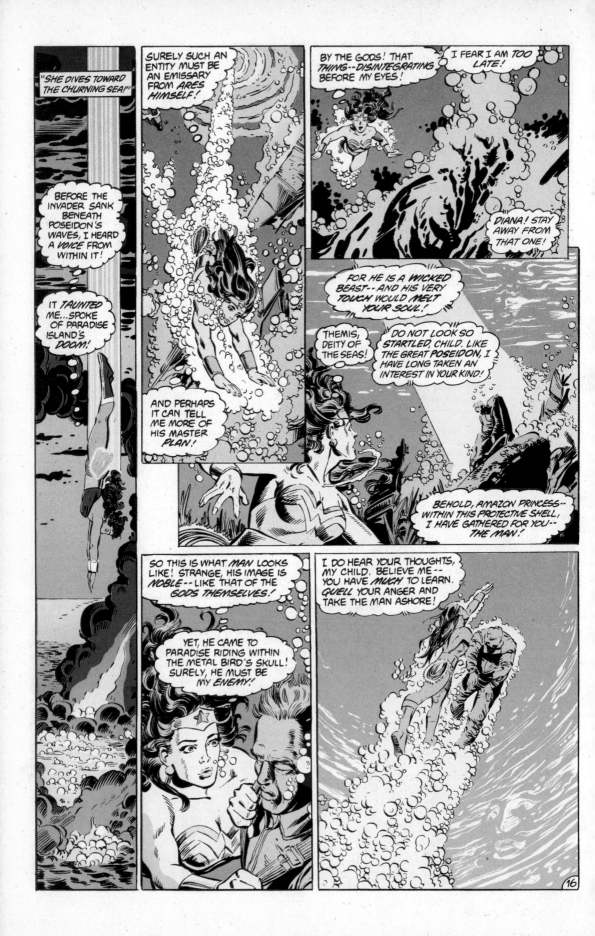

"SHE DIVES TOWARD THE CHURNING SEA!"

BEFORE THE INVADER SANK BENEATH POSEIDON'S WAVES, I HEARD A *VOICE* FROM WITHIN IT!

IT *TAUNTED* ME...SPOKE OF PARADISE ISLAND'S *DOOM!*

SURELY SUCH AN ENTITY MUST BE AN EMISSARY FROM *ARES HIMSELF!*

AND PERHAPS IT CAN TELL ME MORE OF HIS MASTER *PLAN!*

BY THE GODS! THAT *THING*--DISINTEGRATING BEFORE MY EYES!

I FEAR I AM *TOO LATE!*

DIANA! STAY AWAY FROM THAT ONE!

FOR HE IS A *WICKED* BEAST--AND HIS VERY *TOUCH* WOULD *MELT YOUR SOUL!*

THEMIS, DEITY OF THE SEAS!

DO NOT LOOK SO *STARTLED,* CHILD. LIKE THE GREAT *POSEIDON,* I HAVE LONG TAKEN AN INTEREST IN YOUR KIND!

BEHOLD, AMAZON PRINCESS-- WITHIN THIS PROTECTIVE SHELL, I HAVE GATHERED FOR YOU-- THE MAN!

SO THIS IS WHAT *MAN* LOOKS LIKE! STRANGE, HIS IMAGE IS *NOBLE*--LIKE THAT OF THE *GODS THEMSELVES!*

YET, HE CAME TO PARADISE RIDING WITHIN THE METAL BIRD'S SKULL! SURELY, HE MUST BE MY *ENEMY!*

I DO HEAR YOUR THOUGHTS, MY CHILD. BELIEVE ME-- YOU HAVE *MUCH* TO LEARN. *QUELL* YOUR ANGER AND TAKE THE MAN ASHORE!

16

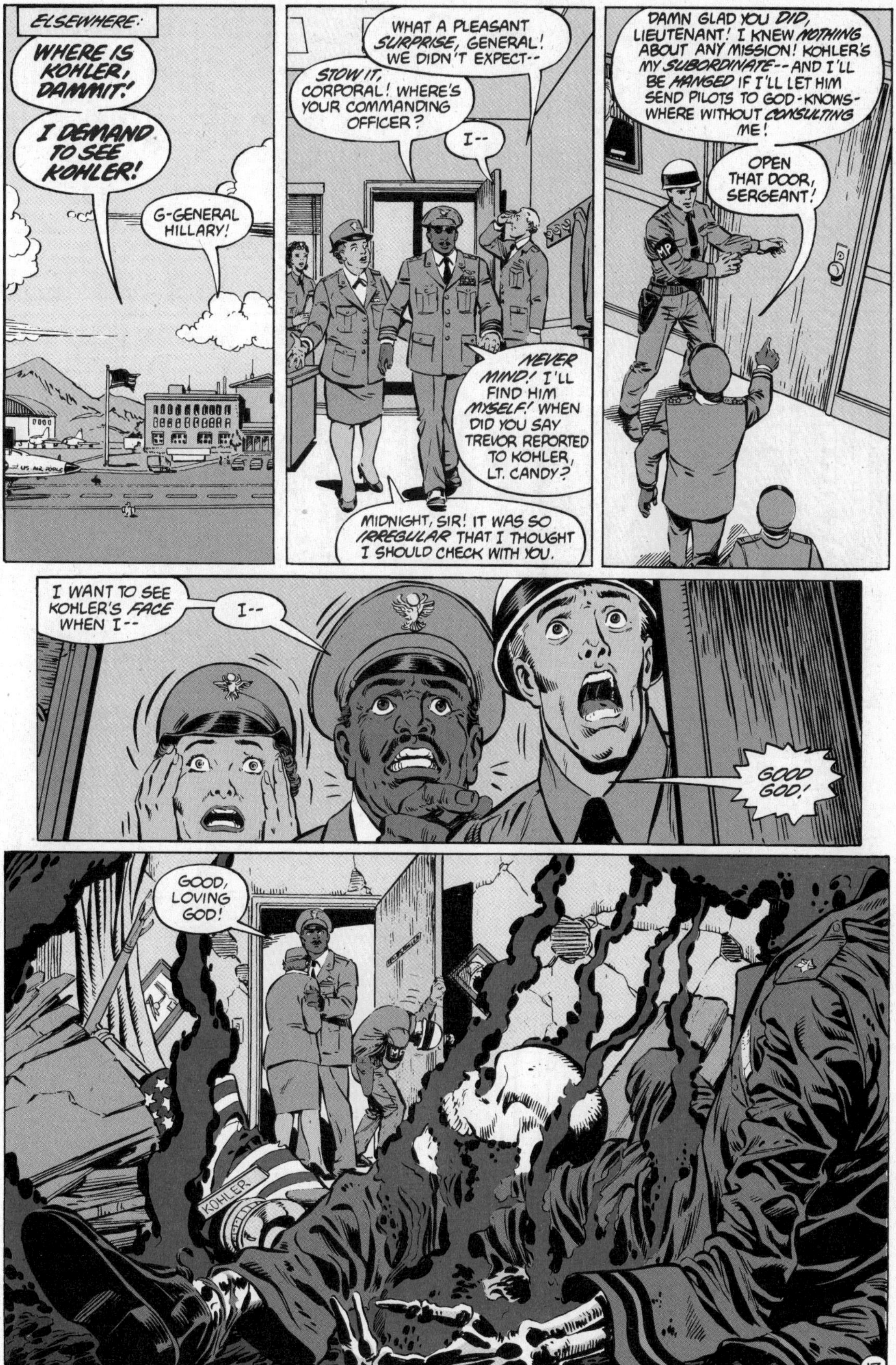
ELSEWHERE:
WHERE IS KOHLER, DAMMIT!
I DEMAND TO SEE KOHLER!
G-GENERAL HILLARY!
US AIR FORCE
WHAT A PLEASANT SURPRISE, GENERAL! WE DIDN'T EXPECT--
STOW IT, CORPORAL! WHERE'S YOUR COMMANDING OFFICER?
I--
NEVER MIND! I'LL FIND HIM MYSELF! WHEN DID YOU SAY TREVOR REPORTED TO KOHLER, LT. CANDY?
MIDNIGHT, SIR! IT WAS SO IRREGULAR THAT I THOUGHT I SHOULD CHECK WITH YOU.
DAMN GLAD YOU DID, LIEUTENANT! I KNEW NOTHING ABOUT ANY MISSION! KOHLER'S MY SUBORDINATE--AND I'LL BE HANGED IF I'LL LET HIM SEND PILOTS TO GOD-KNOWS-WHERE WITHOUT CONSULTING ME!
OPEN THAT DOOR, SERGEANT!
MP
I WANT TO SEE KOHLER'S FACE WHEN I--
I--
GOOD GOD!
GOOD, LOVING GOD!
KOHLER
17

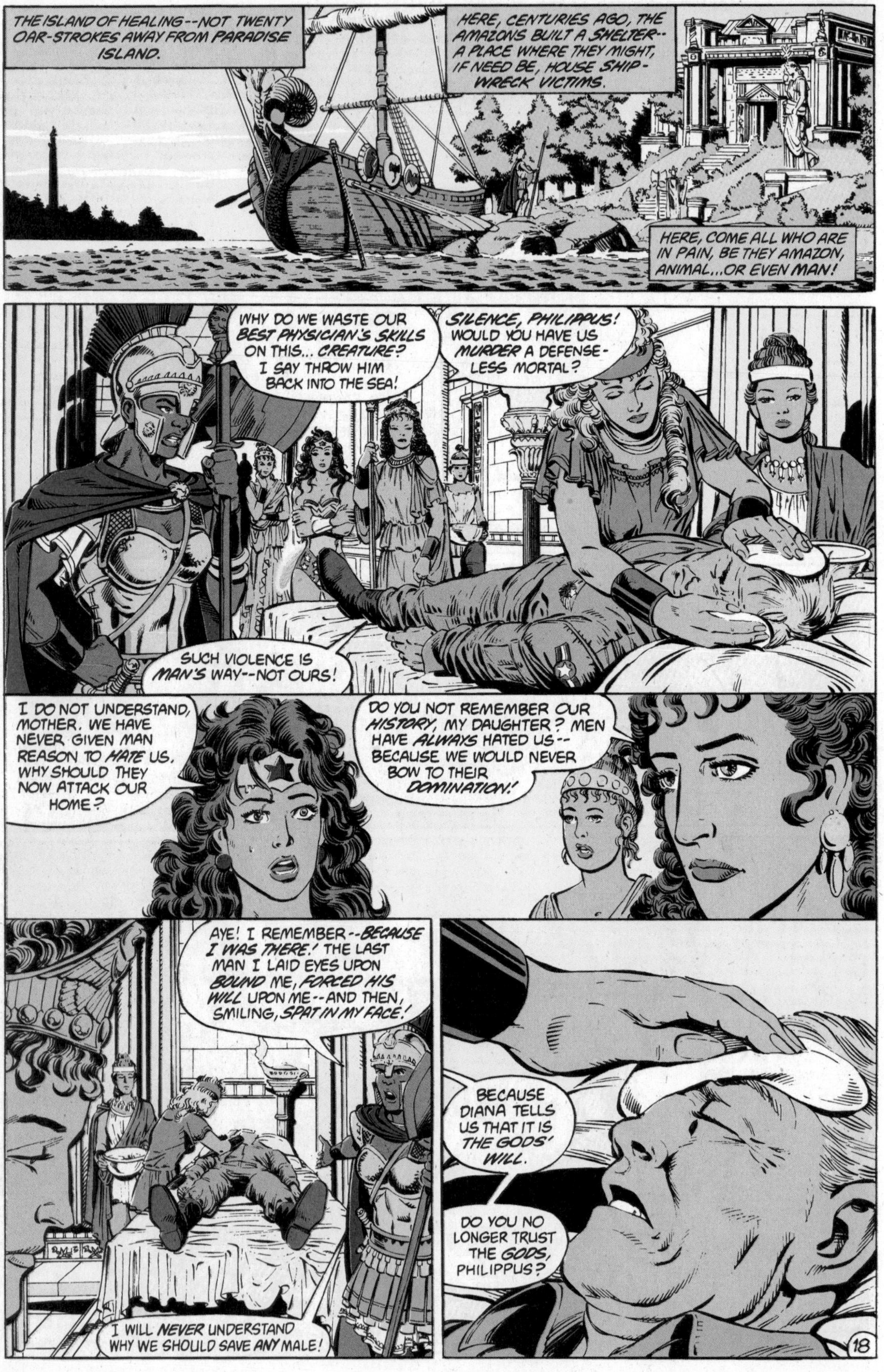
THE ISLAND OF HEALING--NOT TWENTY OAR-STROKES AWAY FROM PARADISE ISLAND.
HERE, CENTURIES AGO, THE AMAZONS BUILT A SHELTER--A PLACE WHERE THEY MIGHT, IF NEED BE, HOUSE SHIP-WRECK VICTIMS.
HERE, COME ALL WHO ARE IN PAIN, BE THEY AMAZON, ANIMAL...OR EVEN MAN!
WHY DO WE WASTE OUR BEST PHYSICIAN'S SKILLS ON THIS... CREATURE? I SAY THROW HIM BACK INTO THE SEA!
SILENCE, PHILIPPUS! WOULD YOU HAVE US MURDER A DEFENSE-LESS MORTAL?
SUCH VIOLENCE IS MAN'S WAY--NOT OURS!
I DO NOT UNDERSTAND, MOTHER. WE HAVE NEVER GIVEN MAN REASON TO HATE US. WHY SHOULD THEY NOW ATTACK OUR HOME?
DO YOU NOT REMEMBER OUR HISTORY, MY DAUGHTER? MEN HAVE ALWAYS HATED US--BECAUSE WE WOULD NEVER BOW TO THEIR DOMINATION!
AYE! I REMEMBER--BECAUSE I WAS THERE! THE LAST MAN I LAID EYES UPON BOUND ME, FORCED HIS WILL UPON ME--AND THEN, SMILING, SPAT IN MY FACE!
I WILL NEVER UNDERSTAND WHY WE SHOULD SAVE ANY MALE!
BECAUSE DIANA TELLS US THAT IT IS THE GODS' WILL.
DO YOU NO LONGER TRUST THE GODS, PHILIPPUS?
18

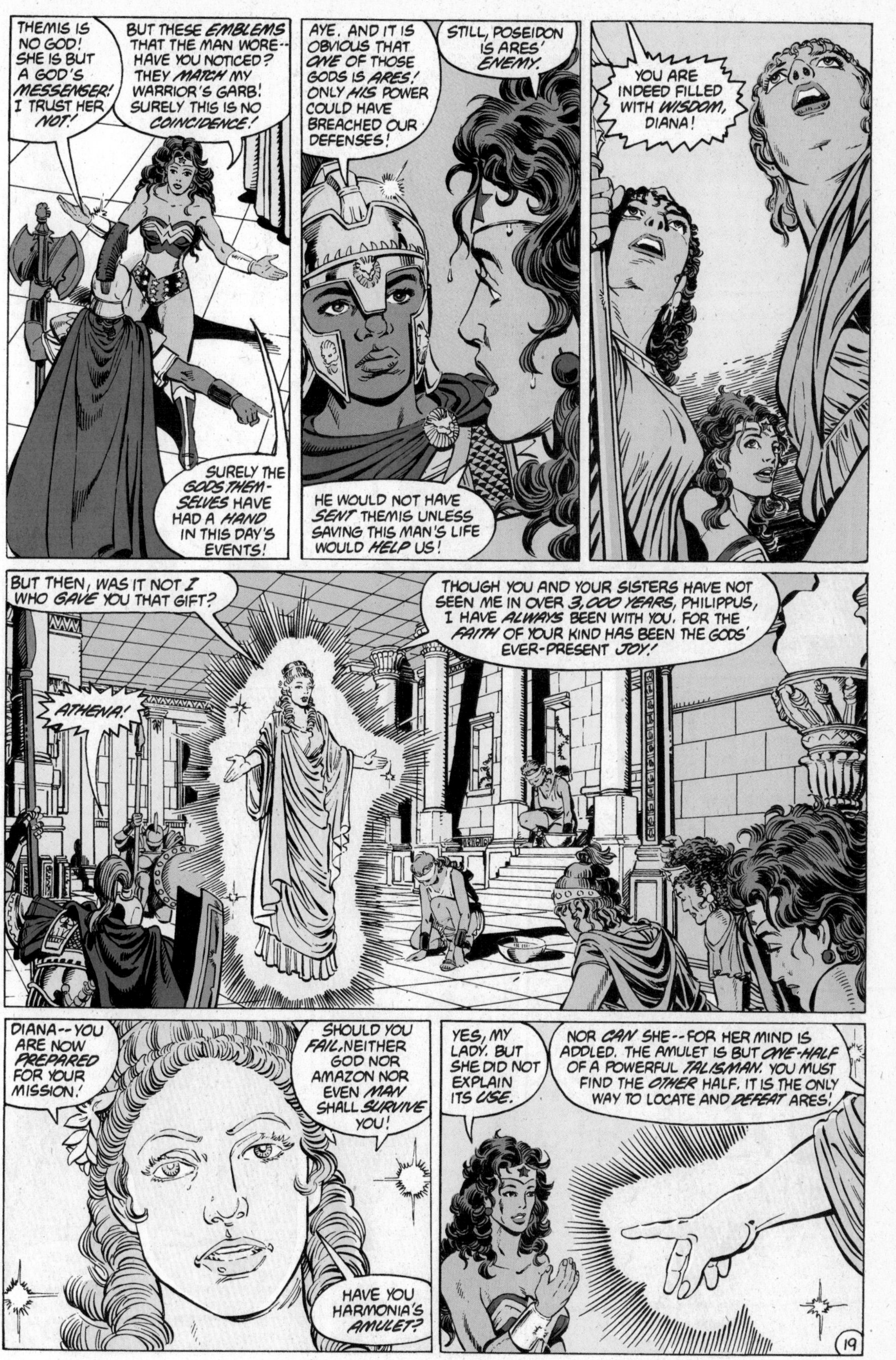
THEMIS IS NO GOD! SHE IS BUT A GOD'S MESSENGER! I TRUST HER NOT!
BUT THESE EMBLEMS THAT THE MAN WORE-- HAVE YOU NOTICED? THEY MATCH MY WARRIOR'S GARB! SURELY THIS IS NO COINCIDENCE!
SURELY THE GODS THEMSELVES HAVE HAD A HAND IN THIS DAY'S EVENTS!
AYE. AND IT IS OBVIOUS THAT ONE OF THOSE GODS IS ARES! ONLY HIS POWER COULD HAVE BREACHED OUR DEFENSES!
STILL, POSEIDON IS ARES' ENEMY.
HE WOULD NOT HAVE SENT THEMIS UNLESS SAVING THIS MAN'S LIFE WOULD HELP US!
YOU ARE INDEED FILLED WITH WISDOM, DIANA!
BUT THEN, WAS IT NOT I WHO GAVE YOU THAT GIFT?
THOUGH YOU AND YOUR SISTERS HAVE NOT SEEN ME IN OVER 3,000 YEARS, PHILIPPUS, I HAVE ALWAYS BEEN WITH YOU. FOR THE FAITH OF YOUR KIND HAS BEEN THE GODS' EVER-PRESENT JOY!
ATHENA!
DIANA--YOU ARE NOW PREPARED FOR YOUR MISSION!
SHOULD YOU FAIL, NEITHER GOD NOR AMAZON NOR EVEN MAN SHALL SURVIVE YOU!
HAVE YOU HARMONIA'S AMULET?
YES, MY LADY. BUT SHE DID NOT EXPLAIN ITS USE.
NOR CAN SHE--FOR HER MIND IS ADDLED. THE AMULET IS BUT ONE-HALF OF A POWERFUL TALISMAN. YOU MUST FIND THE OTHER HALF. IT IS THE ONLY WAY TO LOCATE AND DEFEAT ARES!
19

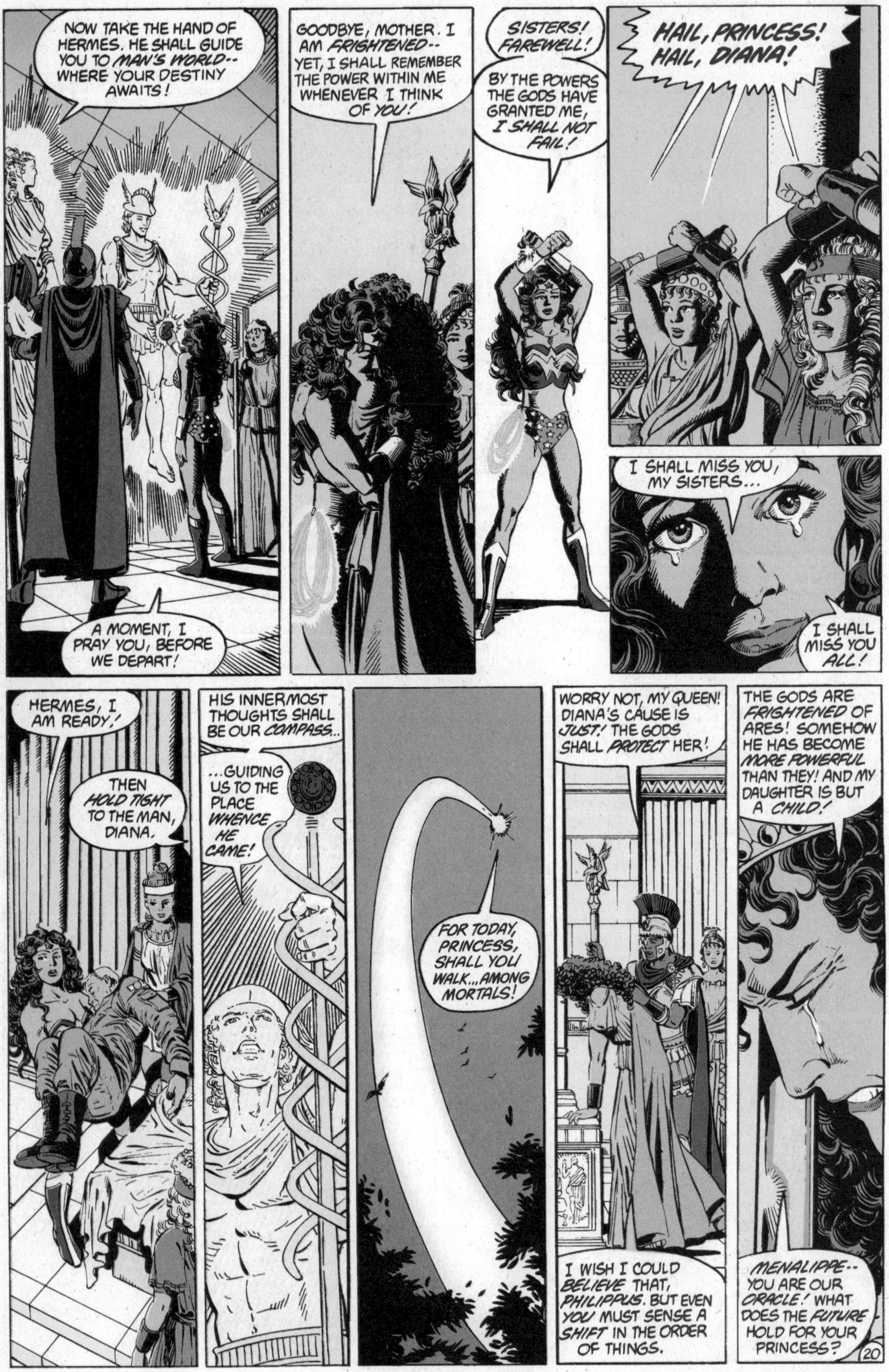
NOW TAKE THE HAND OF HERMES. HE SHALL GUIDE YOU TO MAN'S WORLD-- WHERE YOUR DESTINY AWAITS!
A MOMENT, I PRAY YOU, BEFORE WE DEPART!
GOODBYE, MOTHER. I AM FRIGHTENED-- YET, I SHALL REMEMBER THE POWER WITHIN ME WHENEVER I THINK OF YOU!
SISTERS! FAREWELL!
BY THE POWERS THE GODS HAVE GRANTED ME, I SHALL NOT FAIL!
HAIL, PRINCESS! HAIL, DIANA!
I SHALL MISS YOU, MY SISTERS...
I SHALL MISS YOU ALL!
HERMES, I AM READY!
THEN HOLD TIGHT TO THE MAN, DIANA.
HIS INNERMOST THOUGHTS SHALL BE OUR COMPASS...
...GUIDING US TO THE PLACE WHENCE HE CAME!
FOR TODAY, PRINCESS, SHALL YOU WALK...AMONG MORTALS!
WORRY NOT, MY QUEEN! DIANA'S CAUSE IS JUST! THE GODS SHALL PROTECT HER!
I WISH I COULD BELIEVE THAT, PHILIPPUS. BUT EVEN YOU MUST SENSE A SHIFT IN THE ORDER OF THINGS.
THE GODS ARE FRIGHTENED OF ARES! SOMEHOW HE HAS BECOME MORE POWERFUL THAN THEY! AND MY DAUGHTER IS BUT A CHILD!
MENALIPPE-- YOU ARE OUR ORACLE! WHAT DOES THE FUTURE HOLD FOR YOUR PRINCESS?
20

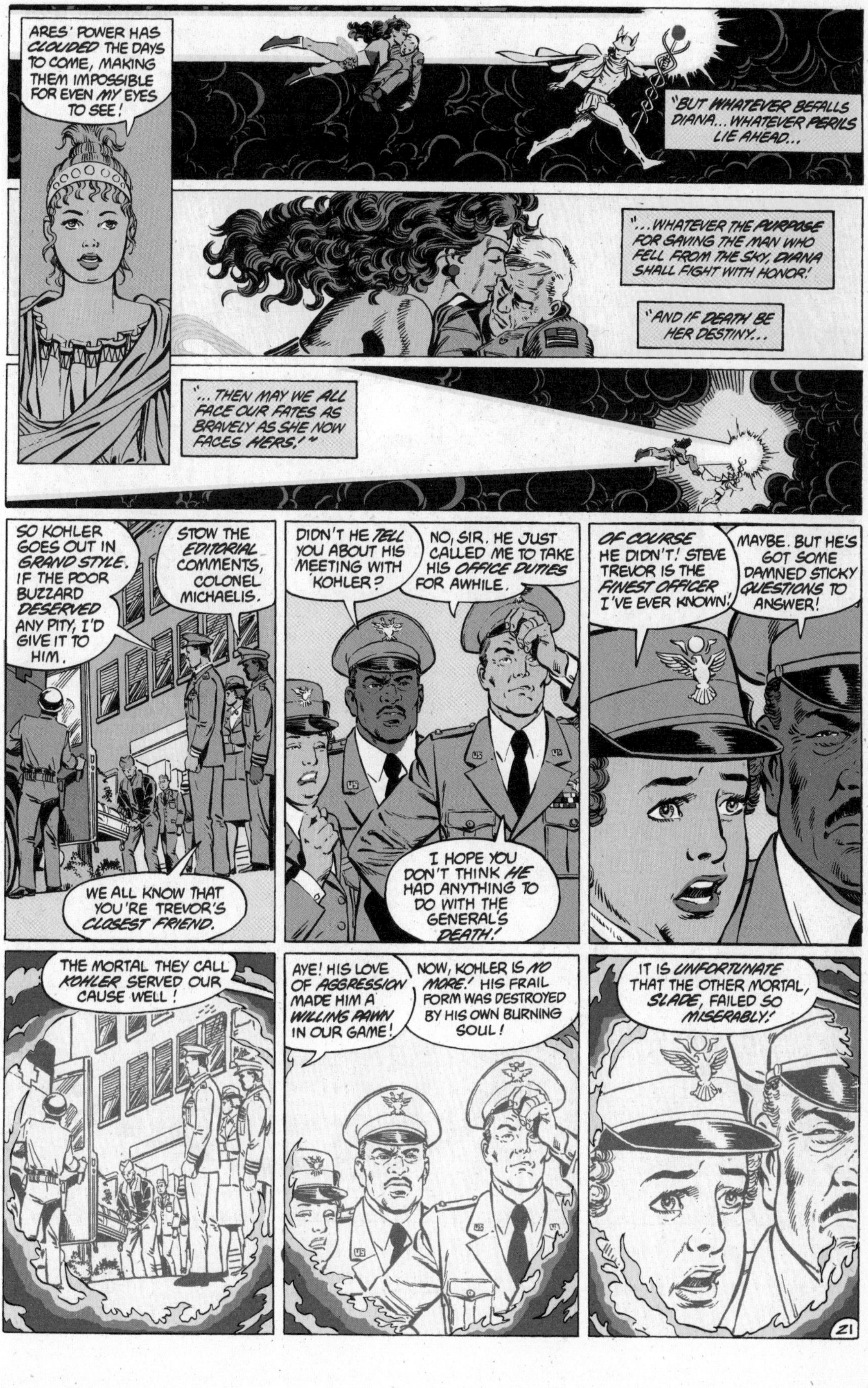

ARES' POWER HAS CLOUDED THE DAYS TO COME, MAKING THEM IMPOSSIBLE FOR EVEN MY EYES TO SEE!
"BUT WHATEVER BEFALLS DIANA... WHATEVER PERILS LIE AHEAD...
"...WHATEVER THE PURPOSE FOR SAVING THE MAN WHO FELL FROM THE SKY, DIANA SHALL FIGHT WITH HONOR!
"AND IF DEATH BE HER DESTINY...
"...THEN MAY WE ALL FACE OUR FATES AS BRAVELY AS SHE NOW FACES HERS!"
SO KOHLER GOES OUT IN GRAND STYLE. IF THE POOR BUZZARD DESERVED ANY PITY, I'D GIVE IT TO HIM.
STOW THE EDITORIAL COMMENTS, COLONEL MICHAELIS.
WE ALL KNOW THAT YOU'RE TREVOR'S CLOSEST FRIEND.
DIDN'T HE TELL YOU ABOUT HIS MEETING WITH KOHLER?
NO, SIR. HE JUST CALLED ME TO TAKE HIS OFFICE DUTIES FOR AWHILE.
I HOPE YOU DON'T THINK HE HAD ANYTHING TO DO WITH THE GENERAL'S DEATH!
OF COURSE HE DIDN'T! STEVE TREVOR IS THE FINEST OFFICER I'VE EVER KNOWN!
MAYBE. BUT HE'S GOT SOME DAMNED STICKY QUESTIONS TO ANSWER!
THE MORTAL THEY CALL KOHLER SERVED OUR CAUSE WELL!
AYE! HIS LOVE OF AGGRESSION MADE HIM A WILLING PAWN IN OUR GAME!
NOW, KOHLER IS NO MORE! HIS FRAIL FORM WAS DESTROYED BY HIS OWN BURNING SOUL!
IT IS UNFORTUNATE THAT THE OTHER MORTAL, SLADE, FAILED SO MISERABLY!
21

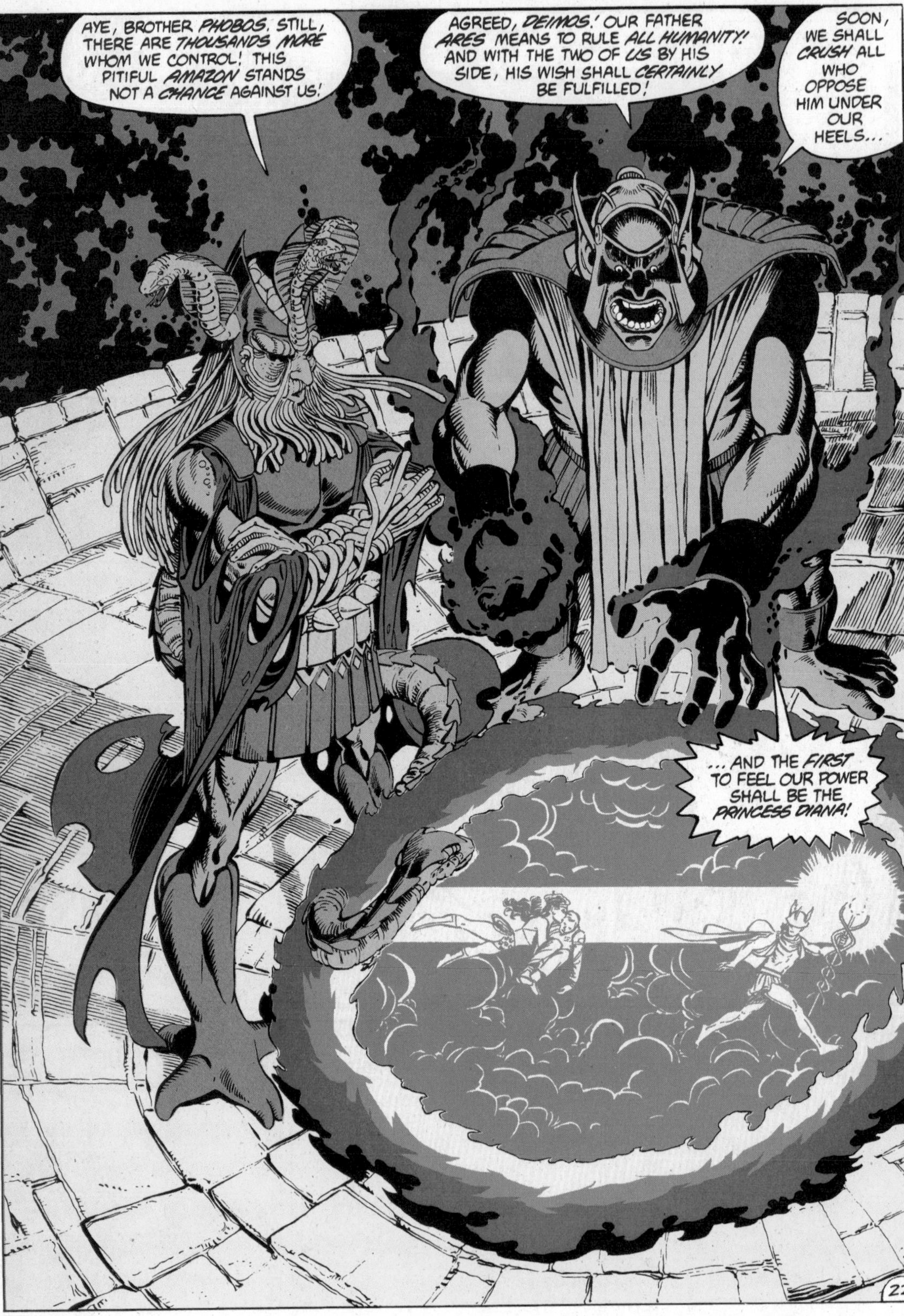
AYE, BROTHER PHOBOS. STILL, THERE ARE THOUSANDS MORE WHOM WE CONTROL! THIS PITIFUL AMAZON STANDS NOT A CHANCE AGAINST US!
AGREED, DEIMOS! OUR FATHER ARES MEANS TO RULE ALL HUMANITY! AND WITH THE TWO OF US BY HIS SIDE, HIS WISH SHALL CERTAINLY BE FULFILLED!
SOON, WE SHALL CRUSH ALL WHO OPPOSE HIM UNDER OUR HEELS...
...AND THE FIRST TO FEEL OUR POWER SHALL BE THE PRINCESS DIANA!

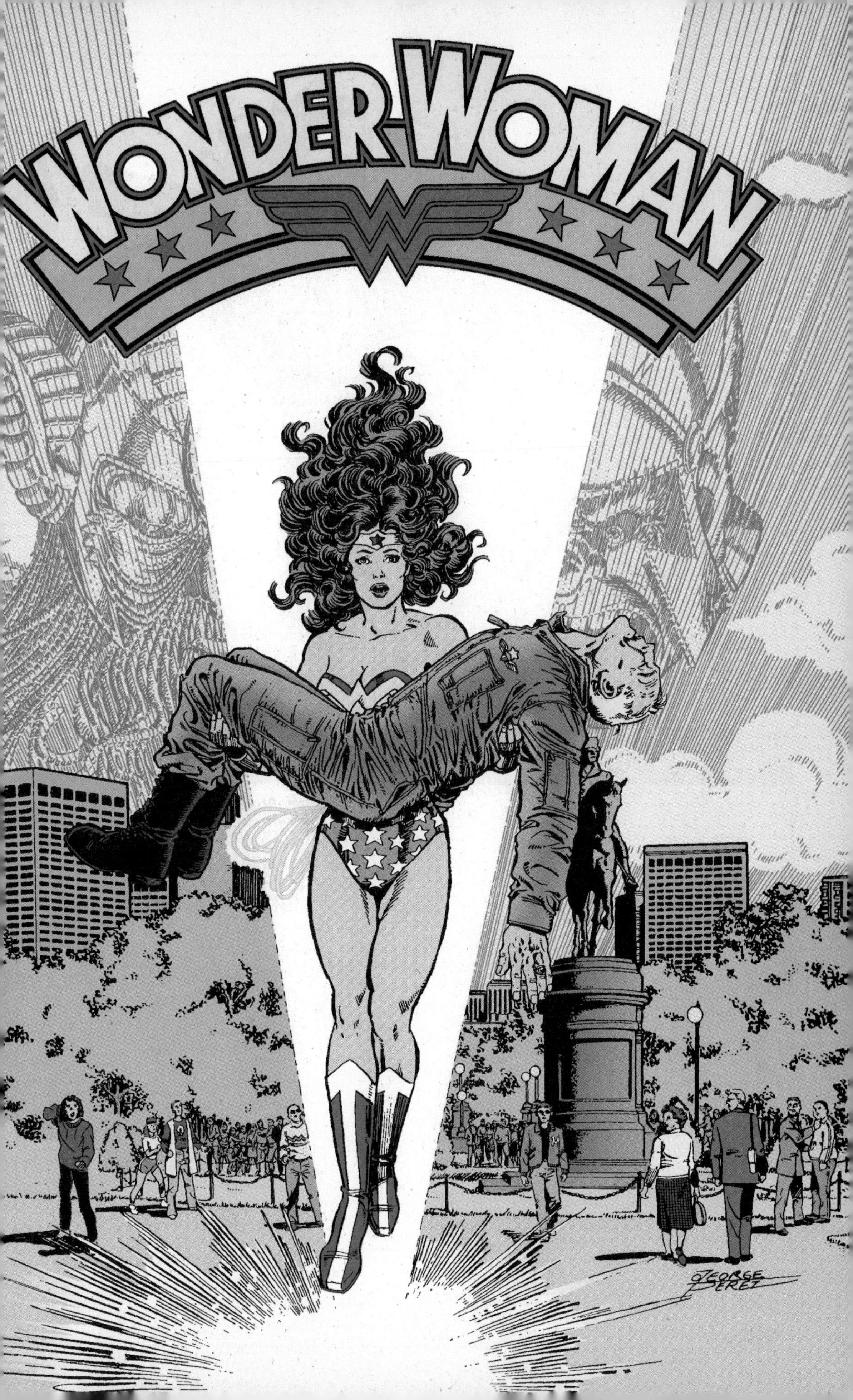
WONDER WOMAN
GEORGE PEREZ

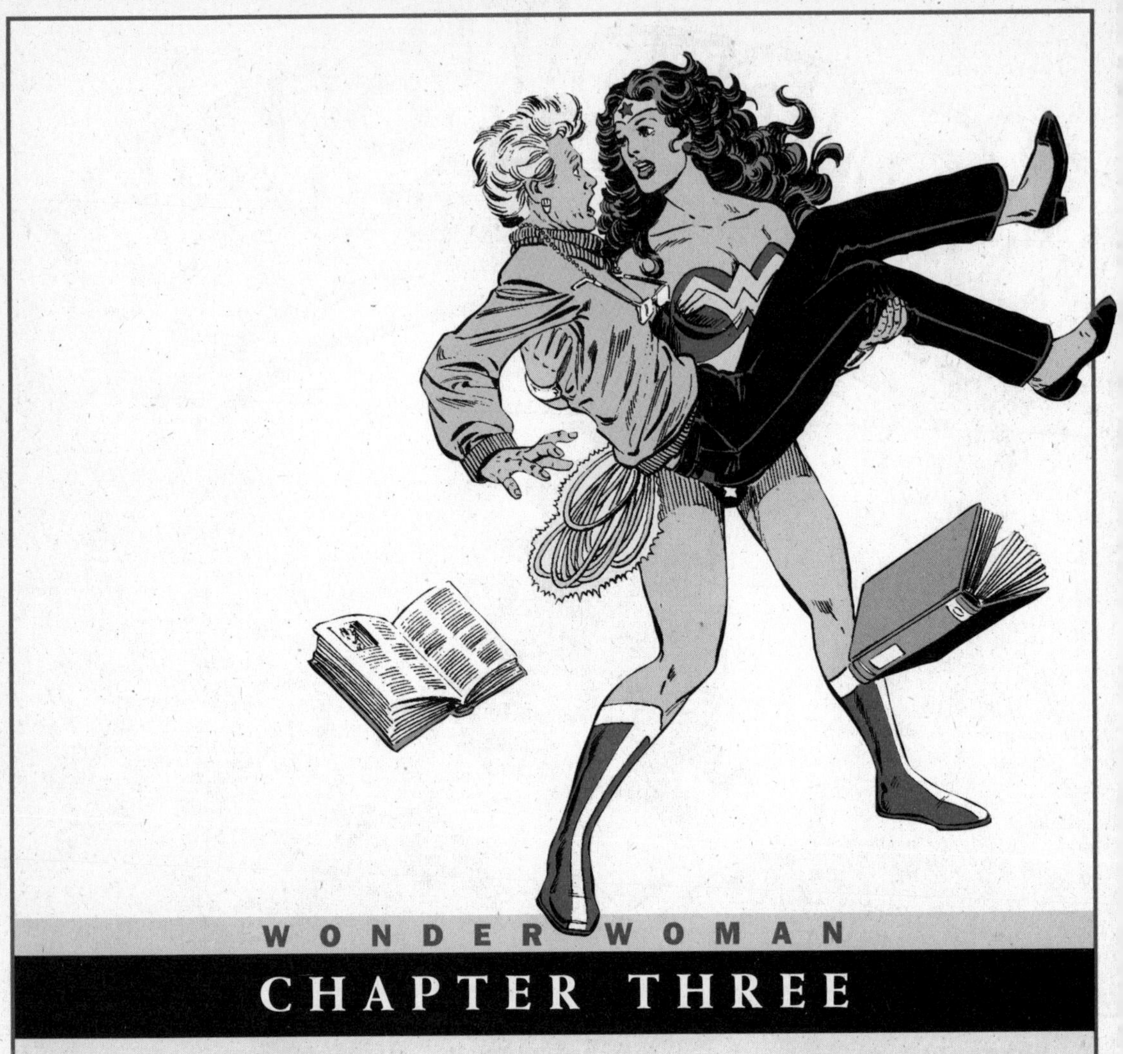

WONDER WOMAN

CHAPTER THREE

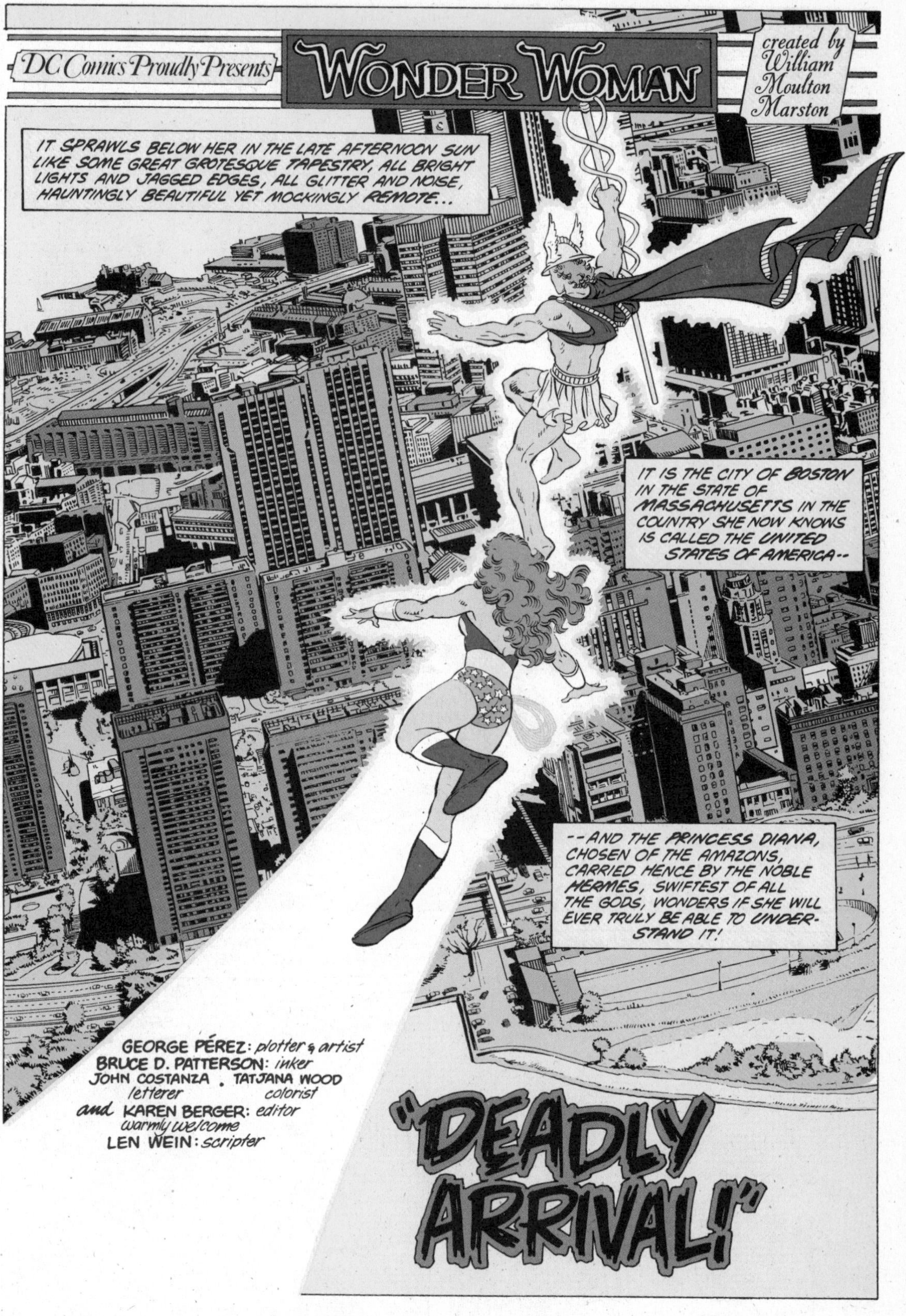

DC Comics Proudly Presents
WONDER WOMAN
created by William Moulton Marston
IT SPRAWLS BELOW HER IN THE LATE AFTERNOON SUN LIKE SOME GREAT GROTESQUE TAPESTRY, ALL BRIGHT LIGHTS AND JAGGED EDGES, ALL GLITTER AND NOISE, HAUNTINGLY BEAUTIFUL YET MOCKINGLY REMOTE...
IT IS THE CITY OF BOSTON IN THE STATE OF MASSACHUSETTS IN THE COUNTRY SHE NOW KNOWS IS CALLED THE UNITED STATES OF AMERICA--
--AND THE PRINCESS DIANA, CHOSEN OF THE AMAZONS, CARRIED HENCE BY THE NOBLE HERMES, SWIFTEST OF ALL THE GODS, WONDERS IF SHE WILL EVER TRULY BE ABLE TO UNDERSTAND IT!
GEORGE PÉREZ: plotter & artist
BRUCE D. PATTERSON: inker
JOHN COSTANZA letterer . TATJANA WOOD colorist
and KAREN BERGER: editor
warmly welcome
LEN WEIN: scripter
"DEADLY ARRIVAL!"

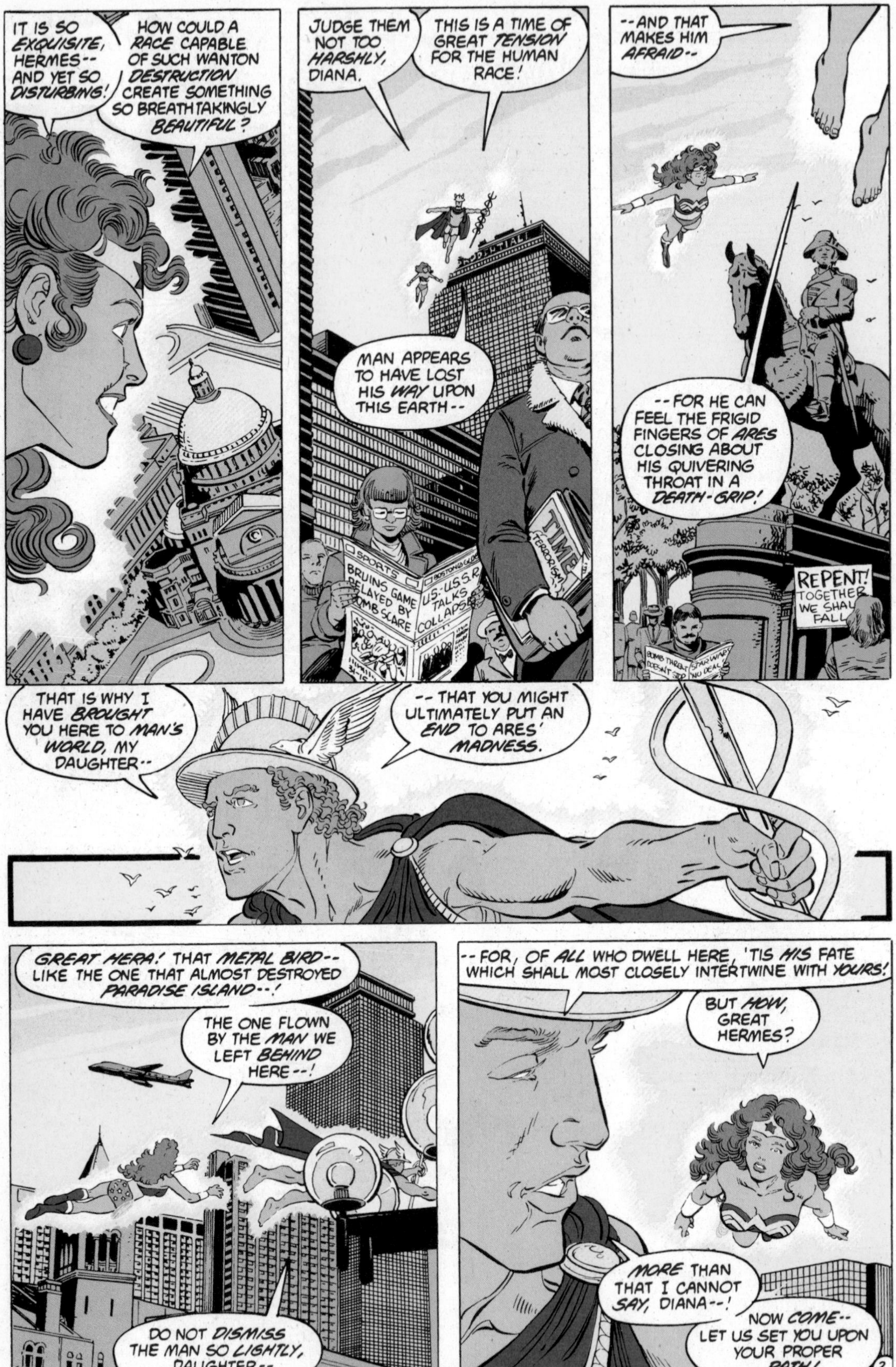
IT IS SO EXQUISITE, HERMES-- AND YET SO DISTURBING!
HOW COULD A RACE CAPABLE OF SUCH WANTON DESTRUCTION CREATE SOMETHING SO BREATHTAKINGLY BEAUTIFUL?
JUDGE THEM NOT TOO HARSHLY, DIANA.
THIS IS A TIME OF GREAT TENSION FOR THE HUMAN RACE!
MAN APPEARS TO HAVE LOST HIS WAY UPON THIS EARTH--
SPORTS
BRUINS GAME DELAYED BY BOMB SCARE
U.S.-U.S.S.R. TALKS COLLAPSE
TIME
TERRORISM
--AND THAT MAKES HIM AFRAID--
--FOR HE CAN FEEL THE FRIGID FINGERS OF ARES CLOSING ABOUT HIS QUIVERING THROAT IN A DEATH-GRIP!
REPENT! TOGETHER WE SHALL FALL
BOMB THREAT DOESN'T STOP
STAR WAR NO DEAL
THAT IS WHY I HAVE BROUGHT YOU HERE TO MAN'S WORLD, MY DAUGHTER--
--THAT YOU MIGHT ULTIMATELY PUT AN END TO ARES' MADNESS.
GREAT HERA! THAT METAL BIRD-- LIKE THE ONE THAT ALMOST DESTROYED PARADISE ISLAND--!
THE ONE FLOWN BY THE MAN WE LEFT BEHIND HERE--!
DO NOT DISMISS THE MAN SO LIGHTLY, DAUGHTER--
--FOR, OF ALL WHO DWELL HERE, 'TIS HIS FATE WHICH SHALL MOST CLOSELY INTERTWINE WITH YOURS!
BUT HOW, GREAT HERMES?
MORE THAN THAT I CANNOT SAY, DIANA--!
NOW COME-- LET US SET YOU UPON YOUR PROPER PATH!
2

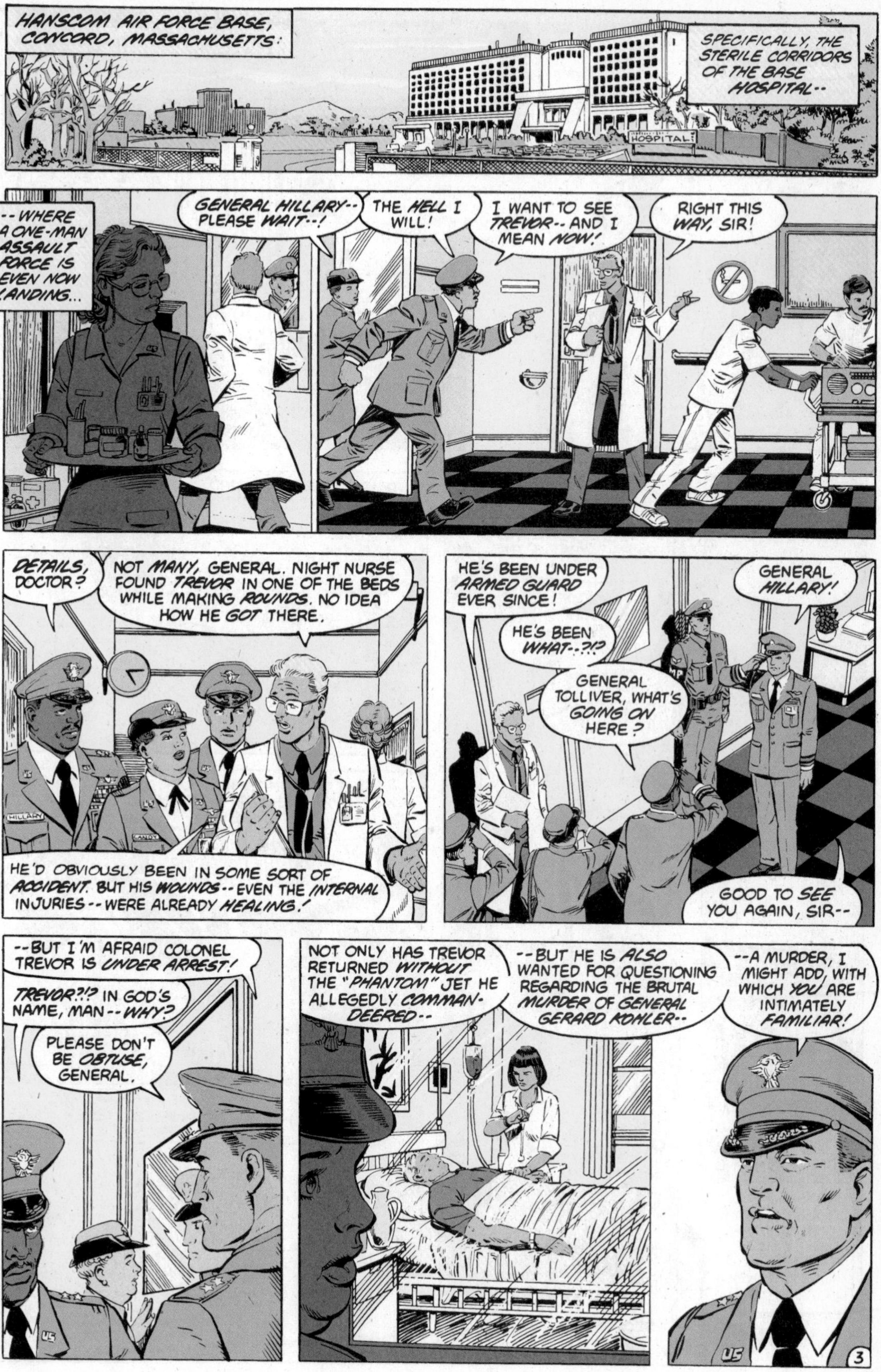

HANSCOM AIR FORCE BASE, CONCORD, MASSACHUSETTS:
SPECIFICALLY, THE STERILE CORRIDORS OF THE BASE HOSPITAL--
HOSPITAL
--WHERE A ONE-MAN ASSAULT FORCE IS EVEN NOW LANDING...
GENERAL HILLARY--PLEASE WAIT--!
THE HELL I WILL!
I WANT TO SEE TREVOR--AND I MEAN NOW!
RIGHT THIS WAY, SIR!
DETAILS, DOCTOR?
NOT MANY, GENERAL. NIGHT NURSE FOUND TREVOR IN ONE OF THE BEDS WHILE MAKING ROUNDS. NO IDEA HOW HE GOT THERE.
HILLARY
CANDY
HE'D OBVIOUSLY BEEN IN SOME SORT OF ACCIDENT. BUT HIS WOUNDS--EVEN THE INTERNAL INJURIES--WERE ALREADY HEALING!
HE'S BEEN UNDER ARMED GUARD EVER SINCE!
HE'S BEEN WHAT--?!?
GENERAL TOLLIVER, WHAT'S GOING ON HERE?
GENERAL HILLARY!
MP
GOOD TO SEE YOU AGAIN, SIR--
--BUT I'M AFRAID COLONEL TREVOR IS UNDER ARREST!
TREVOR?!? IN GOD'S NAME, MAN--WHY?
PLEASE DON'T BE OBTUSE, GENERAL.
US
NOT ONLY HAS TREVOR RETURNED WITHOUT THE "PHANTOM" JET HE ALLEGEDLY COMMANDEERED--
--BUT HE IS ALSO WANTED FOR QUESTIONING REGARDING THE BRUTAL MURDER OF GENERAL GERARD KOHLER--
--A MURDER, I MIGHT ADD, WITH WHICH YOU ARE INTIMATELY FAMILIAR!
US
3

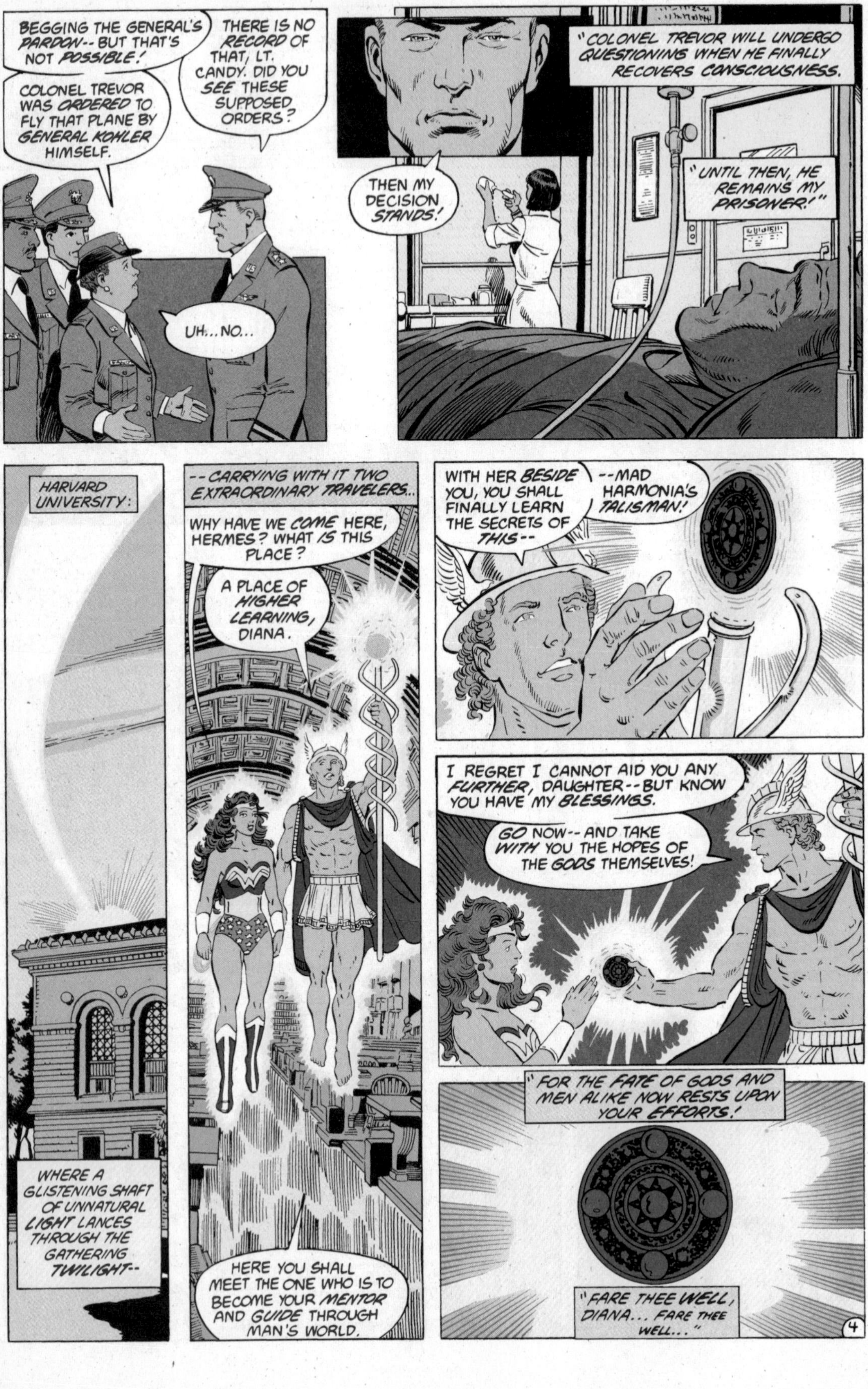
BEGGING THE GENERAL'S PARDON-- BUT THAT'S NOT POSSIBLE!
COLONEL TREVOR WAS ORDERED TO FLY THAT PLANE BY GENERAL KOHLER HIMSELF.
THERE IS NO RECORD OF THAT, LT. CANDY. DID YOU SEE THESE SUPPOSED ORDERS?
UH... NO...
"COLONEL TREVOR WILL UNDERGO QUESTIONING WHEN HE FINALLY RECOVERS CONSCIOUSNESS.
THEN MY DECISION STANDS!
"UNTIL THEN, HE REMAINS MY PRISONER!"
HARVARD UNIVERSITY:
WHERE A GLISTENING SHAFT OF UNNATURAL LIGHT LANCES THROUGH THE GATHERING TWILIGHT--
--CARRYING WITH IT TWO EXTRAORDINARY TRAVELERS...
WHY HAVE WE COME HERE, HERMES? WHAT IS THIS PLACE?
A PLACE OF HIGHER LEARNING, DIANA.
HERE YOU SHALL MEET THE ONE WHO IS TO BECOME YOUR MENTOR AND GUIDE THROUGH MAN'S WORLD.
WITH HER BESIDE YOU, YOU SHALL FINALLY LEARN THE SECRETS OF THIS--
--MAD HARMONIA'S TALISMAN!
I REGRET I CANNOT AID YOU ANY FURTHER, DAUGHTER--BUT KNOW YOU HAVE MY BLESSINGS.
GO NOW--AND TAKE WITH YOU THE HOPES OF THE GODS THEMSELVES!
"FOR THE FATE OF GODS AND MEN ALIKE NOW RESTS UPON YOUR EFFORTS!
"FARE THEE WELL, DIANA... FARE THEE WELL..."
4

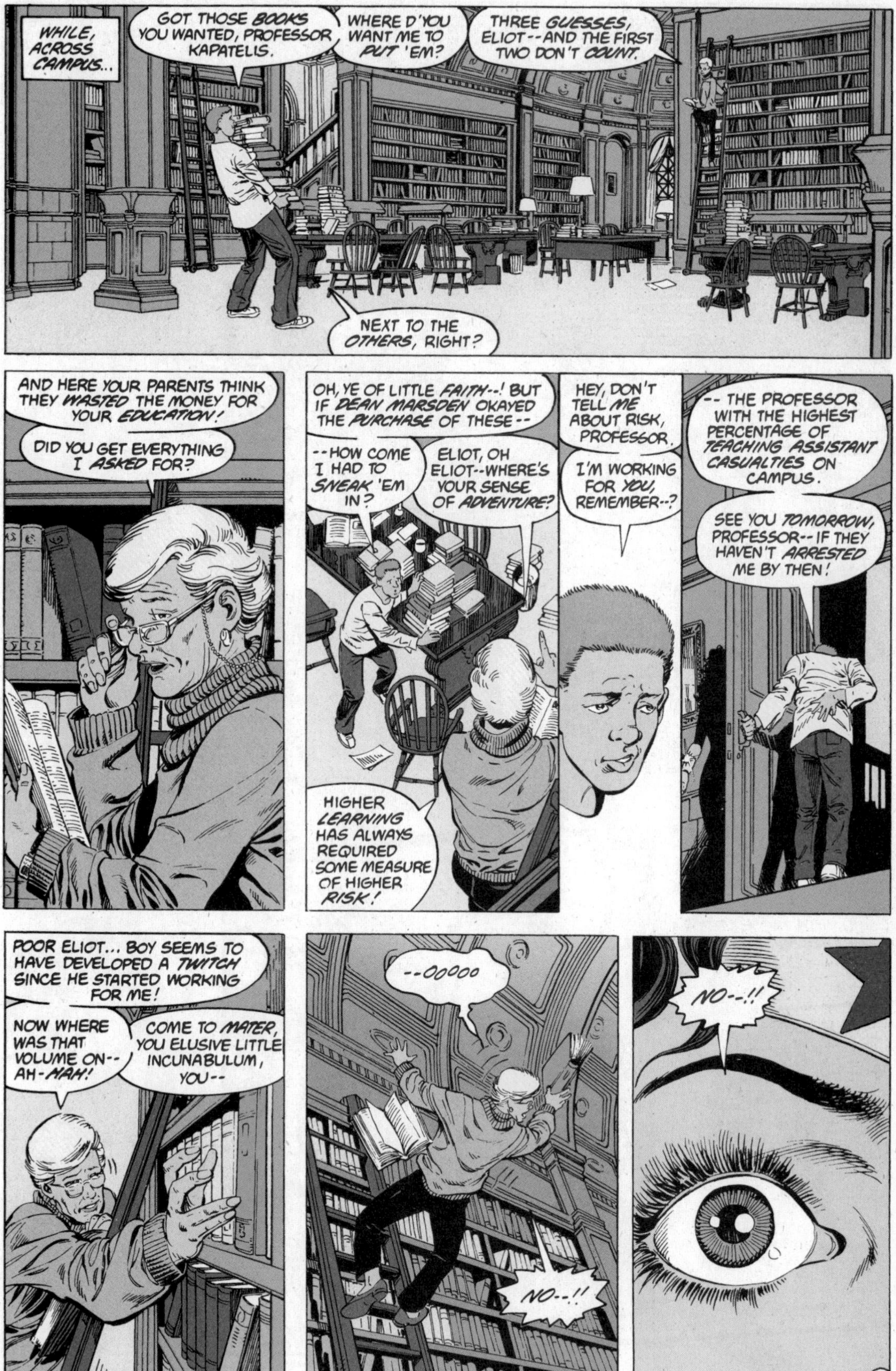

WHILE, ACROSS CAMPUS...
GOT THOSE BOOKS YOU WANTED, PROFESSOR KAPATELIS.
WHERE D'YOU WANT ME TO PUT 'EM?
THREE GUESSES, ELIOT--AND THE FIRST TWO DON'T COUNT.
NEXT TO THE OTHERS, RIGHT?
AND HERE YOUR PARENTS THINK THEY WASTED THE MONEY FOR YOUR EDUCATION!
DID YOU GET EVERYTHING I ASKED FOR?
OH, YE OF LITTLE FAITH--! BUT IF DEAN MARSDEN OKAYED THE PURCHASE OF THESE--
--HOW COME I HAD TO SNEAK 'EM IN?
ELIOT, OH ELIOT--WHERE'S YOUR SENSE OF ADVENTURE?
HIGHER LEARNING HAS ALWAYS REQUIRED SOME MEASURE OF HIGHER RISK!
HEY, DON'T TELL ME ABOUT RISK, PROFESSOR.
I'M WORKING FOR YOU, REMEMBER--?
-- THE PROFESSOR WITH THE HIGHEST PERCENTAGE OF TEACHING ASSISTANT CASUALTIES ON CAMPUS.
SEE YOU TOMORROW, PROFESSOR-- IF THEY HAVEN'T ARRESTED ME BY THEN!
POOR ELIOT... BOY SEEMS TO HAVE DEVELOPED A TWITCH SINCE HE STARTED WORKING FOR ME!
NOW WHERE WAS THAT VOLUME ON-- AH-HAH!
COME TO MATER, YOU ELUSIVE LITTLE INCUNABULUM, YOU--
--OOOOO
NO--!!
NO--!!
5

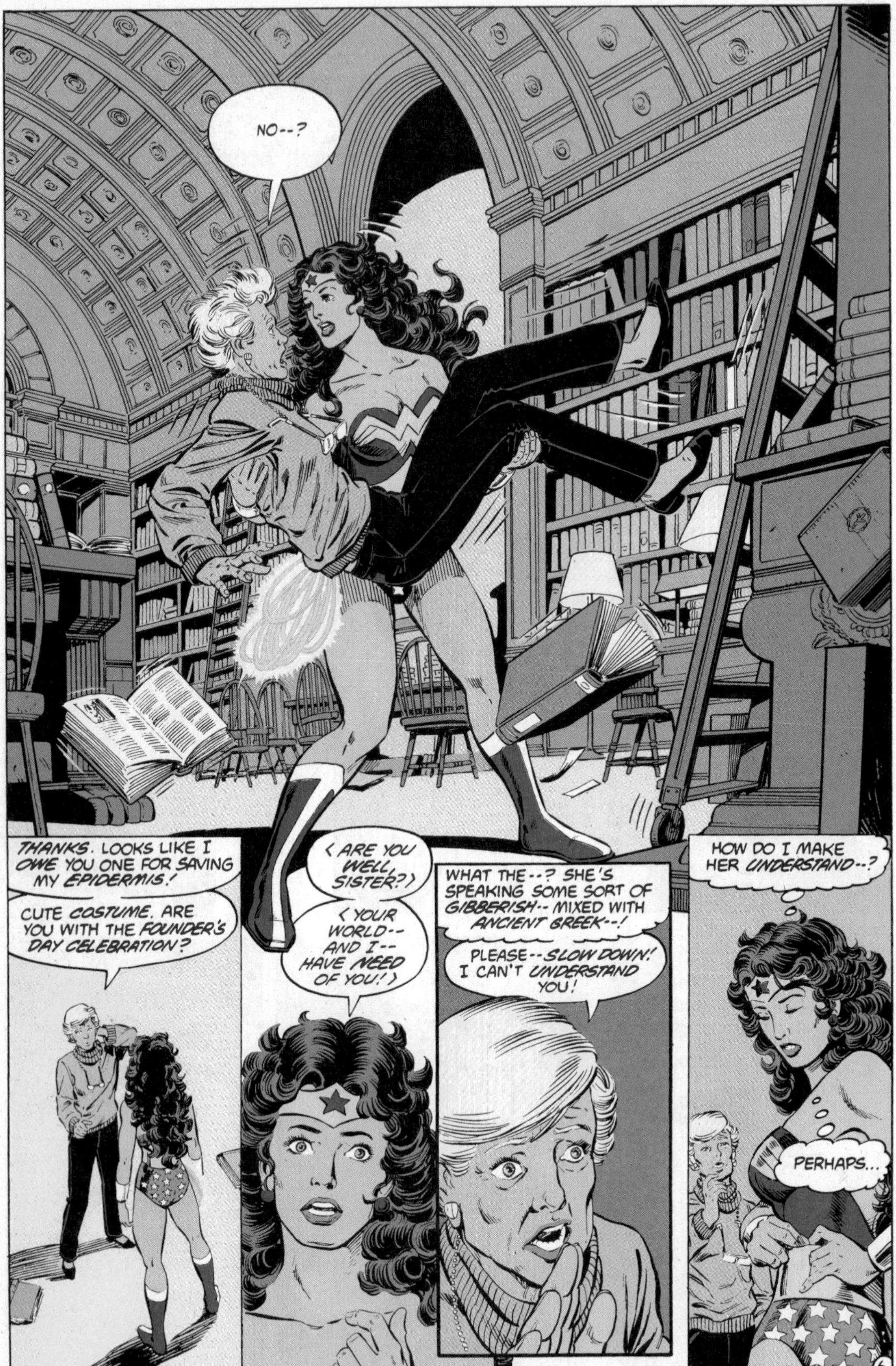

NO--?
THANKS. LOOKS LIKE I OWE YOU ONE FOR SAVING MY EPIDERMIS!
CUTE COSTUME. ARE YOU WITH THE FOUNDER'S DAY CELEBRATION?
< ARE YOU WELL, SISTER? >
< YOUR WORLD-- AND I-- HAVE NEED OF YOU! >
WHAT THE--? SHE'S SPEAKING SOME SORT OF GIBBERISH-- MIXED WITH ANCIENT GREEK--!
PLEASE--SLOW DOWN! I CAN'T UNDERSTAND YOU!
HOW DO I MAKE HER UNDERSTAND--?
PERHAPS...
6

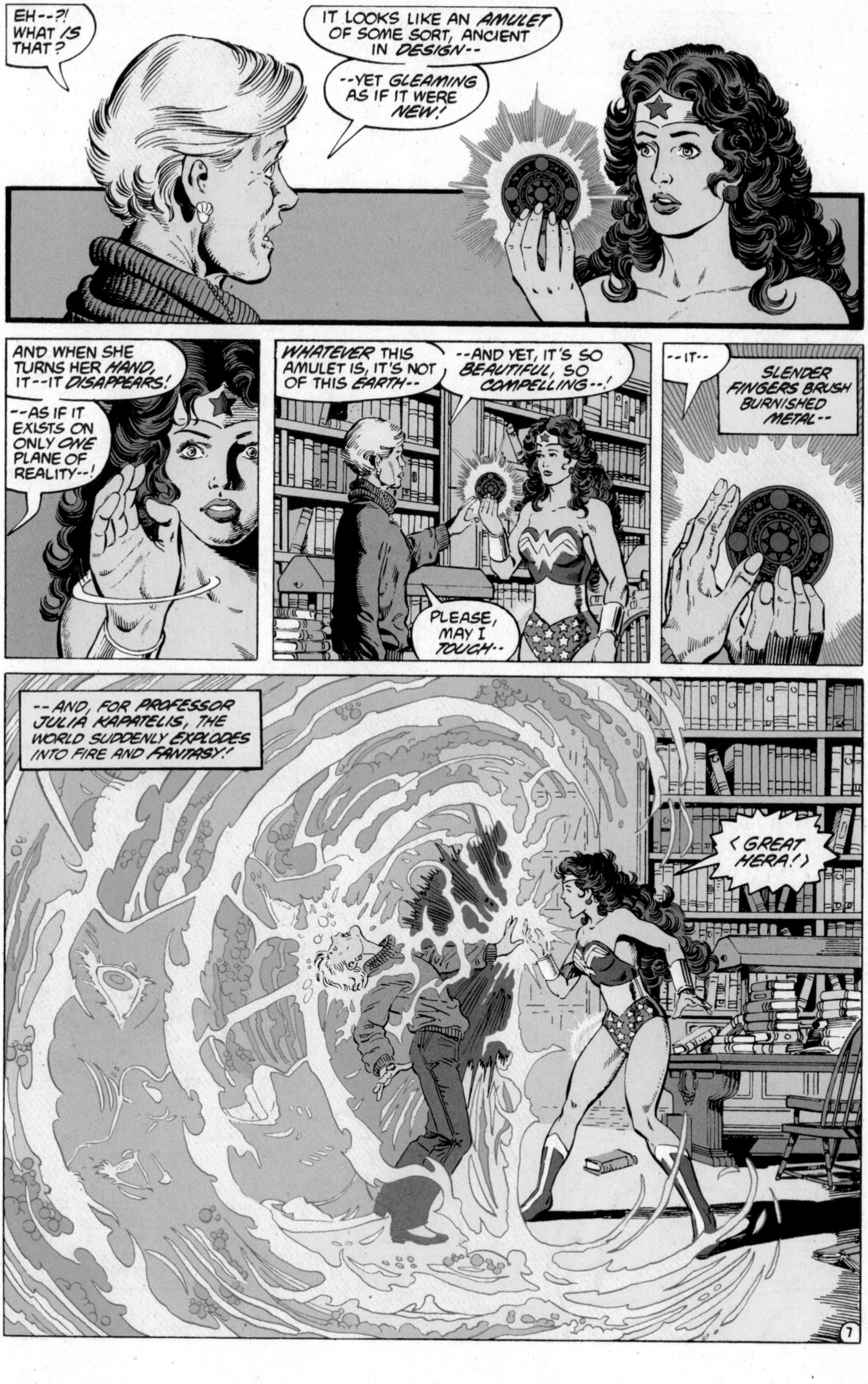
EH--?! WHAT IS THAT?
IT LOOKS LIKE AN AMULET OF SOME SORT, ANCIENT IN DESIGN--
--YET GLEAMING AS IF IT WERE NEW!
AND WHEN SHE TURNS HER HAND, IT--IT DISAPPEARS!
--AS IF IT EXISTS ON ONLY ONE PLANE OF REALITY--!
WHATEVER THIS AMULET IS, IT'S NOT OF THIS EARTH--
--AND YET, IT'S SO BEAUTIFUL, SO COMPELLING--!
PLEASE, MAY I TOUCH--
--IT--
SLENDER FINGERS BRUSH BURNISHED METAL--
--AND, FOR PROFESSOR JULIA KAPATELIS, THE WORLD SUDDENLY EXPLODES INTO FIRE AND FANTASY!
< GREAT HERA! >
7

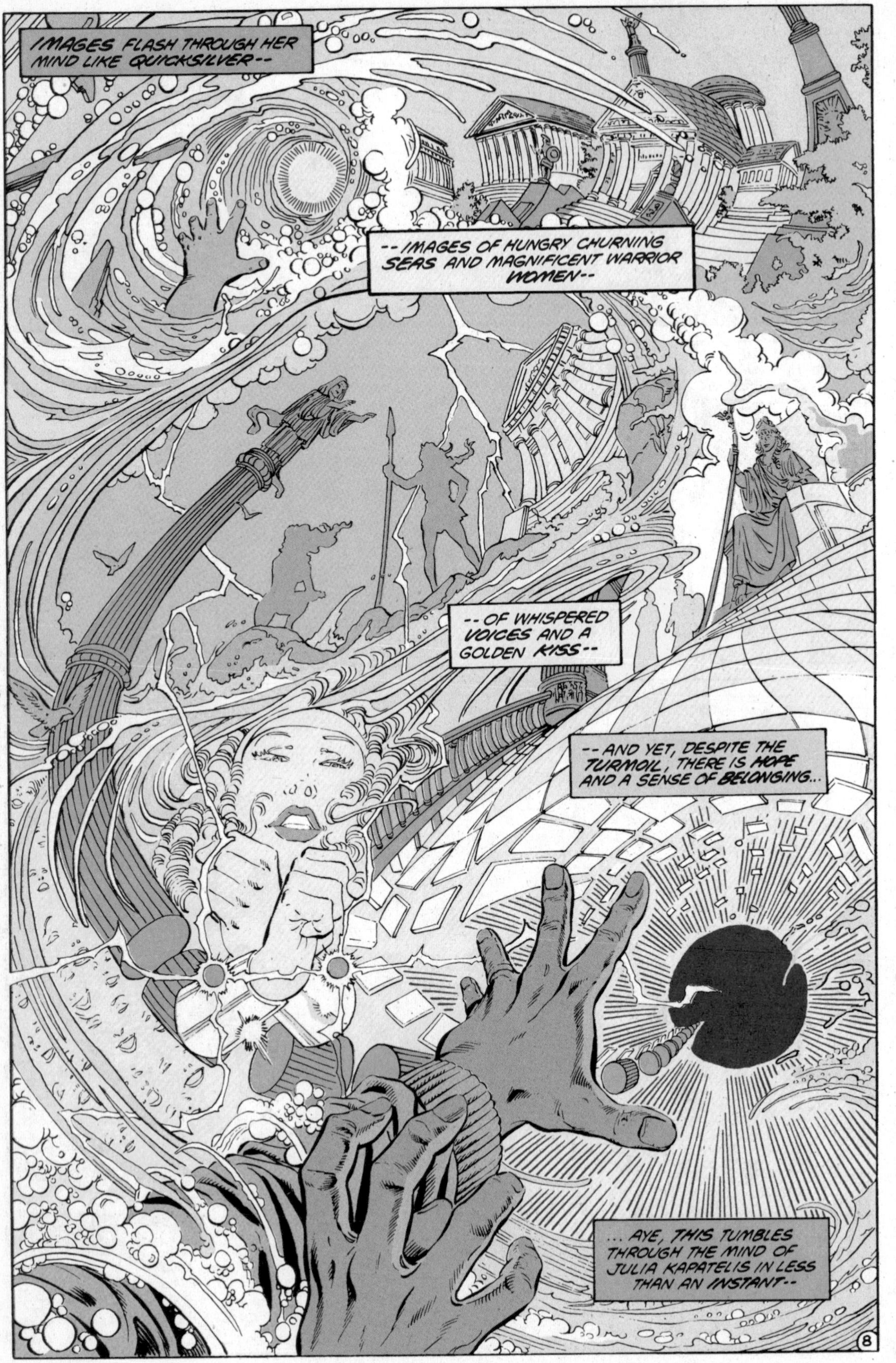
IMAGES FLASH THROUGH HER MIND LIKE QUICKSILVER--
--IMAGES OF HUNGRY CHURNING SEAS AND MAGNIFICENT WARRIOR WOMEN--
--OF WHISPERED VOICES AND A GOLDEN KISS--
--AND YET, DESPITE THE TURMOIL, THERE IS HOPE AND A SENSE OF BELONGING...
...AYE, THIS TUMBLES THROUGH THE MIND OF JULIA KAPATELIS IN LESS THAN AN INSTANT--
8

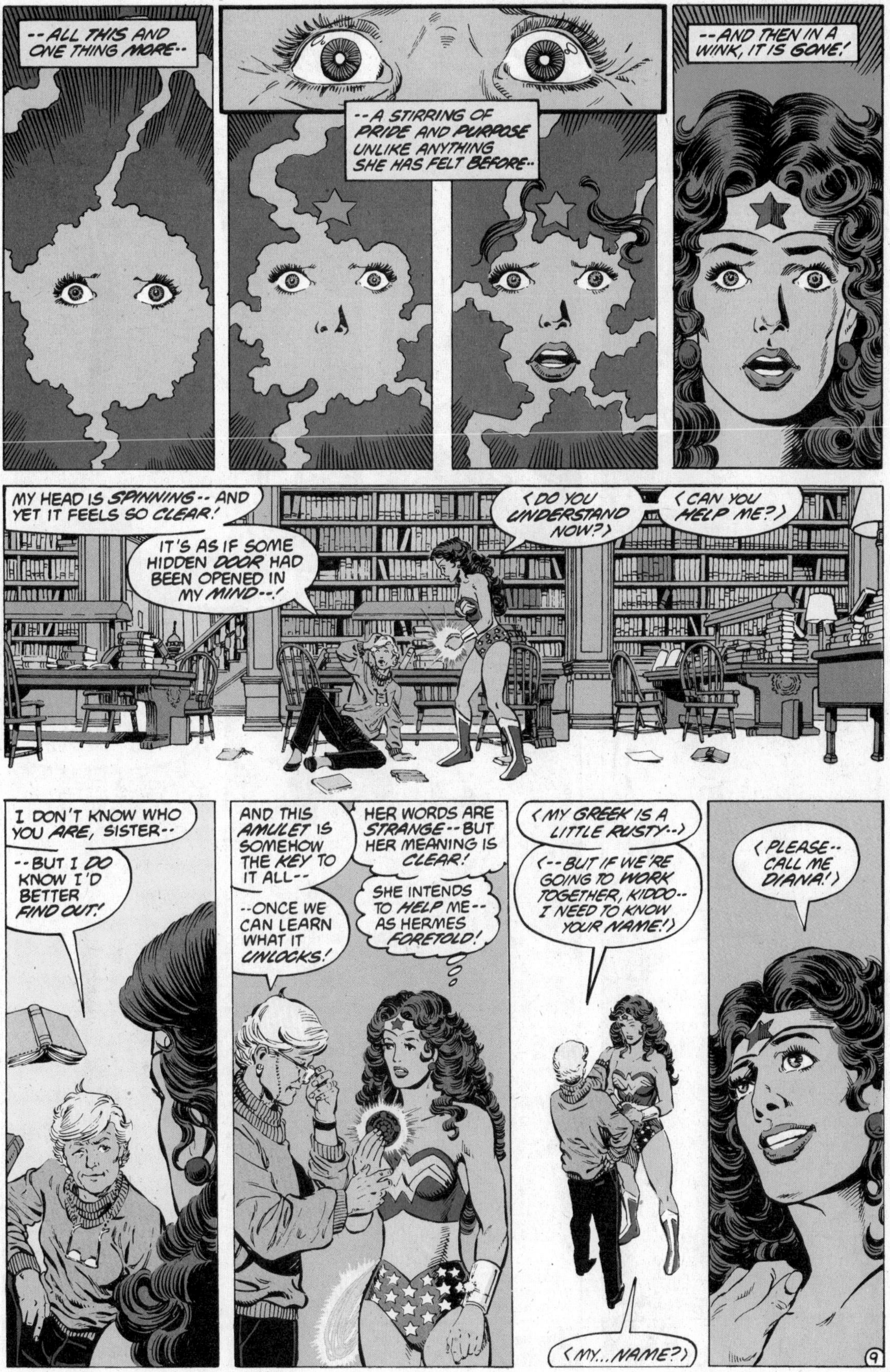
--ALL THIS AND ONE THING MORE--
--A STIRRING OF PRIDE AND PURPOSE UNLIKE ANYTHING SHE HAS FELT BEFORE..
--AND THEN IN A WINK, IT IS GONE!
MY HEAD IS SPINNING-- AND YET IT FEELS SO CLEAR!
IT'S AS IF SOME HIDDEN DOOR HAD BEEN OPENED IN MY MIND--!
⟨DO YOU UNDERSTAND NOW?⟩
⟨CAN YOU HELP ME?⟩
I DON'T KNOW WHO YOU ARE, SISTER--
--BUT I DO KNOW I'D BETTER FIND OUT!
AND THIS AMULET IS SOMEHOW THE KEY TO IT ALL--
--ONCE WE CAN LEARN WHAT IT UNLOCKS!
HER WORDS ARE STRANGE--BUT HER MEANING IS CLEAR!
SHE INTENDS TO HELP ME--AS HERMES FORETOLD!
⟨MY GREEK IS A LITTLE RUSTY--⟩
⟨--BUT IF WE'RE GOING TO WORK TOGETHER, KIDDO--I NEED TO KNOW YOUR NAME!⟩
⟨MY...NAME?⟩
⟨PLEASE--CALL ME DIANA!⟩
9

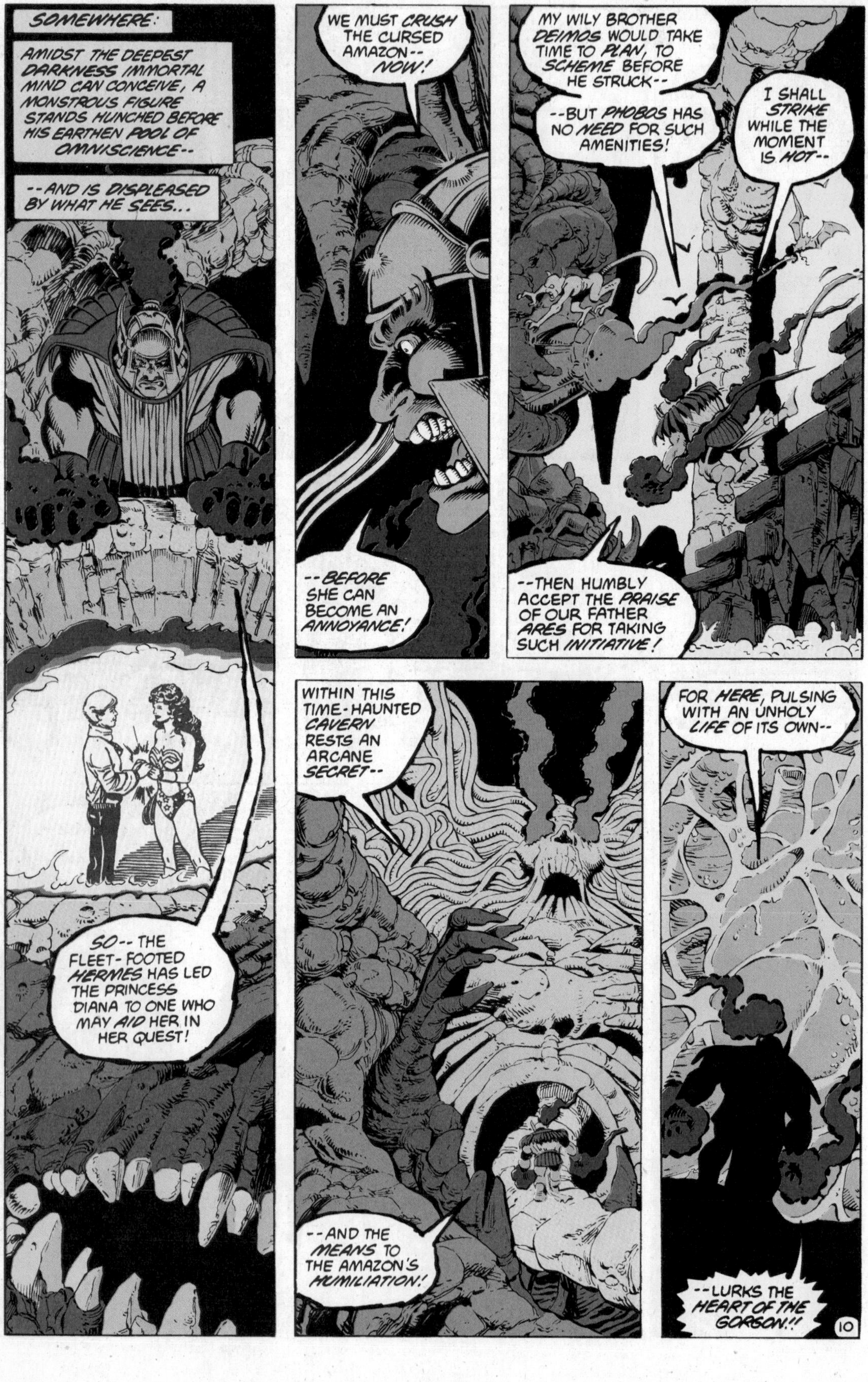
SOMEWHERE:
AMIDST THE DEEPEST DARKNESS IMMORTAL MIND CAN CONCEIVE, A MONSTROUS FIGURE STANDS HUNCHED BEFORE HIS EARTHEN POOL OF OMNISCIENCE--
--AND IS DISPLEASED BY WHAT HE SEES...
SO-- THE FLEET-FOOTED HERMES HAS LED THE PRINCESS DIANA TO ONE WHO MAY AID HER IN HER QUEST!
WE MUST CRUSH THE CURSED AMAZON-- NOW!
--BEFORE SHE CAN BECOME AN ANNOYANCE!
MY WILY BROTHER DEIMOS WOULD TAKE TIME TO PLAN, TO SCHEME BEFORE HE STRUCK--
--BUT PHOBOS HAS NO NEED FOR SUCH AMENITIES!
I SHALL STRIKE WHILE THE MOMENT IS HOT--
--THEN HUMBLY ACCEPT THE PRAISE OF OUR FATHER ARES FOR TAKING SUCH INITIATIVE!
WITHIN THIS TIME-HAUNTED CAVERN RESTS AN ARCANE SECRET--
--AND THE MEANS TO THE AMAZON'S HUMILIATION!
FOR HERE, PULSING WITH AN UNHOLY LIFE OF ITS OWN--
--LURKS THE HEART OF THE GORGON!!
10

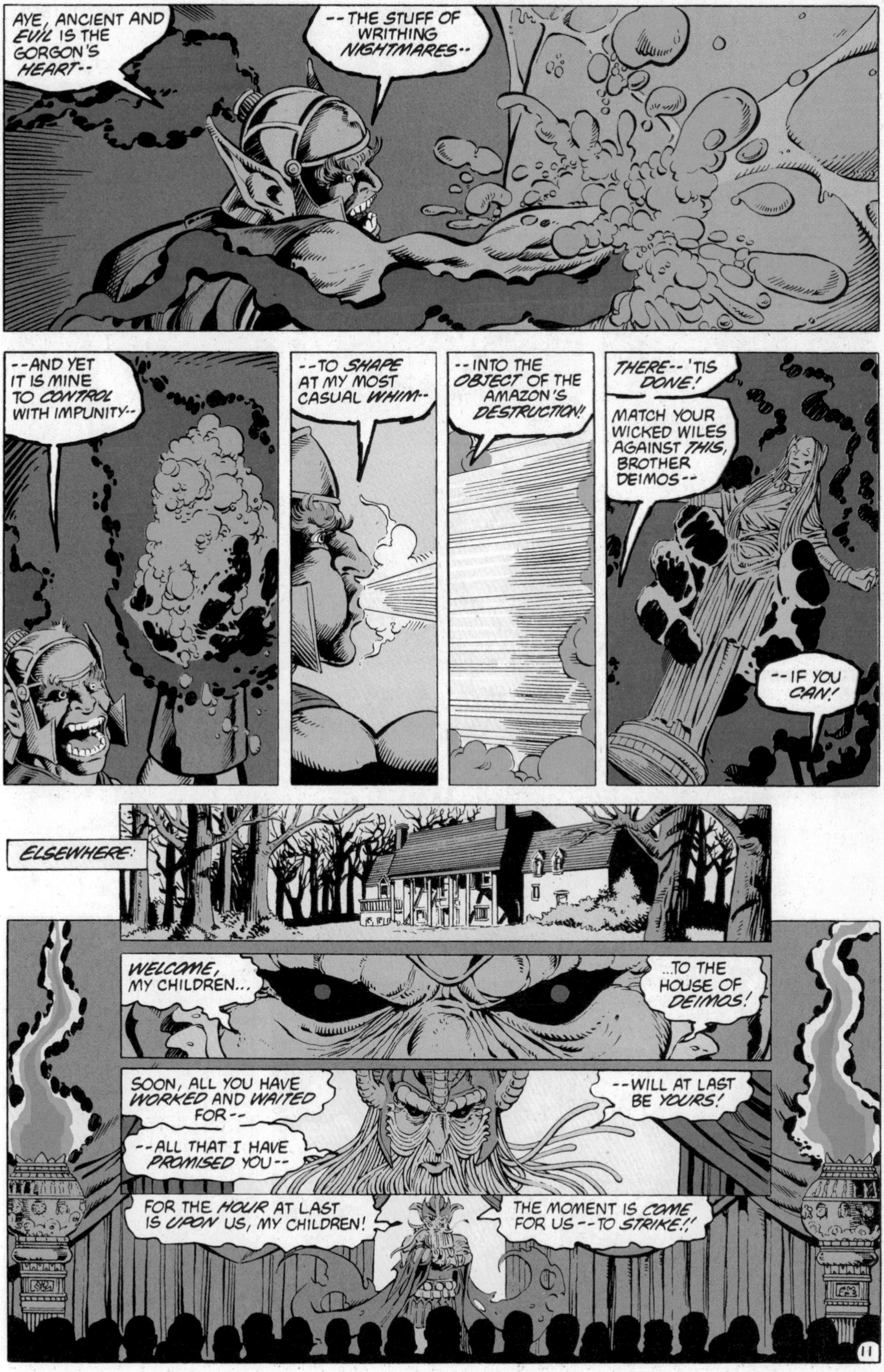
AYE, ANCIENT AND EVIL IS THE GORGON'S HEART--
--THE STUFF OF WRITHING NIGHTMARES--
--AND YET IT IS MINE TO CONTROL WITH IMPUNITY--
--TO SHAPE AT MY MOST CASUAL WHIM--
--INTO THE OBJECT OF THE AMAZON'S DESTRUCTION!
THERE--'TIS DONE!
MATCH YOUR WICKED WILES AGAINST THIS, BROTHER DEIMOS--
--IF YOU CAN!
ELSEWHERE:
WELCOME, MY CHILDREN...
...TO THE HOUSE OF DEIMOS!
SOON, ALL YOU HAVE WORKED AND WAITED FOR--
--ALL THAT I HAVE PROMISED YOU--
--WILL AT LAST BE YOURS!
FOR THE HOUR AT LAST IS UPON US, MY CHILDREN!
THE MOMENT IS COME FOR US--TO STRIKE!!
11

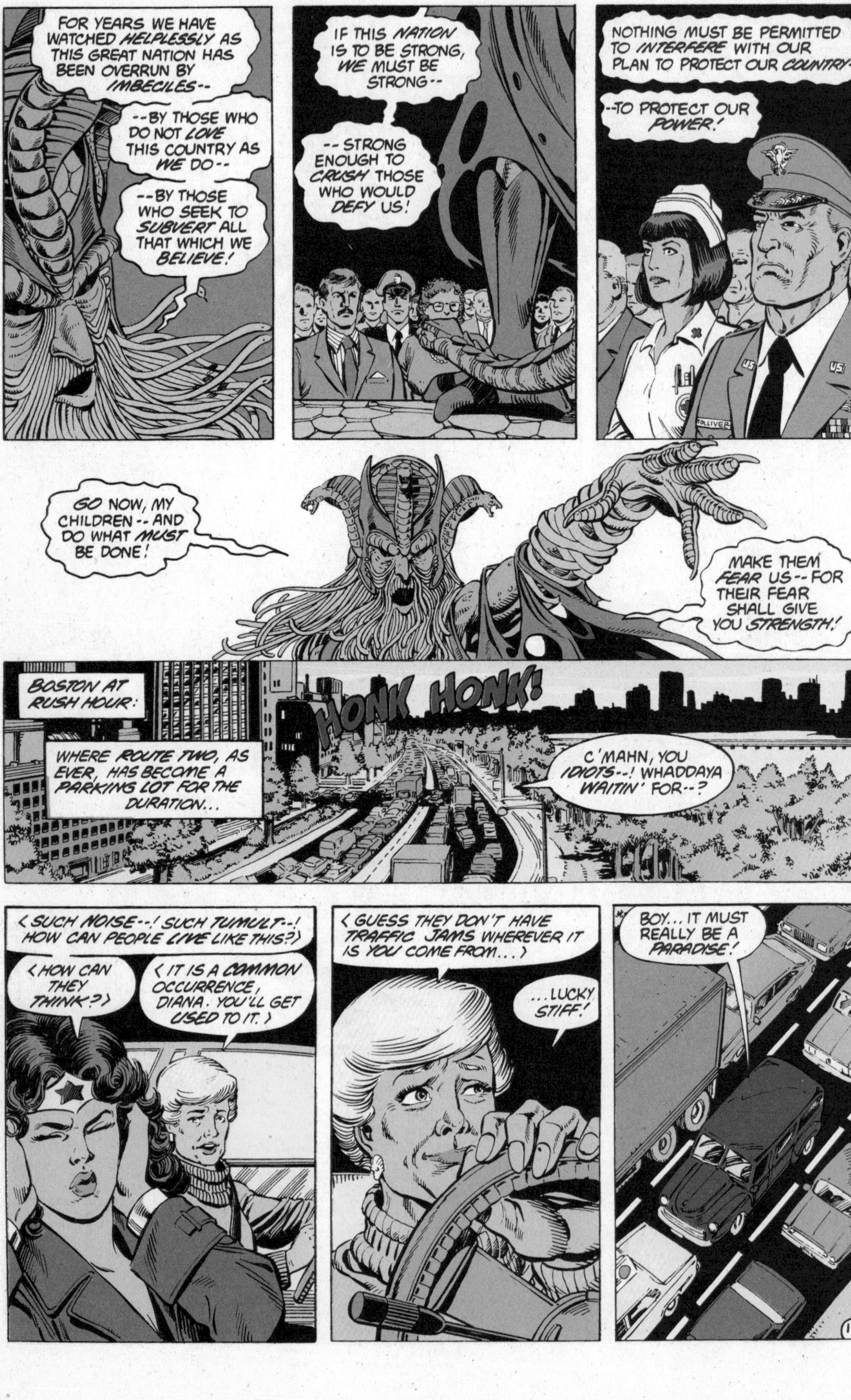

FOR YEARS WE HAVE WATCHED HELPLESSLY AS THIS GREAT NATION HAS BEEN OVERRUN BY IMBECILES--
--BY THOSE WHO DO NOT LOVE THIS COUNTRY AS WE DO--
--BY THOSE WHO SEEK TO SUBVERT ALL THAT WHICH WE BELIEVE!
IF THIS NATION IS TO BE STRONG, WE MUST BE STRONG--
--STRONG ENOUGH TO CRUSH THOSE WHO WOULD DEFY US!
NOTHING MUST BE PERMITTED TO INTERFERE WITH OUR PLAN TO PROTECT OUR COUNTRY--
--TO PROTECT OUR POWER!
TOLLIVER
GO NOW, MY CHILDREN--AND DO WHAT MUST BE DONE!
MAKE THEM FEAR US--FOR THEIR FEAR SHALL GIVE YOU STRENGTH!
BOSTON AT RUSH HOUR:
WHERE ROUTE TWO, AS EVER, HAS BECOME A PARKING LOT FOR THE DURATION...
HONK HONK!
C'MAHN, YOU IDIOTS--! WHADDAYA WAITIN' FOR--?
< SUCH NOISE--! SUCH TUMULT--! HOW CAN PEOPLE LIVE LIKE THIS?>
< HOW CAN THEY THINK?>
< IT IS A COMMON OCCURRENCE, DIANA. YOU'LL GET USED TO IT.>
< GUESS THEY DON'T HAVE TRAFFIC JAMS WHEREVER IT IS YOU COME FROM...>
...LUCKY STIFF!
BOY... IT MUST REALLY BE A PARADISE!
12

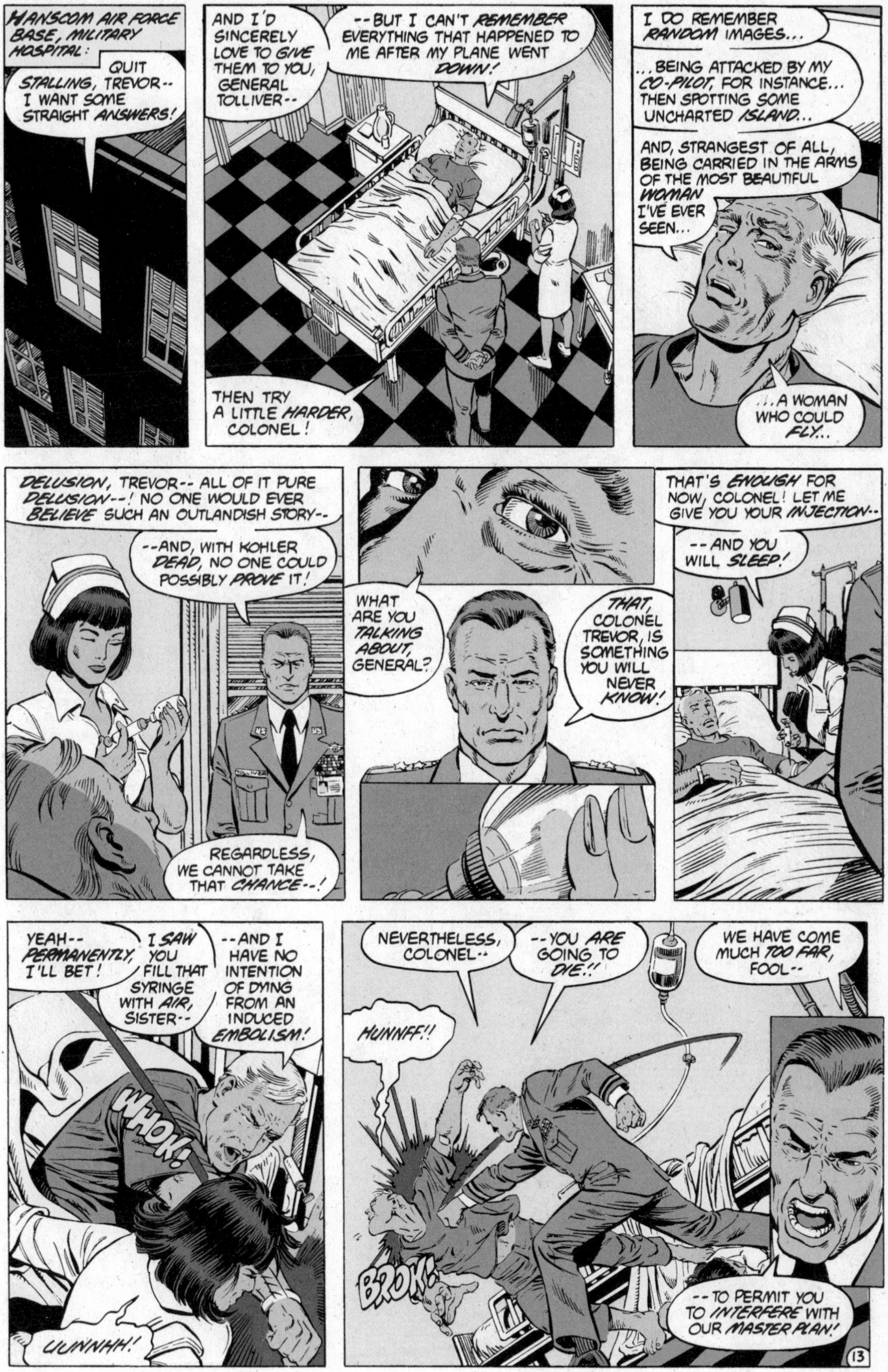
HANSCOM AIR FORCE BASE, MILITARY HOSPITAL:
QUIT STALLING, TREVOR-- I WANT SOME STRAIGHT ANSWERS!
AND I'D SINCERELY LOVE TO GIVE THEM TO YOU, GENERAL TOLLIVER--
--BUT I CAN'T REMEMBER EVERYTHING THAT HAPPENED TO ME AFTER MY PLANE WENT DOWN!
THEN TRY A LITTLE HARDER, COLONEL!
I DO REMEMBER RANDOM IMAGES...
...BEING ATTACKED BY MY CO-PILOT, FOR INSTANCE... THEN SPOTTING SOME UNCHARTED ISLAND...
AND, STRANGEST OF ALL, BEING CARRIED IN THE ARMS OF THE MOST BEAUTIFUL WOMAN I'VE EVER SEEN...
...A WOMAN WHO COULD FLY...
DELUSION, TREVOR-- ALL OF IT PURE DELUSION--! NO ONE WOULD EVER BELIEVE SUCH AN OUTLANDISH STORY--
--AND, WITH KOHLER DEAD, NO ONE COULD POSSIBLY PROVE IT!
REGARDLESS, WE CANNOT TAKE THAT CHANCE--!
WHAT ARE YOU TALKING ABOUT, GENERAL?
THAT, COLONEL TREVOR, IS SOMETHING YOU WILL NEVER KNOW!
THAT'S ENOUGH FOR NOW, COLONEL! LET ME GIVE YOU YOUR INJECTION--
--AND YOU WILL SLEEP!
YEAH-- PERMANENTLY, I'LL BET!
I SAW YOU FILL THAT SYRINGE WITH AIR, SISTER--
--AND I HAVE NO INTENTION OF DYING FROM AN INDUCED EMBOLISM!
WHOK!
UUNNHH!
NEVERTHELESS, COLONEL--
--YOU ARE GOING TO DIE!!
HUNNFF!!
BROK!
WE HAVE COME MUCH TOO FAR, FOOL--
--TO PERMIT YOU TO INTERFERE WITH OUR MASTER PLAN!
13

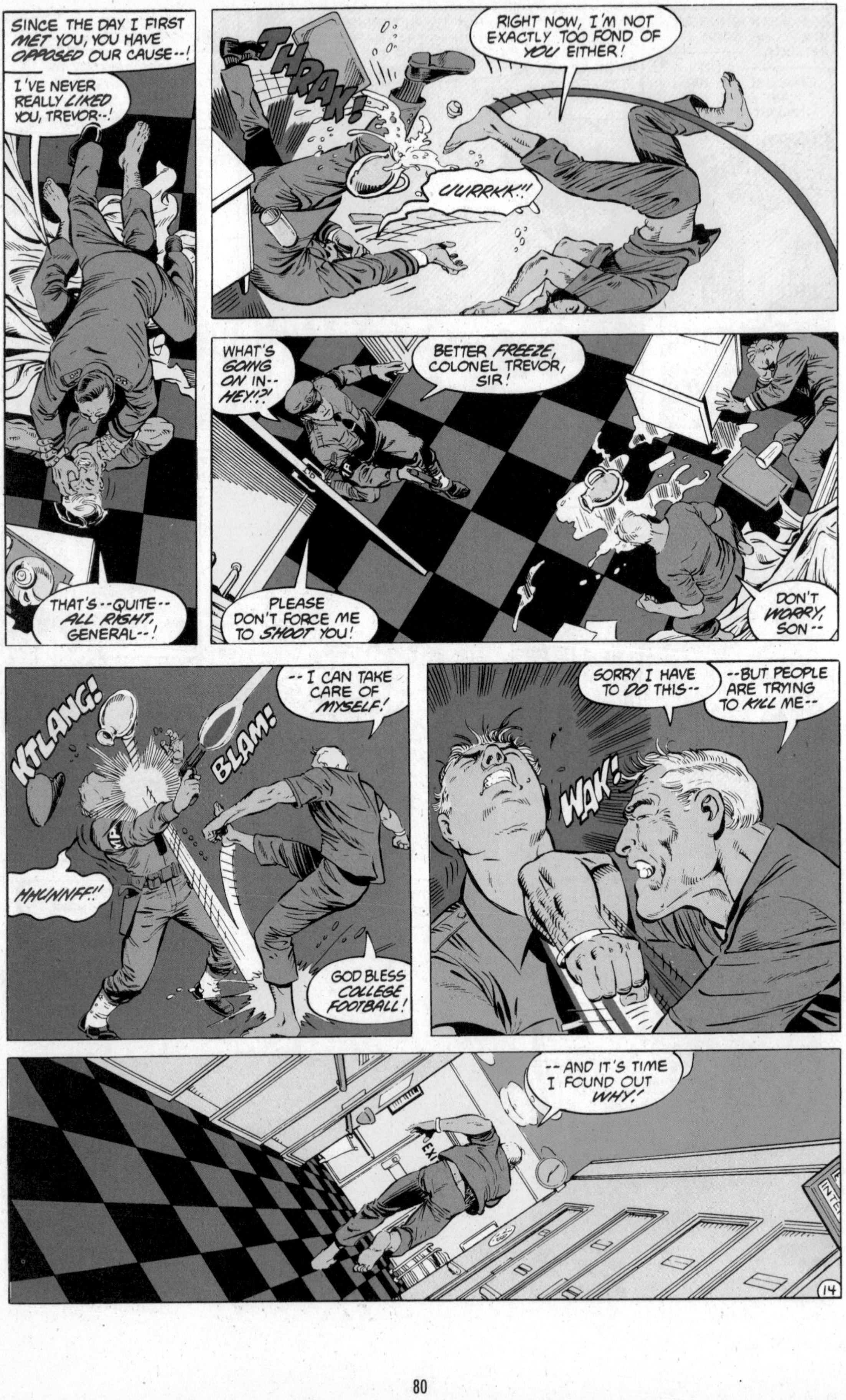
SINCE THE DAY I FIRST MET YOU, YOU HAVE OPPOSED OUR CAUSE--!
I'VE NEVER REALLY LIKED YOU, TREVOR--!
THRAK!
RIGHT NOW, I'M NOT EXACTLY TOO FOND OF YOU EITHER!
UURRKK!!
THAT'S--QUITE--ALL RIGHT, GENERAL--!
WHAT'S GOING ON IN-- HEY!?!
BETTER FREEZE, COLONEL TREVOR, SIR!
PLEASE DON'T FORCE ME TO SHOOT YOU!
DON'T WORRY, SON--
KTLANG!
--I CAN TAKE CARE OF MYSELF!
BLAM!
MMUNNFF!!
GOD BLESS COLLEGE FOOTBALL!
SORRY I HAVE TO DO THIS--
--BUT PEOPLE ARE TRYING TO KILL ME--
WAK!
--AND IT'S TIME I FOUND OUT WHY!
14

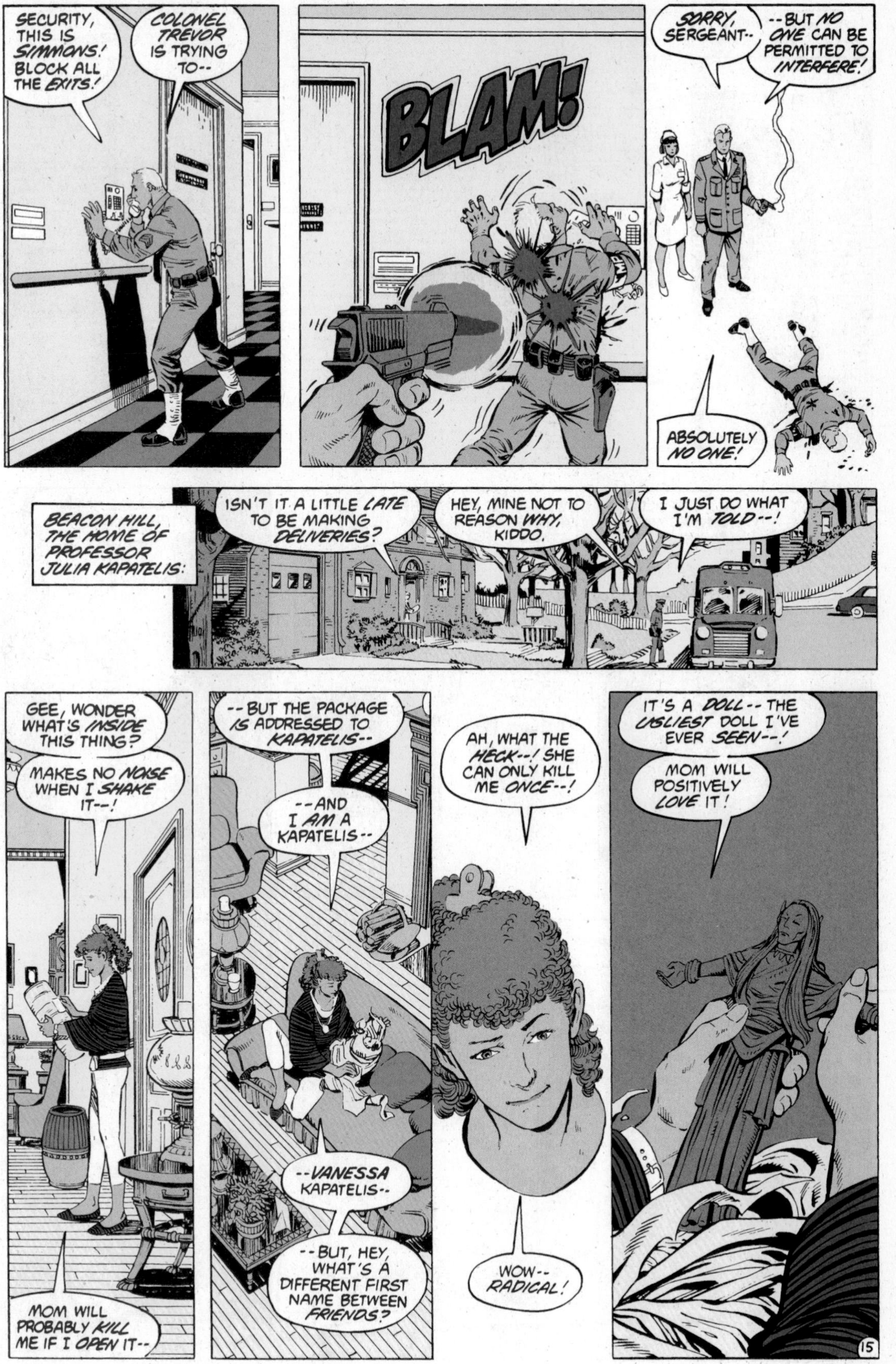
SECURITY, THIS IS SIMMONS! BLOCK ALL THE EXITS!
COLONEL TREVOR IS TRYING TO--
BLAM!
SORRY, SERGEANT--
--BUT NO ONE CAN BE PERMITTED TO INTERFERE!
ABSOLUTELY NO ONE!
BEACON HILL, THE HOME OF PROFESSOR JULIA KAPATELIS:
ISN'T IT A LITTLE LATE TO BE MAKING DELIVERIES?
HEY, MINE NOT TO REASON WHY, KIDDO.
I JUST DO WHAT I'M TOLD--!
GEE, WONDER WHAT'S INSIDE THIS THING?
MAKES NO NOISE WHEN I SHAKE IT--!
MOM WILL PROBABLY KILL ME IF I OPEN IT--
--BUT THE PACKAGE IS ADDRESSED TO KAPATELIS--
--AND I AM A KAPATELIS--
--VANESSA KAPATELIS--
--BUT, HEY, WHAT'S A DIFFERENT FIRST NAME BETWEEN FRIENDS?
AH, WHAT THE HECK--! SHE CAN ONLY KILL ME ONCE--!
WOW--RADICAL!
IT'S A DOLL--THE UGLIEST DOLL I'VE EVER SEEN--!
MOM WILL POSITIVELY LOVE IT!
15

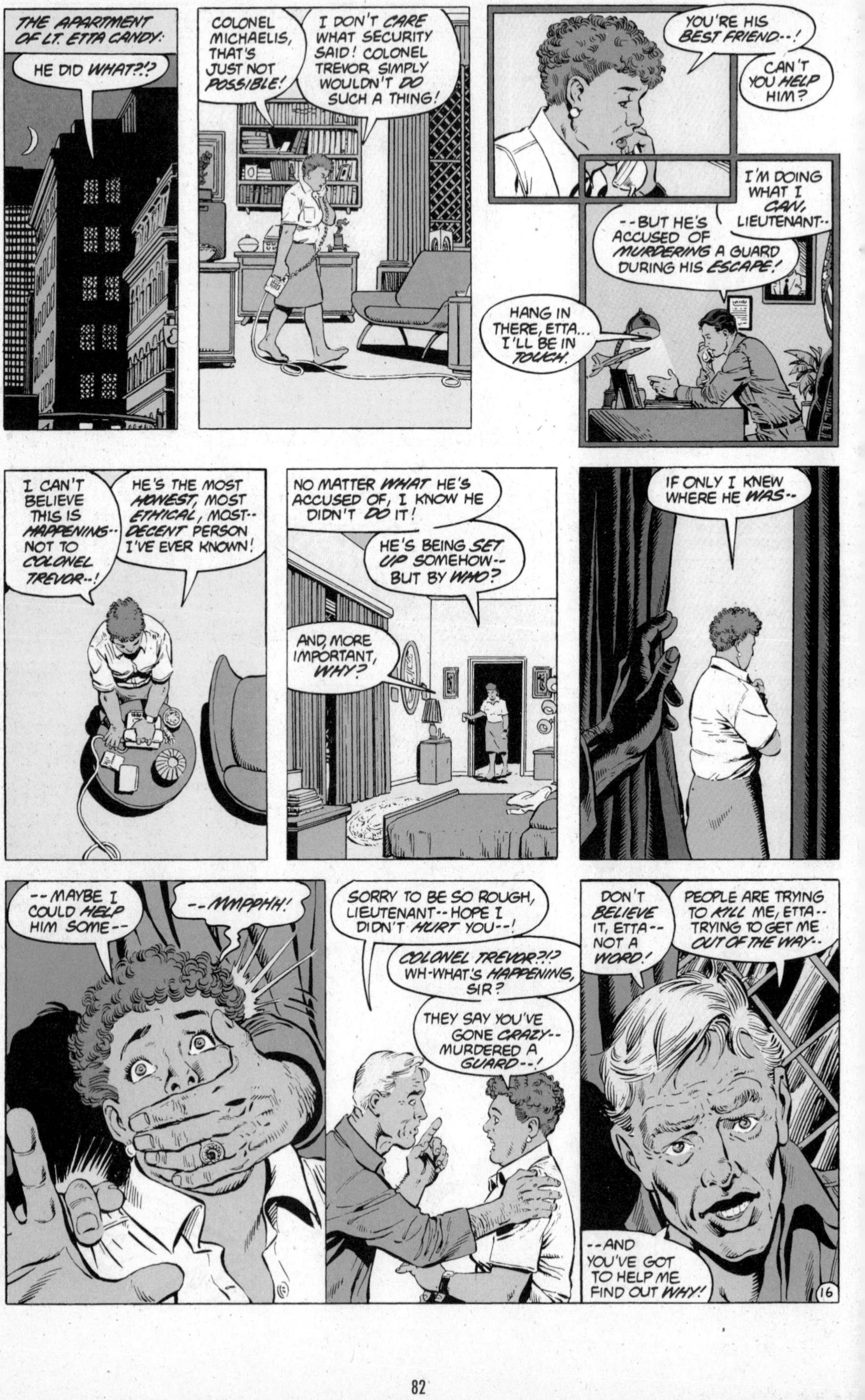
THE APARTMENT OF LT. ETTA CANDY:
HE DID WHAT?!?
COLONEL MICHAELIS, THAT'S JUST NOT POSSIBLE!
I DON'T CARE WHAT SECURITY SAID! COLONEL TREVOR SIMPLY WOULDN'T DO SUCH A THING!
YOU'RE HIS BEST FRIEND--!
CAN'T YOU HELP HIM?
I'M DOING WHAT I CAN, LIEUTENANT--
--BUT HE'S ACCUSED OF MURDERING A GUARD DURING HIS ESCAPE!
HANG IN THERE, ETTA... I'LL BE IN TOUCH.
I CAN'T BELIEVE THIS IS HAPPENING-- NOT TO COLONEL TREVOR--!
HE'S THE MOST HONEST, MOST ETHICAL, MOST-- DECENT PERSON I'VE EVER KNOWN!
NO MATTER WHAT HE'S ACCUSED OF, I KNOW HE DIDN'T DO IT!
HE'S BEING SET UP SOMEHOW-- BUT BY WHO?
AND, MORE IMPORTANT, WHY?
IF ONLY I KNEW WHERE HE WAS--
--MAYBE I COULD HELP HIM SOME--
--MMPPHH!
SORRY TO BE SO ROUGH, LIEUTENANT-- HOPE I DIDN'T HURT YOU--!
COLONEL TREVOR?!? WH-WHAT'S HAPPENING, SIR?
THEY SAY YOU'VE GONE CRAZY-- MURDERED A GUARD--!
DON'T BELIEVE IT, ETTA-- NOT A WORD!
PEOPLE ARE TRYING TO KILL ME, ETTA-- TRYING TO GET ME OUT OF THE WAY--
--AND YOU'VE GOT TO HELP ME FIND OUT WHY!
16

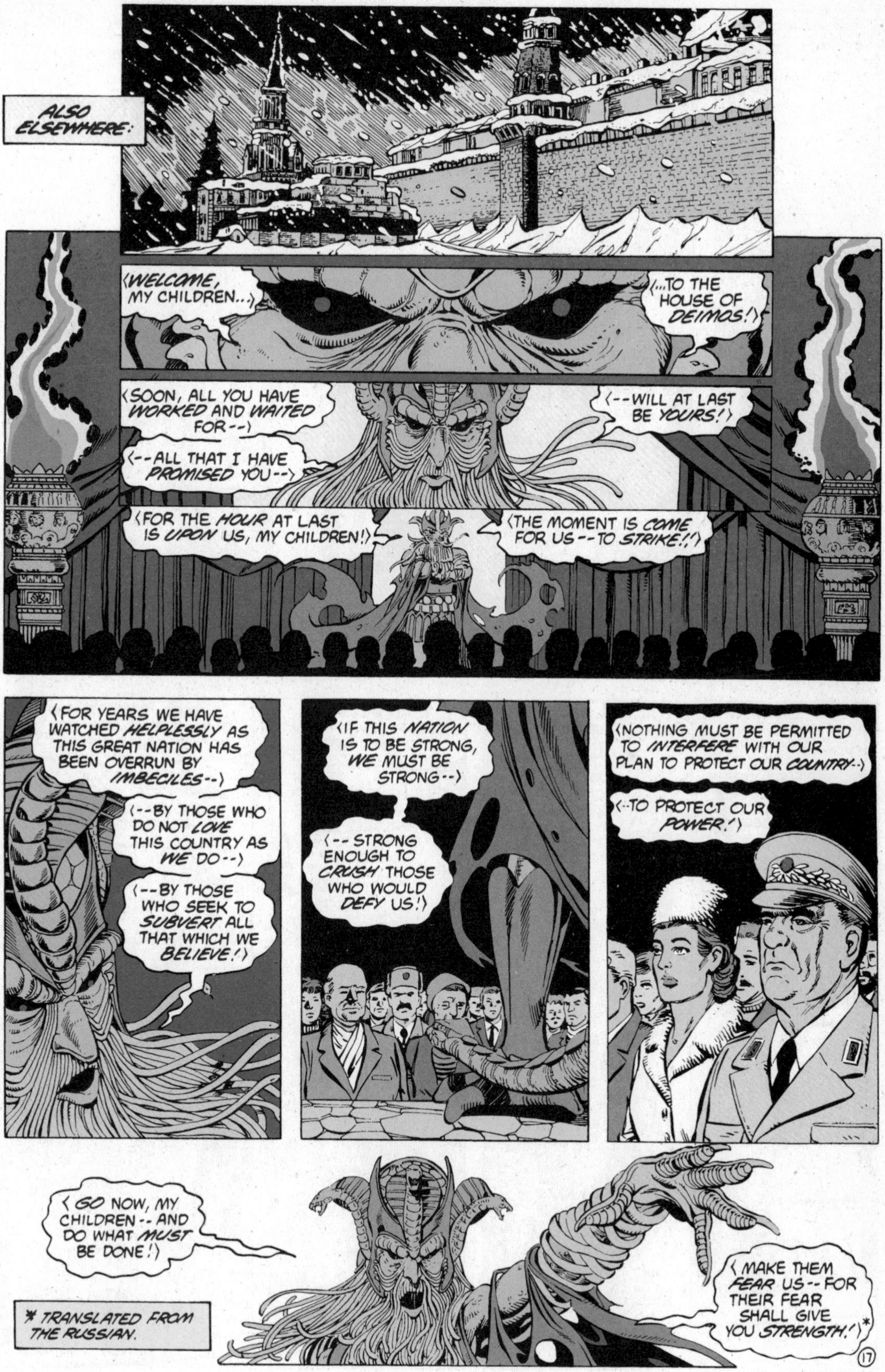
ALSO ELSEWHERE:
⟨WELCOME, MY CHILDREN...⟩
⟨...TO THE HOUSE OF DEIMOS!⟩
⟨SOON, ALL YOU HAVE WORKED AND WAITED FOR--⟩
⟨--ALL THAT I HAVE PROMISED YOU--⟩
⟨--WILL AT LAST BE YOURS!⟩
⟨FOR THE HOUR AT LAST IS UPON US, MY CHILDREN!⟩
⟨THE MOMENT IS COME FOR US--TO STRIKE!!⟩
⟨FOR YEARS WE HAVE WATCHED HELPLESSLY AS THIS GREAT NATION HAS BEEN OVERRUN BY IMBECILES--⟩
⟨--BY THOSE WHO DO NOT LOVE THIS COUNTRY AS WE DO--⟩
⟨--BY THOSE WHO SEEK TO SUBVERT ALL THAT WHICH WE BELIEVE!⟩
⟨IF THIS NATION IS TO BE STRONG, WE MUST BE STRONG--⟩
⟨--STRONG ENOUGH TO CRUSH THOSE WHO WOULD DEFY US!⟩
⟨NOTHING MUST BE PERMITTED TO INTERFERE WITH OUR PLAN TO PROTECT OUR COUNTRY--⟩
⟨--TO PROTECT OUR POWER!⟩
⟨GO NOW, MY CHILDREN--AND DO WHAT MUST BE DONE!⟩
⟨MAKE THEM FEAR US--FOR THEIR FEAR SHALL GIVE YOU STRENGTH!⟩*
*TRANSLATED FROM THE RUSSIAN.
17

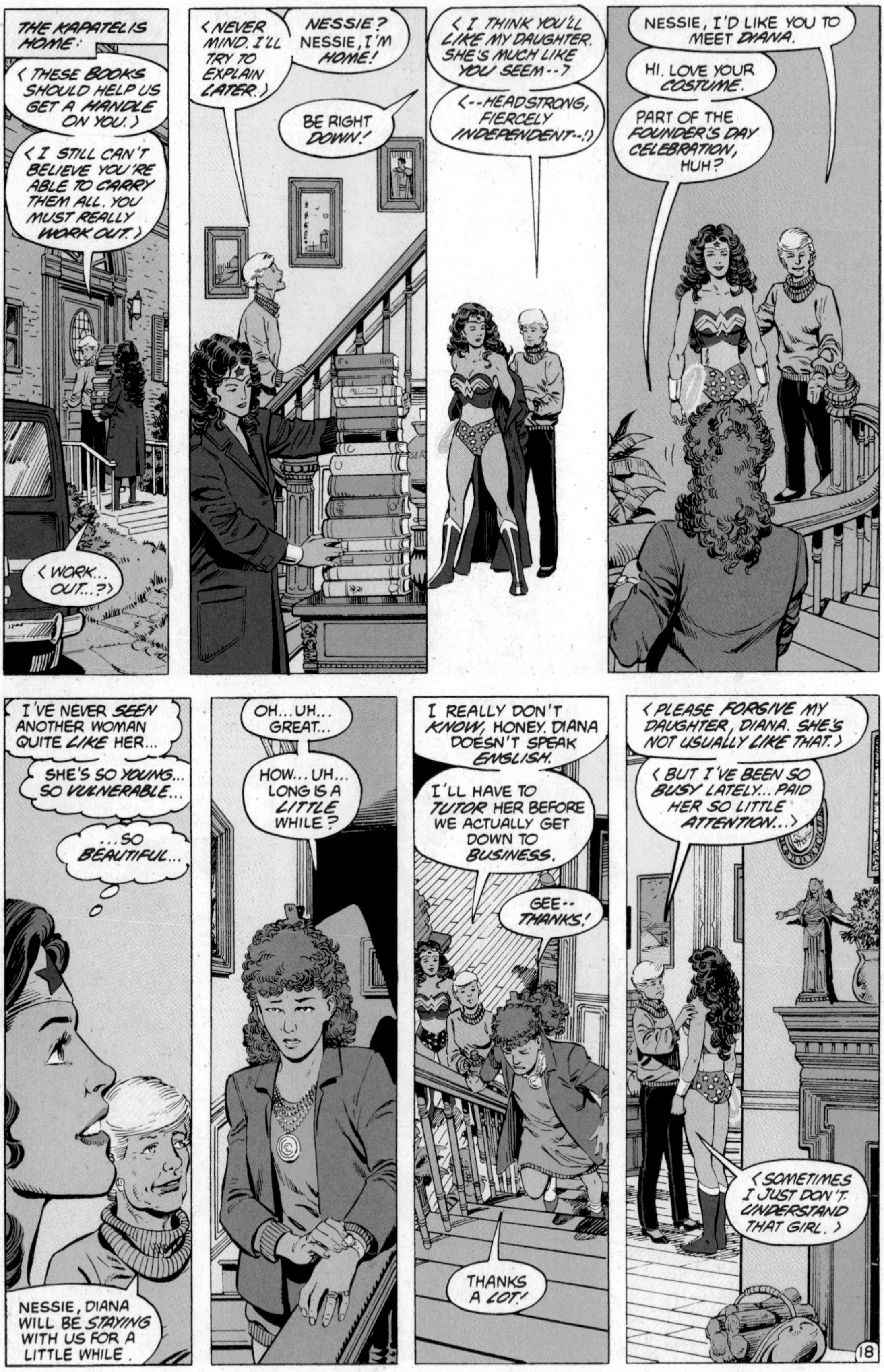
THE KAPATELIS HOME:
< THESE BOOKS SHOULD HELP US GET A HANDLE ON YOU. >
< I STILL CAN'T BELIEVE YOU'RE ABLE TO CARRY THEM ALL. YOU MUST REALLY WORK OUT. >
< WORK... OUT...? >
NESSIE? NESSIE, I'M HOME!
< NEVER MIND. I'LL TRY TO EXPLAIN LATER. >
BE RIGHT DOWN!
< I THINK YOU'LL LIKE MY DAUGHTER. SHE'S MUCH LIKE YOU SEEM-- >
< --HEADSTRONG, FIERCELY INDEPENDENT--! >
NESSIE, I'D LIKE YOU TO MEET DIANA.
HI. LOVE YOUR COSTUME.
PART OF THE FOUNDER'S DAY CELEBRATION, HUH?
NESSIE, DIANA WILL BE STAYING WITH US FOR A LITTLE WHILE.
I'VE NEVER SEEN ANOTHER WOMAN QUITE LIKE HER...
SHE'S SO YOUNG... SO VULNERABLE...
...SO BEAUTIFUL...
OH...UH... GREAT...
HOW...UH... LONG IS A LITTLE WHILE?
I REALLY DON'T KNOW, HONEY. DIANA DOESN'T SPEAK ENGLISH.
I'LL HAVE TO TUTOR HER BEFORE WE ACTUALLY GET DOWN TO BUSINESS.
GEE-- THANKS!
THANKS A LOT!
< PLEASE FORGIVE MY DAUGHTER, DIANA. SHE'S NOT USUALLY LIKE THAT. >
< BUT I'VE BEEN SO BUSY LATELY... PAID HER SO LITTLE ATTENTION... >
< SOMETIMES I JUST DON'T UNDERSTAND THAT GIRL. >
18

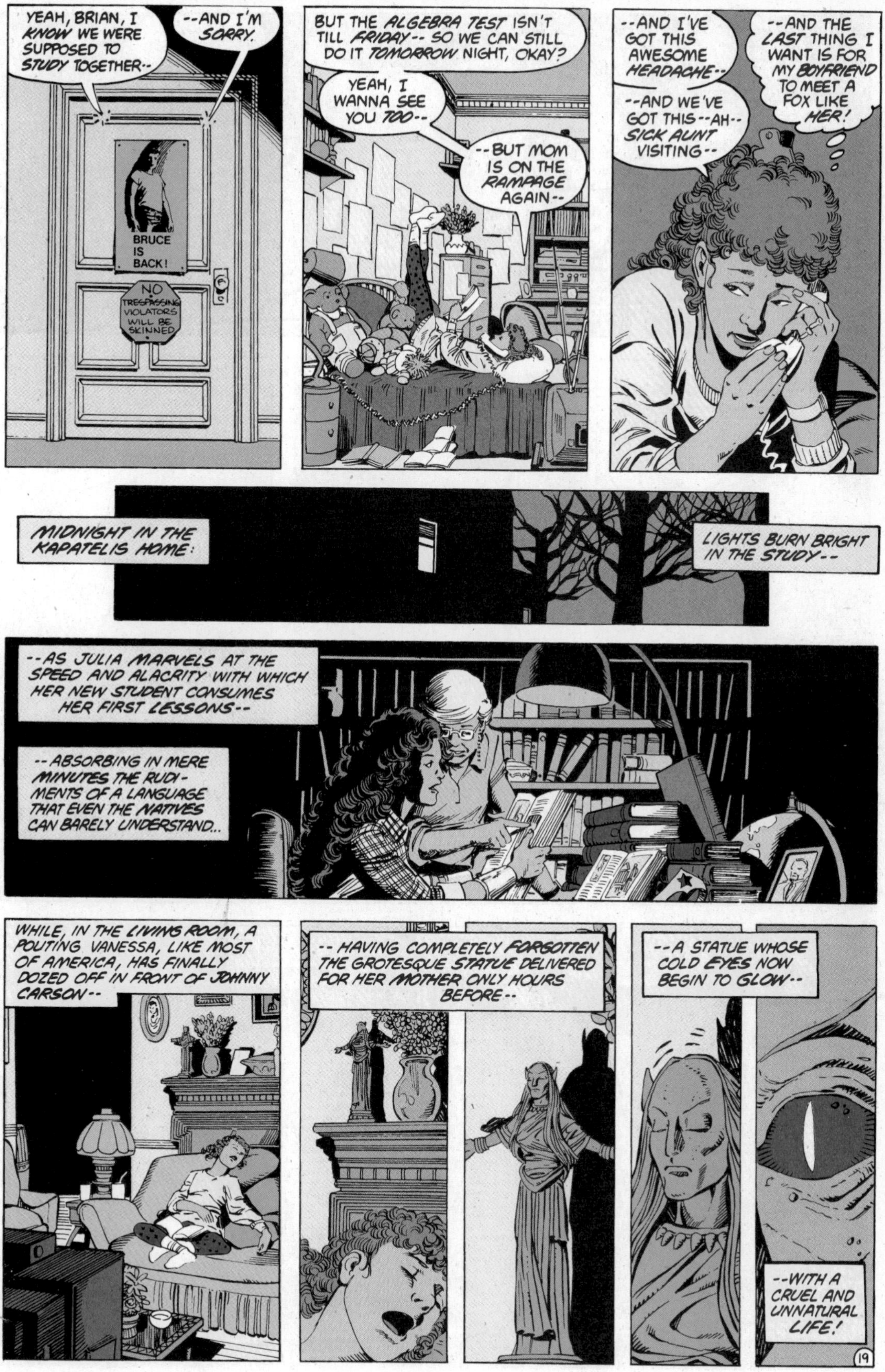
YEAH, BRIAN, I KNOW WE WERE SUPPOSED TO STUDY TOGETHER--
--AND I'M SORRY.
BRUCE IS BACK!
NO TRESPASSING VIOLATORS WILL BE SKINNED
BUT THE ALGEBRA TEST ISN'T TILL FRIDAY-- SO WE CAN STILL DO IT TOMORROW NIGHT, OKAY?
YEAH, I WANNA SEE YOU TOO--
--BUT MOM IS ON THE RAMPAGE AGAIN--
--AND I'VE GOT THIS AWESOME HEADACHE--
--AND WE'VE GOT THIS--AH-- SICK AUNT VISITING--
--AND THE LAST THING I WANT IS FOR MY BOYFRIEND TO MEET A FOX LIKE HER!
MIDNIGHT IN THE KAPATELIS HOME:
LIGHTS BURN BRIGHT IN THE STUDY--
--AS JULIA MARVELS AT THE SPEED AND ALACRITY WITH WHICH HER NEW STUDENT CONSUMES HER FIRST LESSONS--
--ABSORBING IN MERE MINUTES THE RUDIMENTS OF A LANGUAGE THAT EVEN THE NATIVES CAN BARELY UNDERSTAND..
WHILE, IN THE LIVING ROOM, A POUTING VANESSA, LIKE MOST OF AMERICA, HAS FINALLY DOZED OFF IN FRONT OF JOHNNY CARSON--
--HAVING COMPLETELY FORGOTTEN THE GROTESQUE STATUE DELIVERED FOR HER MOTHER ONLY HOURS BEFORE--
--A STATUE WHOSE COLD EYES NOW BEGIN TO GLOW--
--WITH A CRUEL AND UNNATURAL LIFE!
19

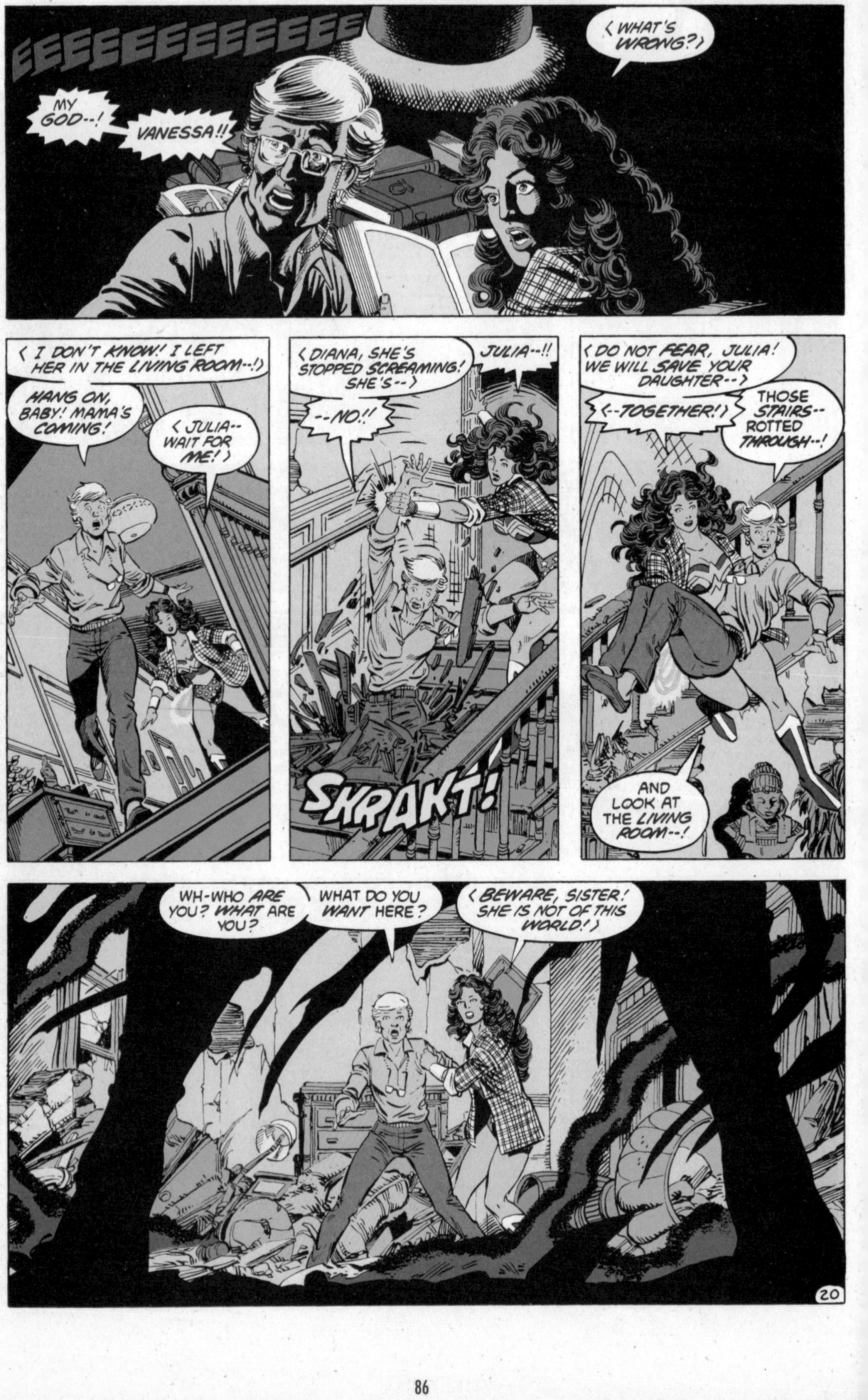
EEEEEEEEEEEE
MY GOD--!
VANESSA!!
⟨WHAT'S WRONG?⟩
⟨I DON'T KNOW! I LEFT HER IN THE LIVING ROOM--!⟩
HANG ON, BABY! MAMA'S COMING!
⟨JULIA-- WAIT FOR ME!⟩
⟨DIANA, SHE'S STOPPED SCREAMING! SHE'S--⟩
JULIA--!!
--NO!!
SKRAKT!
⟨DO NOT FEAR, JULIA! WE WILL SAVE YOUR DAUGHTER--⟩
⟨--TOGETHER!⟩
THOSE STAIRS-- ROTTED THROUGH--!
AND LOOK AT THE LIVING ROOM--!
WH-WHO ARE YOU? WHAT ARE YOU?
WHAT DO YOU WANT HERE?
⟨BEWARE, SISTER! SHE IS NOT OF THIS WORLD!⟩
20

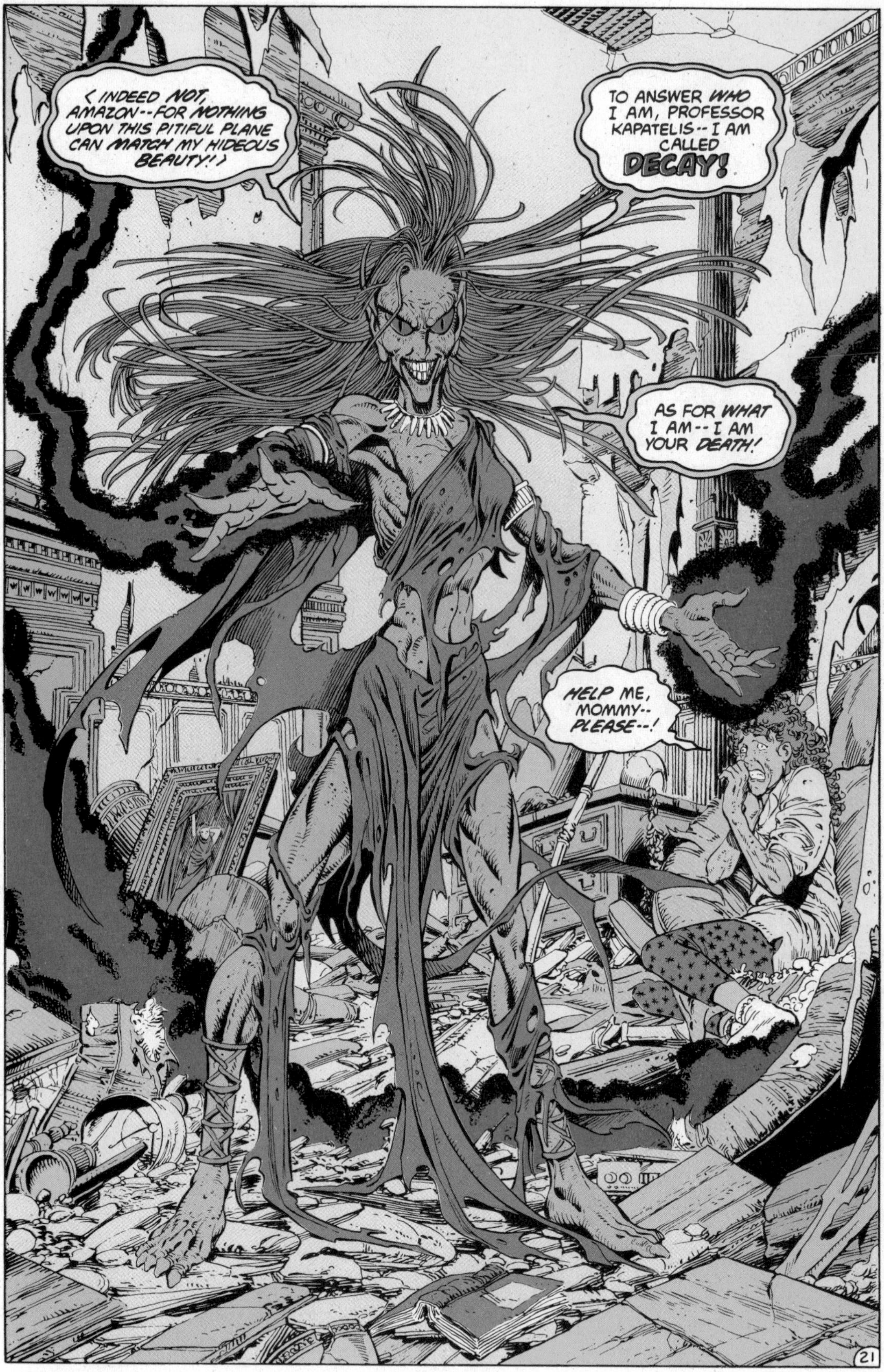

< INDEED NOT, AMAZON--FOR NOTHING UPON THIS PITIFUL PLANE CAN MATCH MY HIDEOUS BEAUTY! >
TO ANSWER WHO I AM, PROFESSOR KAPATELIS-- I AM CALLED DECAY!
AS FOR WHAT I AM-- I AM YOUR DEATH!
HELP ME, MOMMY-- PLEASE--!
21

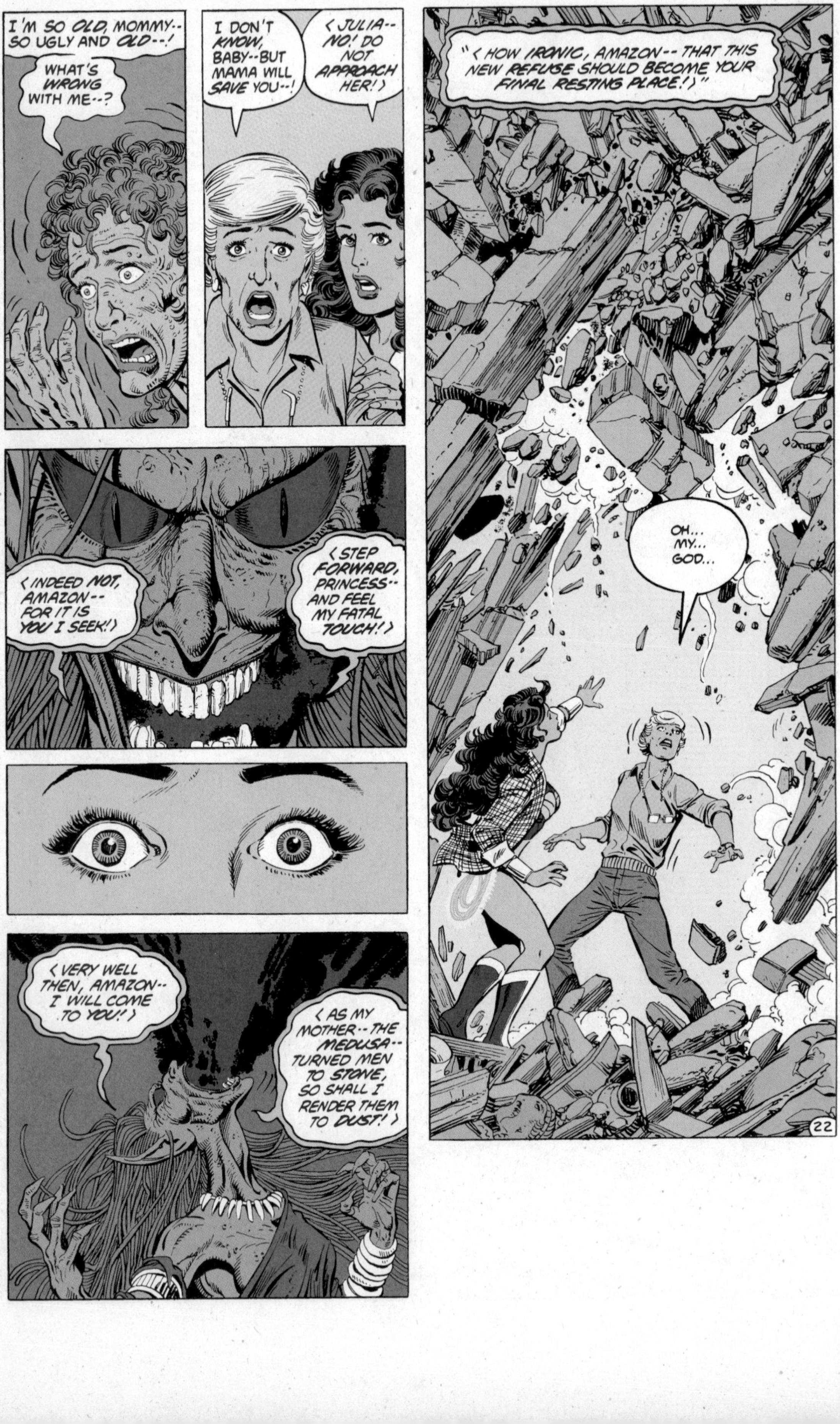
I'M SO OLD, MOMMY-- SO UGLY AND OLD--!
WHAT'S WRONG WITH ME--?
I DON'T KNOW, BABY--BUT MAMA WILL SAVE YOU--!
< JULIA-- NO! DO NOT APPROACH HER! >
< INDEED NOT, AMAZON-- FOR IT IS YOU I SEEK! >
< STEP FORWARD, PRINCESS-- AND FEEL MY FATAL TOUCH! >
< VERY WELL THEN, AMAZON-- I WILL COME TO YOU! >
< AS MY MOTHER--THE MEDUSA-- TURNED MEN TO STONE, SO SHALL I RENDER THEM TO DUST! >
"< HOW IRONIC, AMAZON-- THAT THIS NEW REFUSE SHOULD BECOME YOUR FINAL RESTING PLACE! >"
OH... MY... GOD...

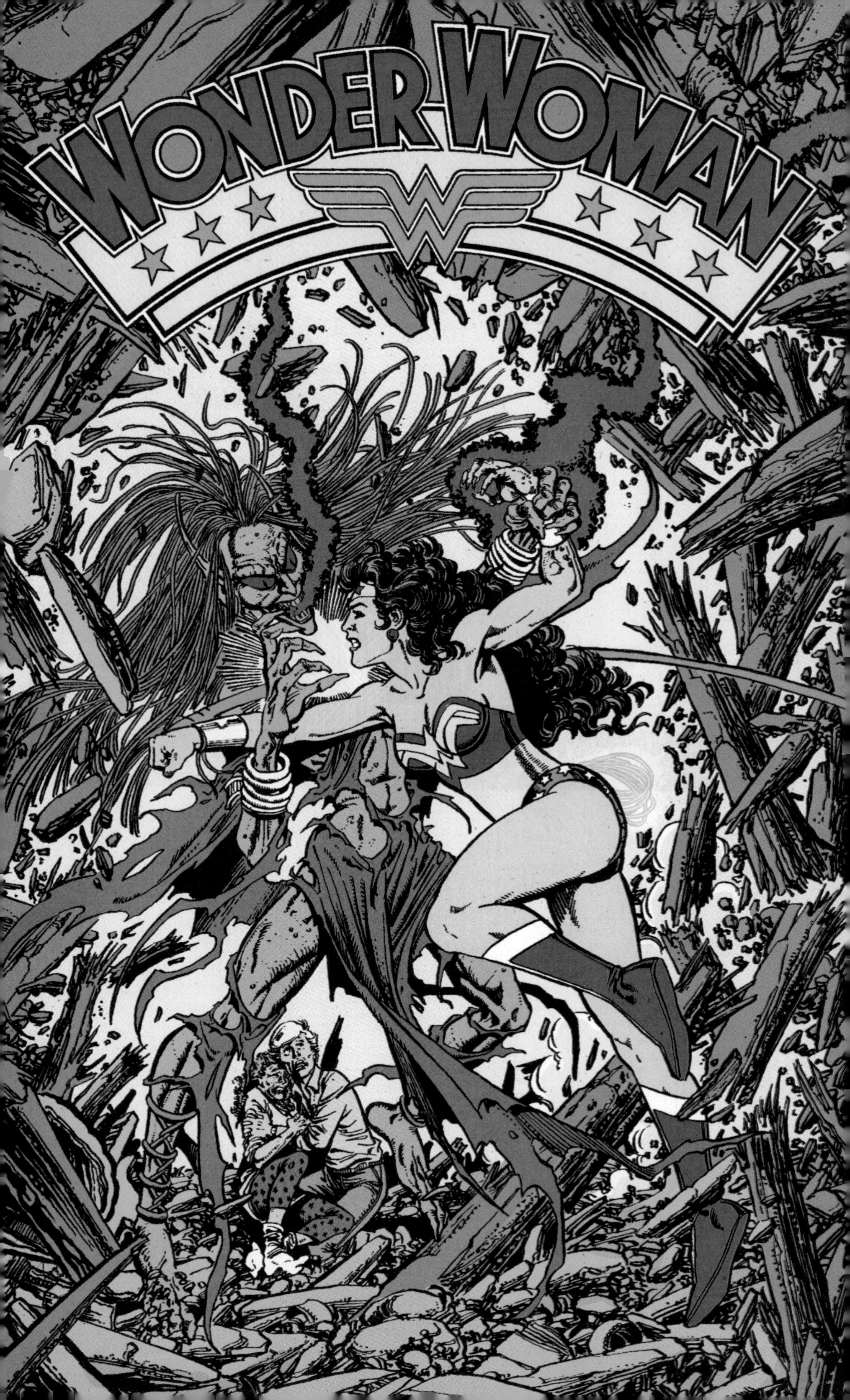
WONDER WOMAN

WONDER WOMAN

CHAPTER FOUR

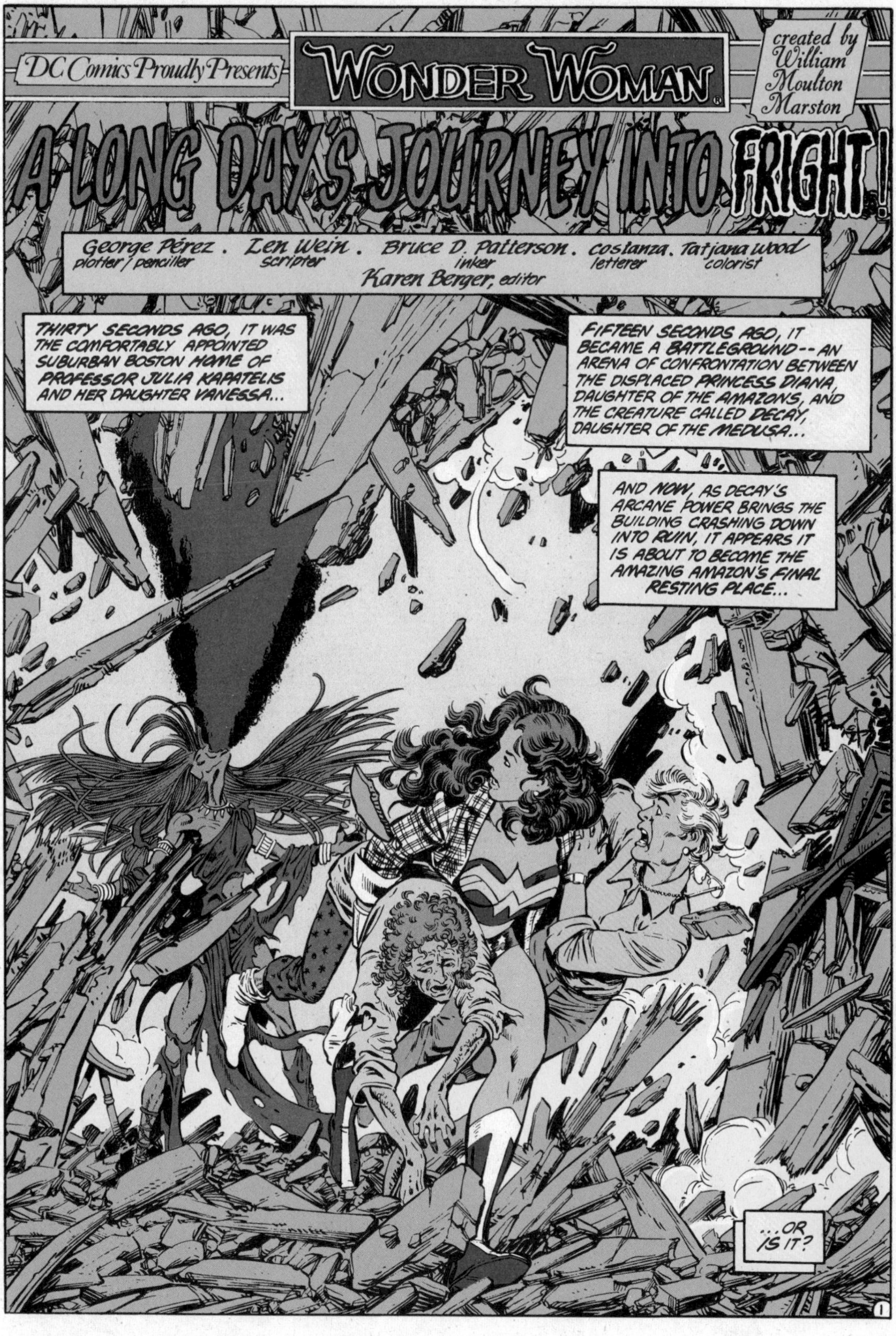
DC Comics Proudly Presents
WONDER WOMAN
created by William Moulton Marston
A LONG DAY'S JOURNEY INTO FRIGHT!
George Pérez . plotter / penciller
Len Wein . scripter
Bruce D. Patterson . inker
costanza . letterer
Tatjana Wood colorist
Karen Berger, editor
THIRTY SECONDS AGO, IT WAS THE COMFORTABLY APPOINTED SUBURBAN BOSTON HOME OF PROFESSOR JULIA KAPATELIS AND HER DAUGHTER VANESSA...
FIFTEEN SECONDS AGO, IT BECAME A BATTLEGROUND -- AN ARENA OF CONFRONTATION BETWEEN THE DISPLACED PRINCESS DIANA, DAUGHTER OF THE AMAZONS, AND THE CREATURE CALLED DECAY, DAUGHTER OF THE MEDUSA...
AND NOW, AS DECAY'S ARCANE POWER BRINGS THE BUILDING CRASHING DOWN INTO RUIN, IT APPEARS IT IS ABOUT TO BECOME THE AMAZING AMAZON'S FINAL RESTING PLACE...
...OR IS IT?
1

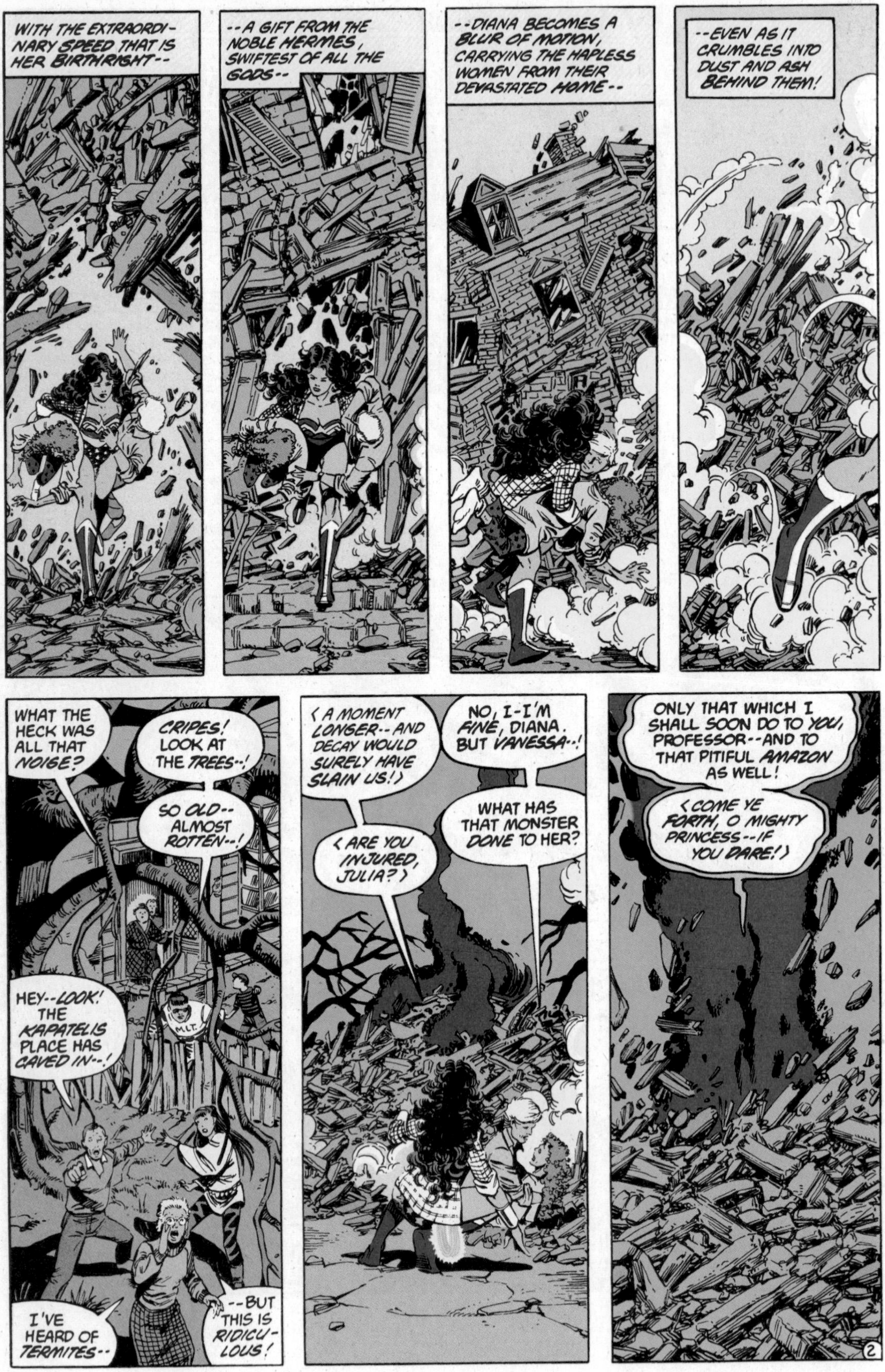
WITH THE EXTRAORDINARY SPEED THAT IS HER BIRTHRIGHT--
--A GIFT FROM THE NOBLE HERMES, SWIFTEST OF ALL THE GODS--
--DIANA BECOMES A BLUR OF MOTION, CARRYING THE HAPLESS WOMEN FROM THEIR DEVASTATED HOME--
--EVEN AS IT CRUMBLES INTO DUST AND ASH BEHIND THEM!
WHAT THE HECK WAS ALL THAT NOISE?
CRIPES! LOOK AT THE TREES--!
SO OLD-- ALMOST ROTTEN--!
HEY--LOOK! THE KAPATELIS PLACE HAS CAVED IN--!
M.I.T.
I'VE HEARD OF TERMITES--
--BUT THIS IS RIDICULOUS!
< A MOMENT LONGER--AND DECAY WOULD SURELY HAVE SLAIN US! >
< ARE YOU INJURED, JULIA? >
NO, I-I'M FINE, DIANA. BUT VANESSA--!
WHAT HAS THAT MONSTER DONE TO HER?
ONLY THAT WHICH I SHALL SOON DO TO YOU, PROFESSOR--AND TO THAT PITIFUL AMAZON AS WELL!
< COME YE FORTH, O MIGHTY PRINCESS--IF YOU DARE! >
2

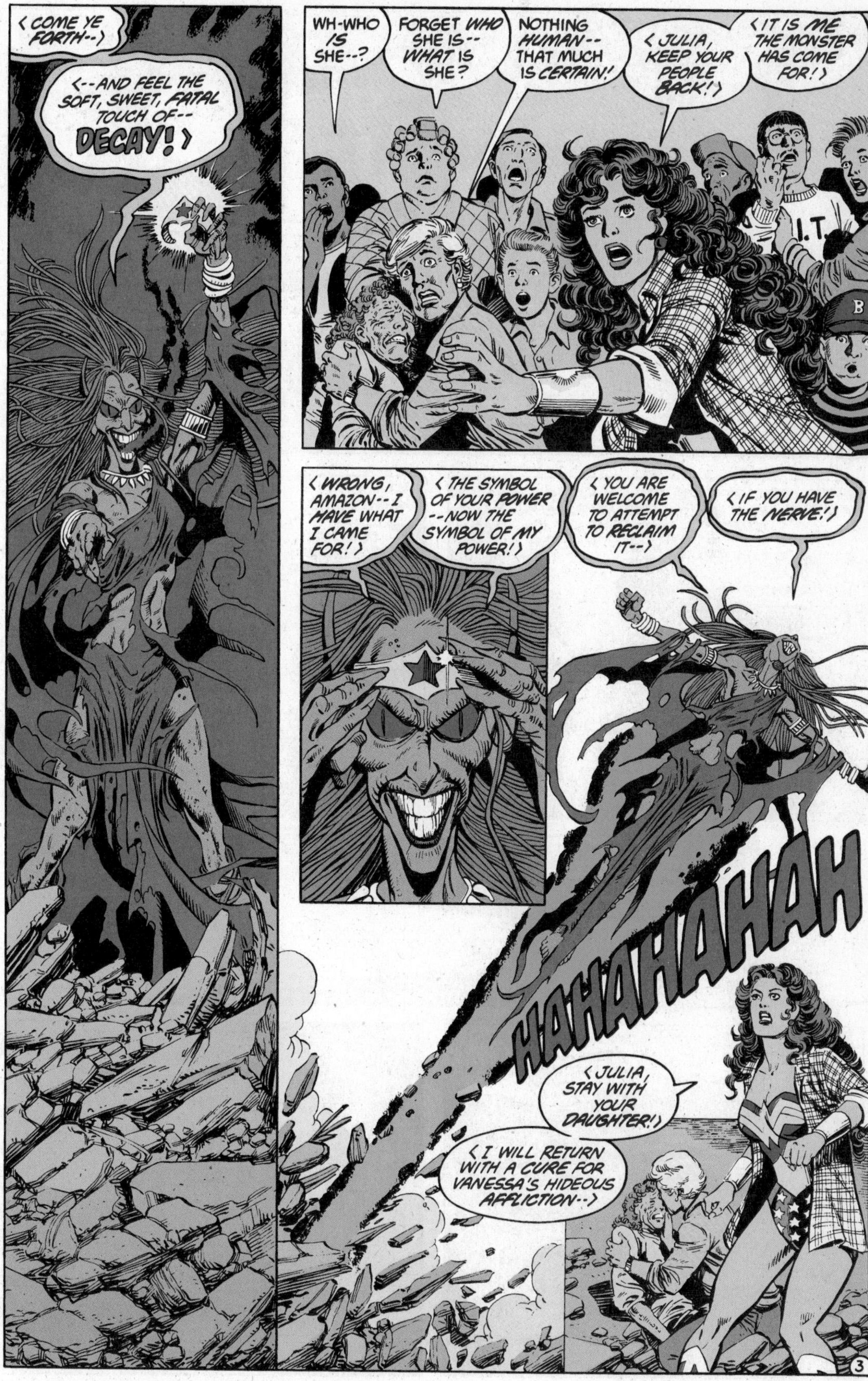
< COME YE FORTH-- >
<--AND FEEL THE SOFT, SWEET, FATAL TOUCH OF-- DECAY! >
WH-WHO IS SHE--?
FORGET WHO SHE IS-- WHAT IS SHE?
NOTHING HUMAN-- THAT MUCH IS CERTAIN!
< JULIA, KEEP YOUR PEOPLE BACK! >
< IT IS ME THE MONSTER HAS COME FOR! >
< WRONG, AMAZON-- I HAVE WHAT I CAME FOR! >
< THE SYMBOL OF YOUR POWER --NOW THE SYMBOL OF MY POWER! >
< YOU ARE WELCOME TO ATTEMPT TO RECLAIM IT-- >
< IF YOU HAVE THE NERVE! >
HAHAHAHAHAH
< JULIA, STAY WITH YOUR DAUGHTER! >
< I WILL RETURN WITH A CURE FOR VANESSA'S HIDEOUS AFFLICTION-- >
3

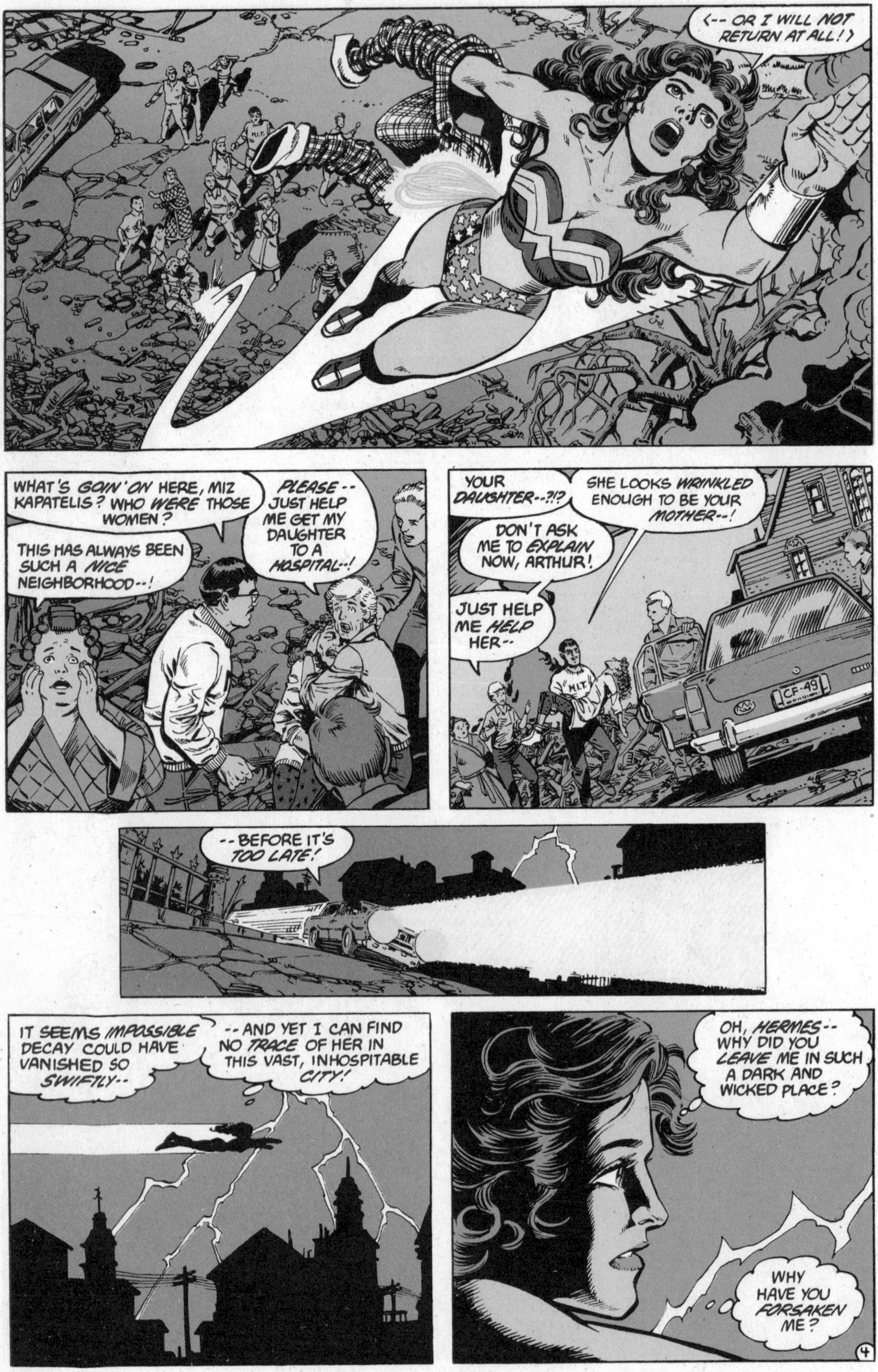

<-- OR I WILL NOT RETURN AT ALL!>
WHAT'S GOIN' ON HERE, MIZ KAPATELIS? WHO WERE THOSE WOMEN?
THIS HAS ALWAYS BEEN SUCH A NICE NEIGHBORHOOD--!
PLEASE-- JUST HELP ME GET MY DAUGHTER TO A HOSPITAL--!
YOUR DAUGHTER--?!?
SHE LOOKS WRINKLED ENOUGH TO BE YOUR MOTHER--!
DON'T ASK ME TO EXPLAIN NOW, ARTHUR!
JUST HELP ME HELP HER--
CF-49
--BEFORE IT'S TOO LATE!
IT SEEMS IMPOSSIBLE DECAY COULD HAVE VANISHED SO SWIFTLY--
--AND YET I CAN FIND NO TRACE OF HER IN THIS VAST, INHOSPITABLE CITY!
OH, HERMES-- WHY DID YOU LEAVE ME IN SUCH A DARK AND WICKED PLACE?
WHY HAVE YOU FORSAKEN ME?
4

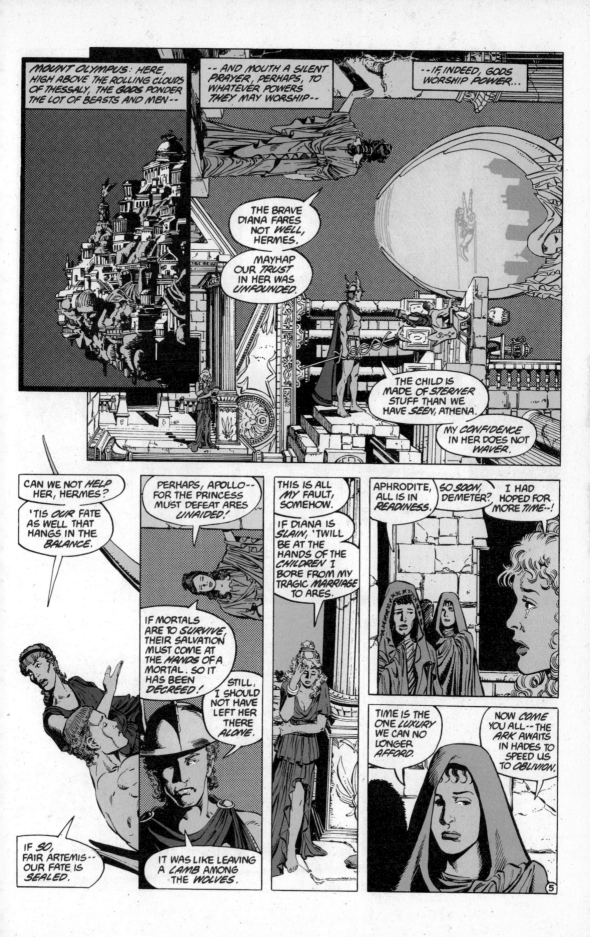

MOUNT OLYMPUS: HERE, HIGH ABOVE THE ROLLING CLOUDS OF THESSALY, THE *GODS* PONDER THE LOT OF BEASTS AND MEN--

-- AND MOUTH A SILENT PRAYER, PERHAPS, TO WHATEVER POWERS THEY MAY WORSHIP--

--IF, INDEED, GODS WORSHIP *POWER*...

THE BRAVE DIANA FARES NOT *WELL*, HERMES.

MAYHAP OUR *TRUST* IN HER WAS *UNFOUNDED.*

THE CHILD IS MADE OF *STERNER* STUFF THAN WE HAVE *SEEN*, ATHENA.

MY *CONFIDENCE* IN HER DOES NOT *WAVER.*

CAN WE NOT *HELP* HER, HERMES?

'TIS *OUR* FATE AS WELL THAT HANGS IN THE *BALANCE.*

PERHAPS, APOLLO-- FOR THE PRINCESS MUST DEFEAT ARES *UNAIDED!*

IF MORTALS ARE TO *SURVIVE*, THEIR SALVATION MUST COME AT THE *HANDS* OF A *MORTAL.* SO IT HAS BEEN *DECREED!*

STILL, I SHOULD NOT HAVE LEFT HER THERE *ALONE.*

THIS IS ALL *MY* FAULT, SOMEHOW.

IF DIANA IS *SLAIN*, 'TWILL BE AT THE HANDS OF THE *CHILDREN* I BORE FROM MY TRAGIC *MARRIAGE* TO ARES.

APHRODITE, ALL IS IN *READINESS.*

SO SOON, DEMETER? I HAD HOPED FOR MORE *TIME*--!

TIME IS THE ONE *LUXURY* WE CAN NO LONGER AFFORD.

NOW *COME* YOU ALL-- THE *ARK* AWAITS IN HADES TO SPEED US TO *OBLIVION.*

IF *SO*, FAIR ARTEMIS-- OUR FATE IS *SEALED.*

IT WAS LIKE LEAVING A *LAMB* AMONG THE *WOLVES.*

95

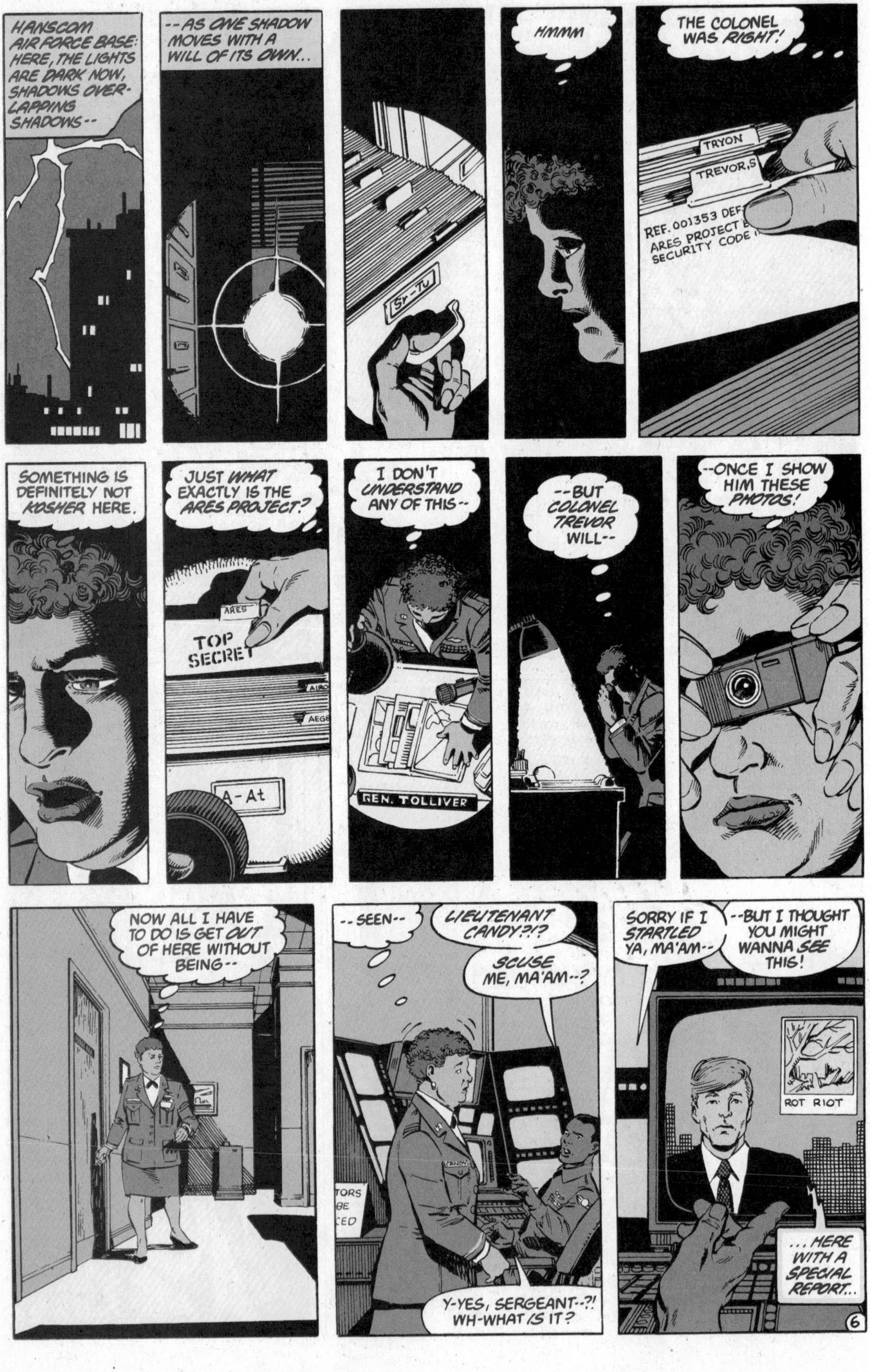
HANSCOM AIR FORCE BASE: HERE, THE LIGHTS ARE DARK NOW, SHADOWS OVERLAPPING SHADOWS--
--AS ONE SHADOW MOVES WITH A WILL OF ITS OWN...
Sr-Tu
HMMM
THE COLONEL WAS RIGHT!
TRYON
TREVOR,S
REF. 001353 DEF
ARES PROJECT
SECURITY CODE
SOMETHING IS DEFINITELY NOT KOSHER HERE.
JUST WHAT EXACTLY IS THE ARES PROJECT?
ARES
TOP SECRET
A-At
I DON'T UNDERSTAND ANY OF THIS--
GEN. TOLLIVER
--BUT COLONEL TREVOR WILL--
--ONCE I SHOW HIM THESE PHOTOS!
NOW ALL I HAVE TO DO IS GET OUT OF HERE WITHOUT BEING--
--SEEN--
LIEUTENANT CANDY?!?
SCUSE ME, MA'AM--?
Y-YES, SERGEANT--?! WH-WHAT IS IT?
SORRY IF I STARTLED YA, MA'AM--
--BUT I THOUGHT YOU MIGHT WANNA SEE THIS!
ROT RIOT
...HERE WITH A SPECIAL REPORT...
6

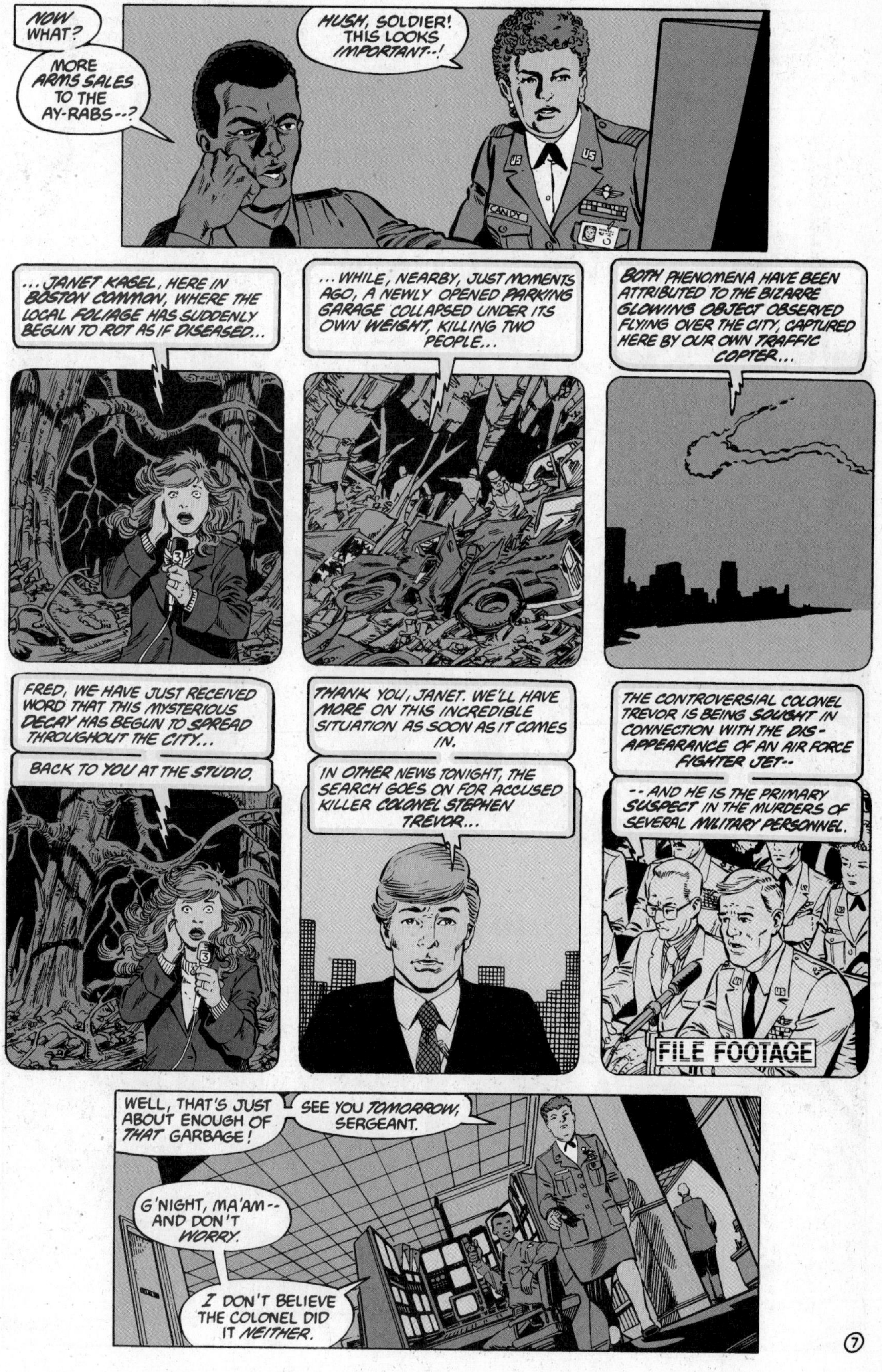

NOW WHAT?
MORE ARMS SALES TO THE AY-RABS--?
HUSH, SOLDIER! THIS LOOKS IMPORTANT--!
CANDY
...JANET KASEL, HERE IN BOSTON COMMON, WHERE THE LOCAL FOLIAGE HAS SUDDENLY BEGUN TO ROT AS IF DISEASED...
...WHILE, NEARBY, JUST MOMENTS AGO, A NEWLY OPENED PARKING GARAGE COLLAPSED UNDER ITS OWN WEIGHT, KILLING TWO PEOPLE...
BOTH PHENOMENA HAVE BEEN ATTRIBUTED TO THE BIZARRE GLOWING OBJECT OBSERVED FLYING OVER THE CITY, CAPTURED HERE BY OUR OWN TRAFFIC COPTER...
FRED, WE HAVE JUST RECEIVED WORD THAT THIS MYSTERIOUS DECAY HAS BEGUN TO SPREAD THROUGHOUT THE CITY...
BACK TO YOU AT THE STUDIO.
THANK YOU, JANET. WE'LL HAVE MORE ON THIS INCREDIBLE SITUATION AS SOON AS IT COMES IN.
IN OTHER NEWS TONIGHT, THE SEARCH GOES ON FOR ACCUSED KILLER COLONEL STEPHEN TREVOR...
THE CONTROVERSIAL COLONEL TREVOR IS BEING SOUGHT IN CONNECTION WITH THE DIS-APPEARANCE OF AN AIR FORCE FIGHTER JET--
--AND HE IS THE PRIMARY SUSPECT IN THE MURDERS OF SEVERAL MILITARY PERSONNEL.
FILE FOOTAGE
WELL, THAT'S JUST ABOUT ENOUGH OF THAT GARBAGE!
SEE YOU TOMORROW, SERGEANT.
G'NIGHT, MA'AM--AND DON'T WORRY.
I DON'T BELIEVE THE COLONEL DID IT NEITHER.

7

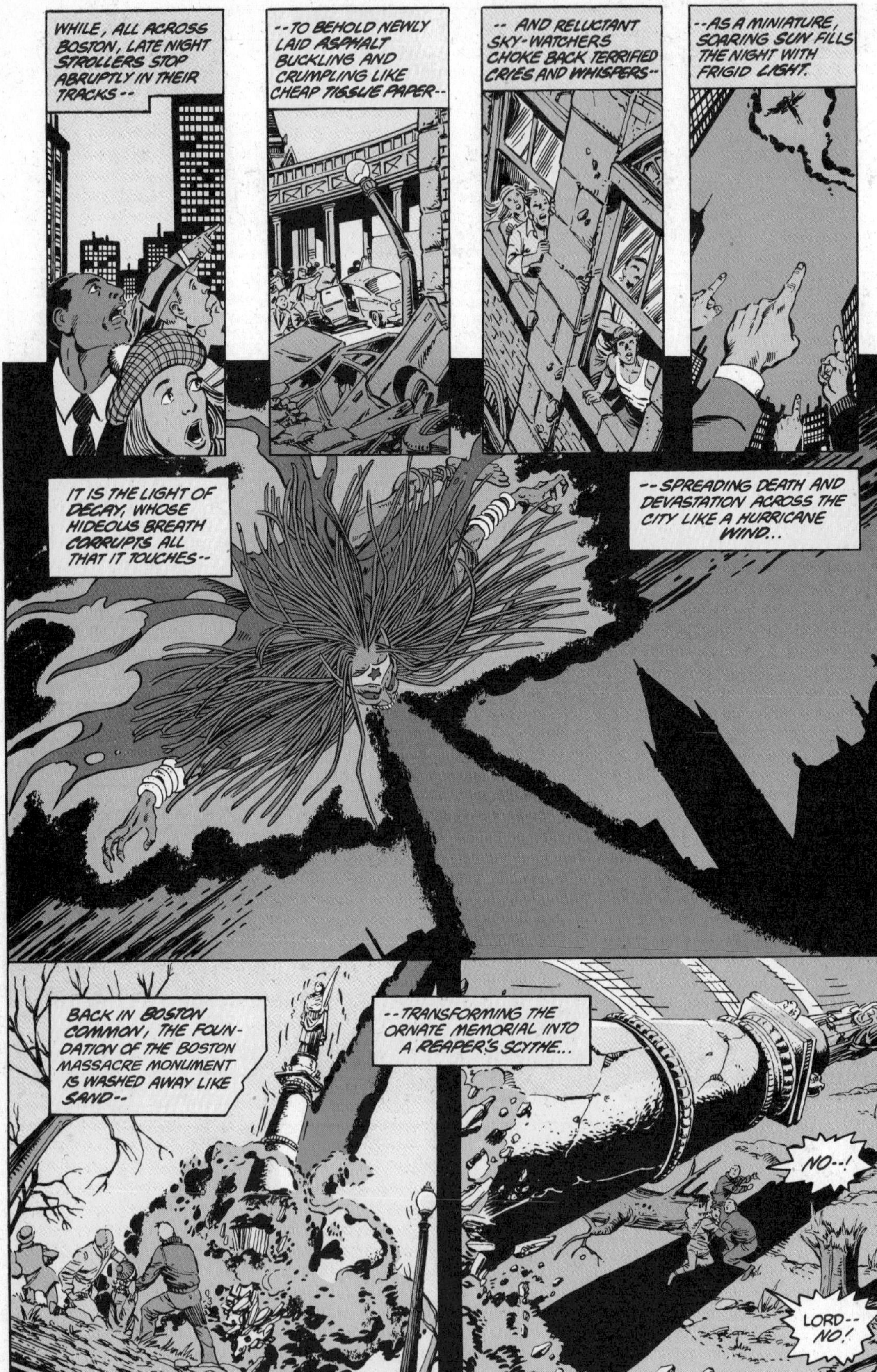
WHILE, ALL ACROSS BOSTON, LATE NIGHT STROLLERS STOP ABRUPTLY IN THEIR TRACKS--
--TO BEHOLD NEWLY LAID ASPHALT BUCKLING AND CRUMPLING LIKE CHEAP TISSUE PAPER--
-- AND RELUCTANT SKY-WATCHERS CHOKE BACK TERRIFIED CRIES AND WHISPERS--
--AS A MINIATURE, SOARING SUN FILLS THE NIGHT WITH FRIGID LIGHT.
IT IS THE LIGHT OF DECAY, WHOSE HIDEOUS BREATH CORRUPTS ALL THAT IT TOUCHES--
--SPREADING DEATH AND DEVASTATION ACROSS THE CITY LIKE A HURRICANE WIND...
BACK IN BOSTON COMMON, THE FOUNDATION OF THE BOSTON MASSACRE MONUMENT IS WASHED AWAY LIKE SAND--
--TRANSFORMING THE ORNATE MEMORIAL INTO A REAPER'S SCYTHE...
NO--!
LORD-- NO!
8

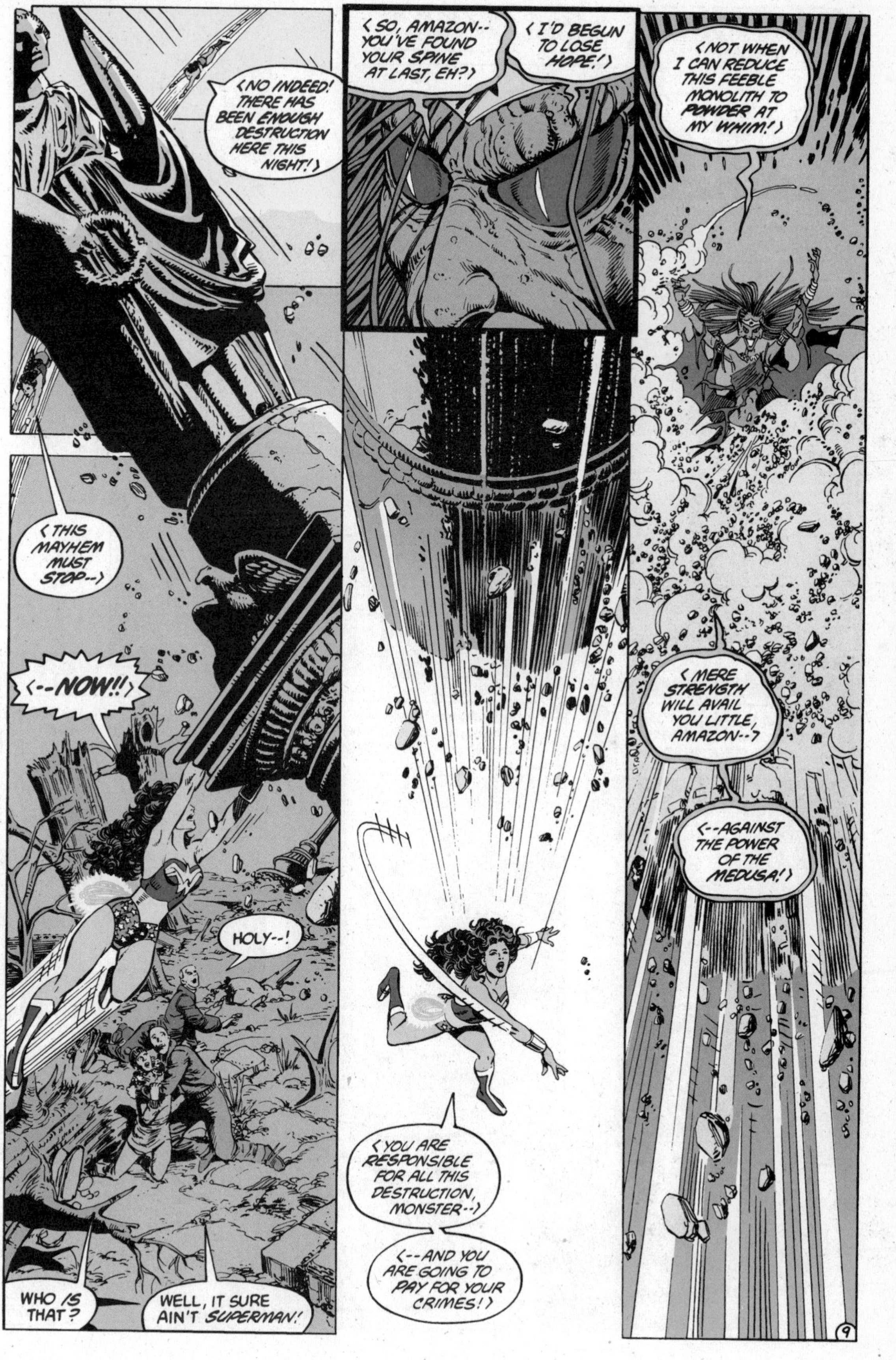

⟨NO INDEED! THERE HAS BEEN ENOUGH DESTRUCTION HERE THIS NIGHT!⟩
⟨THIS MAYHEM MUST STOP--⟩
⟨--NOW!!⟩
HOLY--!
WHO IS THAT?
WELL, IT SURE AIN'T SUPERMAN!
⟨SO, AMAZON-- YOU'VE FOUND YOUR SPINE AT LAST, EH?⟩
⟨I'D BEGUN TO LOSE HOPE!⟩
⟨YOU ARE RESPONSIBLE FOR ALL THIS DESTRUCTION, MONSTER--⟩
⟨--AND YOU ARE GOING TO PAY FOR YOUR CRIMES!⟩
⟨NOT WHEN I CAN REDUCE THIS FEEBLE MONOLITH TO POWDER AT MY WHIM!⟩
⟨MERE STRENGTH WILL AVAIL YOU LITTLE, AMAZON--⟩
⟨--AGAINST THE POWER OF THE MEDUSA!⟩
9

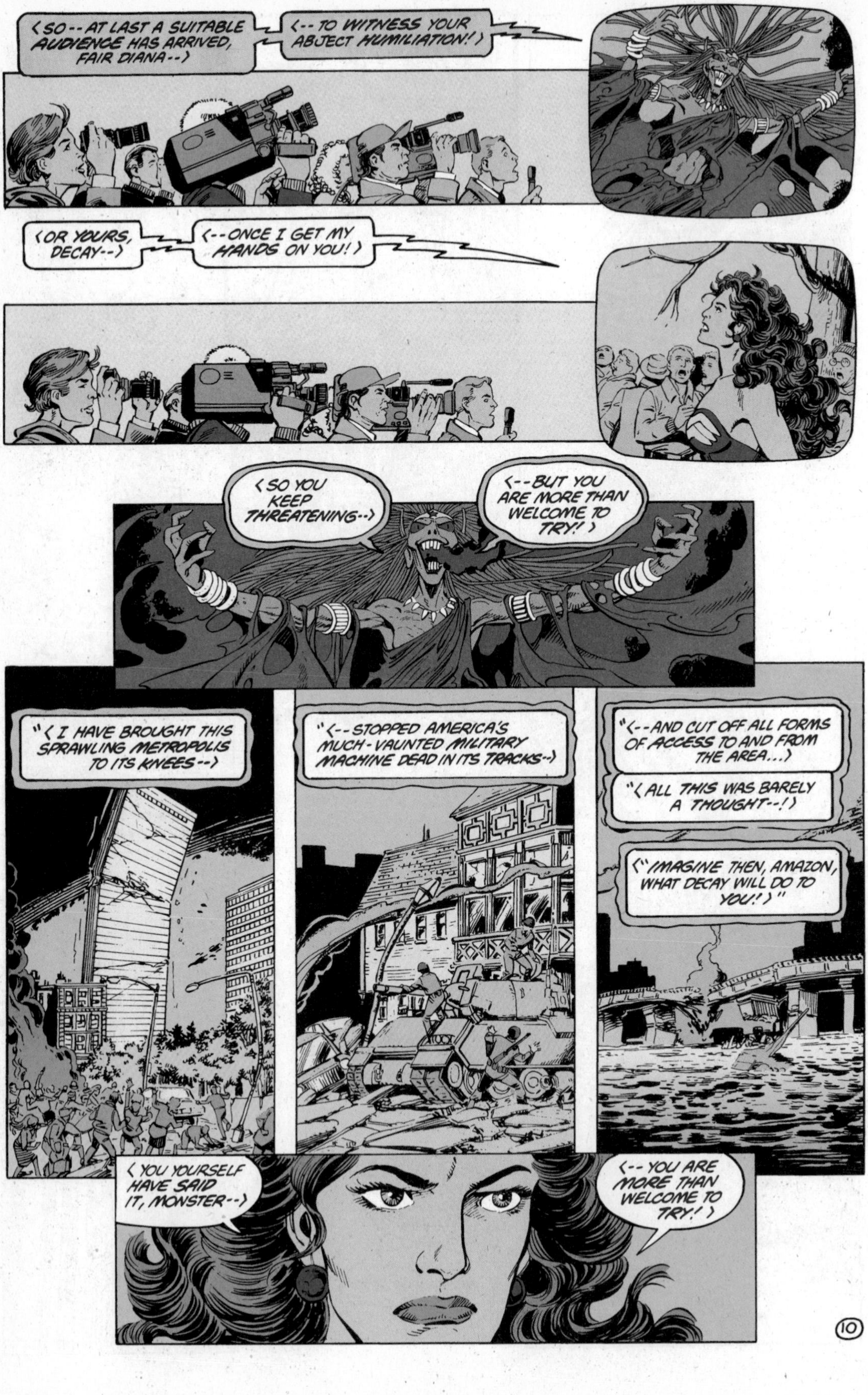

‹SO--AT LAST A SUITABLE AUDIENCE HAS ARRIVED, FAIR DIANA--›
‹--TO WITNESS YOUR ABJECT HUMILIATION!›
‹OR YOURS, DECAY--›
‹--ONCE I GET MY HANDS ON YOU!›
‹SO YOU KEEP THREATENING--›
‹--BUT YOU ARE MORE THAN WELCOME TO TRY!›
"‹I HAVE BROUGHT THIS SPRAWLING METROPOLIS TO ITS KNEES--›
"‹--STOPPED AMERICA'S MUCH-VAUNTED MILITARY MACHINE DEAD IN ITS TRACKS--›
"‹--AND CUT OFF ALL FORMS OF ACCESS TO AND FROM THE AREA...›
"‹ALL THIS WAS BARELY A THOUGHT--!›
‹"IMAGINE THEN, AMAZON, WHAT DECAY WILL DO TO YOU!›"
‹YOU YOURSELF HAVE SAID IT, MONSTER--›
‹--YOU ARE MORE THAN WELCOME TO TRY!›
10

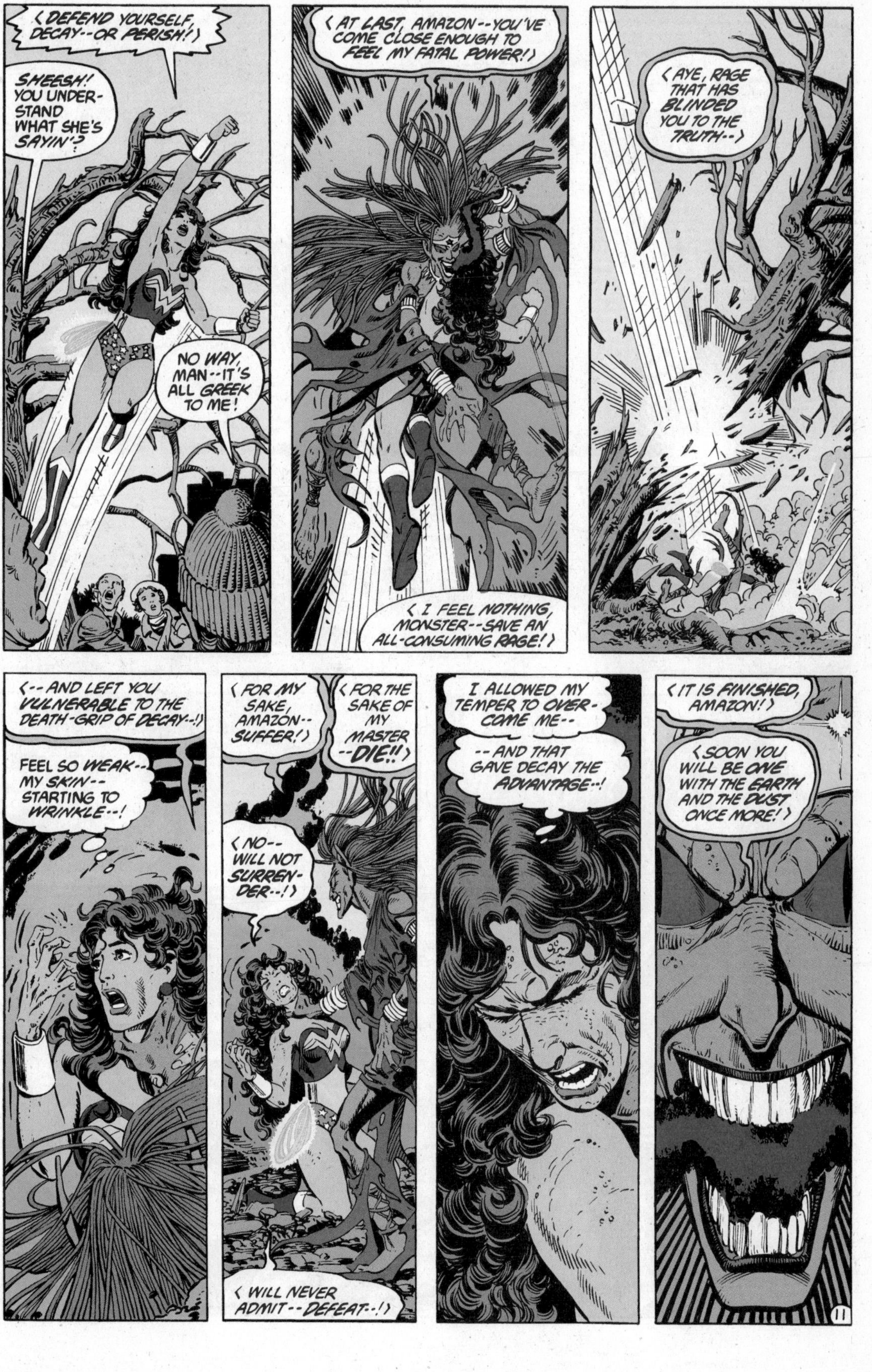

⟨DEFEND YOURSELF, DECAY--OR PERISH!⟩
SHEESH! YOU UNDER-STAND WHAT SHE'S SAYIN'?
NO WAY, MAN--IT'S ALL GREEK TO ME!
⟨AT LAST, AMAZON--YOU'VE COME CLOSE ENOUGH TO FEEL MY FATAL POWER!⟩
⟨I FEEL NOTHING, MONSTER--SAVE AN ALL-CONSUMING RAGE!⟩
⟨AYE, RAGE THAT HAS BLINDED YOU TO THE TRUTH--⟩
⟨--AND LEFT YOU VULNERABLE TO THE DEATH-GRIP OF DECAY--!⟩
FEEL SO WEAK--MY SKIN--STARTING TO WRINKLE--!
⟨FOR MY SAKE, AMAZON--SUFFER!⟩
⟨FOR THE SAKE OF MY MASTER --DIE!!⟩
⟨NO--WILL NOT SURREN-DER--!⟩
⟨WILL NEVER ADMIT--DEFEAT--!⟩
I ALLOWED MY TEMPER TO OVER-COME ME--
--AND THAT GAVE DECAY THE ADVANTAGE--!
⟨IT IS FINISHED, AMAZON!⟩
⟨SOON YOU WILL BE ONE WITH THE EARTH AND THE DUST ONCE MORE!⟩
11

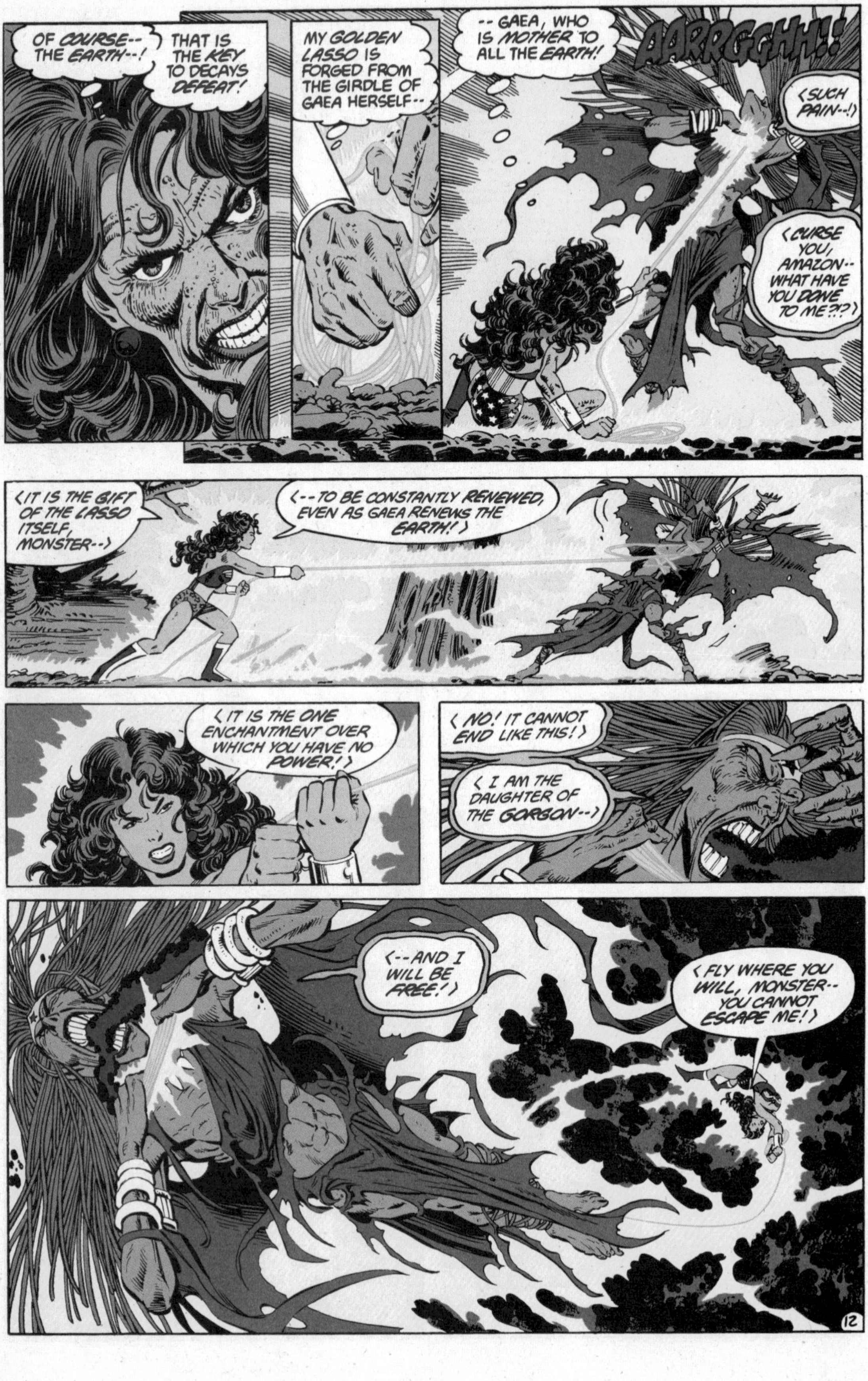
OF COURSE-- THE EARTH--!
THAT IS THE KEY TO DECAYS DEFEAT!
MY GOLDEN LASSO IS FORGED FROM THE GIRDLE OF GAEA HERSELF--
-- GAEA, WHO IS MOTHER TO ALL THE EARTH!
AARRGGHH!!
‹SUCH PAIN--!›
‹CURSE YOU, AMAZON-- WHAT HAVE YOU DONE TO ME?!?›
‹IT IS THE GIFT OF THE LASSO ITSELF, MONSTER--›
‹--TO BE CONSTANTLY RENEWED, EVEN AS GAEA RENEWS THE EARTH!›
‹IT IS THE ONE ENCHANTMENT OVER WHICH YOU HAVE NO POWER!›
‹NO! IT CANNOT END LIKE THIS!›
‹I AM THE DAUGHTER OF THE GORGON--›
‹--AND I WILL BE FREE!›
‹FLY WHERE YOU WILL, MONSTER-- YOU CANNOT ESCAPE ME!›
12

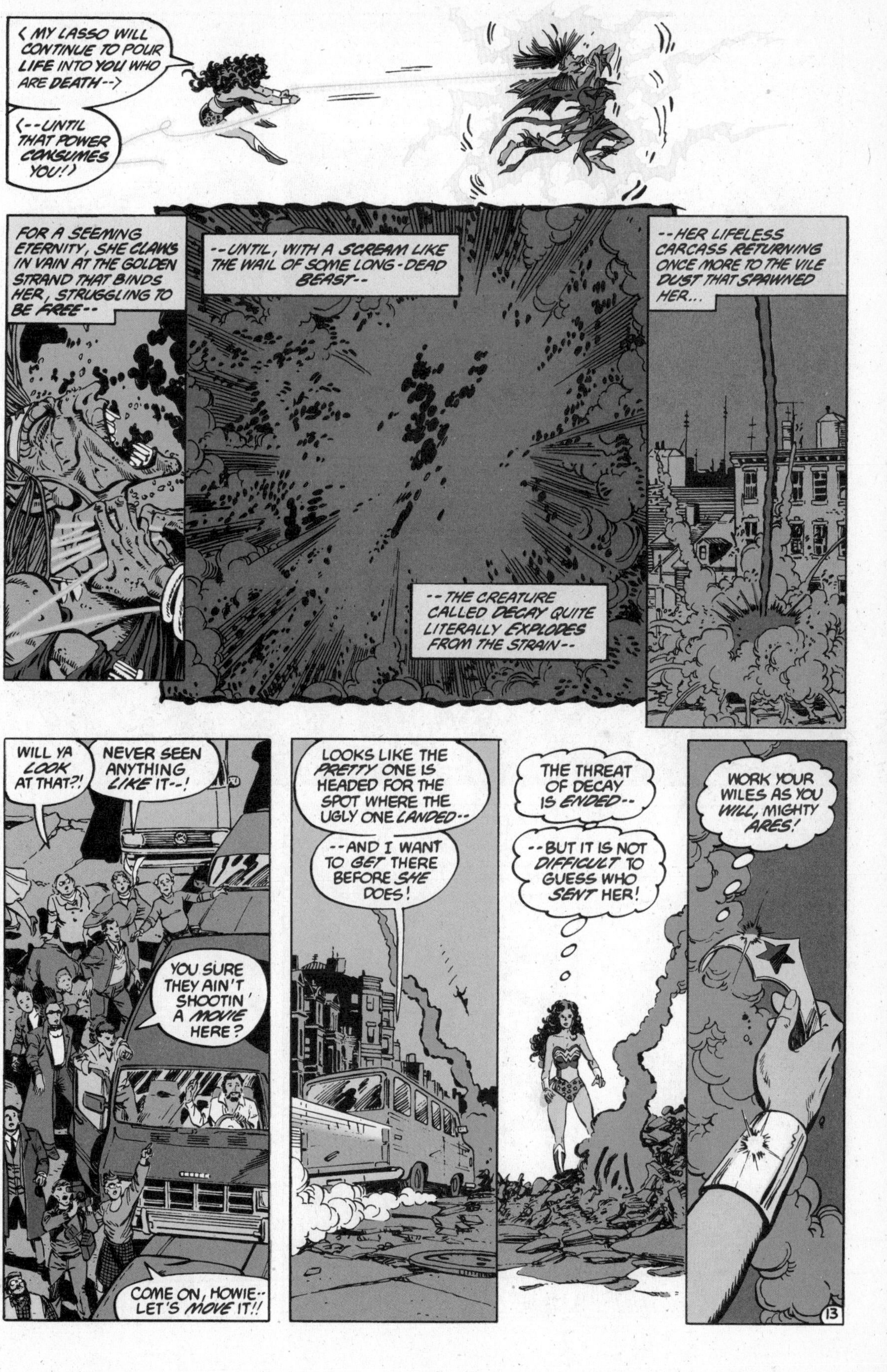

< MY LASSO WILL CONTINUE TO POUR LIFE INTO YOU WHO ARE DEATH-->
<--UNTIL THAT POWER CONSUMES YOU!>
FOR A SEEMING ETERNITY, SHE CLAWS IN VAIN AT THE GOLDEN STRAND THAT BINDS HER, STRUGGLING TO BE FREE--
--UNTIL, WITH A SCREAM LIKE THE WAIL OF SOME LONG-DEAD BEAST--
--THE CREATURE CALLED DECAY QUITE LITERALLY EXPLODES FROM THE STRAIN--
--HER LIFELESS CARCASS RETURNING ONCE MORE TO THE VILE DUST THAT SPAWNED HER...
WILL YA LOOK AT THAT?!
NEVER SEEN ANYTHING LIKE IT--!
YOU SURE THEY AIN'T SHOOTIN' A MOVIE HERE?
COME ON, HOWIE-- LET'S MOVE IT!!
LOOKS LIKE THE PRETTY ONE IS HEADED FOR THE SPOT WHERE THE UGLY ONE LANDED--
--AND I WANT TO GET THERE BEFORE SHE DOES!
THE THREAT OF DECAY IS ENDED--
--BUT IT IS NOT DIFFICULT TO GUESS WHO SENT HER!
WORK YOUR WILES AS YOU WILL, MIGHTY ARES!
13

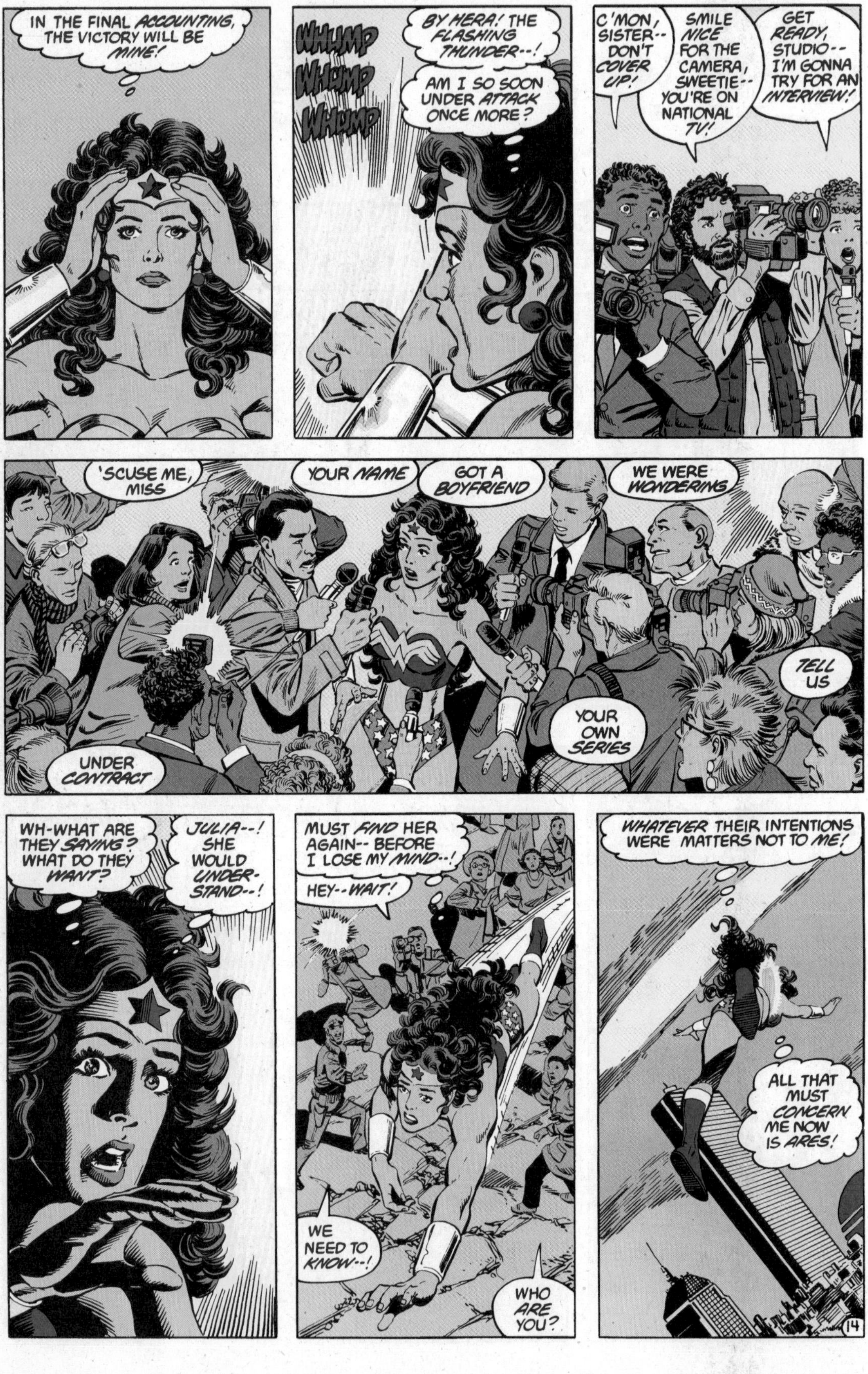
IN THE FINAL ACCOUNTING, THE VICTORY WILL BE MINE!
WHUMP WHUMP WHUMP
BY HERA! THE FLASHING THUNDER--!
AM I SO SOON UNDER ATTACK ONCE MORE?
C'MON, SISTER-- DON'T COVER UP!
SMILE NICE FOR THE CAMERA, SWEETIE-- YOU'RE ON NATIONAL TV!
GET READY, STUDIO-- I'M GONNA TRY FOR AN INTERVIEW!
'SCUSE ME, MISS
YOUR NAME
GOT A BOYFRIEND
WE WERE WONDERING
TELL US
YOUR OWN SERIES
UNDER CONTRACT
WH-WHAT ARE THEY SAYING? WHAT DO THEY WANT?
JULIA--! SHE WOULD UNDER-STAND--!
MUST FIND HER AGAIN-- BEFORE I LOSE MY MIND--!
HEY--WAIT!
WE NEED TO KNOW--!
WHO ARE YOU?
WHATEVER THEIR INTENTIONS WERE MATTERS NOT TO ME!
ALL THAT MUST CONCERN ME NOW IS ARES!
14

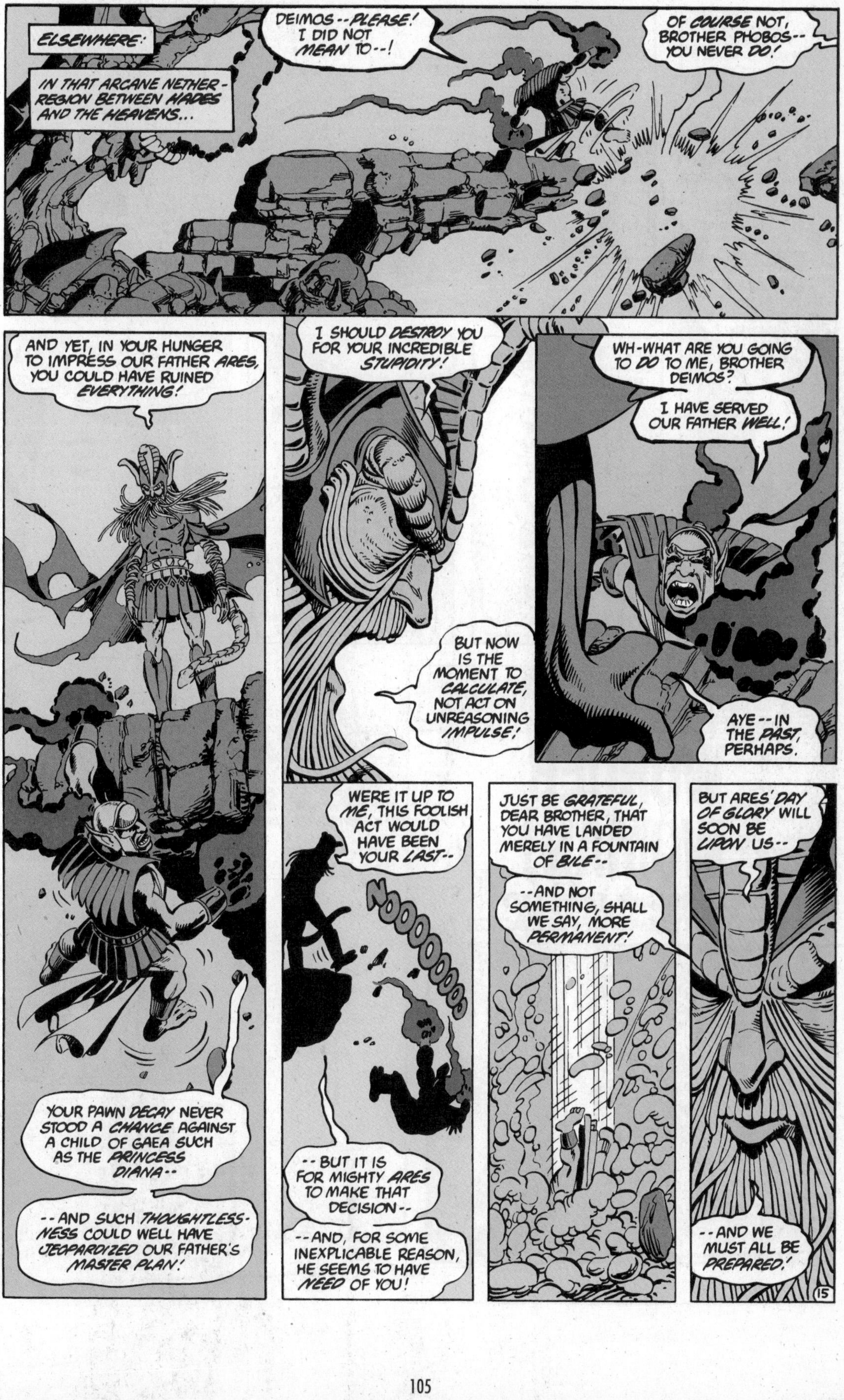
ELSEWHERE:
IN THAT ARCANE NETHER-REGION BETWEEN HADES AND THE HEAVENS...
DEIMOS--PLEASE! I DID NOT MEAN TO--!
OF COURSE NOT, BROTHER PHOBOS--YOU NEVER DO!
AND YET, IN YOUR HUNGER TO IMPRESS OUR FATHER ARES, YOU COULD HAVE RUINED EVERYTHING!
YOUR PAWN DECAY NEVER STOOD A CHANCE AGAINST A CHILD OF GAEA SUCH AS THE PRINCESS DIANA--
--AND SUCH THOUGHTLESS-NESS COULD WELL HAVE JEOPARDIZED OUR FATHER'S MASTER PLAN!
I SHOULD DESTROY YOU FOR YOUR INCREDIBLE STUPIDITY!
BUT NOW IS THE MOMENT TO CALCULATE, NOT ACT ON UNREASONING IMPULSE!
WH-WHAT ARE YOU GOING TO DO TO ME, BROTHER DEIMOS?
I HAVE SERVED OUR FATHER WELL!
AYE--IN THE PAST, PERHAPS.
WERE IT UP TO ME, THIS FOOLISH ACT WOULD HAVE BEEN YOUR LAST--
NOOOOOOOOO
--BUT IT IS FOR MIGHTY ARES TO MAKE THAT DECISION--
--AND, FOR SOME INEXPLICABLE REASON, HE SEEMS TO HAVE NEED OF YOU!
JUST BE GRATEFUL, DEAR BROTHER, THAT YOU HAVE LANDED MERELY IN A FOUNTAIN OF BILE--
--AND NOT SOMETHING, SHALL WE SAY, MORE PERMANENT!
BUT ARES' DAY OF GLORY WILL SOON BE UPON US--
--AND WE MUST ALL BE PREPARED!
15

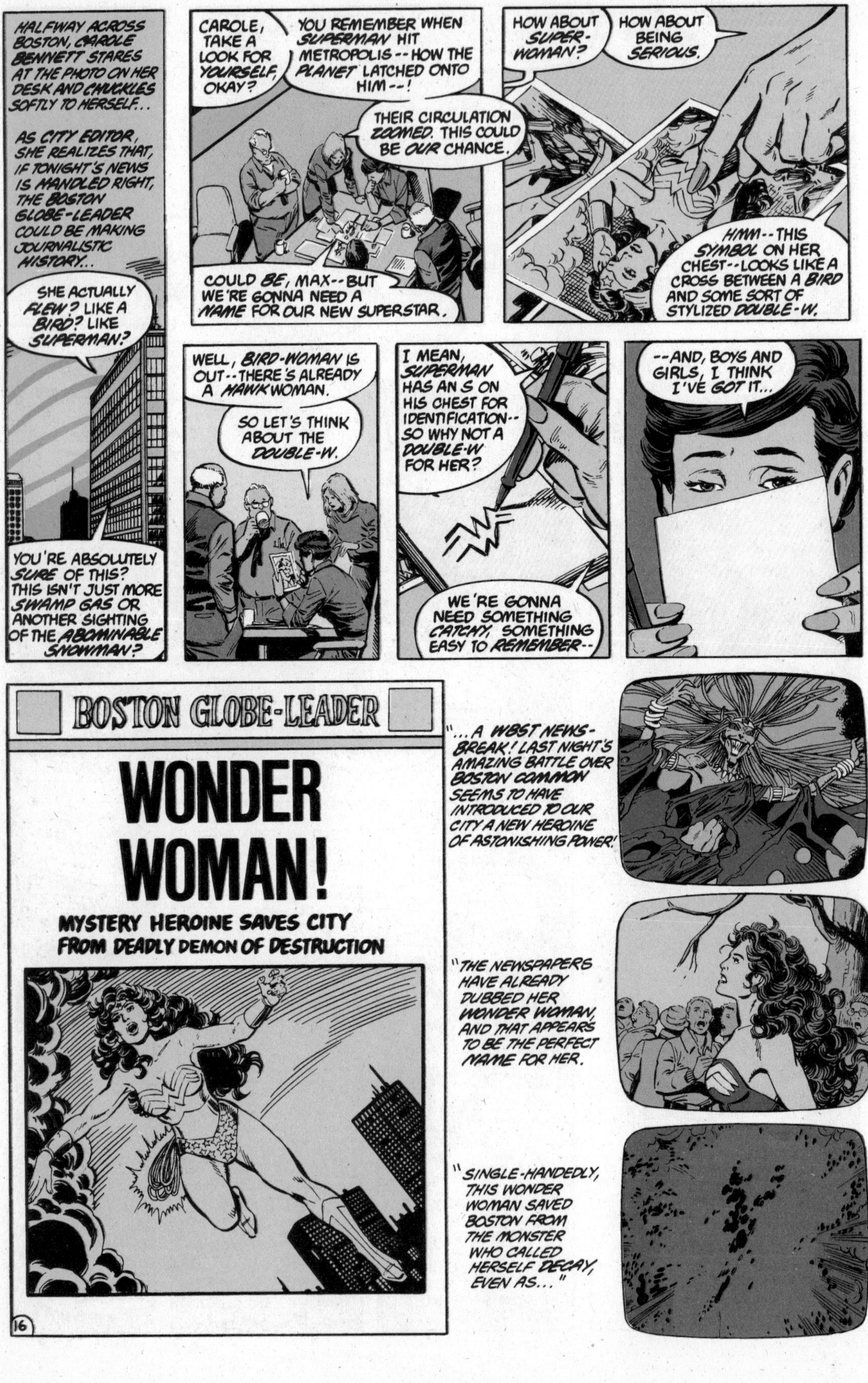
HALFWAY ACROSS BOSTON, CAROLE BENNETT STARES AT THE PHOTO ON HER DESK AND CHUCKLES SOFTLY TO HERSELF...
AS CITY EDITOR, SHE REALIZES THAT, IF TONIGHT'S NEWS IS HANDLED RIGHT, THE BOSTON GLOBE-LEADER COULD BE MAKING JOURNALISTIC HISTORY...
SHE ACTUALLY FLEW? LIKE A BIRD? LIKE SUPERMAN?
YOU'RE ABSOLUTELY SURE OF THIS? THIS ISN'T JUST MORE SWAMP GAS OR ANOTHER SIGHTING OF THE ABOMINABLE SNOWMAN?
CAROLE, TAKE A LOOK FOR YOURSELF, OKAY?
YOU REMEMBER WHEN SUPERMAN HIT METROPOLIS--HOW THE PLANET LATCHED ONTO HIM--!
THEIR CIRCULATION ZOOMED. THIS COULD BE OUR CHANCE.
COULD BE, MAX--BUT WE'RE GONNA NEED A NAME FOR OUR NEW SUPERSTAR.
HOW ABOUT SUPER-WOMAN?
HOW ABOUT BEING SERIOUS.
HMM--THIS SYMBOL ON HER CHEST--LOOKS LIKE A CROSS BETWEEN A BIRD AND SOME SORT OF STYLIZED DOUBLE-W.
WELL, BIRD-WOMAN IS OUT--THERE'S ALREADY A HAWKWOMAN.
SO LET'S THINK ABOUT THE DOUBLE-W.
I MEAN, SUPERMAN HAS AN S ON HIS CHEST FOR IDENTIFICATION--SO WHY NOT A DOUBLE-W FOR HER?
WE'RE GONNA NEED SOMETHING CATCHY, SOMETHING EASY TO REMEMBER--
--AND, BOYS AND GIRLS, I THINK I'VE GOT IT...
BOSTON GLOBE-LEADER
WONDER WOMAN!
MYSTERY HEROINE SAVES CITY FROM DEADLY DEMON OF DESTRUCTION
"...A WBST NEWS-BREAK! LAST NIGHT'S AMAZING BATTLE OVER BOSTON COMMON SEEMS TO HAVE INTRODUCED TO OUR CITY A NEW HEROINE OF ASTONISHING POWER!
"THE NEWSPAPERS HAVE ALREADY DUBBED HER WONDER WOMAN, AND THAT APPEARS TO BE THE PERFECT NAME FOR HER.
"SINGLE-HANDEDLY, THIS WONDER WOMAN SAVED BOSTON FROM THE MONSTER WHO CALLED HERSELF DECAY, EVEN AS..."
16

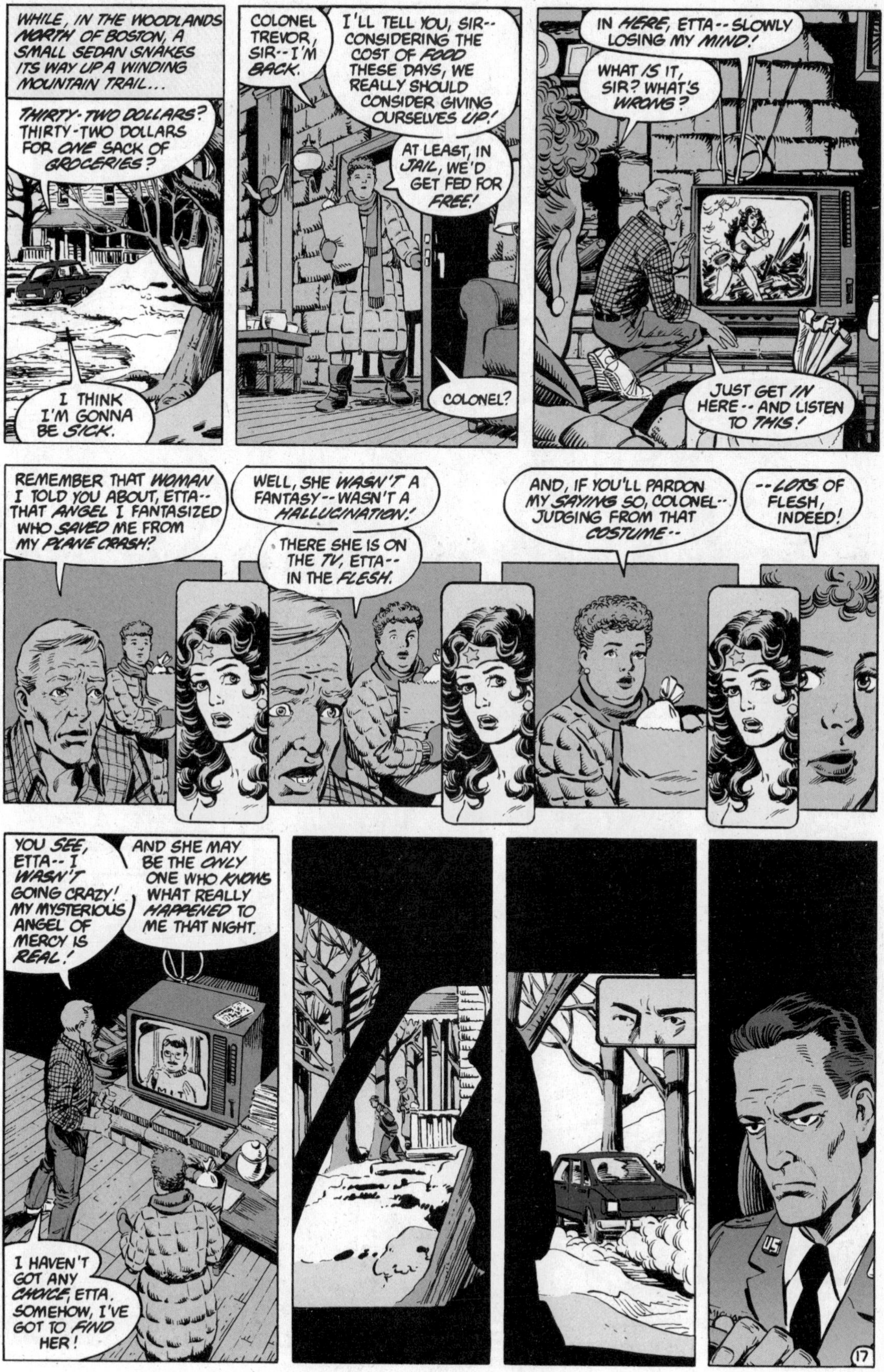
WHILE, IN THE WOODLANDS NORTH OF BOSTON, A SMALL SEDAN SNAKES ITS WAY UP A WINDING MOUNTAIN TRAIL...
THIRTY-TWO DOLLARS? THIRTY-TWO DOLLARS FOR ONE SACK OF GROCERIES?
I THINK I'M GONNA BE SICK.
COLONEL TREVOR, SIR--I'M BACK.
I'LL TELL YOU, SIR--CONSIDERING THE COST OF FOOD THESE DAYS, WE REALLY SHOULD CONSIDER GIVING OURSELVES UP!
AT LEAST, IN JAIL, WE'D GET FED FOR FREE!
COLONEL?
IN HERE, ETTA--SLOWLY LOSING MY MIND!
WHAT IS IT, SIR? WHAT'S WRONG?
JUST GET IN HERE--AND LISTEN TO THIS!
REMEMBER THAT WOMAN I TOLD YOU ABOUT, ETTA--THAT ANGEL I FANTASIZED WHO SAVED ME FROM MY PLANE CRASH?
WELL, SHE WASN'T A FANTASY--WASN'T A HALLUCINATION!
THERE SHE IS ON THE TV, ETTA--IN THE FLESH.
AND, IF YOU'LL PARDON MY SAYING SO, COLONEL--JUDGING FROM THAT COSTUME--
--LOTS OF FLESH, INDEED!
YOU SEE, ETTA--I WASN'T GOING CRAZY! MY MYSTERIOUS ANGEL OF MERCY IS REAL!
AND SHE MAY BE THE ONLY ONE WHO KNOWS WHAT REALLY HAPPENED TO ME THAT NIGHT.
I HAVEN'T GOT ANY CHOICE, ETTA. SOMEHOW, I'VE GOT TO FIND HER!
17

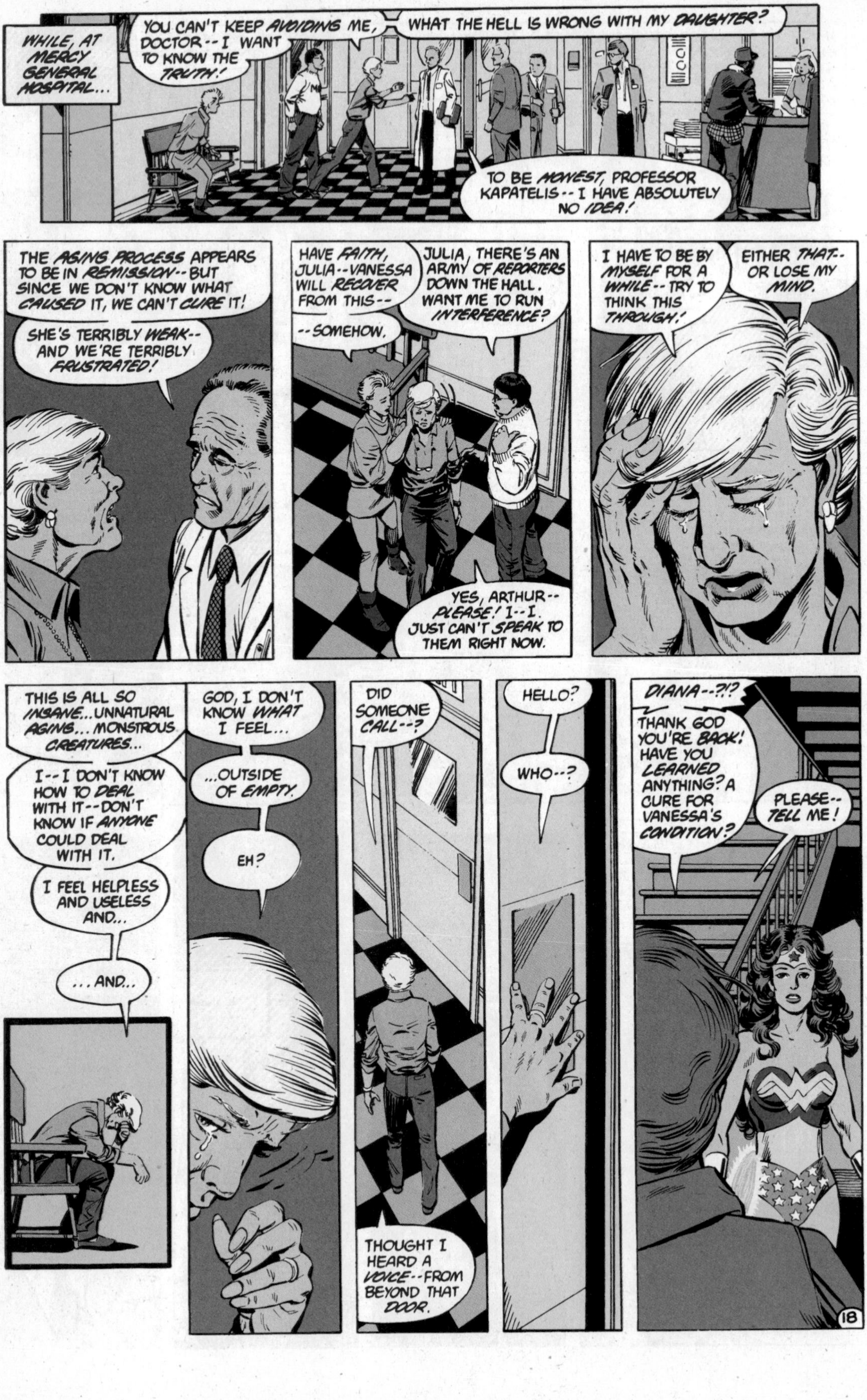
WHILE, AT MERCY GENERAL HOSPITAL...
YOU CAN'T KEEP AVOIDING ME, DOCTOR--I WANT TO KNOW THE TRUTH!
WHAT THE HELL IS WRONG WITH MY DAUGHTER?
TO BE HONEST, PROFESSOR KAPATELIS--I HAVE ABSOLUTELY NO IDEA!
THE AGING PROCESS APPEARS TO BE IN REMISSION--BUT SINCE WE DON'T KNOW WHAT CAUSED IT, WE CAN'T CURE IT!
SHE'S TERRIBLY WEAK--AND WE'RE TERRIBLY FRUSTRATED!
HAVE FAITH, JULIA--VANESSA WILL RECOVER FROM THIS--
--SOMEHOW.
JULIA, THERE'S AN ARMY OF REPORTERS DOWN THE HALL. WANT ME TO RUN INTERFERENCE?
YES, ARTHUR--PLEASE! I--I. JUST CAN'T SPEAK TO THEM RIGHT NOW.
I HAVE TO BE BY MYSELF FOR A WHILE--TRY TO THINK THIS THROUGH!
EITHER THAT--OR LOSE MY MIND.
THIS IS ALL SO INSANE...UNNATURAL AGING...MONSTROUS CREATURES...
I--I DON'T KNOW HOW TO DEAL WITH IT--DON'T KNOW IF ANYONE COULD DEAL WITH IT.
I FEEL HELPLESS AND USELESS AND...
...AND...
GOD, I DON'T KNOW WHAT I FEEL...
...OUTSIDE OF EMPTY.
EH?
DID SOMEONE CALL--?
THOUGHT I HEARD A VOICE--FROM BEYOND THAT DOOR.
HELLO?
WHO--?
DIANA--?!?
THANK GOD YOU'RE BACK! HAVE YOU LEARNED ANYTHING? A CURE FOR VANESSA'S CONDITION?
PLEASE--TELL ME!
18

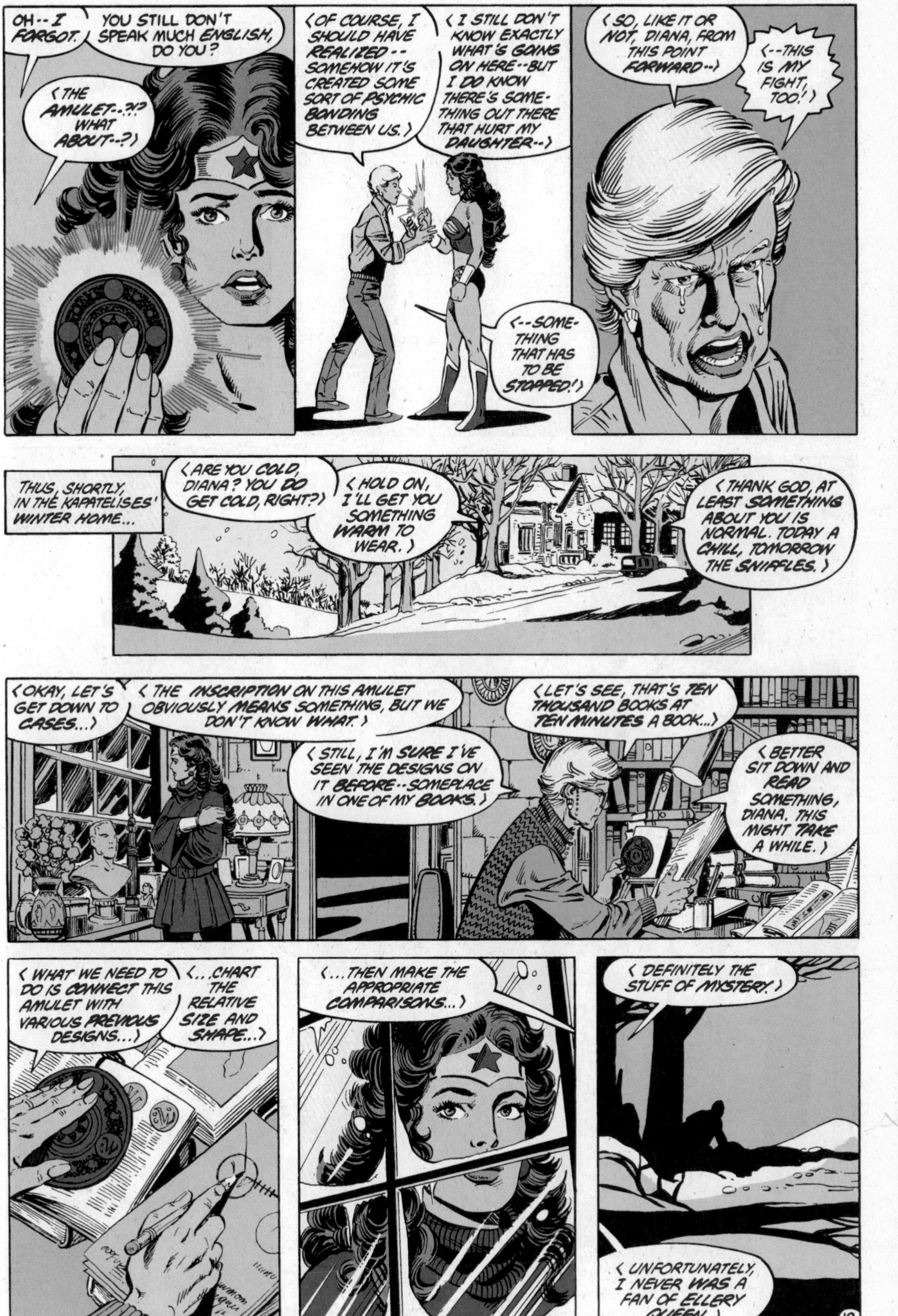
OH-- I FORGOT.
YOU STILL DON'T SPEAK MUCH ENGLISH, DO YOU?
⟨THE AMULET--?!? WHAT ABOUT--?⟩
⟨OF COURSE, I SHOULD HAVE REALIZED-- SOMEHOW IT'S CREATED SOME SORT OF PSYCHIC BONDING BETWEEN US.⟩
⟨I STILL DON'T KNOW EXACTLY WHAT'S GOING ON HERE--BUT I DO KNOW THERE'S SOMETHING OUT THERE THAT HURT MY DAUGHTER--⟩
⟨--SOMETHING THAT HAS TO BE STOPPED!⟩
⟨SO, LIKE IT OR NOT, DIANA, FROM THIS POINT FORWARD--⟩
⟨--THIS IS MY FIGHT, TOO!⟩
THUS, SHORTLY, IN THE KAPATELISES' WINTER HOME...
⟨ARE YOU COLD, DIANA? YOU DO GET COLD, RIGHT?⟩
⟨HOLD ON, I'LL GET YOU SOMETHING WARM TO WEAR.⟩
⟨THANK GOD, AT LEAST SOMETHING ABOUT YOU IS NORMAL. TODAY A CHILL, TOMORROW THE SNIFFLES.⟩
⟨OKAY, LET'S GET DOWN TO CASES...⟩
⟨THE INSCRIPTION ON THIS AMULET OBVIOUSLY MEANS SOMETHING, BUT WE DON'T KNOW WHAT.⟩
⟨STILL, I'M SURE I'VE SEEN THE DESIGNS ON IT BEFORE--SOMEPLACE IN ONE OF MY BOOKS.⟩
⟨LET'S SEE, THAT'S TEN THOUSAND BOOKS AT TEN MINUTES A BOOK...⟩
⟨BETTER SIT DOWN AND READ SOMETHING, DIANA. THIS MIGHT TAKE A WHILE.⟩
⟨WHAT WE NEED TO DO IS CONNECT THIS AMULET WITH VARIOUS PREVIOUS DESIGNS...⟩
⟨...CHART THE RELATIVE SIZE AND SHAPE...⟩
⟨...THEN MAKE THE APPROPRIATE COMPARISONS...⟩
⟨DEFINITELY THE STUFF OF MYSTERY.⟩
⟨UNFORTUNATELY, I NEVER WAS A FAN OF ELLERY QUEEN.⟩
19

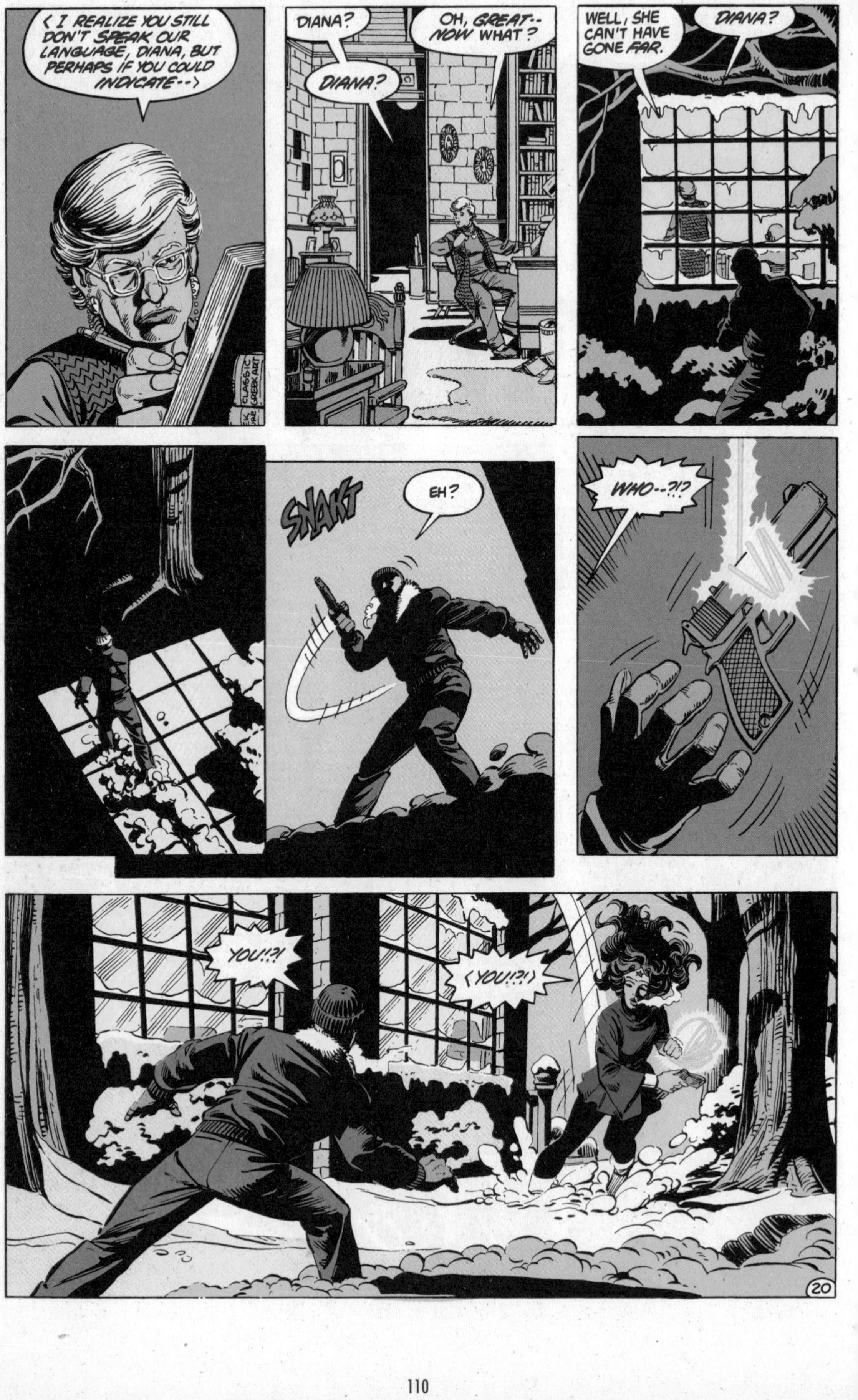

< I REALIZE YOU STILL DON'T SPEAK OUR LANGUAGE, DIANA, BUT PERHAPS IF YOU COULD INDICATE-- >
CLASSIC GREEK ART
DIANA?
DIANA?
OH, GREAT-- NOW WHAT?
WELL, SHE CAN'T HAVE GONE FAR.
DIANA?
SNAKT
EH?
WHO--?!?
YOU!?!
< YOU!?! >
20

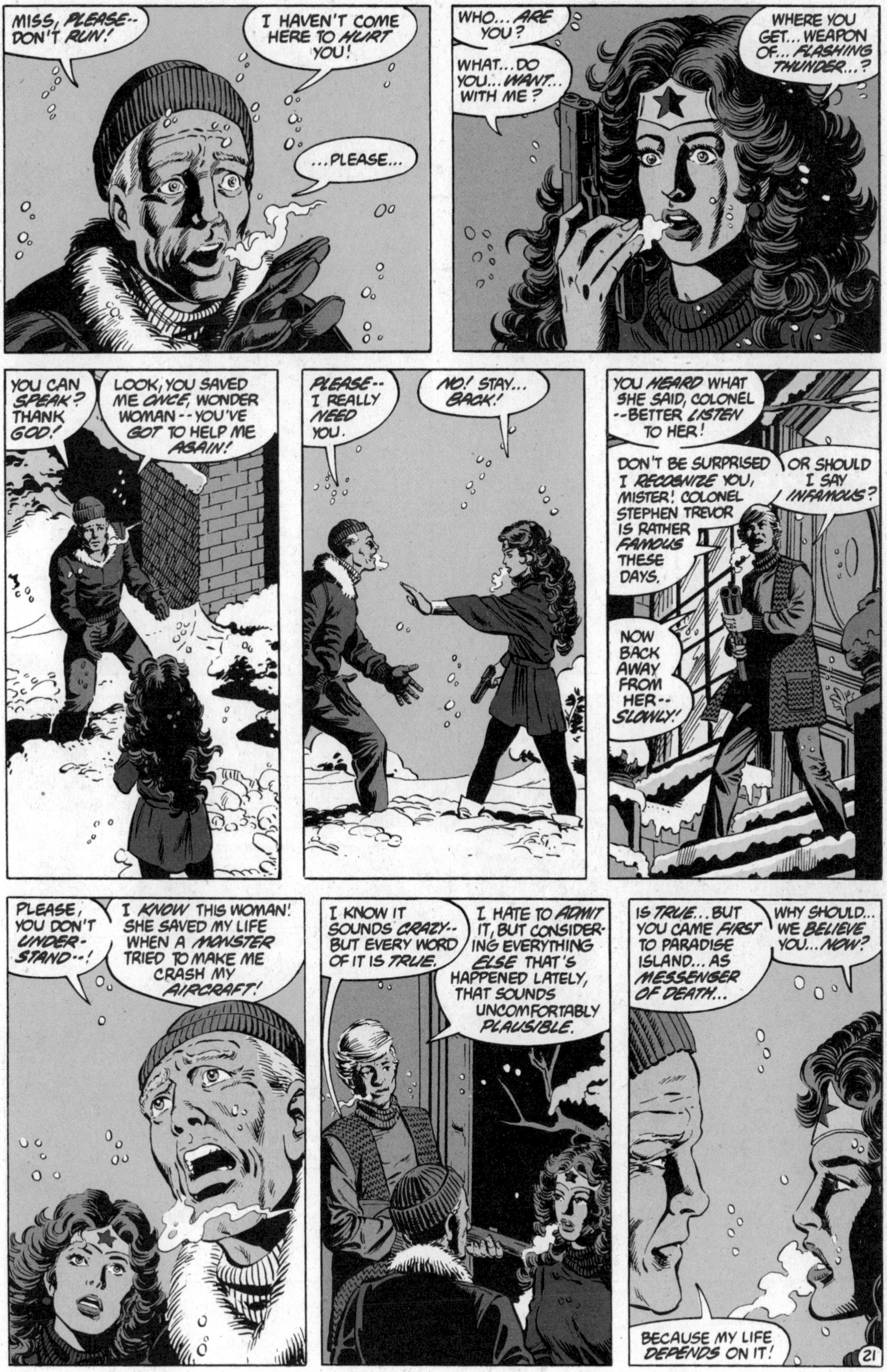
MISS, PLEASE-- DON'T RUN!
I HAVEN'T COME HERE TO HURT YOU!
...PLEASE...
WHO... ARE YOU?
WHAT... DO YOU... WANT... WITH ME?
WHERE YOU GET... WEAPON OF... FLASHING THUNDER...?
YOU CAN SPEAK? THANK GOD!
LOOK, YOU SAVED ME ONCE, WONDER WOMAN -- YOU'VE GOT TO HELP ME AGAIN!
PLEASE-- I REALLY NEED YOU.
NO! STAY... BACK!
YOU HEARD WHAT SHE SAID, COLONEL --BETTER LISTEN TO HER!
DON'T BE SURPRISED I RECOGNIZE YOU, MISTER! COLONEL STEPHEN TREVOR IS RATHER FAMOUS THESE DAYS.
OR SHOULD I SAY INFAMOUS?
NOW BACK AWAY FROM HER-- SLOWLY!
PLEASE, YOU DON'T UNDER-STAND--!
I KNOW THIS WOMAN! SHE SAVED MY LIFE WHEN A MONSTER TRIED TO MAKE ME CRASH MY AIRCRAFT!
I KNOW IT SOUNDS CRAZY-- BUT EVERY WORD OF IT IS TRUE.
I HATE TO ADMIT IT, BUT CONSIDER-ING EVERYTHING ELSE THAT'S HAPPENED LATELY, THAT SOUNDS UNCOMFORTABLY PLAUSIBLE.
IS TRUE... BUT YOU CAME FIRST TO PARADISE ISLAND... AS MESSENGER OF DEATH...
WHY SHOULD... WE BELIEVE YOU... NOW?
BECAUSE MY LIFE DEPENDS ON IT!
21

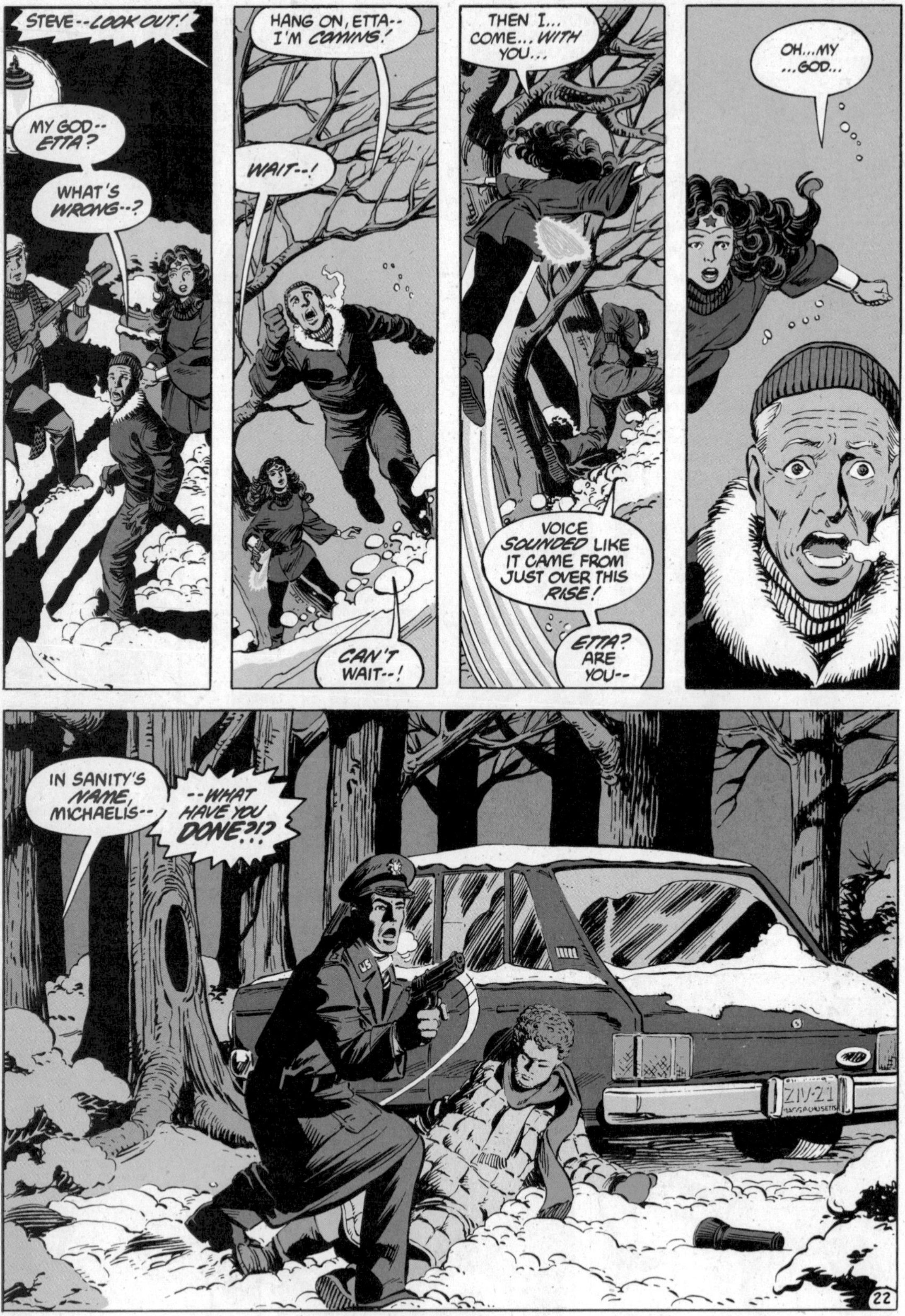

STEVE--LOOK OUT!
MY GOD--ETTA?
WHAT'S WRONG--?
HANG ON, ETTA--I'M COMING!
WAIT--!
CAN'T WAIT--!
THEN I... COME... WITH YOU...
VOICE SOUNDED LIKE IT CAME FROM JUST OVER THIS RISE!
ETTA? ARE YOU--
OH...MY ...GOD...
IN SANITY'S NAME, MICHAELIS--
--WHAT HAVE YOU DONE?!?

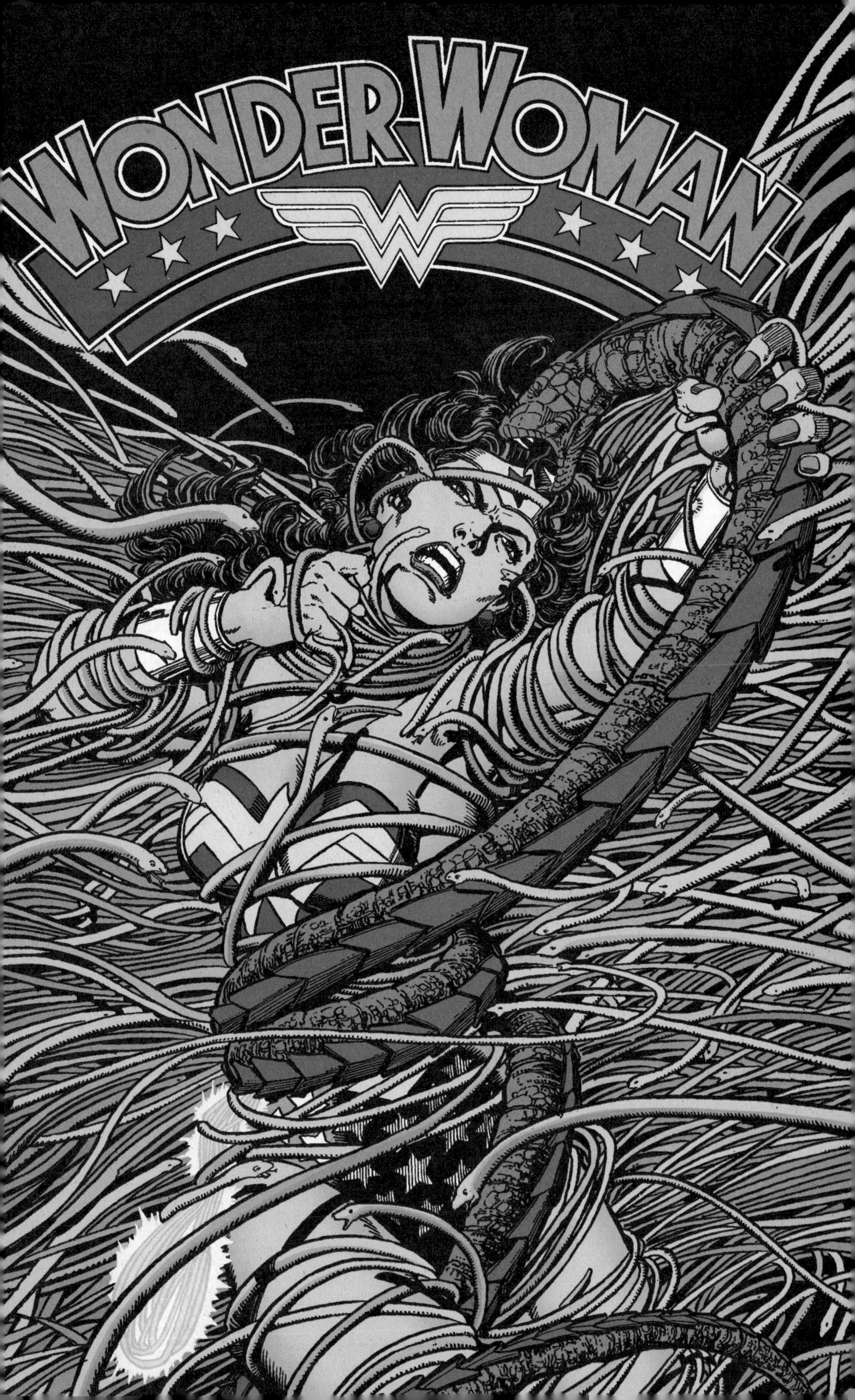
WONDER WOMAN

WONDER WOMAN

CHAPTER FIVE

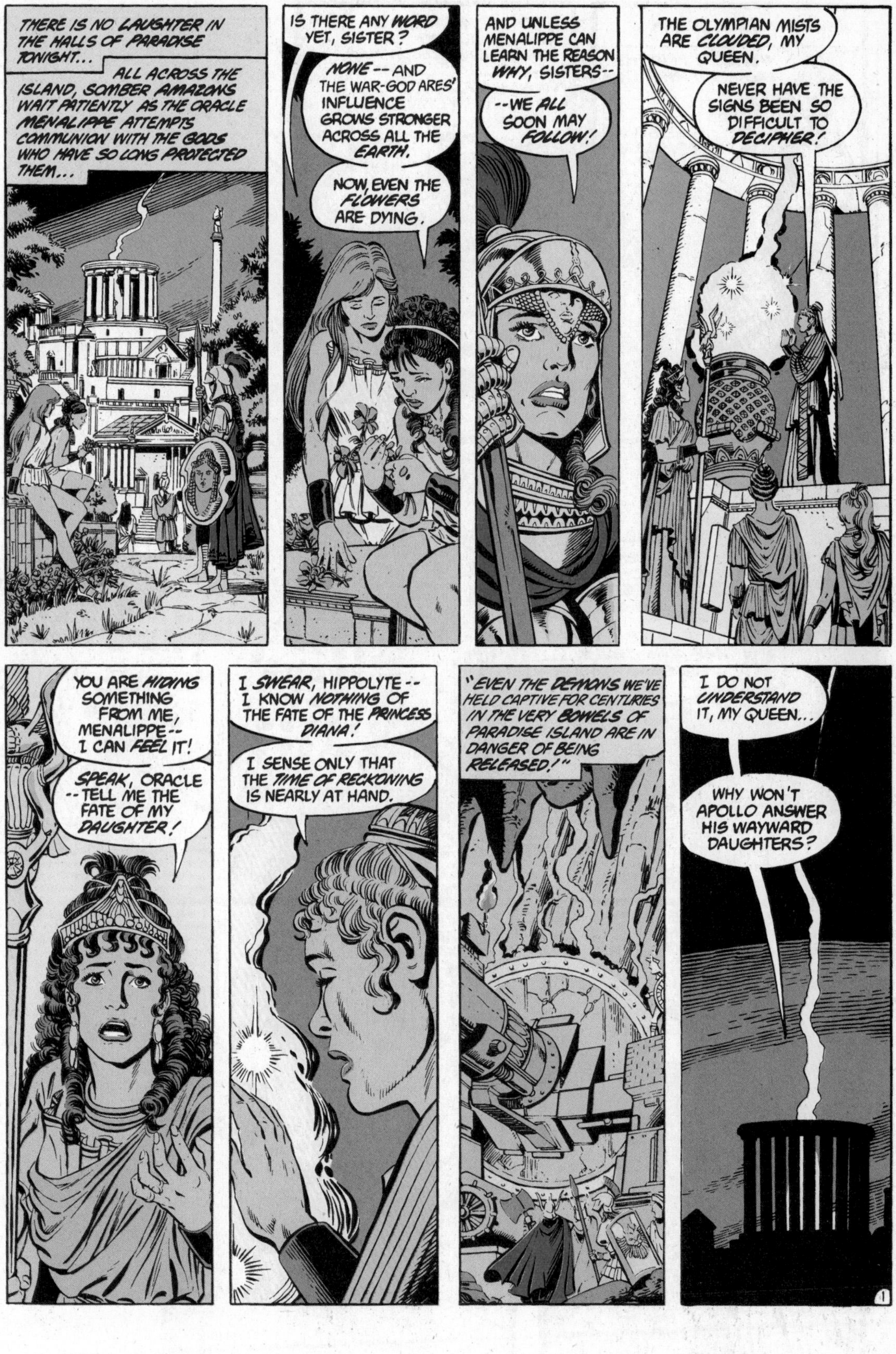
THERE IS NO LAUGHTER IN THE HALLS OF PARADISE TONIGHT...
ALL ACROSS THE ISLAND, SOMBER AMAZONS WAIT PATIENTLY AS THE ORACLE MENALIPPE ATTEMPTS COMMUNION WITH THE GODS WHO HAVE SO LONG PROTECTED THEM...
IS THERE ANY WORD YET, SISTER?
NONE -- AND THE WAR-GOD ARES' INFLUENCE GROWS STRONGER ACROSS ALL THE EARTH.
NOW, EVEN THE FLOWERS ARE DYING.
AND UNLESS MENALIPPE CAN LEARN THE REASON WHY, SISTERS--
--WE ALL SOON MAY FOLLOW!
THE OLYMPIAN MISTS ARE CLOUDED, MY QUEEN.
NEVER HAVE THE SIGNS BEEN SO DIFFICULT TO DECIPHER!
YOU ARE HIDING SOMETHING FROM ME, MENALIPPE-- I CAN FEEL IT!
SPEAK, ORACLE --TELL ME THE FATE OF MY DAUGHTER!
I SWEAR, HIPPOLYTE-- I KNOW NOTHING OF THE FATE OF THE PRINCESS DIANA!
I SENSE ONLY THAT THE TIME OF RECKONING IS NEARLY AT HAND.
"EVEN THE DEMONS WE'VE HELD CAPTIVE FOR CENTURIES IN THE VERY BOWELS OF PARADISE ISLAND ARE IN DANGER OF BEING RELEASED!"
I DO NOT UNDERSTAND IT, MY QUEEN...
WHY WON'T APOLLO ANSWER HIS WAYWARD DAUGHTERS?
1

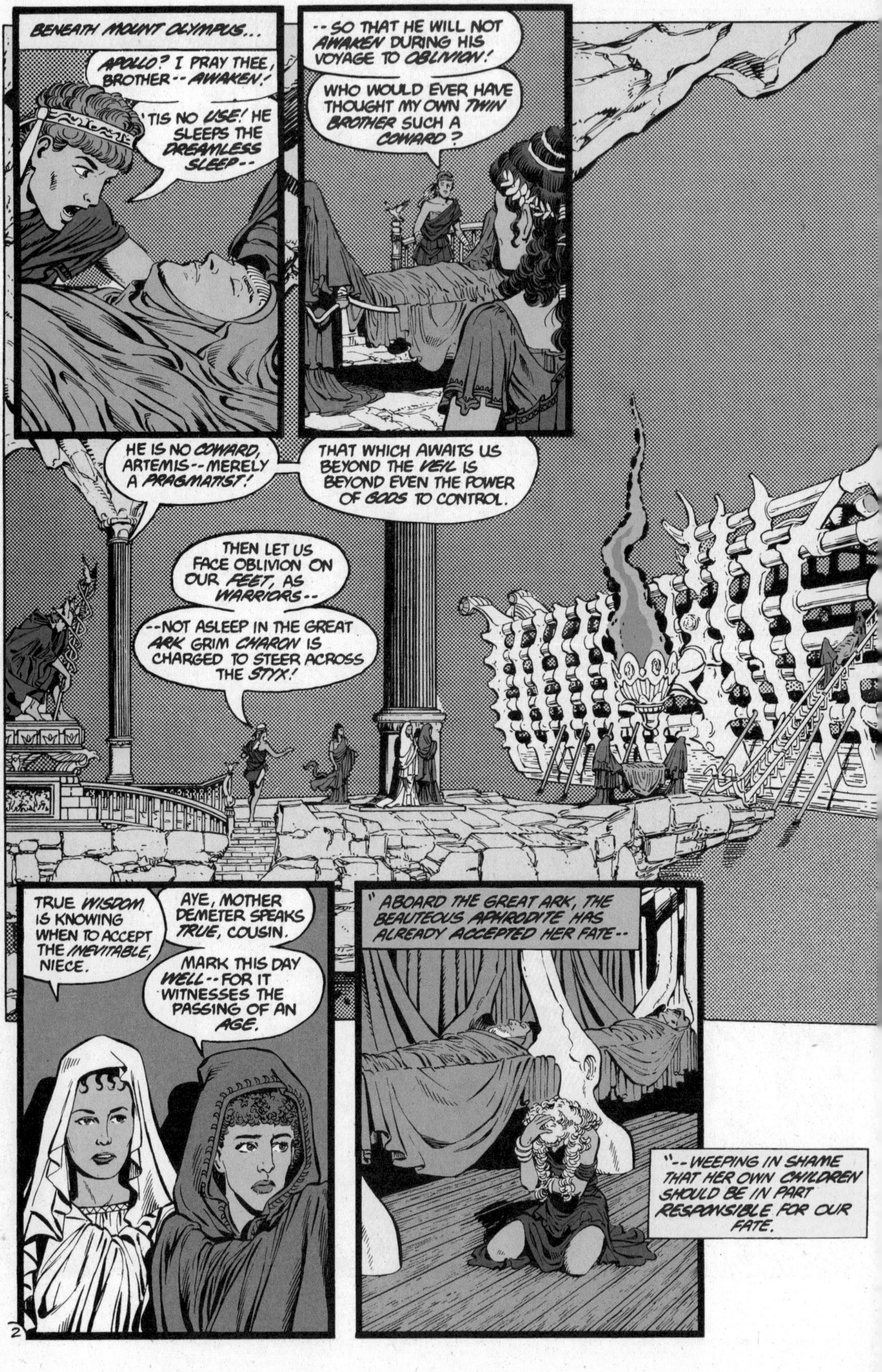
BENEATH MOUNT OLYMPUS...
APOLLO? I PRAY THEE, BROTHER--AWAKEN!
'TIS NO USE! HE SLEEPS THE DREAMLESS SLEEP--
--SO THAT HE WILL NOT AWAKEN DURING HIS VOYAGE TO OBLIVION!
WHO WOULD EVER HAVE THOUGHT MY OWN TWIN BROTHER SUCH A COWARD?
HE IS NO COWARD, ARTEMIS--MERELY A PRAGMATIST!
THAT WHICH AWAITS US BEYOND THE VEIL IS BEYOND EVEN THE POWER OF GODS TO CONTROL.
THEN LET US FACE OBLIVION ON OUR FEET, AS WARRIORS--
--NOT ASLEEP IN THE GREAT ARK GRIM CHARON IS CHARGED TO STEER ACROSS THE STYX!
TRUE WISDOM IS KNOWING WHEN TO ACCEPT THE INEVITABLE, NIECE.
AYE, MOTHER DEMETER SPEAKS TRUE, COUSIN.
MARK THIS DAY WELL--FOR IT WITNESSES THE PASSING OF AN AGE.
"ABOARD THE GREAT ARK, THE BEAUTEOUS APHRODITE HAS ALREADY ACCEPTED HER FATE--
"--WEEPING IN SHAME THAT HER OWN CHILDREN SHOULD BE IN PART RESPONSIBLE FOR OUR FATE.
2

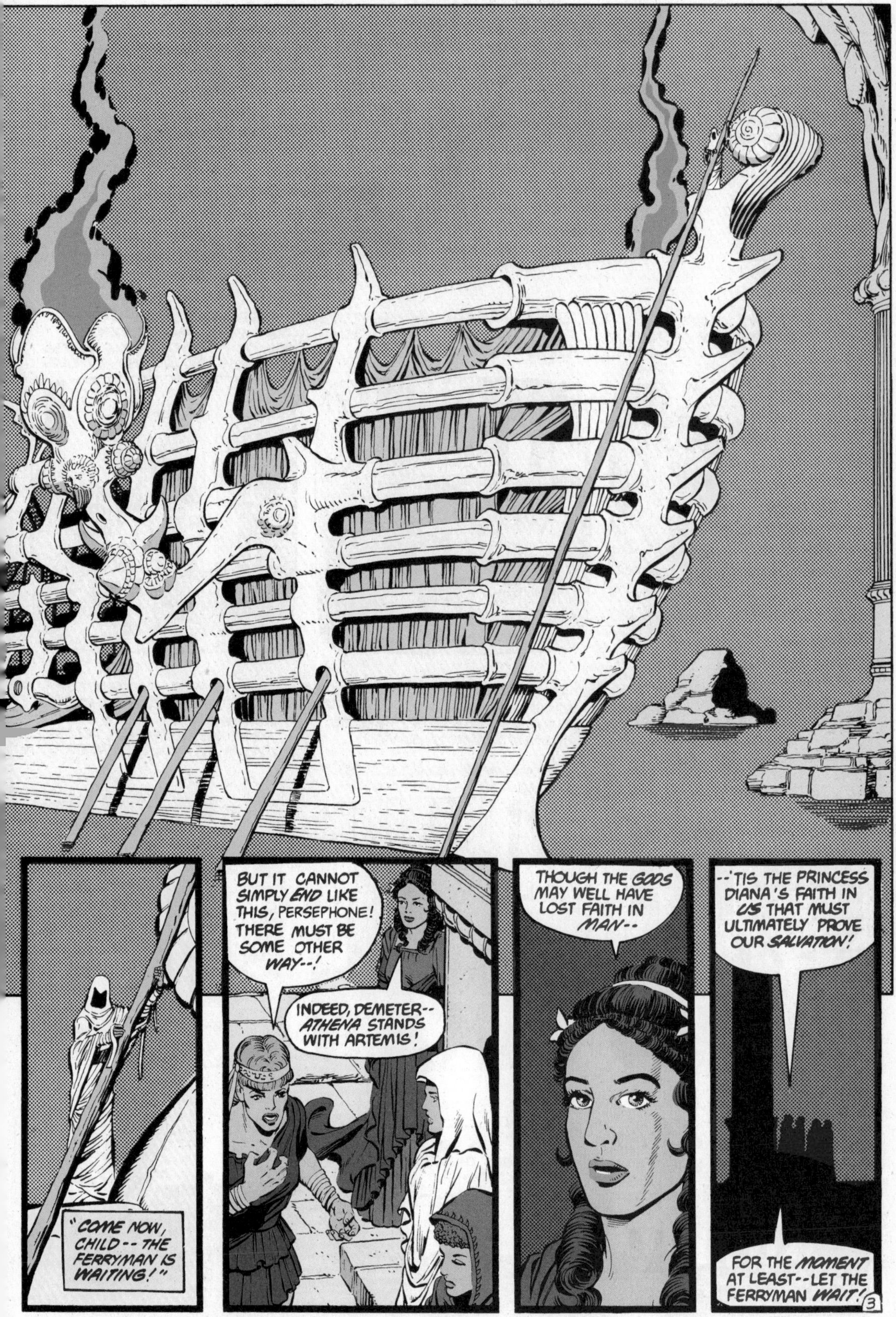
"COME NOW, CHILD -- THE FERRYMAN IS WAITING!"
BUT IT CANNOT SIMPLY END LIKE THIS, PERSEPHONE! THERE MUST BE SOME OTHER WAY--!
INDEED, DEMETER-- ATHENA STANDS WITH ARTEMIS!
THOUGH THE GODS MAY WELL HAVE LOST FAITH IN MAN--
--'TIS THE PRINCESS DIANA'S FAITH IN US THAT MUST ULTIMATELY PROVE OUR SALVATION!
FOR THE MOMENT AT LEAST--LET THE FERRYMAN WAIT!
3

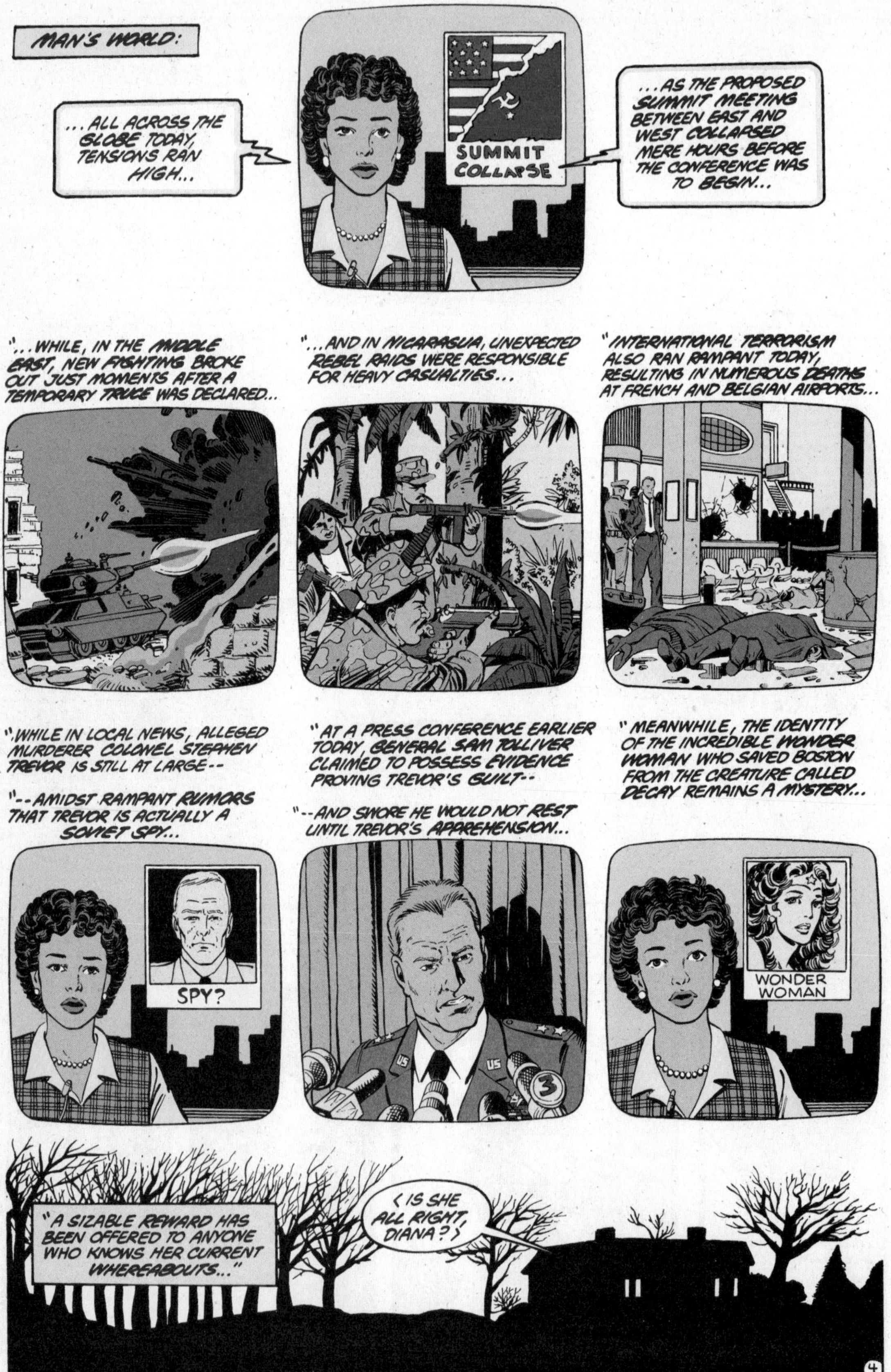
MAN'S WORLD:
...ALL ACROSS THE GLOBE TODAY, TENSIONS RAN HIGH...
SUMMIT COLLAPSE
...AS THE PROPOSED SUMMIT MEETING BETWEEN EAST AND WEST COLLAPSED MERE HOURS BEFORE THE CONFERENCE WAS TO BEGIN...
"...WHILE, IN THE MIDDLE EAST, NEW FIGHTING BROKE OUT JUST MOMENTS AFTER A TEMPORARY TRUCE WAS DECLARED...
"...AND IN NICARAGUA, UNEXPECTED REBEL RAIDS WERE RESPONSIBLE FOR HEAVY CASUALTIES...
"INTERNATIONAL TERRORISM ALSO RAN RAMPANT TODAY, RESULTING IN NUMEROUS DEATHS AT FRENCH AND BELGIAN AIRPORTS...
"WHILE IN LOCAL NEWS, ALLEGED MURDERER COLONEL STEPHEN TREVOR IS STILL AT LARGE--
"--AMIDST RAMPANT RUMORS THAT TREVOR IS ACTUALLY A SOVIET SPY...
SPY?
"AT A PRESS CONFERENCE EARLIER TODAY, GENERAL SAM TOLLIVER CLAIMED TO POSSESS EVIDENCE PROVING TREVOR'S GUILT--
"--AND SWORE HE WOULD NOT REST UNTIL TREVOR'S APPREHENSION...
US
US
3
"MEANWHILE, THE IDENTITY OF THE INCREDIBLE WONDER WOMAN WHO SAVED BOSTON FROM THE CREATURE CALLED DECAY REMAINS A MYSTERY...
WONDER WOMAN
"A SIZABLE REWARD HAS BEEN OFFERED TO ANYONE WHO KNOWS HER CURRENT WHEREABOUTS..."
‹IS SHE ALL RIGHT, DIANA?›
4

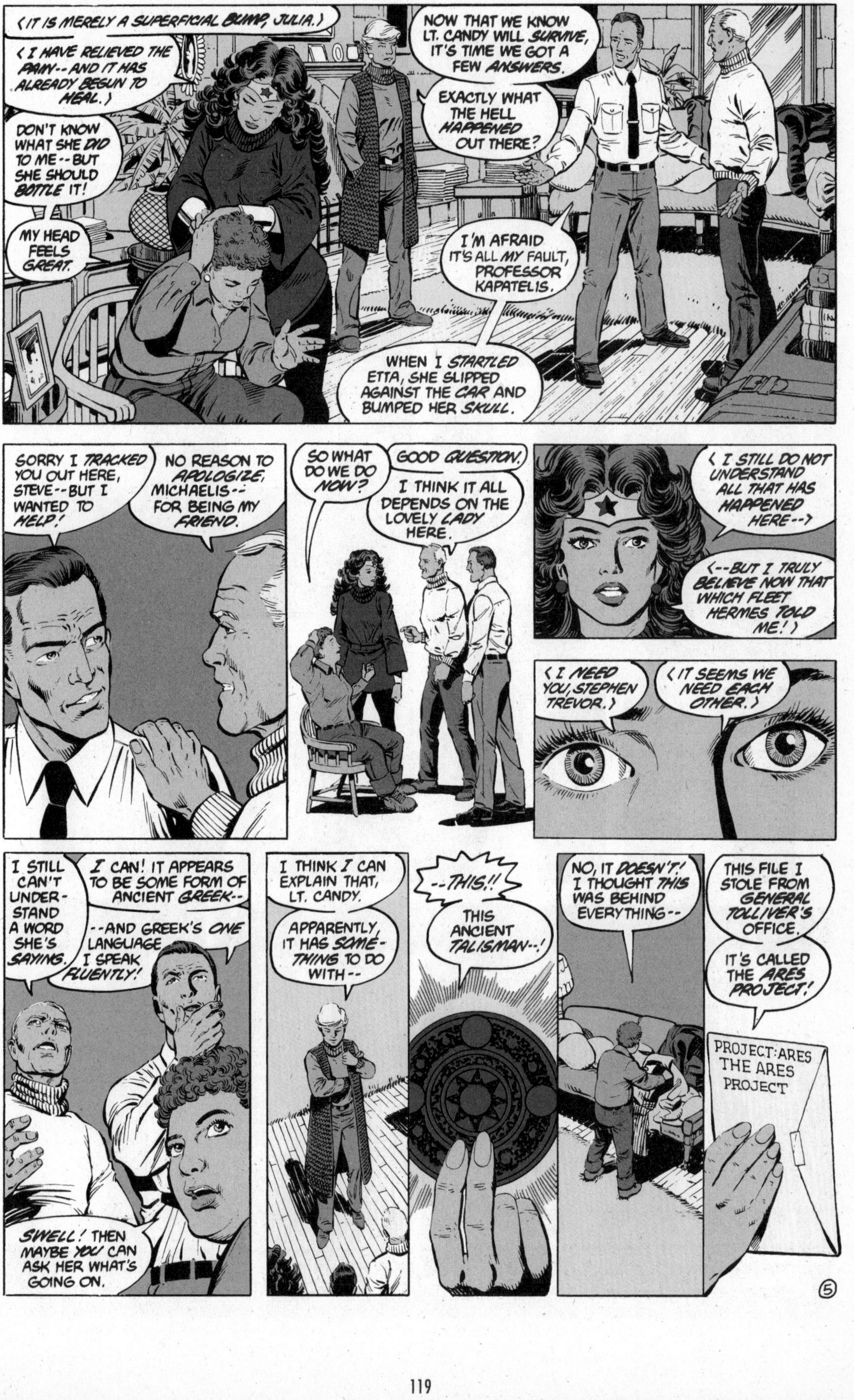
‹IT IS MERELY A SUPERFICIAL BUMP, JULIA.›
‹I HAVE RELIEVED THE PAIN--AND IT HAS ALREADY BEGUN TO HEAL.›
DON'T KNOW WHAT SHE DID TO ME--BUT SHE SHOULD BOTTLE IT!
MY HEAD FEELS GREAT.
NOW THAT WE KNOW LT. CANDY WILL SURVIVE, IT'S TIME WE GOT A FEW ANSWERS.
EXACTLY WHAT THE HELL HAPPENED OUT THERE?
I'M AFRAID IT'S ALL MY FAULT, PROFESSOR KAPATELIS.
WHEN I STARTLED ETTA, SHE SLIPPED AGAINST THE CAR AND BUMPED HER SKULL.
SORRY I TRACKED YOU OUT HERE, STEVE--BUT I WANTED TO HELP!
NO REASON TO APOLOGIZE, MICHAELIS--FOR BEING MY FRIEND.
SO WHAT DO WE DO NOW?
GOOD QUESTION.
I THINK IT ALL DEPENDS ON THE LOVELY LADY HERE.
‹I STILL DO NOT UNDERSTAND ALL THAT HAS HAPPENED HERE--›
‹--BUT I TRULY BELIEVE NOW THAT WHICH FLEET HERMES TOLD ME!›
‹I NEED YOU, STEPHEN TREVOR.›
‹IT SEEMS WE NEED EACH OTHER.›
I STILL CAN'T UNDERSTAND A WORD SHE'S SAYING.
I CAN! IT APPEARS TO BE SOME FORM OF ANCIENT GREEK--
--AND GREEK'S ONE LANGUAGE I SPEAK FLUENTLY!
SWELL! THEN MAYBE YOU CAN ASK HER WHAT'S GOING ON.
I THINK I CAN EXPLAIN THAT, LT. CANDY.
APPARENTLY, IT HAS SOMETHING TO DO WITH--
--THIS!!
THIS ANCIENT TALISMAN--!
NO, IT DOESN'T! I THOUGHT THIS WAS BEHIND EVERYTHING--
THIS FILE I STOLE FROM GENERAL TOLLIVER'S OFFICE.
IT'S CALLED THE ARES PROJECT!
PROJECT: ARES
THE ARES PROJECT
5

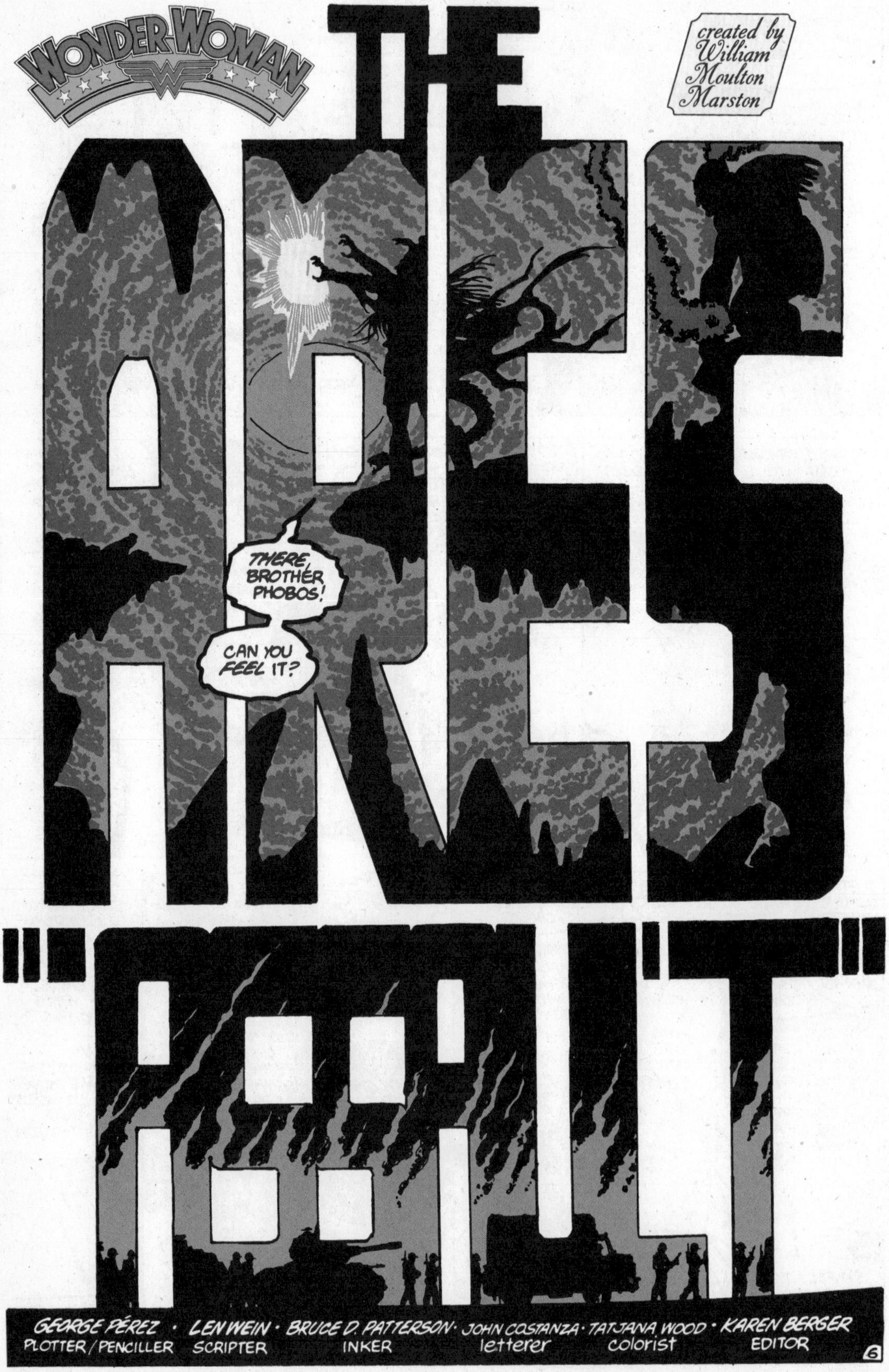
WONDER WOMAN
created by William Moulton Marston
THE ARES "BUSINESS"
THERE, BROTHER PHOBOS!
CAN YOU FEEL IT?
GEORGE PÉREZ PLOTTER/PENCILLER · LEN WEIN SCRIPTER · BRUCE D. PATTERSON INKER · JOHN COSTANZA letterer · TATJANA WOOD colorist · KAREN BERGER EDITOR
6

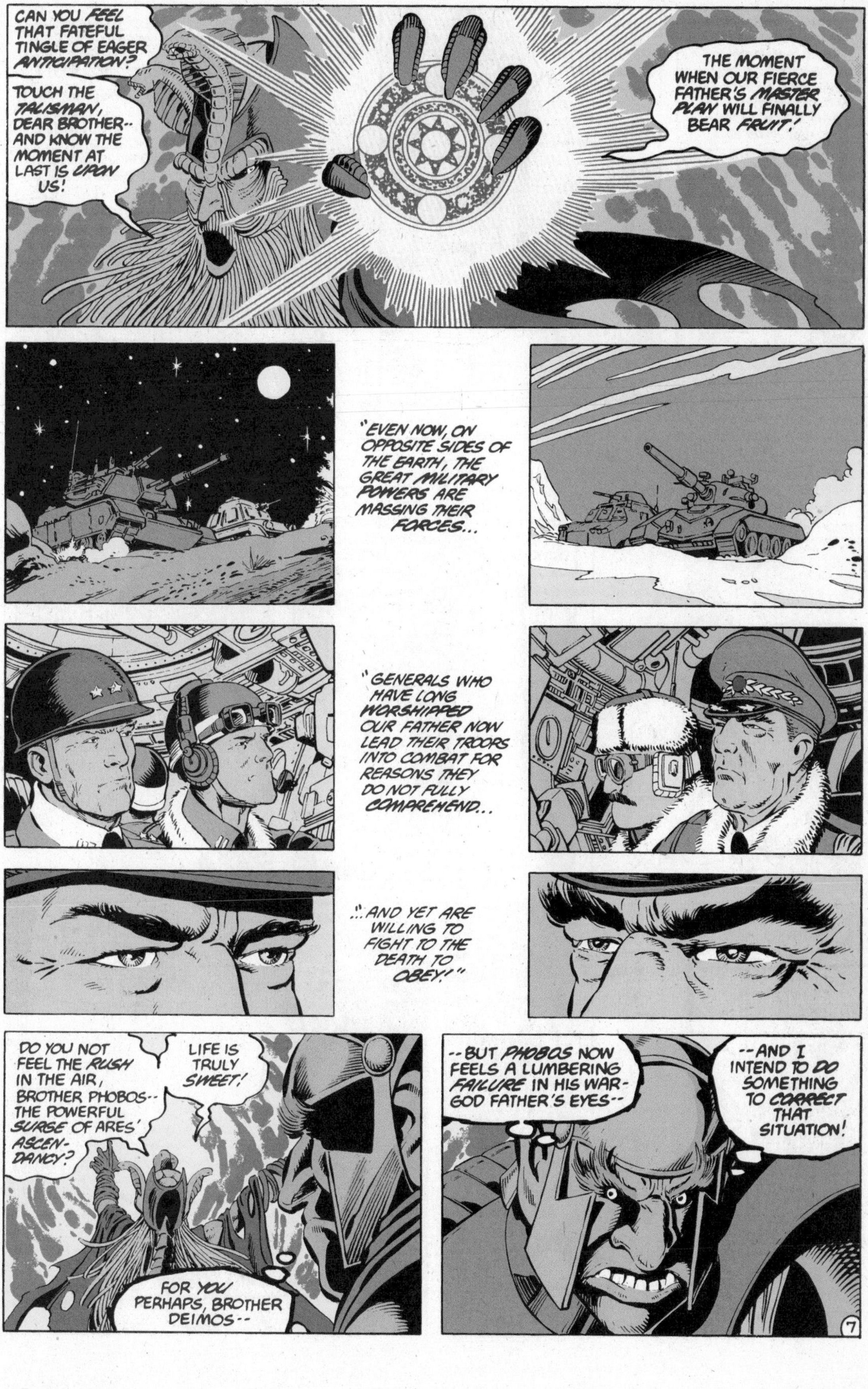

CAN YOU FEEL THAT FATEFUL TINGLE OF EAGER ANTICIPATION?
TOUCH THE TALISMAN, DEAR BROTHER-- AND KNOW THE MOMENT AT LAST IS UPON US!
THE MOMENT WHEN OUR FIERCE FATHER'S MASTER PLAN WILL FINALLY BEAR FRUIT!
"EVEN NOW, ON OPPOSITE SIDES OF THE EARTH, THE GREAT MILITARY POWERS ARE MASSING THEIR FORCES...
"GENERALS WHO HAVE LONG WORSHIPPED OUR FATHER NOW LEAD THEIR TROOPS INTO COMBAT FOR REASONS THEY DO NOT FULLY COMPREHEND...
"...AND YET ARE WILLING TO FIGHT TO THE DEATH TO OBEY!"
DO YOU NOT FEEL THE RUSH IN THE AIR, BROTHER PHOBOS-- THE POWERFUL SURGE OF ARES' ASCEN-DANCY?
LIFE IS TRULY SWEET!
FOR YOU PERHAPS, BROTHER DEIMOS--
--BUT PHOBOS NOW FEELS A LUMBERING FAILURE IN HIS WAR-GOD FATHER'S EYES--
--AND I INTEND TO DO SOMETHING TO CORRECT THAT SITUATION!
7

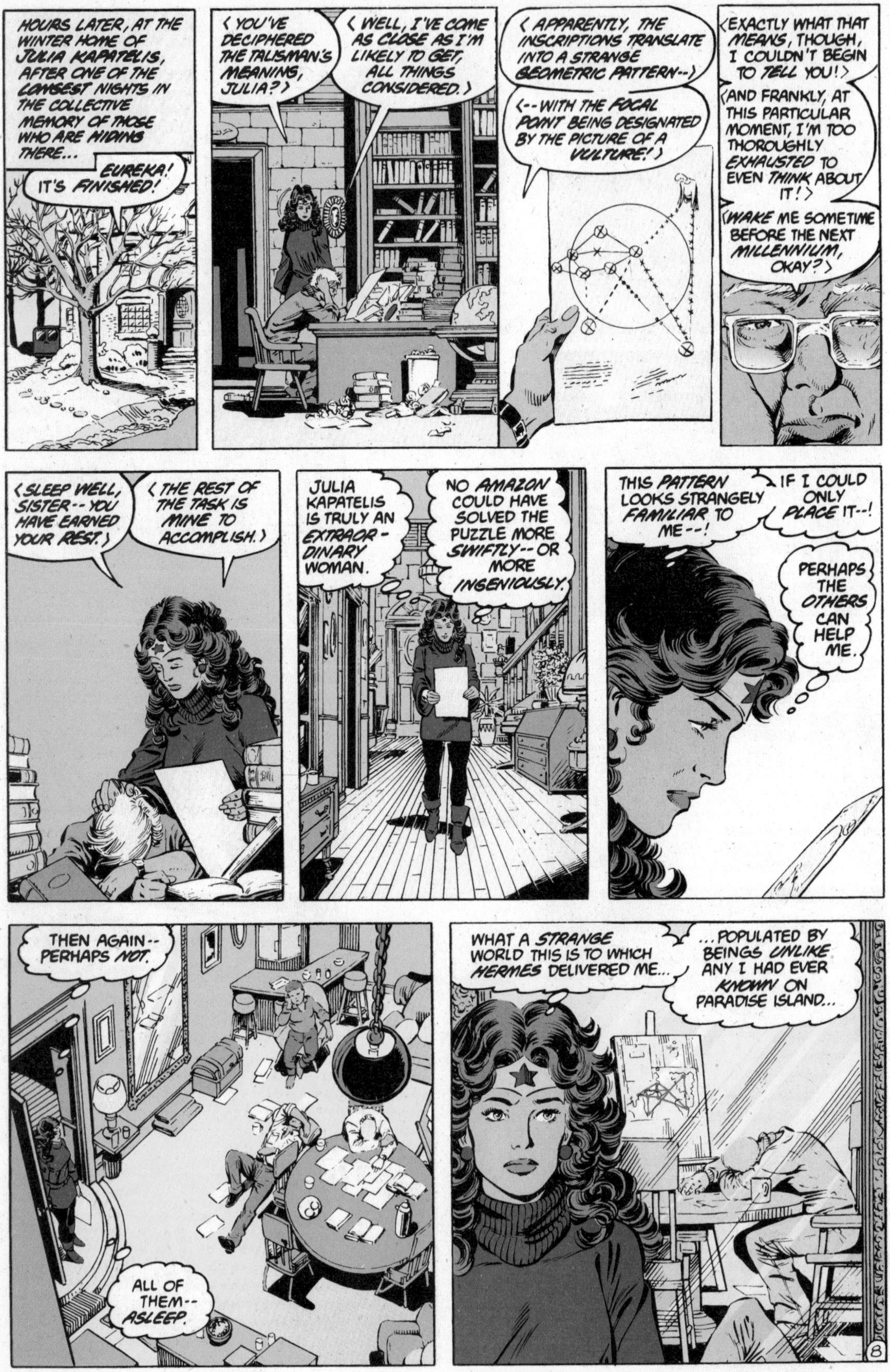
HOURS LATER, AT THE WINTER HOME OF JULIA KAPATELIS, AFTER ONE OF THE LONGEST NIGHTS IN THE COLLECTIVE MEMORY OF THOSE WHO ARE HIDING THERE...
EUREKA! IT'S FINISHED!
‹YOU'VE DECIPHERED THE TALISMAN'S MEANING, JULIA?›
‹WELL, I'VE COME AS CLOSE AS I'M LIKELY TO GET, ALL THINGS CONSIDERED.›
‹APPARENTLY, THE INSCRIPTIONS TRANSLATE INTO A STRANGE GEOMETRIC PATTERN--›
‹--WITH THE FOCAL POINT BEING DESIGNATED BY THE PICTURE OF A VULTURE!›
‹EXACTLY WHAT THAT MEANS, THOUGH, I COULDN'T BEGIN TO TELL YOU!›
‹AND FRANKLY, AT THIS PARTICULAR MOMENT, I'M TOO THOROUGHLY EXHAUSTED TO EVEN THINK ABOUT IT!›
‹WAKE ME SOMETIME BEFORE THE NEXT MILLENNIUM, OKAY?›
‹SLEEP WELL, SISTER-- YOU HAVE EARNED YOUR REST.›
‹THE REST OF THE TASK IS MINE TO ACCOMPLISH.›
JULIA KAPATELIS IS TRULY AN EXTRAOR-DINARY WOMAN.
NO AMAZON COULD HAVE SOLVED THE PUZZLE MORE SWIFTLY-- OR MORE INGENIOUSLY.
THIS PATTERN LOOKS STRANGELY FAMILIAR TO ME--!
IF I COULD ONLY PLACE IT--!
PERHAPS THE OTHERS CAN HELP ME.
THEN AGAIN-- PERHAPS NOT.
ALL OF THEM-- ASLEEP.
WHAT A STRANGE WORLD THIS IS TO WHICH HERMES DELIVERED ME...
...POPULATED BY BEINGS UNLIKE ANY I HAD EVER KNOWN ON PARADISE ISLAND...
8

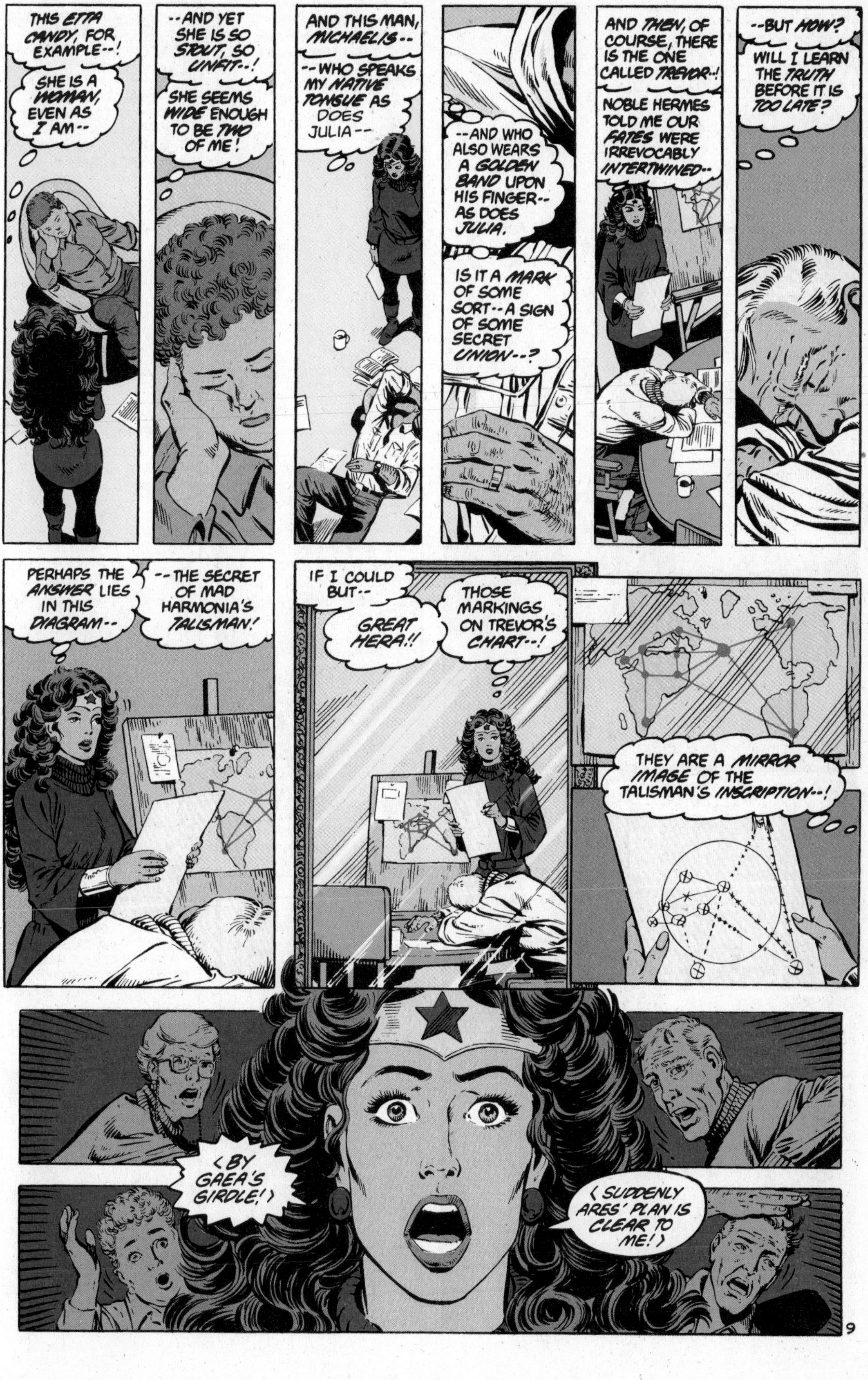
THIS ETTA CANDY, FOR EXAMPLE--!
SHE IS A WOMAN, EVEN AS I AM--
--AND YET SHE IS SO STOUT, SO UNFIT--!
SHE SEEMS WIDE ENOUGH TO BE TWO OF ME!
AND THIS MAN, MICHAELIS--
--WHO SPEAKS MY NATIVE TONGUE AS DOES JULIA--
--AND WHO ALSO WEARS A GOLDEN BAND UPON HIS FINGER--AS DOES JULIA.
IS IT A MARK OF SOME SORT--A SIGN OF SOME SECRET UNION--?
AND THEN, OF COURSE, THERE IS THE ONE CALLED TREVOR--!
NOBLE HERMES TOLD ME OUR FATES WERE IRREVOCABLY INTERTWINED--
--BUT HOW?
WILL I LEARN THE TRUTH BEFORE IT IS TOO LATE?
PERHAPS THE ANSWER LIES IN THIS DIAGRAM--
--THE SECRET OF MAD HARMONIA'S TALISMAN!
IF I COULD BUT--
GREAT HERA!!
THOSE MARKINGS ON TREVOR'S CHART--!
THEY ARE A MIRROR IMAGE OF THE TALISMAN'S INSCRIPTION--!
(BY GAEA'S GIRDLE!)
(SUDDENLY ARES' PLAN IS CLEAR TO ME!)
9

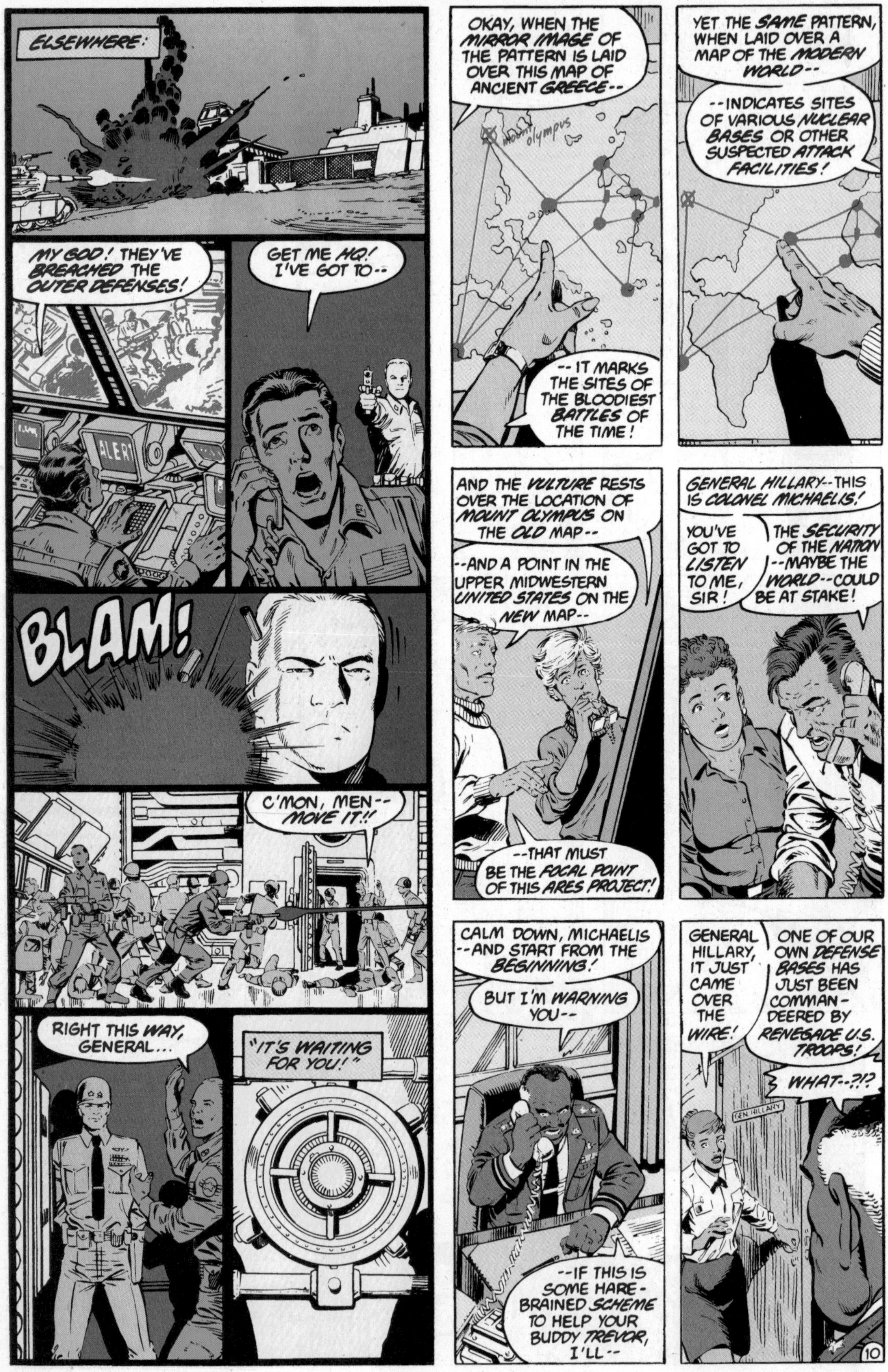
ELSEWHERE:
MY GOD! THEY'VE BREACHED THE OUTER DEFENSES!
GET ME HQ! I'VE GOT TO--
BLAM!
C'MON, MEN-- MOVE IT!!
RIGHT THIS WAY, GENERAL...
"IT'S WAITING FOR YOU!"
OKAY, WHEN THE MIRROR IMAGE OF THE PATTERN IS LAID OVER THIS MAP OF ANCIENT GREECE--
mount olympus
--IT MARKS THE SITES OF THE BLOODIEST BATTLES OF THE TIME!
YET THE SAME PATTERN, WHEN LAID OVER A MAP OF THE MODERN WORLD--
--INDICATES SITES OF VARIOUS NUCLEAR BASES OR OTHER SUSPECTED ATTACK FACILITIES!
AND THE VULTURE RESTS OVER THE LOCATION OF MOUNT OLYMPUS ON THE OLD MAP--
--AND A POINT IN THE UPPER MIDWESTERN UNITED STATES ON THE NEW MAP--
--THAT MUST BE THE FOCAL POINT OF THIS ARES PROJECT!
GENERAL HILLARY--THIS IS COLONEL MICHAELIS!
YOU'VE GOT TO LISTEN TO ME, SIR!
THE SECURITY OF THE NATION --MAYBE THE WORLD--COULD BE AT STAKE!
CALM DOWN, MICHAELIS --AND START FROM THE BEGINNING!
BUT I'M WARNING YOU--
--IF THIS IS SOME HARE-BRAINED SCHEME TO HELP YOUR BUDDY TREVOR, I'LL--
GENERAL HILLARY, IT JUST CAME OVER THE WIRE!
ONE OF OUR OWN DEFENSE BASES HAS JUST BEEN COMMAN-DEERED BY RENEGADE U.S. TROOPS!
WHAT--?!?
GEN HILLARY
10

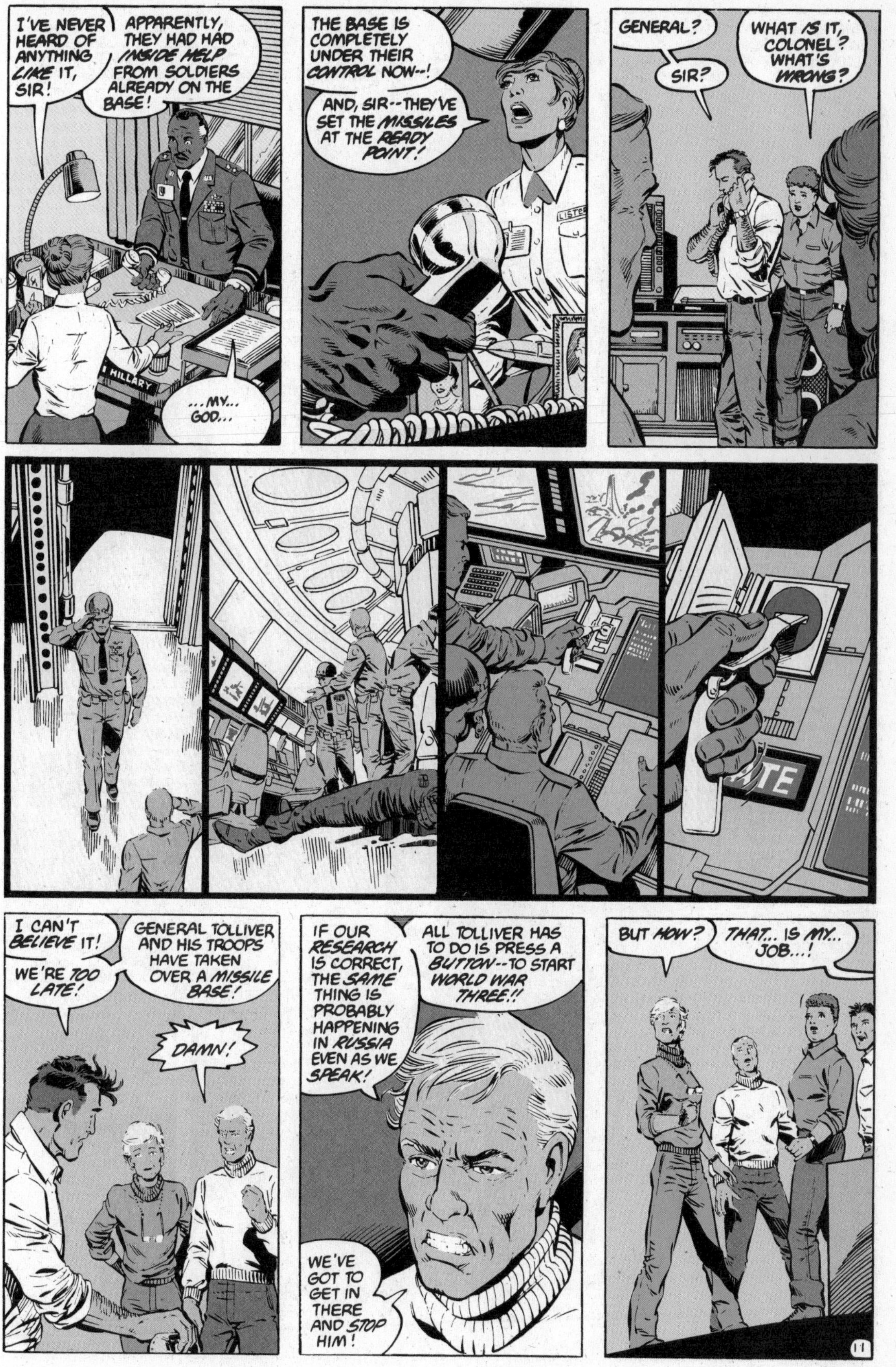
I'VE NEVER HEARD OF ANYTHING LIKE IT, SIR!
APPARENTLY, THEY HAD HAD INSIDE HELP FROM SOLDIERS ALREADY ON THE BASE!
...MY... GOD...
THE BASE IS COMPLETELY UNDER THEIR CONTROL NOW--!
AND, SIR--THEY'VE SET THE MISSILES AT THE READY POINT!
GENERAL?
SIR?
WHAT IS IT, COLONEL? WHAT'S WRONG?
I CAN'T BELIEVE IT!
WE'RE TOO LATE!
GENERAL TOLLIVER AND HIS TROOPS HAVE TAKEN OVER A MISSILE BASE!
DAMN!
IF OUR RESEARCH IS CORRECT, THE SAME THING IS PROBABLY HAPPENING IN RUSSIA EVEN AS WE SPEAK!
ALL TOLLIVER HAS TO DO IS PRESS A BUTTON--TO START WORLD WAR THREE!!
WE'VE GOT TO GET IN THERE AND STOP HIM!
BUT HOW?
THAT... IS MY... JOB...!
11

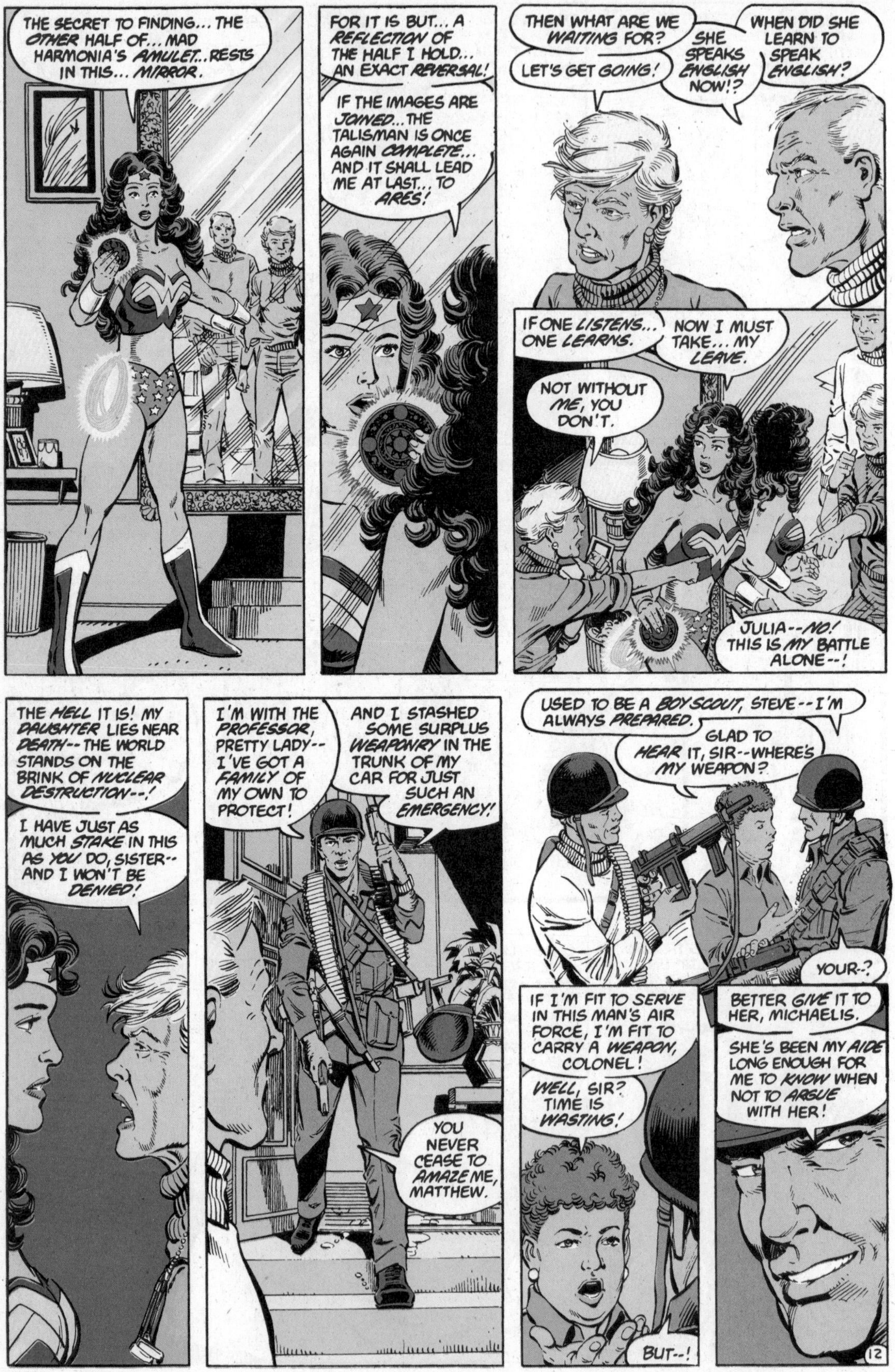
THE SECRET TO FINDING... THE OTHER HALF OF... MAD HARMONIA'S AMULET... RESTS IN THIS... MIRROR.
FOR IT IS BUT... A REFLECTION OF THE HALF I HOLD... AN EXACT REVERSAL!
IF THE IMAGES ARE JOINED... THE TALISMAN IS ONCE AGAIN COMPLETE... AND IT SHALL LEAD ME AT LAST... TO ARES!
THEN WHAT ARE WE WAITING FOR?
LET'S GET GOING!
SHE SPEAKS ENGLISH NOW!?
WHEN DID SHE LEARN TO SPEAK ENGLISH?
IF ONE LISTENS... ONE LEARNS.
NOW I MUST TAKE... MY LEAVE.
NOT WITHOUT ME, YOU DON'T.
JULIA--NO! THIS IS MY BATTLE ALONE--!
THE HELL IT IS! MY DAUGHTER LIES NEAR DEATH-- THE WORLD STANDS ON THE BRINK OF NUCLEAR DESTRUCTION--!
I HAVE JUST AS MUCH STAKE IN THIS AS YOU DO, SISTER-- AND I WON'T BE DENIED!
I'M WITH THE PROFESSOR, PRETTY LADY-- I'VE GOT A FAMILY OF MY OWN TO PROTECT!
AND I STASHED SOME SURPLUS WEAPONRY IN THE TRUNK OF MY CAR FOR JUST SUCH AN EMERGENCY!
YOU NEVER CEASE TO AMAZE ME, MATTHEW.
USED TO BE A BOY SCOUT, STEVE--I'M ALWAYS PREPARED.
GLAD TO HEAR IT, SIR--WHERE'S MY WEAPON?
YOUR--?
IF I'M FIT TO SERVE IN THIS MAN'S AIR FORCE, I'M FIT TO CARRY A WEAPON, COLONEL!
WELL, SIR? TIME IS WASTING!
BUT--!
BETTER GIVE IT TO HER, MICHAELIS.
SHE'S BEEN MY AIDE LONG ENOUGH FOR ME TO KNOW WHEN NOT TO ARGUE WITH HER!
12

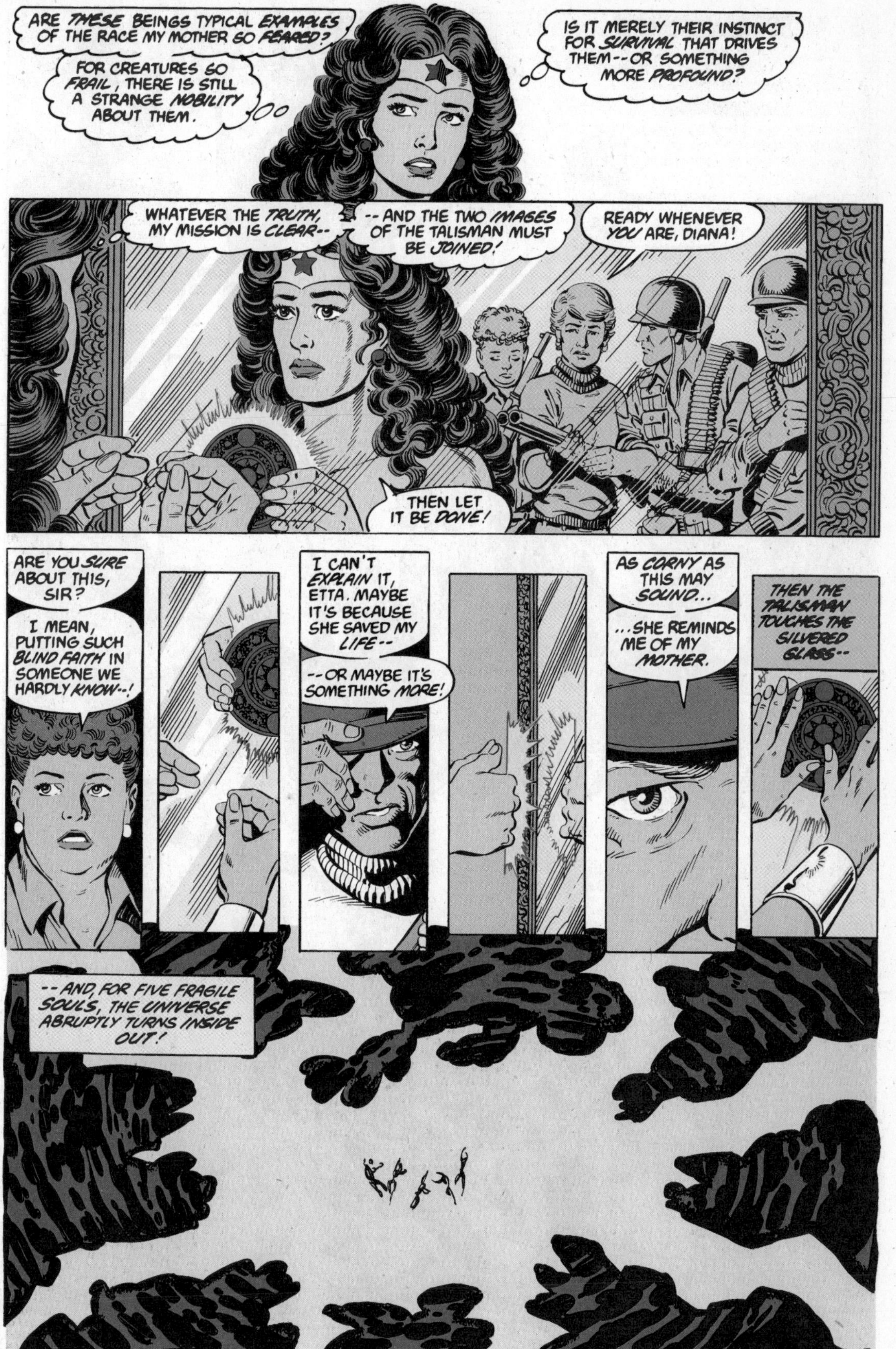

ARE THESE BEINGS TYPICAL EXAMPLES OF THE RACE MY MOTHER SO FEARED?
FOR CREATURES SO FRAIL, THERE IS STILL A STRANGE NOBILITY ABOUT THEM.
IS IT MERELY THEIR INSTINCT FOR SURVIVAL THAT DRIVES THEM--OR SOMETHING MORE PROFOUND?
WHATEVER THE TRUTH, MY MISSION IS CLEAR--
--AND THE TWO IMAGES OF THE TALISMAN MUST BE JOINED!
READY WHENEVER YOU ARE, DIANA!
THEN LET IT BE DONE!
ARE YOU SURE ABOUT THIS, SIR?
I MEAN, PUTTING SUCH BLIND FAITH IN SOMEONE WE HARDLY KNOW--!
I CAN'T EXPLAIN IT, ETTA. MAYBE IT'S BECAUSE SHE SAVED MY LIFE--
--OR MAYBE IT'S SOMETHING MORE!
AS CORNY AS THIS MAY SOUND...
...SHE REMINDS ME OF MY MOTHER.
THEN THE TALISMAN TOUCHES THE SILVERED GLASS--
--AND, FOR FIVE FRAGILE SOULS, THE UNIVERSE ABRUPTLY TURNS INSIDE OUT!
13

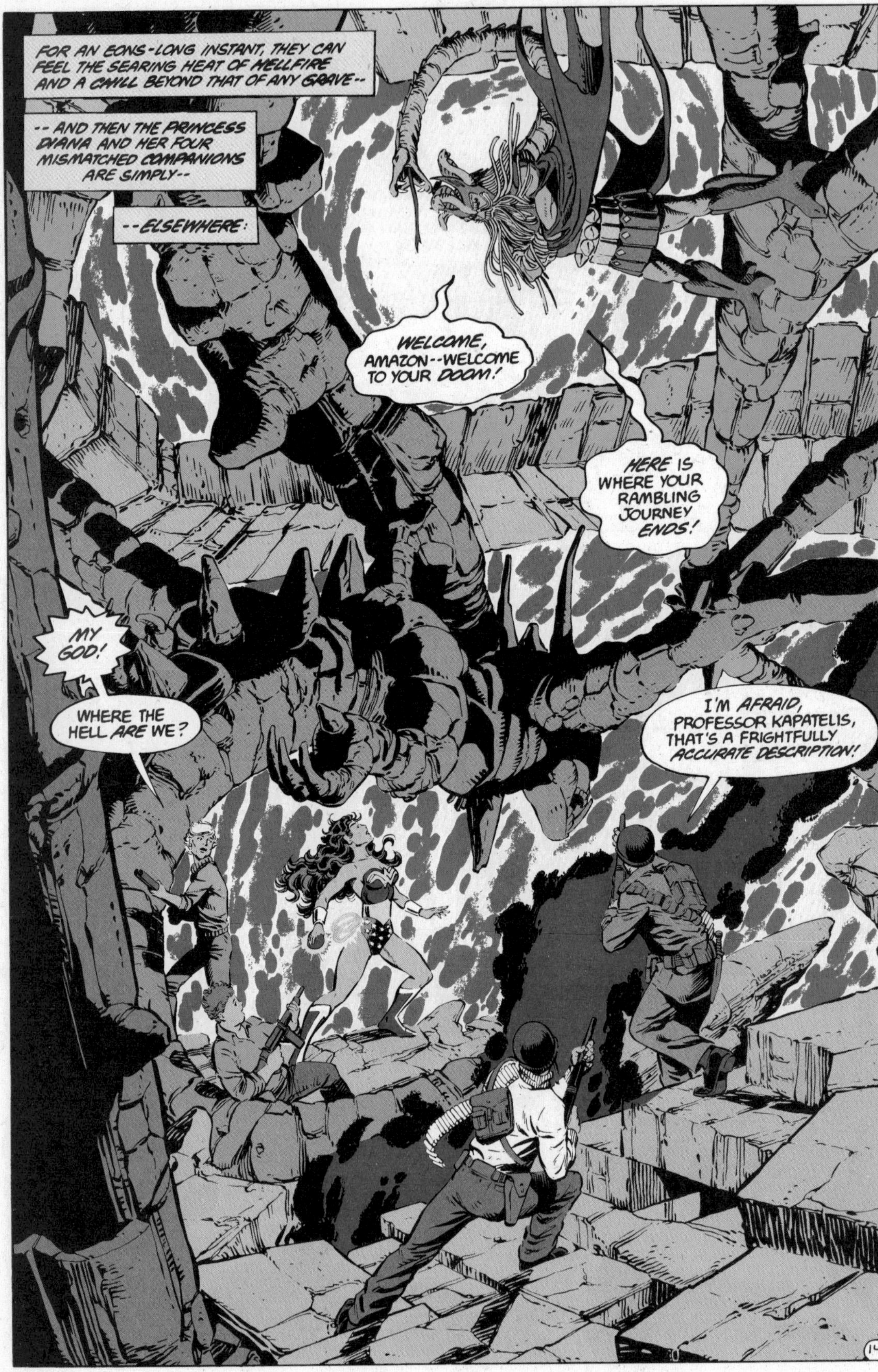

FOR AN EONS-LONG INSTANT, THEY CAN FEEL THE SEARING HEAT OF HELLFIRE AND A CHILL BEYOND THAT OF ANY GRAVE--
-- AND THEN THE PRINCESS DIANA AND HER FOUR MISMATCHED COMPANIONS ARE SIMPLY--
--ELSEWHERE!
WELCOME, AMAZON--WELCOME TO YOUR DOOM!
HERE IS WHERE YOUR RAMBLING JOURNEY ENDS!
MY GOD!
WHERE THE HELL ARE WE?
I'M AFRAID, PROFESSOR KAPATELIS, THAT'S A FRIGHTFULLY ACCURATE DESCRIPTION!
14

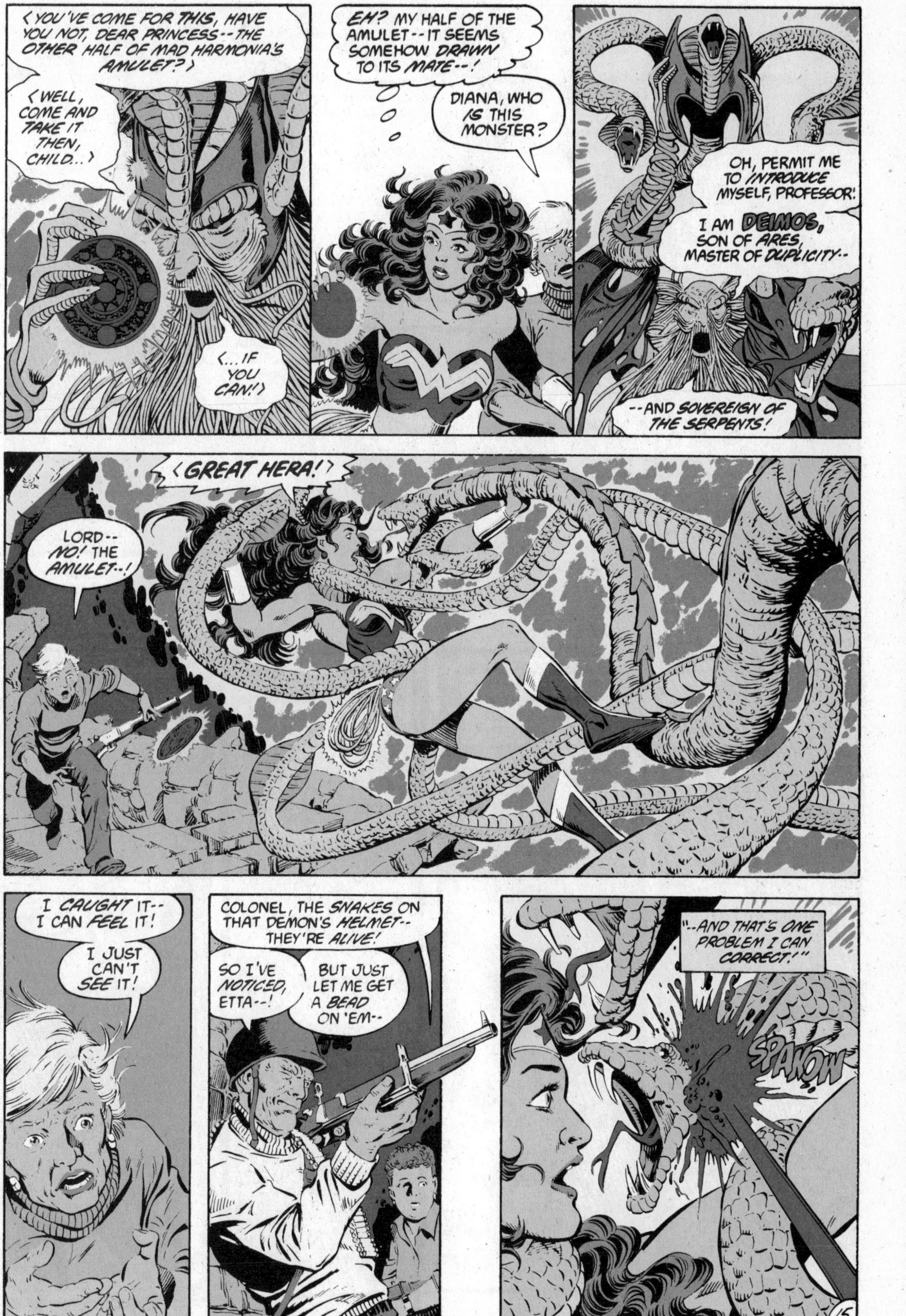

<YOU'VE COME FOR THIS, HAVE YOU NOT, DEAR PRINCESS--THE OTHER HALF OF MAD HARMONIA'S AMULET?>
<WELL, COME AND TAKE IT THEN, CHILD...>
<...IF YOU CAN!>
EH? MY HALF OF THE AMULET--IT SEEMS SOMEHOW DRAWN TO ITS MATE--!
DIANA, WHO IS THIS MONSTER?
OH, PERMIT ME TO INTRODUCE MYSELF, PROFESSOR!
I AM DEIMOS, SON OF ARES, MASTER OF DUPLICITY--
--AND SOVEREIGN OF THE SERPENTS!
<GREAT HERA!>
LORD--NO! THE AMULET--!
I CAUGHT IT--I CAN FEEL IT!
I JUST CAN'T SEE IT!
COLONEL, THE SNAKES ON THAT DEMON'S HELMET--THEY'RE ALIVE!
SO I'VE NOTICED, ETTA--!
BUT JUST LET ME GET A BEAD ON 'EM--
"--AND THAT'S ONE PROBLEM I CAN CORRECT!"
SPAKOW
15

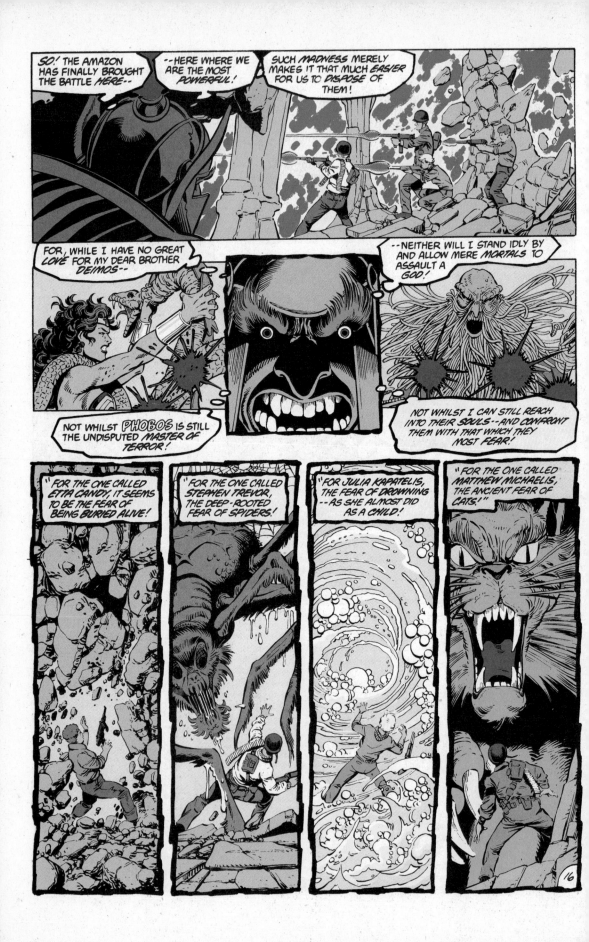

SO! THE AMAZON HAS FINALLY BROUGHT THE BATTLE *HERE*--

--HERE WHERE WE ARE THE MOST *POWERFUL!*

SUCH *MADNESS* MERELY MAKES IT THAT MUCH *EASIER* FOR US TO *DISPOSE* OF THEM!

FOR, WHILE I HAVE NO GREAT *LOVE* FOR MY DEAR BROTHER *DEIMOS*--

--NEITHER WILL I STAND IDLY BY AND ALLOW MERE *MORTALS* TO ASSAULT A *GOD!*

NOT WHILST *PHOBOS* IS STILL THE UNDISPUTED *MASTER OF TERROR!*

NOT WHILST I CAN STILL REACH INTO THEIR *SOULS*--AND CONFRONT THEM WITH THAT WHICH THEY *MOST FEAR!*

"FOR THE ONE CALLED *ETTA CANDY*, IT SEEMS TO BE THE FEAR OF BEING *BURIED ALIVE!*

"FOR THE ONE CALLED *STEPHEN TREVOR*, THE DEEP-ROOTED FEAR OF *SPIDERS!*

"FOR *JULIA KAPATELIS*, THE FEAR OF *DROWNING* --AS SHE ALMOST DID AS A *CHILD!*

"FOR THE ONE CALLED *MATTHEW MICHAELIS*, THE ANCIENT FEAR OF *CATS!*"

16

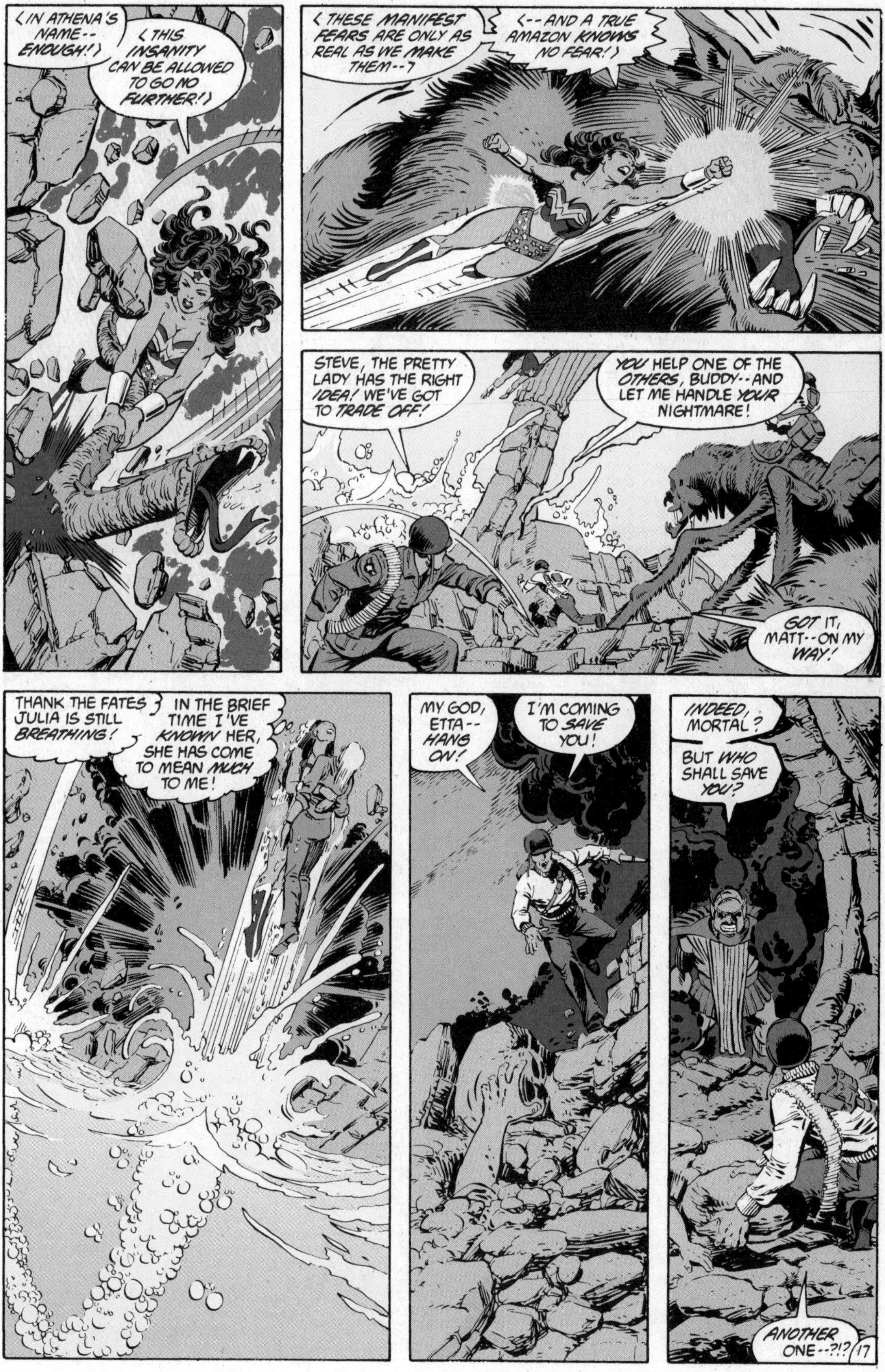

<IN ATHENA'S NAME--ENOUGH!>
<THIS INSANITY CAN BE ALLOWED TO GO NO FURTHER!>
<THESE MANIFEST FEARS ARE ONLY AS REAL AS WE MAKE THEM-->
<--AND A TRUE AMAZON KNOWS NO FEAR!>
STEVE, THE PRETTY LADY HAS THE RIGHT IDEA! WE'VE GOT TO TRADE OFF!
YOU HELP ONE OF THE OTHERS, BUDDY--AND LET ME HANDLE YOUR NIGHTMARE!
GOT IT, MATT--ON MY WAY!
THANK THE FATES JULIA IS STILL BREATHING!
IN THE BRIEF TIME I'VE KNOWN HER, SHE HAS COME TO MEAN MUCH TO ME!
MY GOD, ETTA--HANG ON!
I'M COMING TO SAVE YOU!
INDEED, MORTAL?
BUT WHO SHALL SAVE YOU?
ANOTHER ONE--?!?
17

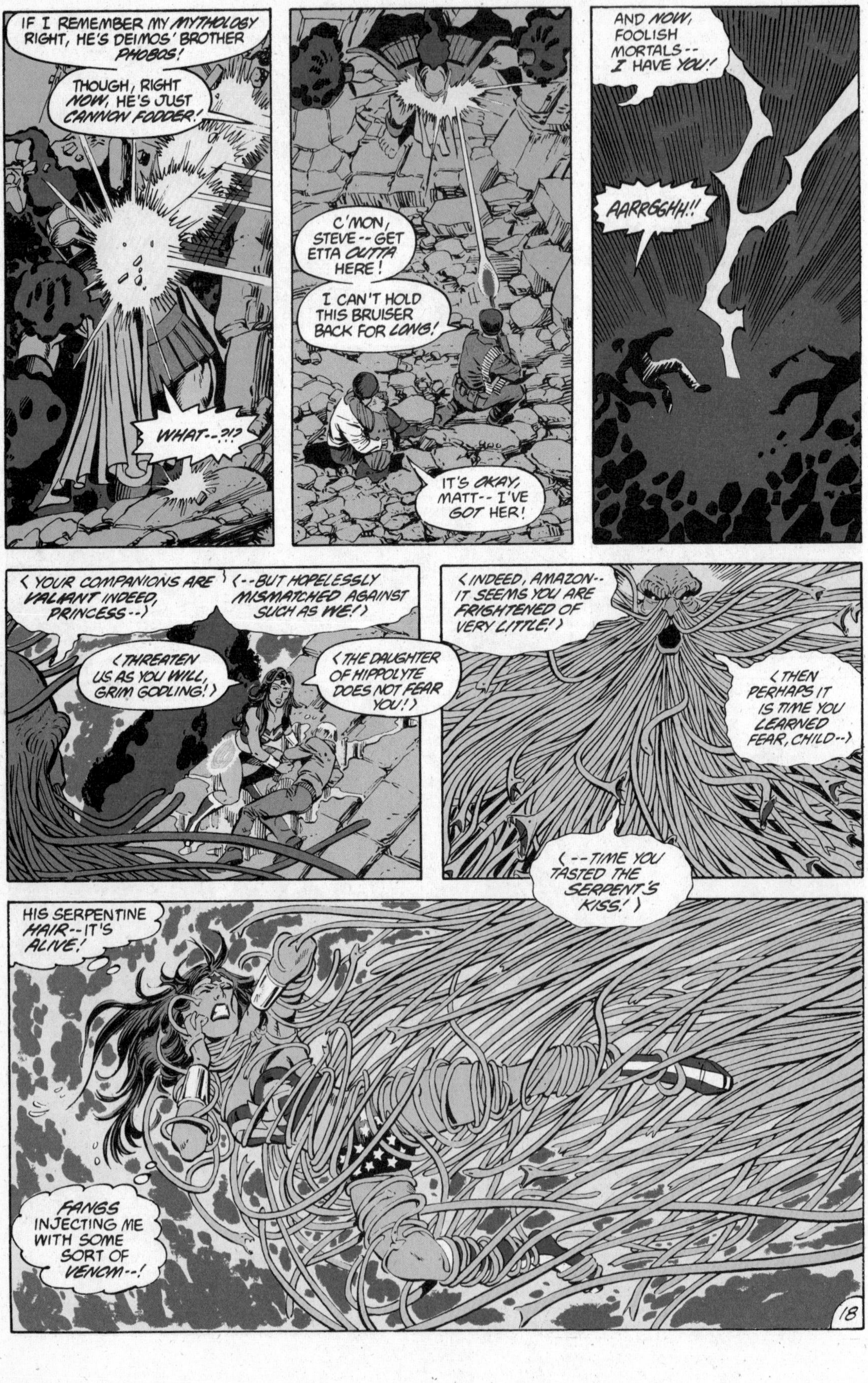
IF I REMEMBER MY MYTHOLOGY RIGHT, HE'S DEIMOS' BROTHER PHOBOS!
THOUGH, RIGHT NOW, HE'S JUST CANNON FODDER!
WHAT--?!?
C'MON, STEVE--GET ETTA OUTTA HERE!
I CAN'T HOLD THIS BRUISER BACK FOR LONG!
IT'S OKAY, MATT-- I'VE GOT HER!
AND NOW, FOOLISH MORTALS-- I HAVE YOU!
AARRGGHH!!
<YOUR COMPANIONS ARE VALIANT INDEED, PRINCESS-->
<--BUT HOPELESSLY MISMATCHED AGAINST SUCH AS WE!>
<THREATEN US AS YOU WILL, GRIM GODLING!>
<THE DAUGHTER OF HIPPOLYTE DOES NOT FEAR YOU!>
<INDEED, AMAZON-- IT SEEMS YOU ARE FRIGHTENED OF VERY LITTLE!>
<THEN PERHAPS IT IS TIME YOU LEARNED FEAR, CHILD-->
<--TIME YOU TASTED THE SERPENT'S KISS!>
HIS SERPENTINE HAIR--IT'S ALIVE!
FANGS INJECTING ME WITH SOME SORT OF VENOM--!
18

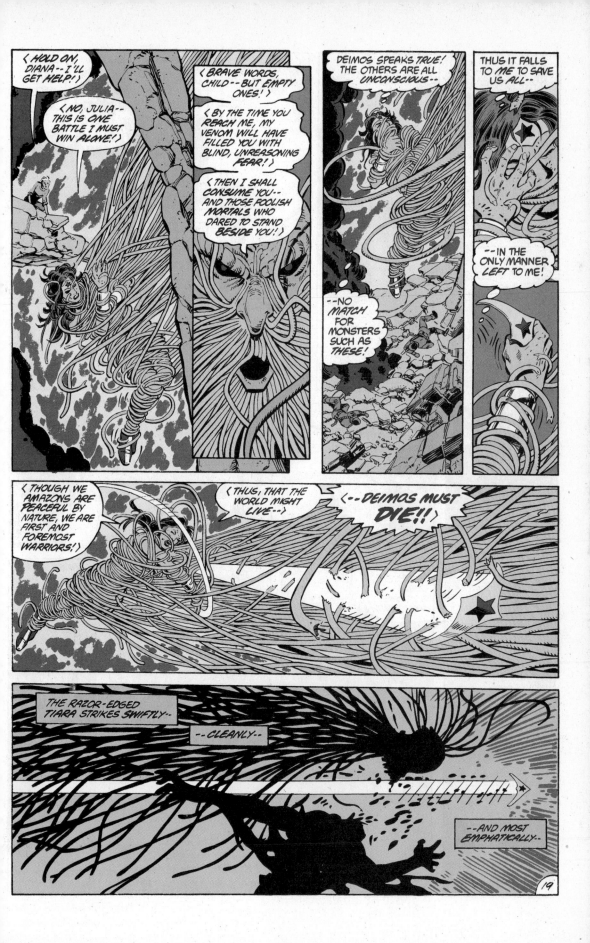

< HOLD ON, DIANA -- I'LL GET HELP! >

< NO, JULIA -- THIS IS ONE BATTLE I MUST WIN ALONE! >

< BRAVE WORDS, CHILD -- BUT EMPTY ONES! >

< BY THE TIME YOU REACH ME, MY VENOM WILL HAVE FILLED YOU WITH BLIND, UNREASONING FEAR! >

< THEN I SHALL CONSUME YOU -- AND THOSE FOOLISH MORTALS WHO DARED TO STAND BESIDE YOU! >

DEIMOS SPEAKS TRUE! THE OTHERS ARE ALL UNCONSCIOUS --

-- NO MATCH FOR MONSTERS SUCH AS THESE!

THUS IT FALLS TO ME TO SAVE US ALL --

-- IN THE ONLY MANNER LEFT TO ME!

< THOUGH WE AMAZONS ARE PEACEFUL BY NATURE, WE ARE FIRST AND FOREMOST WARRIORS! >

< THUS, THAT THE WORLD MIGHT LIVE -- >

< -- DEIMOS MUST DIE!! >

THE RAZOR-EDGED TIARA STRIKES SWIFTLY --

-- CLEANLY --

-- AND MOST EMPHATICALLY --

19

133

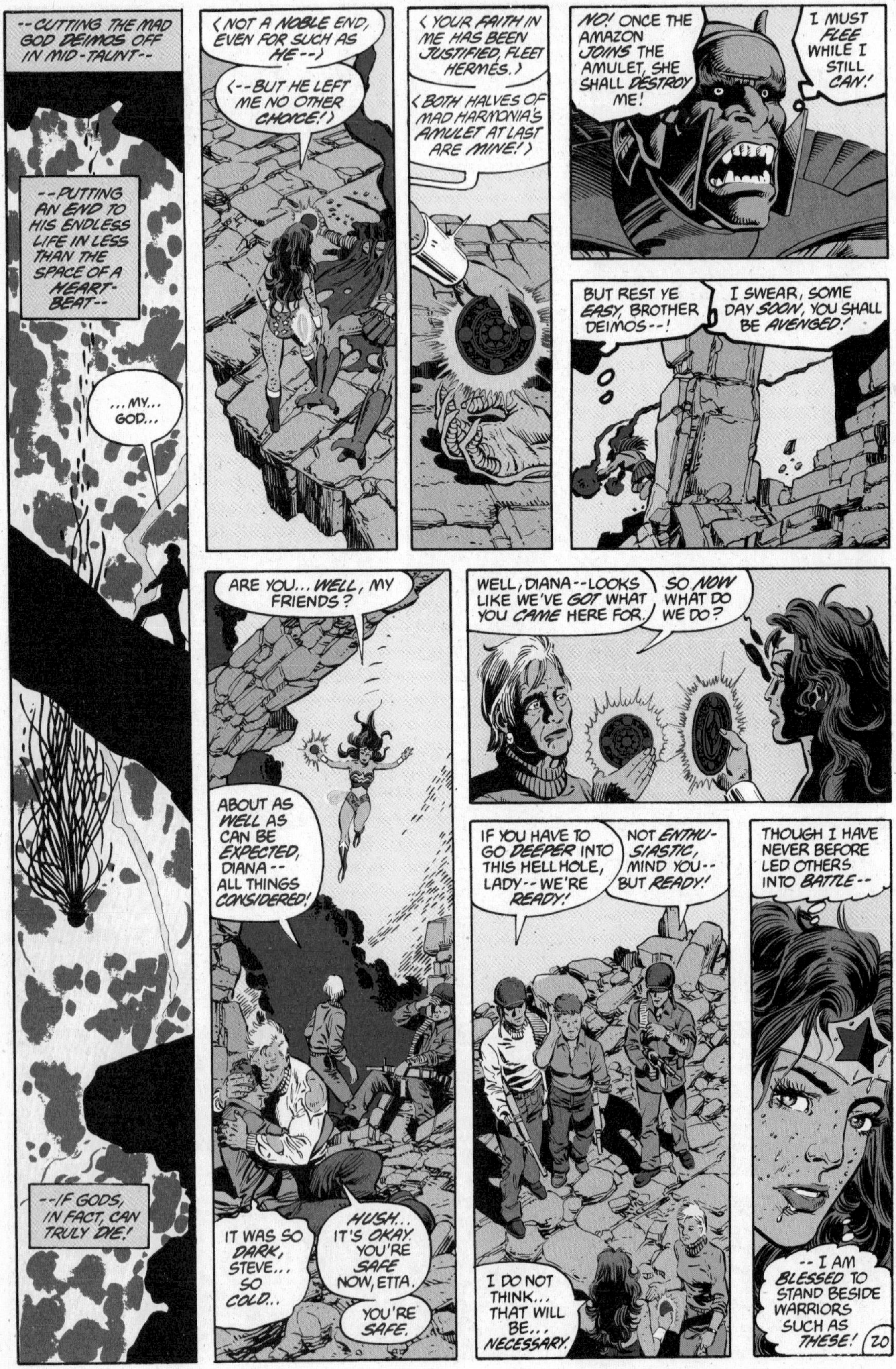
--CUTTING THE MAD GOD DEIMOS OFF IN MID-TAUNT--
--PUTTING AN END TO HIS ENDLESS LIFE IN LESS THAN THE SPACE OF A HEART-BEAT--
...MY... GOD...
--IF GODS, IN FACT, CAN TRULY DIE!
‹NOT A NOBLE END, EVEN FOR SUCH AS HE--›
‹--BUT HE LEFT ME NO OTHER CHOICE!›
‹YOUR FAITH IN ME HAS BEEN JUSTIFIED, FLEET HERMÉS.›
‹BOTH HALVES OF MAD HARMONIA'S AMULET AT LAST ARE MINE!›
NO! ONCE THE AMAZON JOINS THE AMULET, SHE SHALL DESTROY ME!
I MUST FLEE WHILE I STILL CAN!
BUT REST YE EASY, BROTHER DEIMOS--!
I SWEAR, SOME DAY SOON, YOU SHALL BE AVENGED!
ARE YOU... WELL, MY FRIENDS?
ABOUT AS WELL AS CAN BE EXPECTED, DIANA--ALL THINGS CONSIDERED!
IT WAS SO DARK, STEVE... SO COLD...
HUSH... IT'S OKAY. YOU'RE SAFE NOW, ETTA.
YOU'RE SAFE.
WELL, DIANA--LOOKS LIKE WE'VE GOT WHAT YOU CAME HERE FOR.
SO NOW WHAT DO WE DO?
IF YOU HAVE TO GO DEEPER INTO THIS HELLHOLE, LADY--WE'RE READY!
NOT ENTHU-SIASTIC, MIND YOU--BUT READY!
I DO NOT THINK... THAT WILL BE... NECESSARY.
THOUGH I HAVE NEVER BEFORE LED OTHERS INTO BATTLE--
--I AM BLESSED TO STAND BESIDE WARRIORS SUCH AS THESE!
20

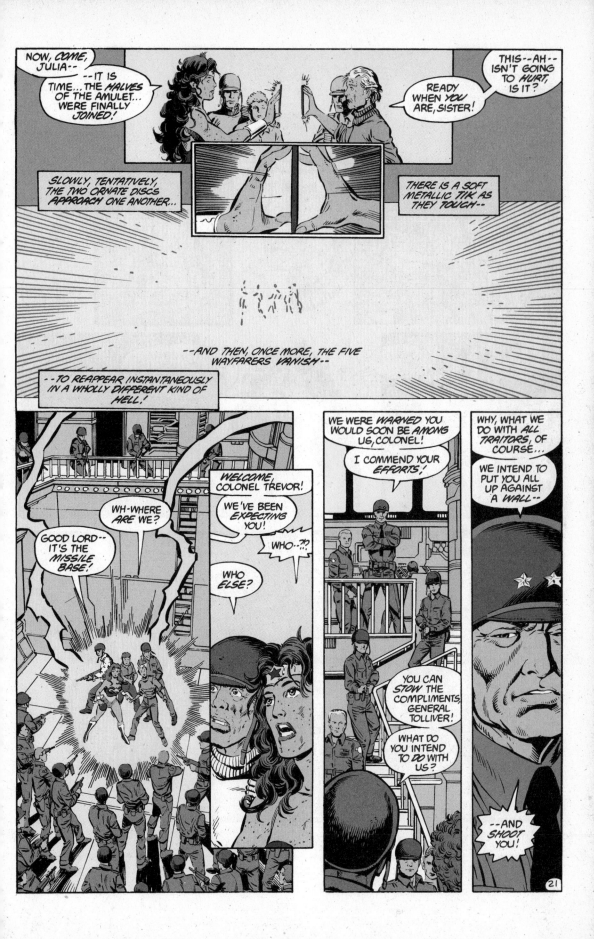

NOW, COME, JULIA-- --IT IS TIME...THE HALVES OF THE AMULET... WERE FINALLY JOINED!

READY WHEN YOU ARE, SISTER!

THIS--AH-- ISN'T GOING TO HURT, IS IT?

SLOWLY, TENTATIVELY, THE TWO ORNATE DISCS APPROACH ONE ANOTHER...

THERE IS A SOFT METALLIC TIK AS THEY TOUCH--

--AND THEN, ONCE MORE, THE FIVE WAYFARERS VANISH--

--TO REAPPEAR INSTANTANEOUSLY IN A WHOLLY DIFFERENT KIND OF HELL!

WH-WHERE ARE WE?

GOOD LORD-- IT'S THE MISSILE BASE!

WELCOME, COLONEL TREVOR!

WE'VE BEEN EXPECTING YOU!

WHO--?!?

WHO ELSE?

WE WERE WARNED YOU WOULD SOON BE AMONG US, COLONEL!

I COMMEND YOUR EFFORTS!

YOU CAN STOW THE COMPLIMENTS, GENERAL TOLLIVER!

WHAT DO YOU INTEND TO DO WITH US?

WHY, WHAT WE DO WITH ALL TRAITORS, OF COURSE...

WE INTEND TO PUT YOU ALL UP AGAINST A WALL--

--AND SHOOT YOU!

21

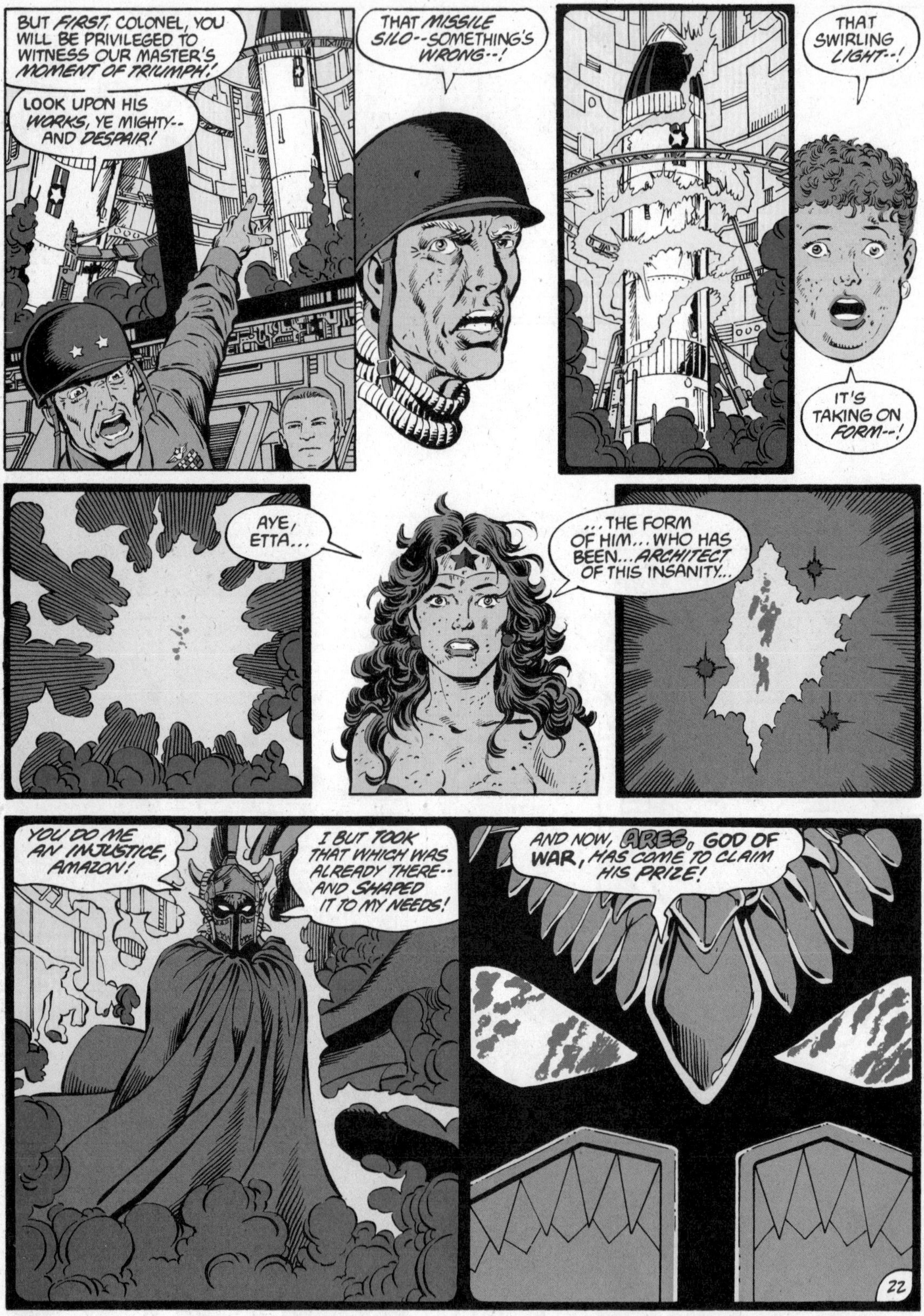
BUT FIRST, COLONEL, YOU WILL BE PRIVILEGED TO WITNESS OUR MASTER'S MOMENT OF TRIUMPH!
LOOK UPON HIS WORKS, YE MIGHTY-- AND DESPAIR!
THAT MISSILE SILO--SOMETHING'S WRONG--!
THAT SWIRLING LIGHT--!
IT'S TAKING ON FORM--!
AYE, ETTA...
...THE FORM OF HIM...WHO HAS BEEN...ARCHITECT OF THIS INSANITY...
YOU DO ME AN INJUSTICE, AMAZON!
I BUT TOOK THAT WHICH WAS ALREADY THERE-- AND SHAPED IT TO MY NEEDS!
AND NOW, ARES, GOD OF WAR, HAS COME TO CLAIM HIS PRIZE!
22

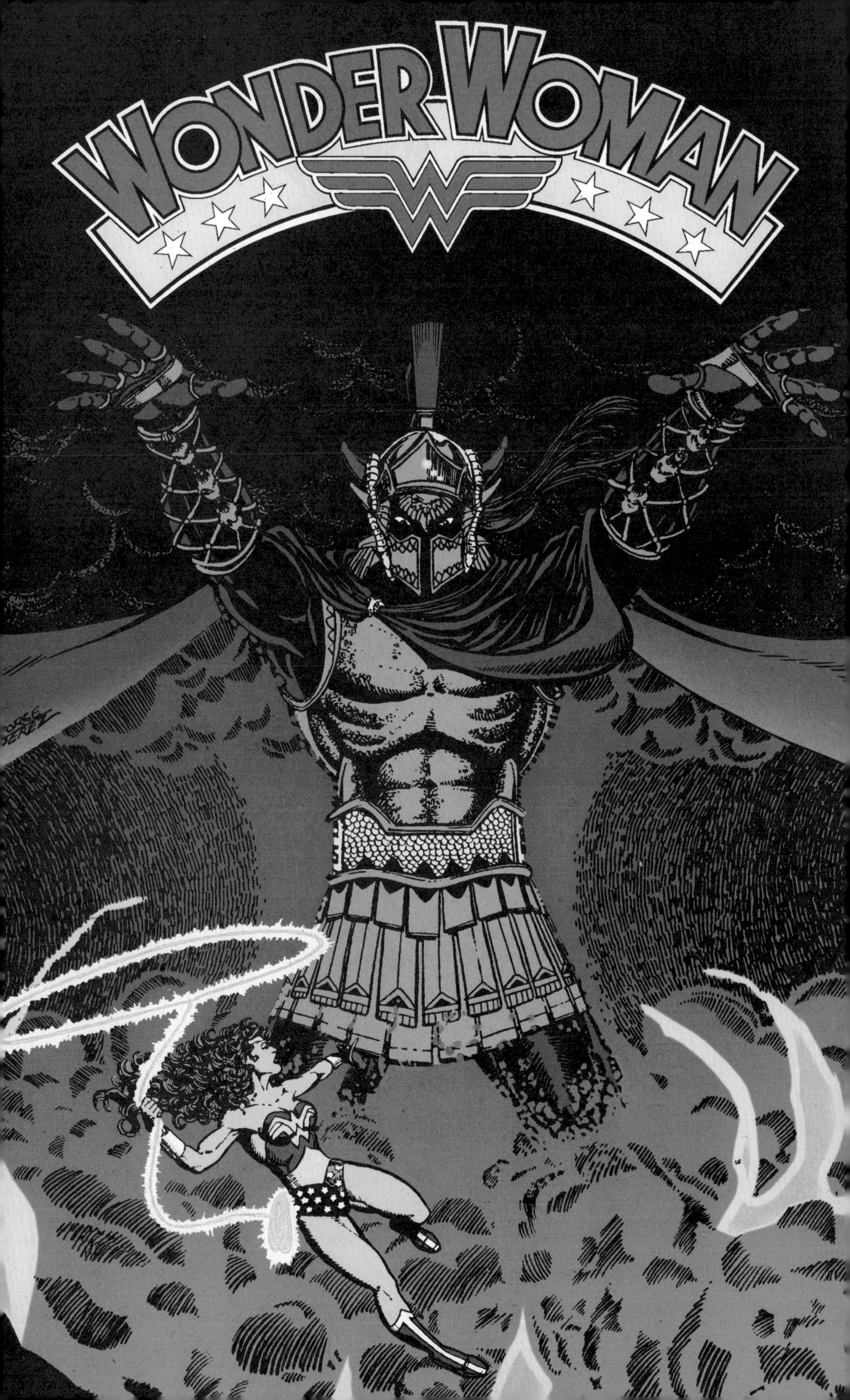
WONDER WOMAN

WONDER WOMAN
CHAPTER SIX

"WE INTERRUPT OUR REGULAR PROGRAMMING TO BRING YOU A SPECIAL CHANNEL 35 NOW-NEWS BULLETIN! HERE IS ANCHOR-WOMAN CONNIE CONLEY IN OUR NEWSROOM WITH AN UPDATE REPORT..."

"REPORTS ARE STILL COMING IN CONCERNING THIS MORNING'S ASTONISHING TAKEOVER OF A FEDERAL MISSILE BASE BY A BAND OF RENEGADE MILITARY PERSONNEL LED BY AIR FORCE GENERAL SAMUEL TOLLIVER..."

"APPARENTLY, TOLLIVER AND HIS TROOPS HAD INSIDE HELP IN ACCOMPLISHING THEIR INFILTRATION-- THOUGH NO SPECIFIC DETAILS ARE YET KNOWN. WE SWITCH YOU NOW TO CHAUNCEY STARK, LIVE IN WASHINGTON..."

SPECIAL NEWS BULLETIN

TV35

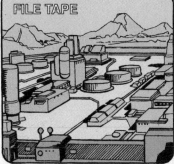

FILE TAPE

"THANK YOU, CONNIE. A HURRIED PRESS CONFERENCE HAS BEEN CALLED HERE TO REPORT ON THE PRESIDENT'S RECENT EFFORTS TO DISSUADE GENERAL TOLLIVER FROM HIS PLANS TO LAUNCH A NUCLEAR MISSILE STRIKE DIRECTLY AT MOSCOW..."

"MISTER REAGAN HAS ATTEMPTED REPEATEDLY TO TALK WITH TOLLIVER, WHO CLAIMS CERTAIN KNOWLEDGE OF SOVIET PLANS TO LAUNCH A NUCLEAR FIRST STRIKE AGAINST AMERICA..."

"SINCE WE WERE NOT REACTING QUICKLY ENOUGH, ACCORDING TO TOLLIVER, HE CLAIMS HE HAS NO CHOICE BUT TO PROTECT AMERICA IN HIS OWN WAY AT THIS TIME, TOLLIVER REFUSES TO RESPOND TO ANY FURTHER COMMUNICATION..."

"THOUGH MEETINGS WERE HELD EARLIER TODAY TO DEAL WITH THE TOLLIVER AFFAIR-- WHICH GENERAL JOHN HILLARY CALLS THE ARES ASSAULT-- THE GOVERNMENT HAS NO OFFICIAL STATEMENT FOR THE PRESS, AND THE RESULTS OF THE MEETINGS REMAIN UNKNOWN.

"MEANWHILE, RUMORS HAVE REACHED US THAT A RENEGADE SOVIET GENERAL AND HIS TROOPS HAVE NOW TAKEN CONTROL OF A RUSSIAN MISSILE SILO AT THIS TIME, THE SOVIETS HAVE REFUSED TO SUBSTANTIATE THESE RUMORS..."

"CHANNEL 35 WILL KEEP YOU INFORMED OF ANY LATE-BREAKING DEVELOPMENTS IN THIS DESPERATE SITUATION AS THEY OCCUR. MEANWHILE, WE NOW RETURN YOU TO 'ME AND THE CHIMP'..."

SOVIET SIEGE

SPECIAL NEWS BULLETIN

TV35

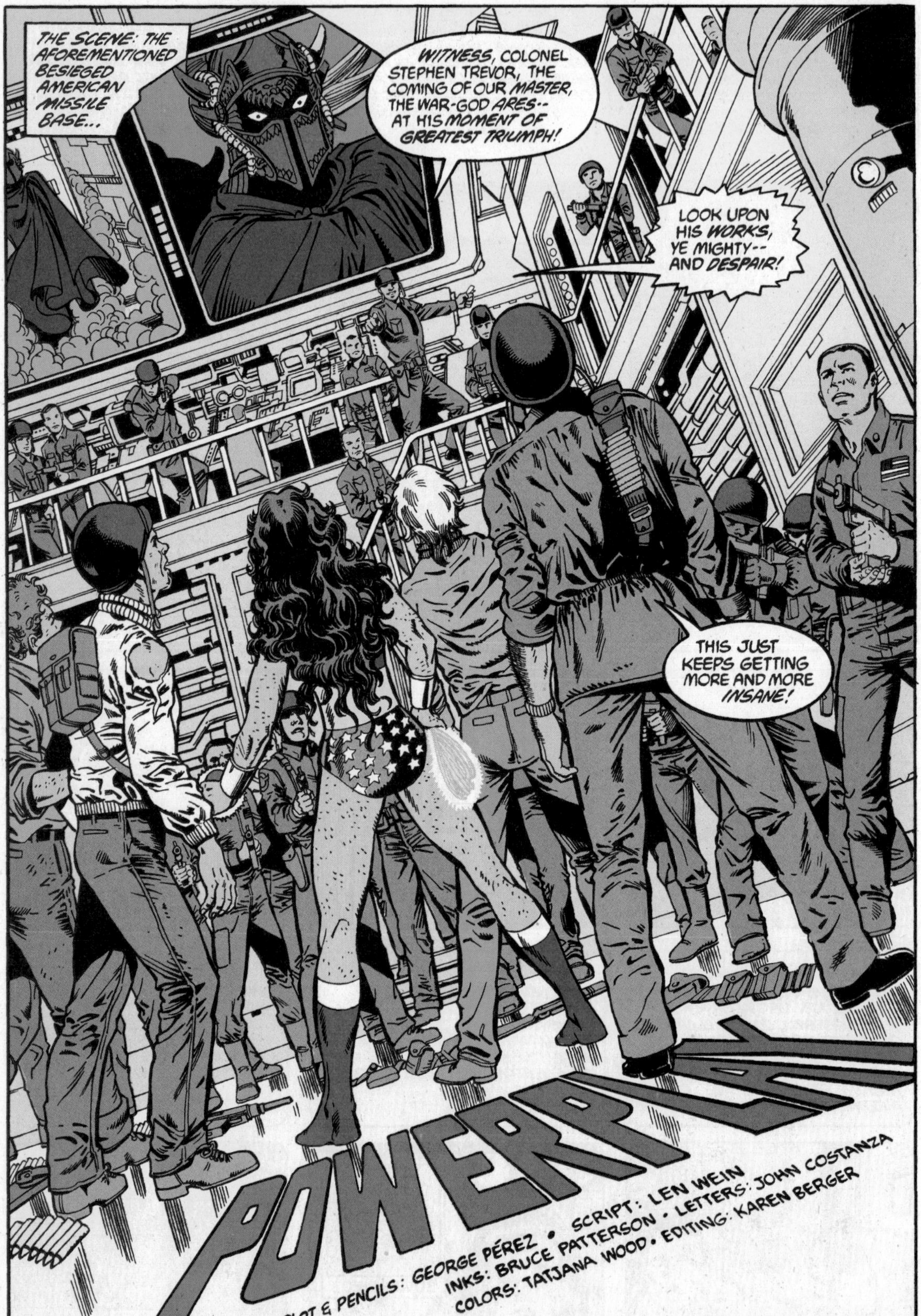
THE SCENE: THE AFOREMENTIONED BESIEGED AMERICAN MISSILE BASE...
WITNESS, COLONEL STEPHEN TREVOR, THE COMING OF OUR MASTER, THE WAR-GOD ARES-- AT HIS MOMENT OF GREATEST TRIUMPH!
LOOK UPON HIS WORKS, YE MIGHTY-- AND DESPAIR!
THIS JUST KEEPS GETTING MORE AND MORE INSANE!
POWERPLAY
PLOT & PENCILS: GEORGE PÉREZ • SCRIPT: LEN WEIN
INKS: BRUCE PATTERSON • LETTERS: JOHN COSTANZA
COLORS: TATJANA WOOD • EDITING: KAREN BERGER

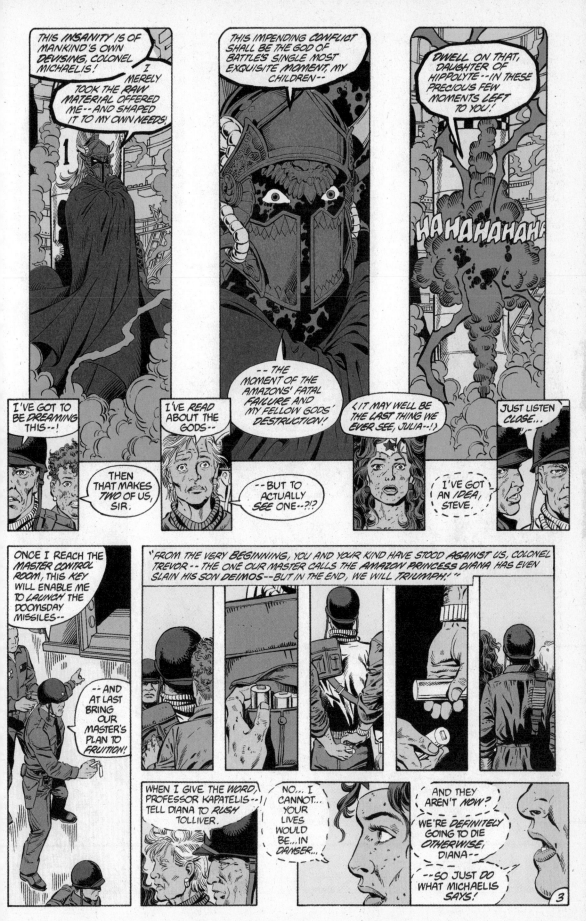

THIS INSANITY IS OF MANKIND'S OWN DEVISING, COLONEL MICHAELIS! I MERELY TOOK THE RAW MATERIAL OFFERED ME--AND SHAPED IT TO MY OWN NEEDS!

THIS IMPENDING CONFLICT SHALL BE THE GOD OF BATTLE'S SINGLE MOST EXQUISITE MOMENT, MY CHILDREN--

DWELL ON THAT, DAUGHTER OF HIPPOLYTE--IN THESE PRECIOUS FEW MOMENTS LEFT TO YOU!

HAHAHAHAH

I'VE GOT TO BE DREAMING THIS--!

THEN THAT MAKES TWO OF US, SIR.

I'VE READ ABOUT THE GODS--

--THE MOMENT OF THE AMAZONS' FATAL FAILURE AND MY FELLOW GODS' DESTRUCTION!

--BUT TO ACTUALLY SEE ONE--?!?

‹IT MAY WELL BE THE LAST THING WE EVER SEE, JULIA--!›

I'VE GOT AN IDEA, STEVE.

JUST LISTEN CLOSE...

ONCE I REACH THE MASTER CONTROL ROOM, THIS KEY WILL ENABLE ME TO LAUNCH THE DOOMSDAY MISSILES--

--AND AT LAST BRING OUR MASTER'S PLAN TO FRUITION!

"FROM THE VERY BEGINNING, YOU AND YOUR KIND HAVE STOOD AGAINST US, COLONEL TREVOR -- THE ONE OUR MASTER CALLS THE AMAZON PRINCESS DIANA HAS EVEN SLAIN HIS SON DEIMOS--BUT IN THE END, WE WILL TRIUMPH!"

WHEN I GIVE THE WORD, PROFESSOR KAPATELIS--! TELL DIANA TO RUSH TOLLIVER.

NO... I CANNOT... YOUR LIVES WOULD BE... IN DANGER...

AND THEY AREN'T NOW?

WE'RE DEFINITELY GOING TO DIE OTHERWISE, DIANA--

--SO JUST DO WHAT MICHAELIS SAYS!

3

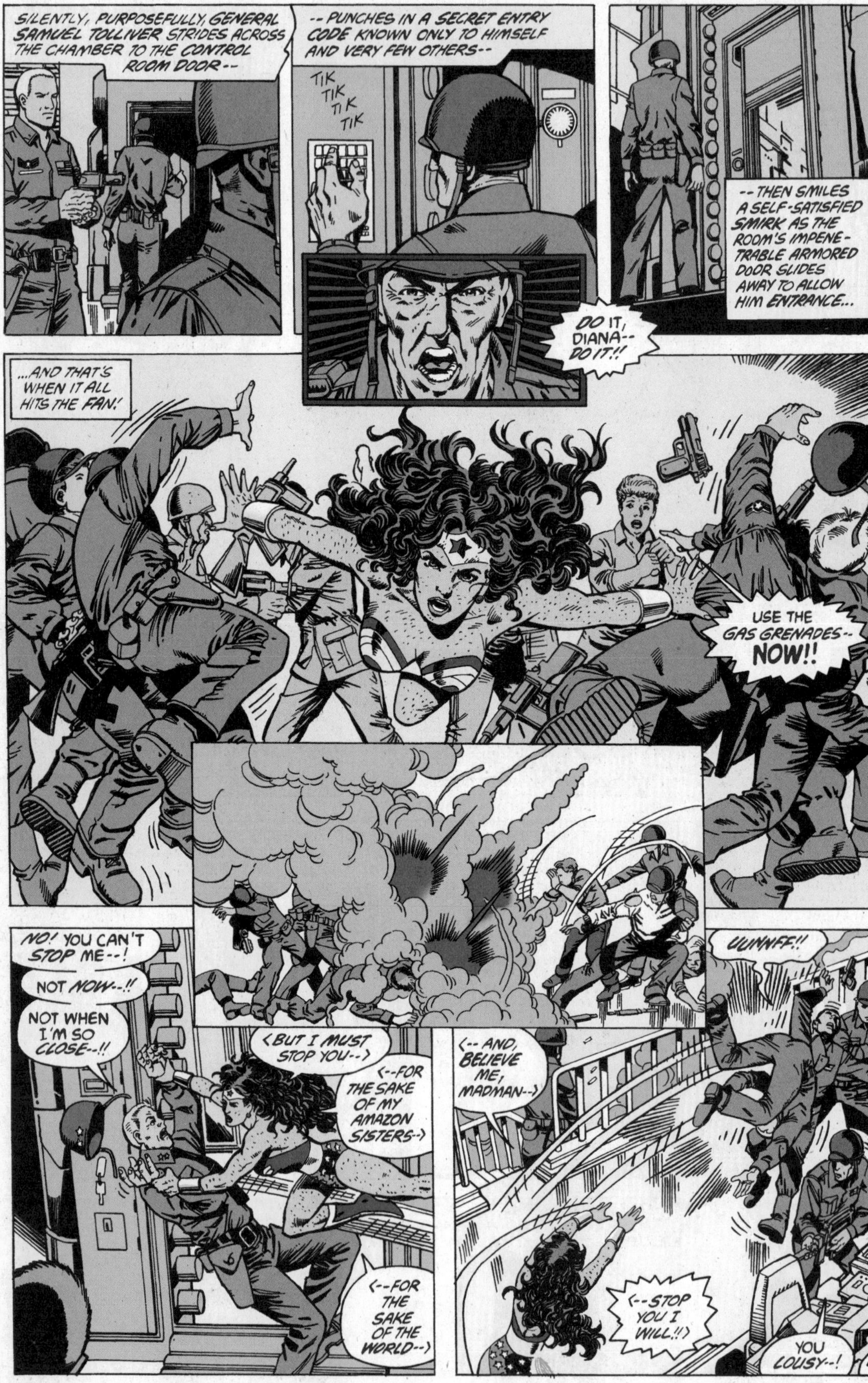
SILENTLY, PURPOSEFULLY, GENERAL SAMUEL TOLLIVER STRIDES ACROSS THE CHAMBER TO THE CONTROL ROOM DOOR--
--PUNCHES IN A SECRET ENTRY CODE KNOWN ONLY TO HIMSELF AND VERY FEW OTHERS--
TIK TIK TIK TIK
--THEN SMILES A SELF-SATISFIED SMIRK AS THE ROOM'S IMPENE-TRABLE ARMORED DOOR SLIDES AWAY TO ALLOW HIM ENTRANCE...
DO IT, DIANA-- DO IT!!
...AND THAT'S WHEN IT ALL HITS THE FAN!
USE THE GAS GRENADES-- NOW!!
NO! YOU CAN'T STOP ME--!
NOT NOW--!!
NOT WHEN I'M SO CLOSE--!!
<BUT I MUST STOP YOU-->
<--FOR THE SAKE OF MY AMAZON SISTERS-->
<--FOR THE SAKE OF THE WORLD-->
UUNNFF!!
<--AND, BELIEVE ME, MADMAN-->
<--STOP YOU I WILL!!>
YOU LOUSY--!
4

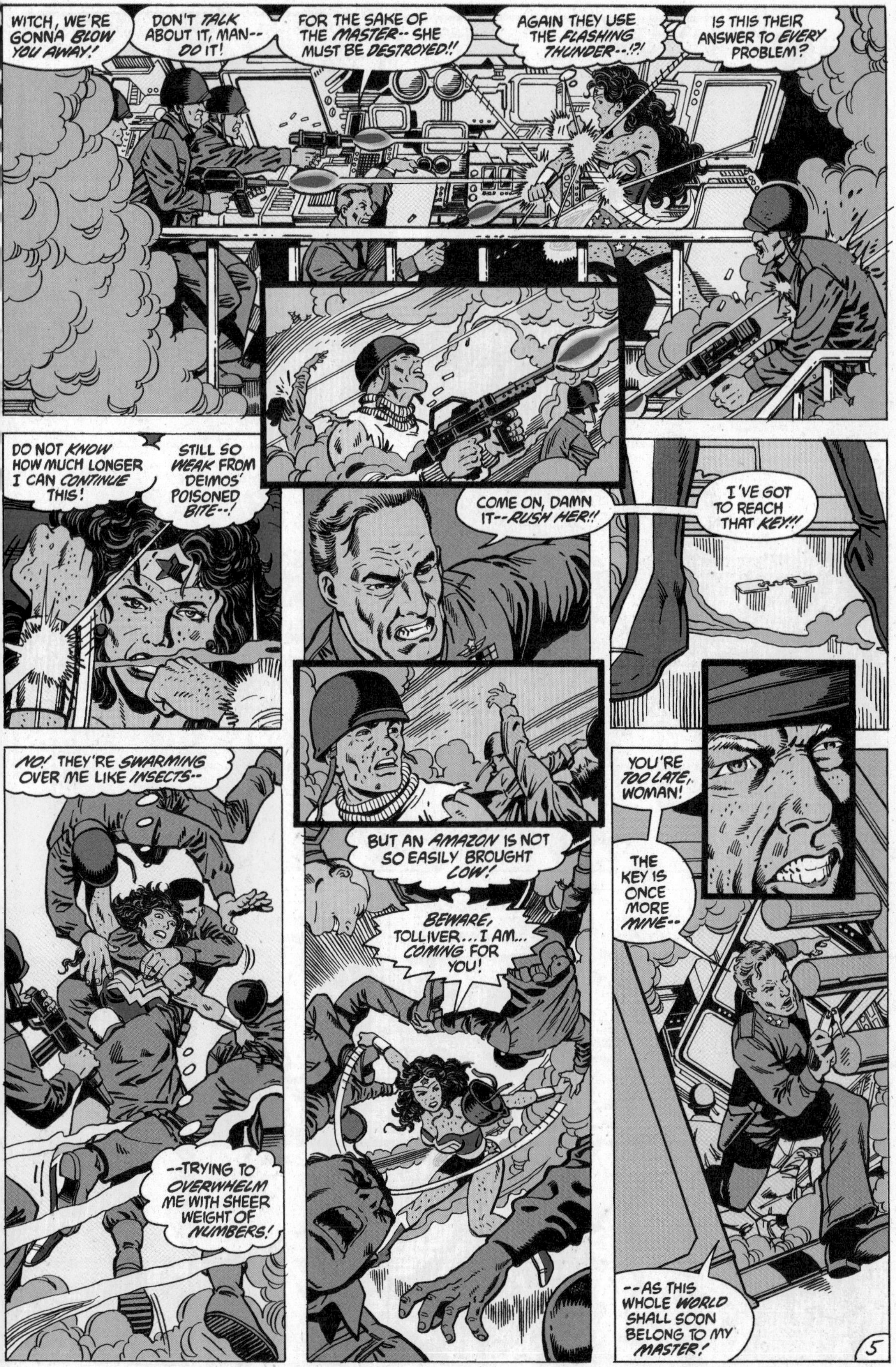

WITCH, WE'RE GONNA BLOW YOU AWAY!
DON'T TALK ABOUT IT, MAN-- DO IT!
FOR THE SAKE OF THE MASTER-- SHE MUST BE DESTROYED!!
AGAIN THEY USE THE FLASHING THUNDER--!?!
IS THIS THEIR ANSWER TO EVERY PROBLEM?
DO NOT KNOW HOW MUCH LONGER I CAN CONTINUE THIS!
STILL SO WEAK FROM DEIMOS' POISONED BITE--!
COME ON, DAMN IT--RUSH HER!!
I'VE GOT TO REACH THAT KEY!!
NO! THEY'RE SWARMING OVER ME LIKE INSECTS--
--TRYING TO OVERWHELM ME WITH SHEER WEIGHT OF NUMBERS!
BUT AN AMAZON IS NOT SO EASILY BROUGHT LOW!
BEWARE, TOLLIVER...I AM... COMING FOR YOU!
YOU'RE TOO LATE, WOMAN!
THE KEY IS ONCE MORE MINE--
--AS THIS WHOLE WORLD SHALL SOON BELONG TO MY MASTER!
5

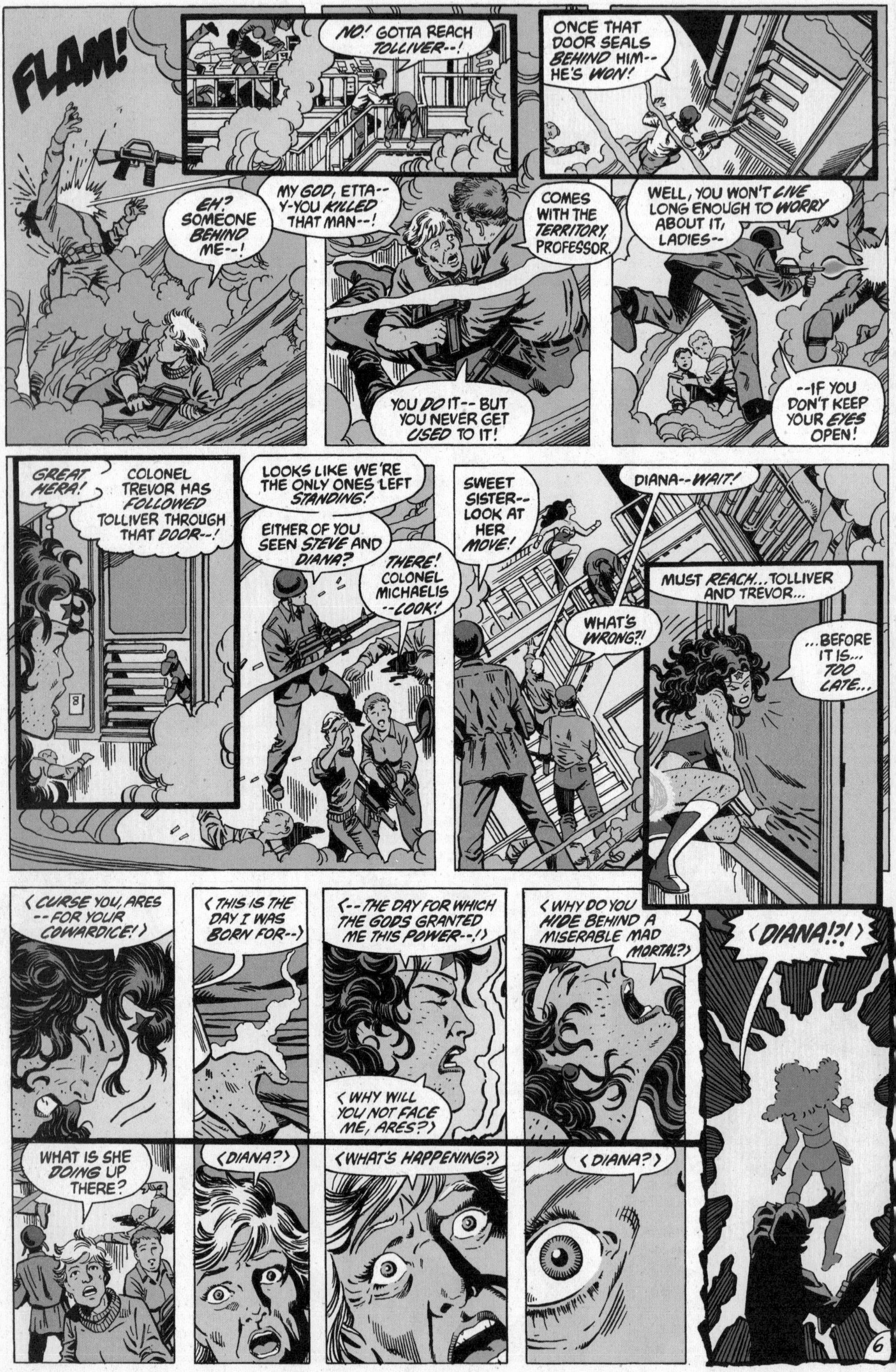

FLAM!
NO! GOTTA REACH TOLLIVER--!
ONCE THAT DOOR SEALS BEHIND HIM-- HE'S WON!
EH? SOMEONE BEHIND ME--!
MY GOD, ETTA-- Y-YOU KILLED THAT MAN--!
YOU DO IT-- BUT YOU NEVER GET USED TO IT!
COMES WITH THE TERRITORY, PROFESSOR.
WELL, YOU WON'T LIVE LONG ENOUGH TO WORRY ABOUT IT, LADIES--
--IF YOU DON'T KEEP YOUR EYES OPEN!
GREAT HERA!
COLONEL TREVOR HAS FOLLOWED TOLLIVER THROUGH THAT DOOR--!
LOOKS LIKE WE'RE THE ONLY ONES LEFT STANDING!
EITHER OF YOU SEEN STEVE AND DIANA?
THERE! COLONEL MICHAELIS --LOOK!
SWEET SISTER-- LOOK AT HER MOVE!
DIANA--WAIT!
WHAT'S WRONG?!
MUST REACH...TOLLIVER AND TREVOR...
...BEFORE IT IS... TOO LATE...
<CURSE YOU, ARES --FOR YOUR COWARDICE!>
<THIS IS THE DAY I WAS BORN FOR-->
<--THE DAY FOR WHICH THE GODS GRANTED ME THIS POWER--!>
<WHY WILL YOU NOT FACE ME, ARES?>
<WHY DO YOU HIDE BEHIND A MISERABLE MAD MORTAL?>
<DIANA!?!>
WHAT IS SHE DOING UP THERE?
<DIANA?>
<WHAT'S HAPPENING?>
<DIANA?>
6

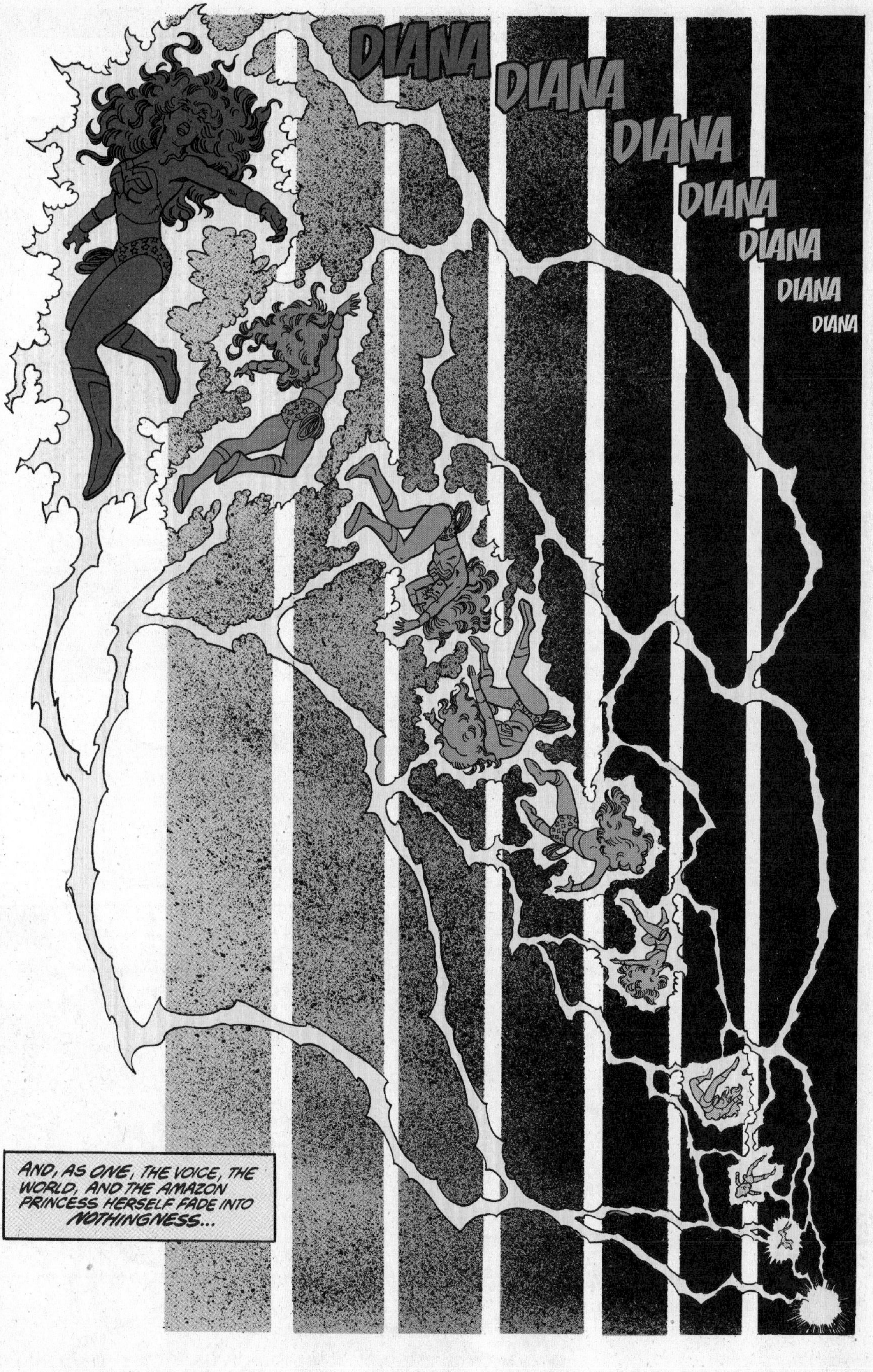
DIANA
DIANA
DIANA
DIANA
DIANA
DIANA
DIANA
AND, AS ONE, THE VOICE, THE WORLD, AND THE AMAZON PRINCESS HERSELF FADE INTO NOTHINGNESS...

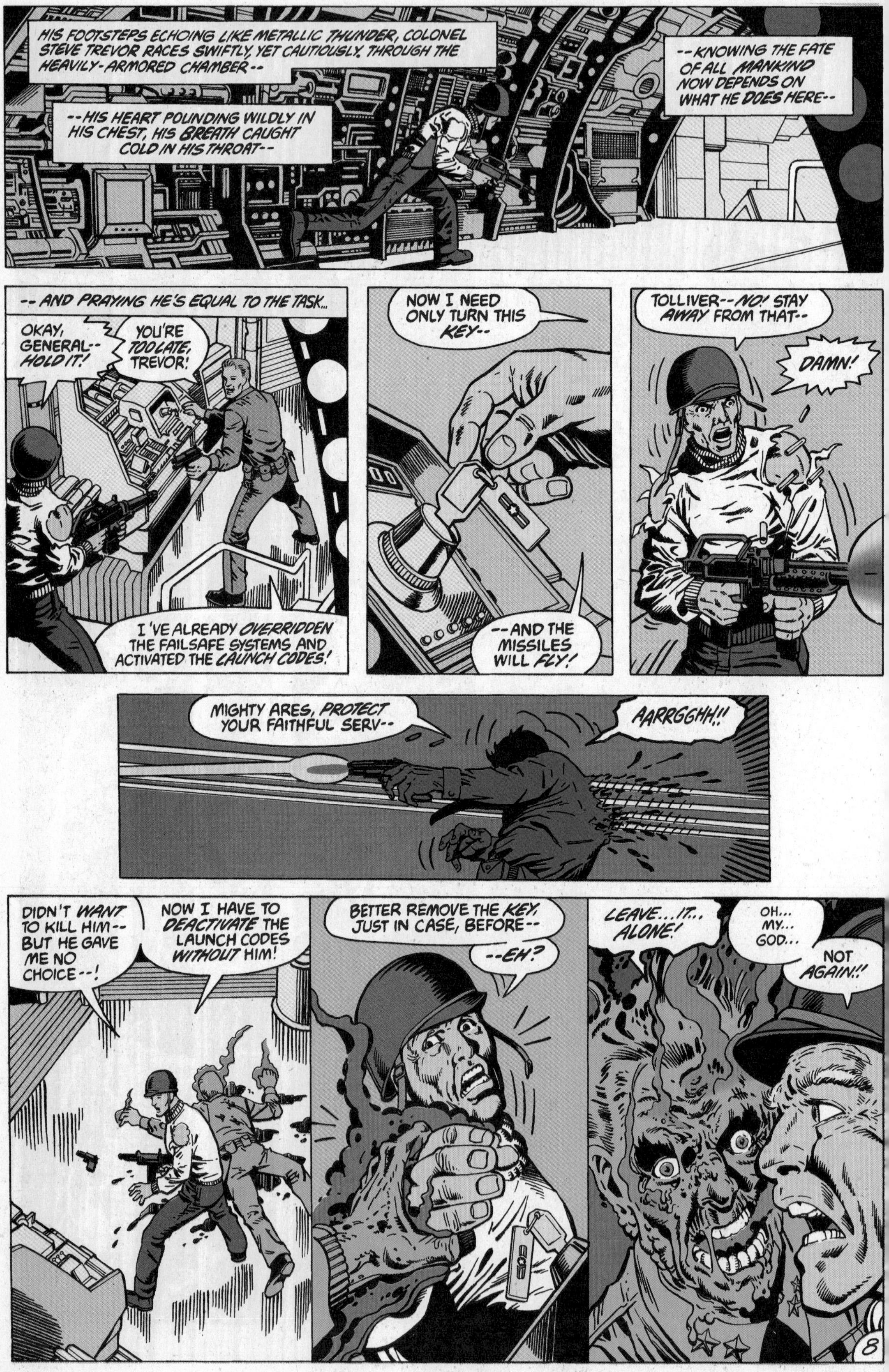
HIS FOOTSTEPS ECHOING LIKE METALLIC THUNDER, COLONEL STEVE TREVOR RACES SWIFTLY, YET CAUTIOUSLY, THROUGH THE HEAVILY-ARMORED CHAMBER--
--HIS HEART POUNDING WILDLY IN HIS CHEST, HIS BREATH CAUGHT COLD IN HIS THROAT--
--KNOWING THE FATE OF ALL MANKIND NOW DEPENDS ON WHAT HE DOES HERE--
--AND PRAYING HE'S EQUAL TO THE TASK...
OKAY, GENERAL-- HOLD IT!
YOU'RE TOO LATE, TREVOR!
I'VE ALREADY OVERRIDDEN THE FAILSAFE SYSTEMS AND ACTIVATED THE LAUNCH CODES!
NOW I NEED ONLY TURN THIS KEY--
--AND THE MISSILES WILL FLY!
TOLLIVER--NO! STAY AWAY FROM THAT--
DAMN!
MIGHTY ARES, PROTECT YOUR FAITHFUL SERV--
AARRGGHH!!
DIDN'T WANT TO KILL HIM-- BUT HE GAVE ME NO CHOICE--!
NOW I HAVE TO DEACTIVATE THE LAUNCH CODES WITHOUT HIM!
BETTER REMOVE THE KEY, JUST IN CASE, BEFORE--
--EH?
LEAVE... IT... ALONE!
OH... MY... GOD...
NOT AGAIN!!
8

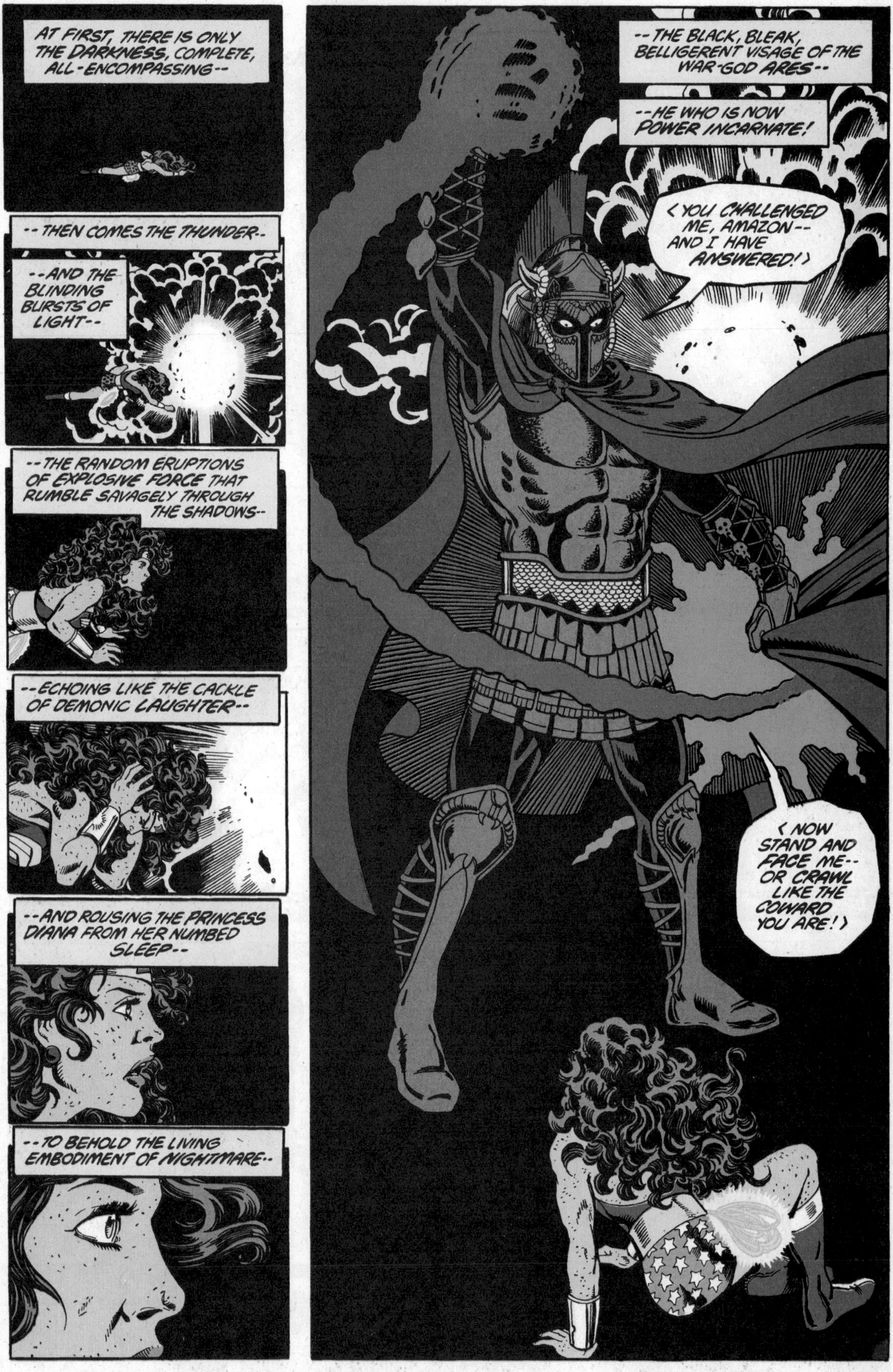
AT FIRST, THERE IS ONLY THE DARKNESS, COMPLETE, ALL-ENCOMPASSING--
--THEN COMES THE THUNDER--
--AND THE BLINDING BURSTS OF LIGHT--
--THE RANDOM ERUPTIONS OF EXPLOSIVE FORCE THAT RUMBLE SAVAGELY THROUGH THE SHADOWS--
--ECHOING LIKE THE CACKLE OF DEMONIC LAUGHTER--
--AND ROUSING THE PRINCESS DIANA FROM HER NUMBED SLEEP--
--TO BEHOLD THE LIVING EMBODIMENT OF NIGHTMARE--
--THE BLACK, BLEAK, BELLIGERENT VISAGE OF THE WAR-GOD ARES--
--HE WHO IS NOW POWER INCARNATE!
<YOU CHALLENGED ME, AMAZON-- AND I HAVE ANSWERED!>
<NOW STAND AND FACE ME-- OR CRAWL LIKE THE COWARD YOU ARE!>

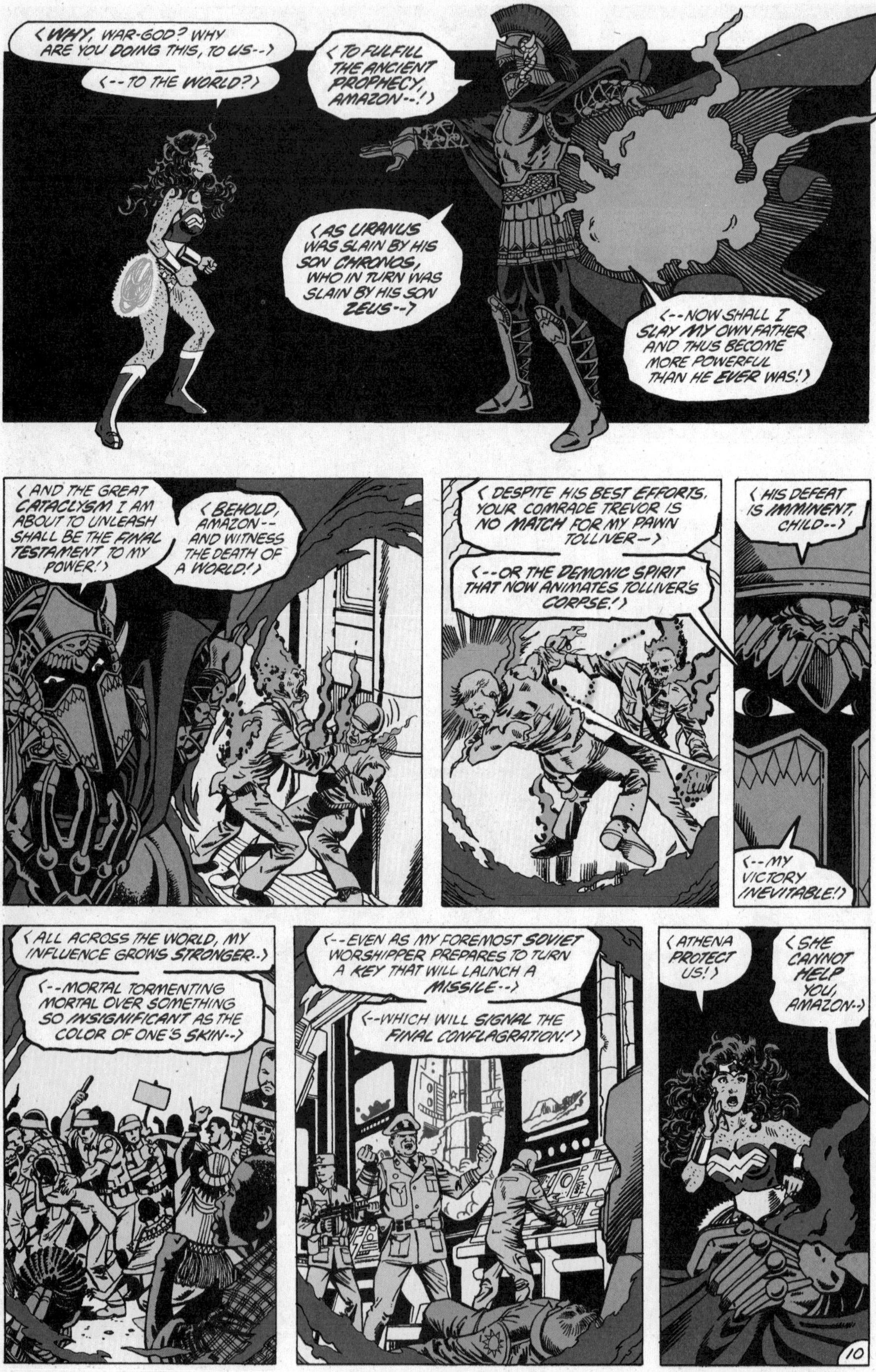

‹WHY, WAR-GOD? WHY ARE YOU DOING THIS, TO US--›
‹--TO THE WORLD?›
‹TO FULFILL THE ANCIENT PROPHECY, AMAZON--!›
‹AS URANUS WAS SLAIN BY HIS SON CHRONOS, WHO IN TURN WAS SLAIN BY HIS SON ZEUS--›
‹--NOW SHALL I SLAY MY OWN FATHER AND THUS BECOME MORE POWERFUL THAN HE EVER WAS!›
‹AND THE GREAT CATACLYSM I AM ABOUT TO UNLEASH SHALL BE THE FINAL TESTAMENT TO MY POWER!›
‹BEHOLD, AMAZON-- AND WITNESS THE DEATH OF A WORLD!›
‹DESPITE HIS BEST EFFORTS, YOUR COMRADE TREVOR IS NO MATCH FOR MY PAWN TOLLIVER--›
‹--OR THE DEMONIC SPIRIT THAT NOW ANIMATES TOLLIVER'S CORPSE!›
‹HIS DEFEAT IS IMMINENT, CHILD--›
‹--MY VICTORY INEVITABLE!›
‹ALL ACROSS THE WORLD, MY INFLUENCE GROWS STRONGER..›
‹--MORTAL TORMENTING MORTAL OVER SOMETHING SO INSIGNIFICANT AS THE COLOR OF ONE'S SKIN--›
‹--EVEN AS MY FOREMOST SOVIET WORSHIPPER PREPARES TO TURN A KEY THAT WILL LAUNCH A MISSILE--›
‹--WHICH WILL SIGNAL THE FINAL CONFLAGRATION!›
‹ATHENA PROTECT US!›
‹SHE CANNOT HELP YOU, AMAZON--›
10

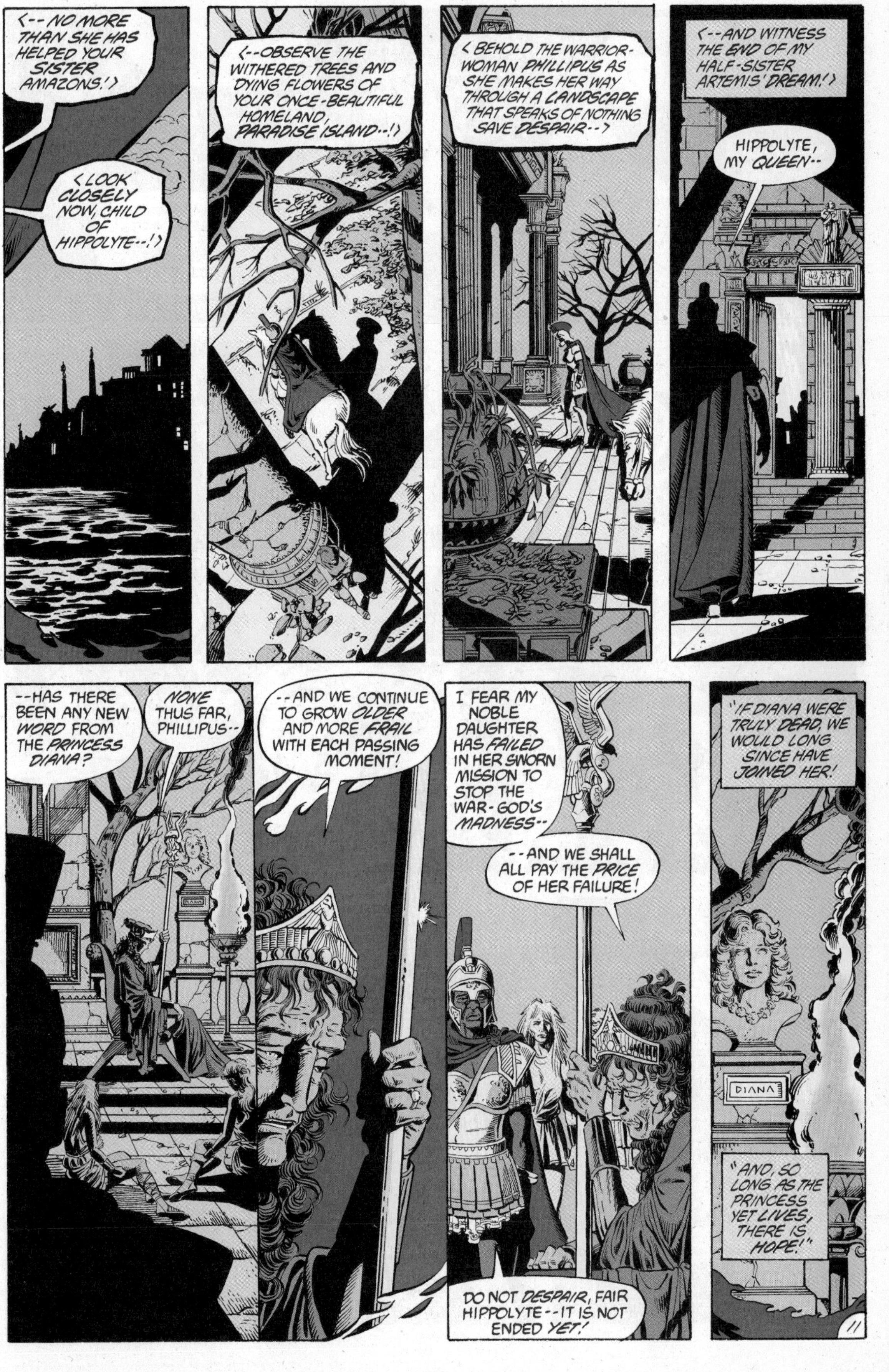
<--NO MORE THAN SHE HAS HELPED YOUR SISTER AMAZONS.!>
<LOOK CLOSELY NOW, CHILD OF HIPPOLYTE--!>
<--OBSERVE THE WITHERED TREES AND DYING FLOWERS OF YOUR ONCE-BEAUTIFUL HOMELAND, PARADISE ISLAND--!>
<BEHOLD THE WARRIOR-WOMAN PHILLIPUS AS SHE MAKES HER WAY THROUGH A LANDSCAPE THAT SPEAKS OF NOTHING SAVE DESPAIR-->
<--AND WITNESS THE END OF MY HALF-SISTER ARTEMIS' DREAM!>
HIPPOLYTE, MY QUEEN--
--HAS THERE BEEN ANY NEW WORD FROM THE PRINCESS DIANA?
NONE THUS FAR, PHILLIPUS--
--AND WE CONTINUE TO GROW OLDER AND MORE FRAIL WITH EACH PASSING MOMENT!
I FEAR MY NOBLE DAUGHTER HAS FAILED IN HER SWORN MISSION TO STOP THE WAR-GOD'S MADNESS--
--AND WE SHALL ALL PAY THE PRICE OF HER FAILURE!
DO NOT DESPAIR, FAIR HIPPOLYTE--IT IS NOT ENDED YET!
"IF DIANA WERE TRULY DEAD, WE WOULD LONG SINCE HAVE JOINED HER!
DIANA
"AND, SO LONG AS THE PRINCESS YET LIVES, THERE IS HOPE!"
11

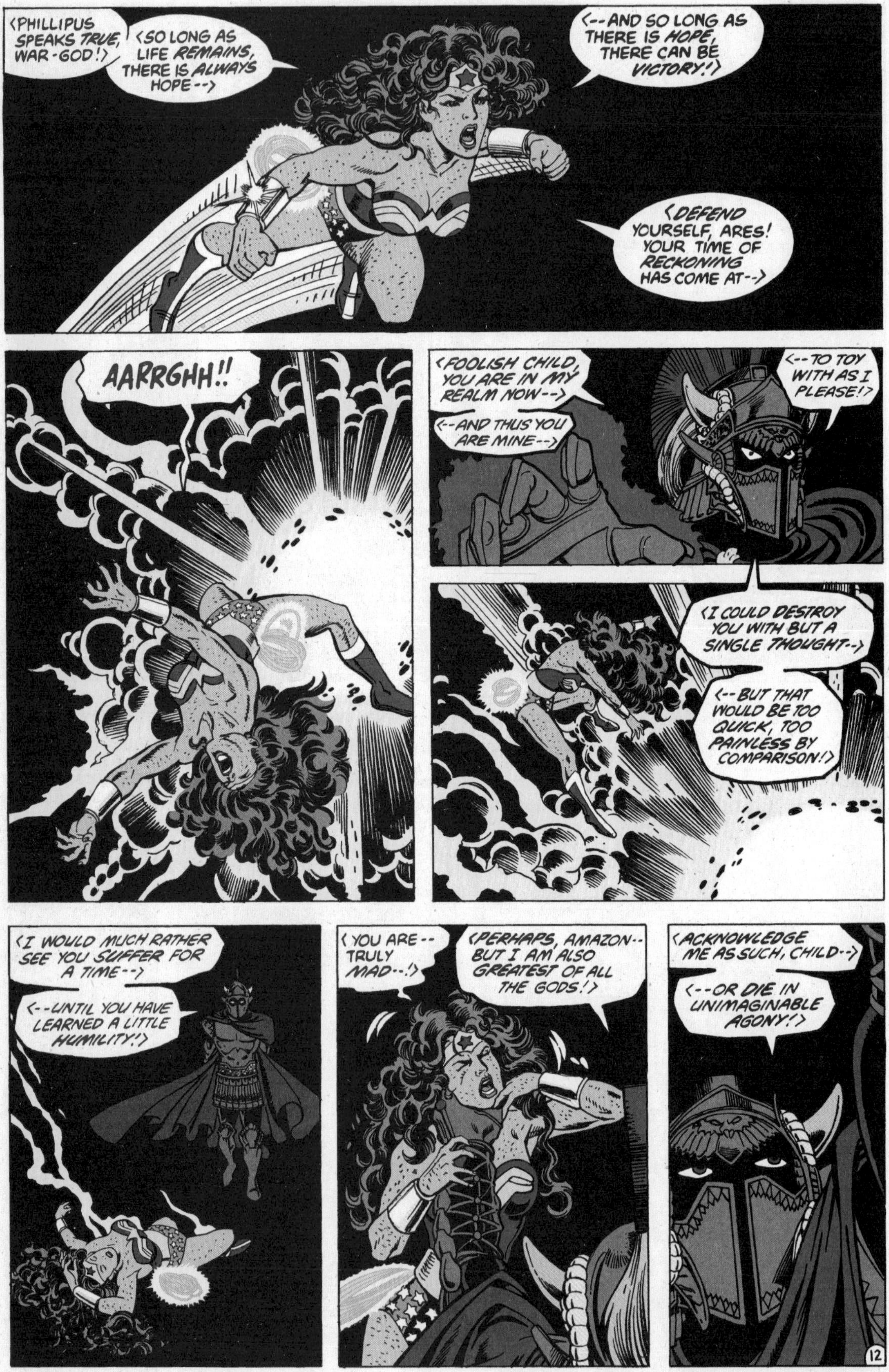

‹PHILLIPUS SPEAKS TRUE, WAR-GOD!›
‹SO LONG AS LIFE REMAINS, THERE IS ALWAYS HOPE--›
‹--AND SO LONG AS THERE IS HOPE, THERE CAN BE VICTORY!›
‹DEFEND YOURSELF, ARES! YOUR TIME OF RECKONING HAS COME AT--›
AARRGHH!!
‹FOOLISH CHILD, YOU ARE IN MY REALM NOW--›
‹--AND THUS YOU ARE MINE--›
‹--TO TOY WITH AS I PLEASE!›
‹I COULD DESTROY YOU WITH BUT A SINGLE THOUGHT--›
‹--BUT THAT WOULD BE TOO QUICK, TOO PAINLESS BY COMPARISON!›
‹I WOULD MUCH RATHER SEE YOU SUFFER FOR A TIME--›
‹--UNTIL YOU HAVE LEARNED A LITTLE HUMILITY!›
‹YOU ARE-- TRULY MAD--!›
‹PERHAPS, AMAZON-- BUT I AM ALSO GREATEST OF ALL THE GODS!›
‹ACKNOWLEDGE ME AS SUCH, CHILD--›
‹--OR DIE IN UNIMAGINABLE AGONY!›
12

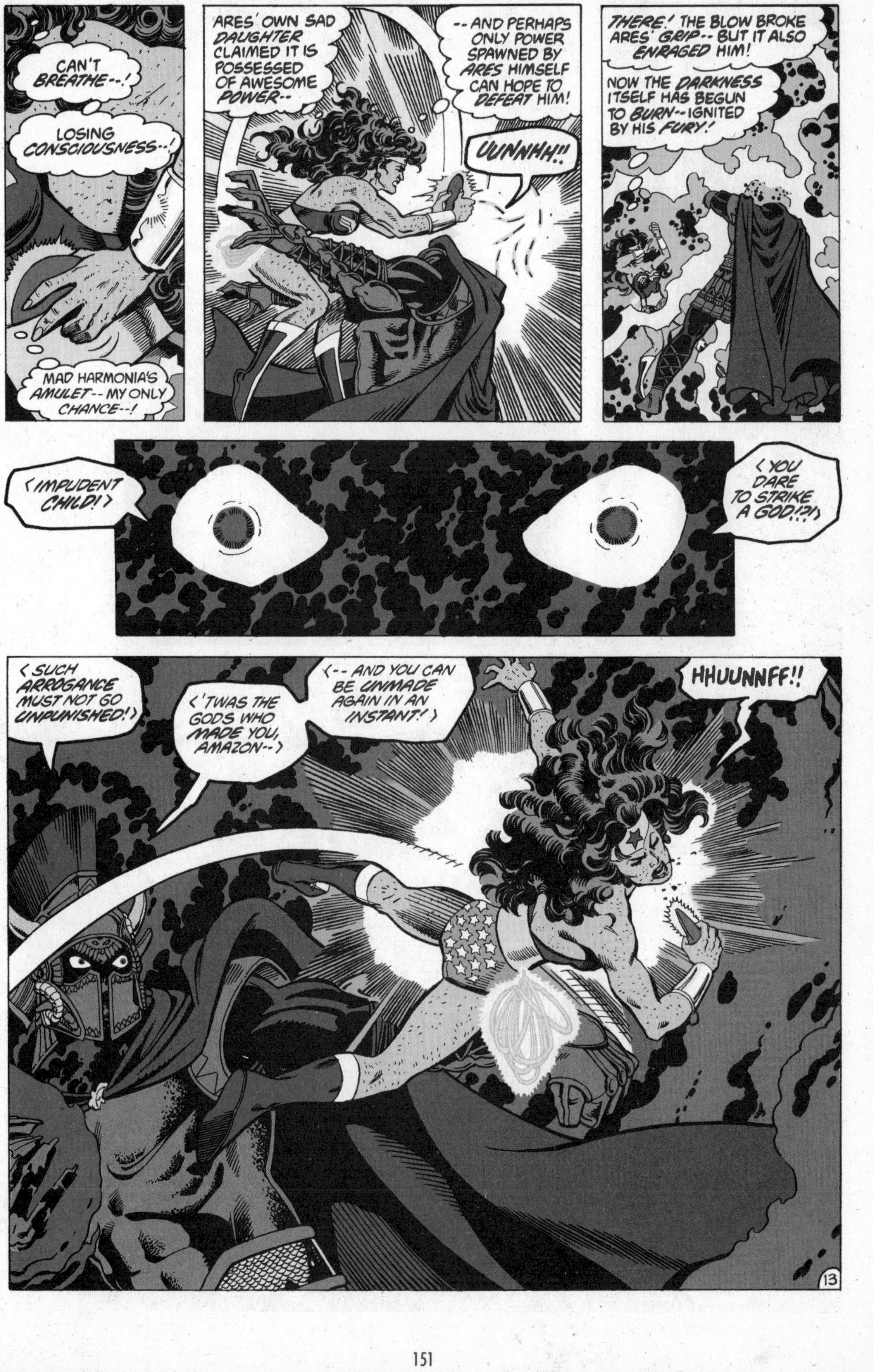
CAN'T BREATHE--!
LOSING CONSCIOUSNESS--!
MAD HARMONIA'S AMULET-- MY ONLY CHANCE--!
ARES' OWN SAD DAUGHTER CLAIMED IT IS POSSESSED OF AWESOME POWER--
--AND PERHAPS ONLY POWER SPAWNED BY ARES HIMSELF CAN HOPE TO DEFEAT HIM!
UUNNHH!!
THERE! THE BLOW BROKE ARES' GRIP-- BUT IT ALSO ENRAGED HIM!
NOW THE DARKNESS ITSELF HAS BEGUN TO BURN--IGNITED BY HIS FURY!
⟨IMPUDENT CHILD!⟩
⟨YOU DARE TO STRIKE A GOD!?!⟩
⟨SUCH ARROGANCE MUST NOT GO UNPUNISHED!⟩
⟨'TWAS THE GODS WHO MADE YOU, AMAZON--⟩
⟨--AND YOU CAN BE UNMADE AGAIN IN AN INSTANT!⟩
HHUUNNFF!!
13

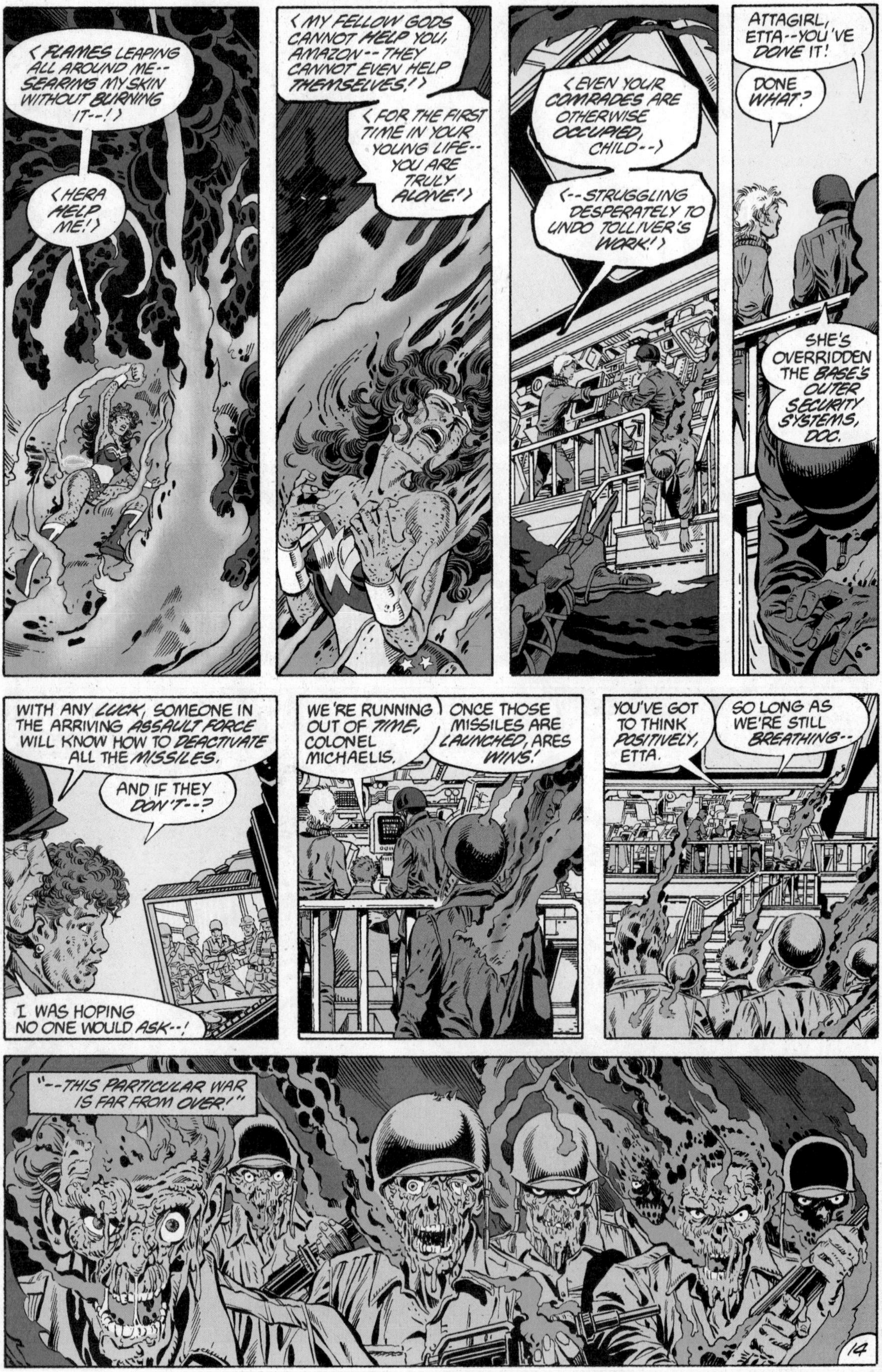
<FLAMES LEAPING ALL AROUND ME-- SEARING MY SKIN WITHOUT BURNING IT--!>
<HERA HELP ME!>
<MY FELLOW GODS CANNOT HELP YOU, AMAZON--THEY CANNOT EVEN HELP THEMSELVES!>
<FOR THE FIRST TIME IN YOUR YOUNG LIFE-- YOU ARE TRULY ALONE!>
<EVEN YOUR COMRADES ARE OTHERWISE OCCUPIED, CHILD-->
<--STRUGGLING DESPERATELY TO UNDO TOLLIVER'S WORK!>
ATTAGIRL, ETTA--YOU'VE DONE IT!
DONE WHAT?
SHE'S OVERRIDDEN THE BASE'S OUTER SECURITY SYSTEMS, DOC.
WITH ANY LUCK, SOMEONE IN THE ARRIVING ASSAULT FORCE WILL KNOW HOW TO DEACTIVATE ALL THE MISSILES.
AND IF THEY DON'T--?
I WAS HOPING NO ONE WOULD ASK--!
WE'RE RUNNING OUT OF TIME, COLONEL MICHAELIS.
ONCE THOSE MISSILES ARE LAUNCHED, ARES WINS!
YOU'VE GOT TO THINK POSITIVELY, ETTA.
SO LONG AS WE'RE STILL BREATHING--
"--THIS PARTICULAR WAR IS FAR FROM OVER!"
14

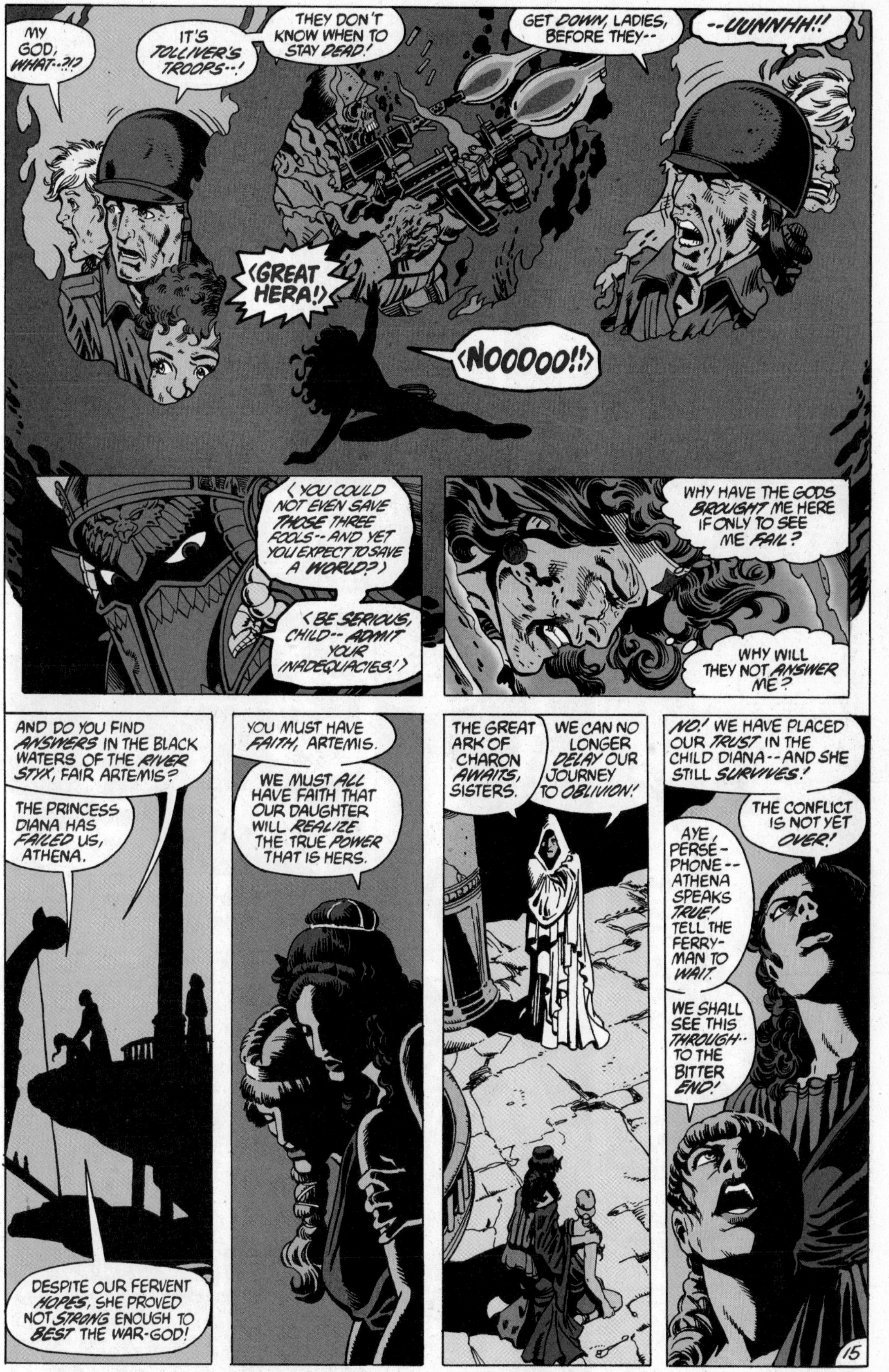
MY GOD, WHAT--?!?
IT'S TOLLIVER'S TROOPS--!
THEY DON'T KNOW WHEN TO STAY DEAD!
GET DOWN, LADIES, BEFORE THEY--
--UUNNHH!!
‹GREAT HERA!›
‹NOOOOO!!›
‹YOU COULD NOT EVEN SAVE THOSE THREE FOOLS--AND YET YOU EXPECT TO SAVE A WORLD?›
‹BE SERIOUS, CHILD--ADMIT YOUR INADEQUACIES!›
WHY HAVE THE GODS BROUGHT ME HERE IF ONLY TO SEE ME FAIL?
WHY WILL THEY NOT ANSWER ME?
AND DO YOU FIND ANSWERS IN THE BLACK WATERS OF THE RIVER STYX, FAIR ARTEMIS?
THE PRINCESS DIANA HAS FAILED US, ATHENA.
DESPITE OUR FERVENT HOPES, SHE PROVED NOT STRONG ENOUGH TO BEST THE WAR-GOD!
YOU MUST HAVE FAITH, ARTEMIS.
WE MUST ALL HAVE FAITH THAT OUR DAUGHTER WILL REALIZE THE TRUE POWER THAT IS HERS.
THE GREAT ARK OF CHARON AWAITS, SISTERS.
WE CAN NO LONGER DELAY OUR JOURNEY TO OBLIVION!
NO! WE HAVE PLACED OUR TRUST IN THE CHILD DIANA--AND SHE STILL SURVIVES!
THE CONFLICT IS NOT YET OVER!
AYE, PERSÉPHONE--ATHENA SPEAKS TRUE! TELL THE FERRYMAN TO WAIT.
WE SHALL SEE THIS THROUGH--TO THE BITTER END!
15

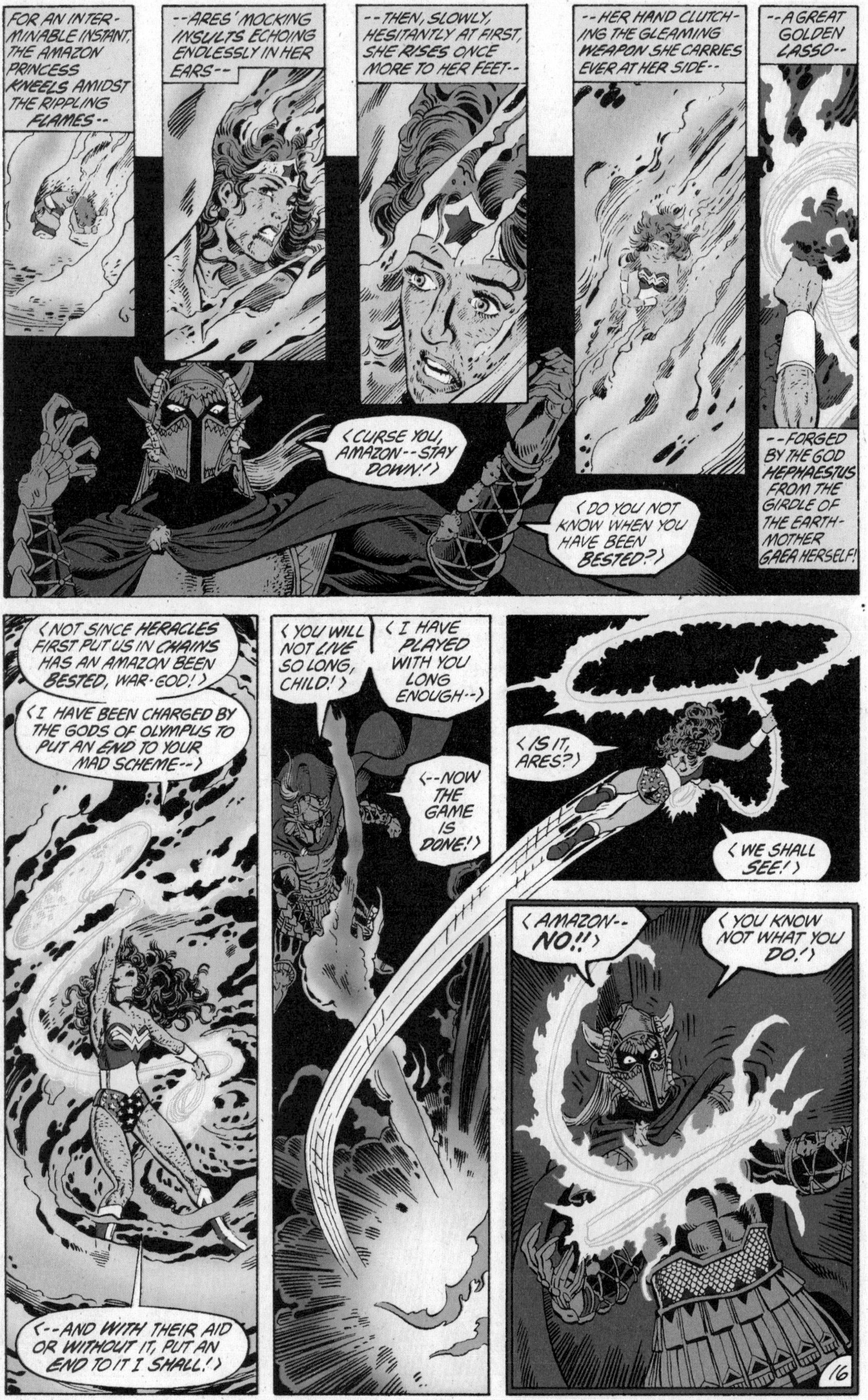
FOR AN INTERMINABLE INSTANT, THE AMAZON PRINCESS KNEELS AMIDST THE RIPPLING FLAMES--
--ARES' MOCKING INSULTS ECHOING ENDLESSLY IN HER EARS--
--THEN, SLOWLY, HESITANTLY AT FIRST, SHE RISES ONCE MORE TO HER FEET--
--HER HAND CLUTCHING THE GLEAMING WEAPON SHE CARRIES EVER AT HER SIDE--
--A GREAT GOLDEN LASSO--
--FORGED BY THE GOD HEPHAESTUS FROM THE GIRDLE OF THE EARTH-MOTHER GAEA HERSELF!
‹CURSE YOU, AMAZON--STAY DOWN!›
‹DO YOU NOT KNOW WHEN YOU HAVE BEEN BESTED?›
‹NOT SINCE HERACLES FIRST PUT US IN CHAINS HAS AN AMAZON BEEN BESTED, WAR-GOD!›
‹I HAVE BEEN CHARGED BY THE GODS OF OLYMPUS TO PUT AN END TO YOUR MAD SCHEME--›
‹--AND WITH THEIR AID OR WITHOUT IT, PUT AN END TO IT I SHALL!›
‹YOU WILL NOT LIVE SO LONG, CHILD!›
‹I HAVE PLAYED WITH YOU LONG ENOUGH--›
‹--NOW THE GAME IS DONE!›
‹IS IT, ARES?›
‹WE SHALL SEE!›
‹AMAZON--NO!!›
‹YOU KNOW NOT WHAT YOU DO!›
16

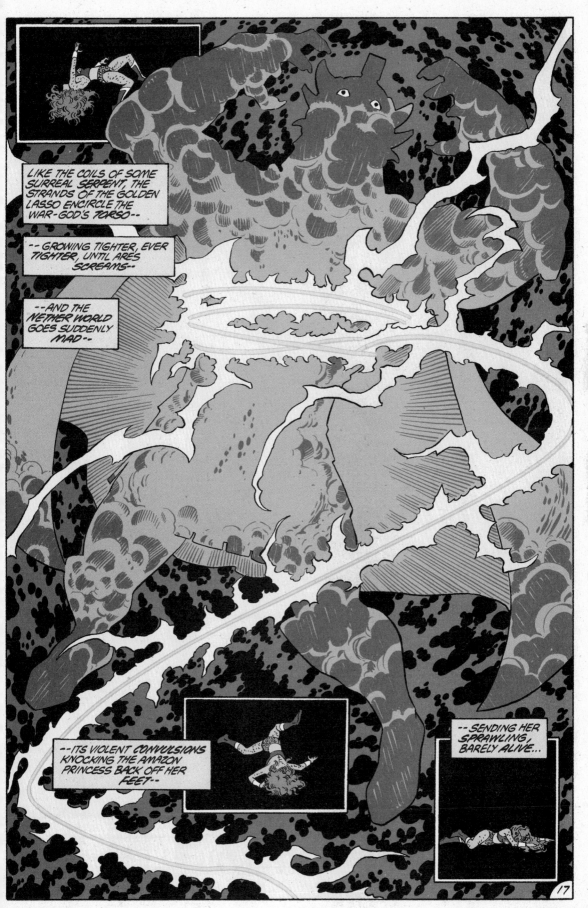

LIKE THE COILS OF SOME SURREAL *SERPENT*, THE STRANDS OF THE GOLDEN LASSO ENCIRCLE THE WAR-GOD'S *TORSO*--

--GROWING TIGHTER, EVER TIGHTER, UNTIL ARES *SCREAMS*--

--AND THE *NETHER WORLD* GOES SUDDENLY *MAD*--

--ITS VIOLENT *CONVULSIONS* KNOCKING THE AMAZON PRINCESS BACK OFF HER *FEET*--

--SENDING HER *SPRAWLING*, BARELY *ALIVE*...

17

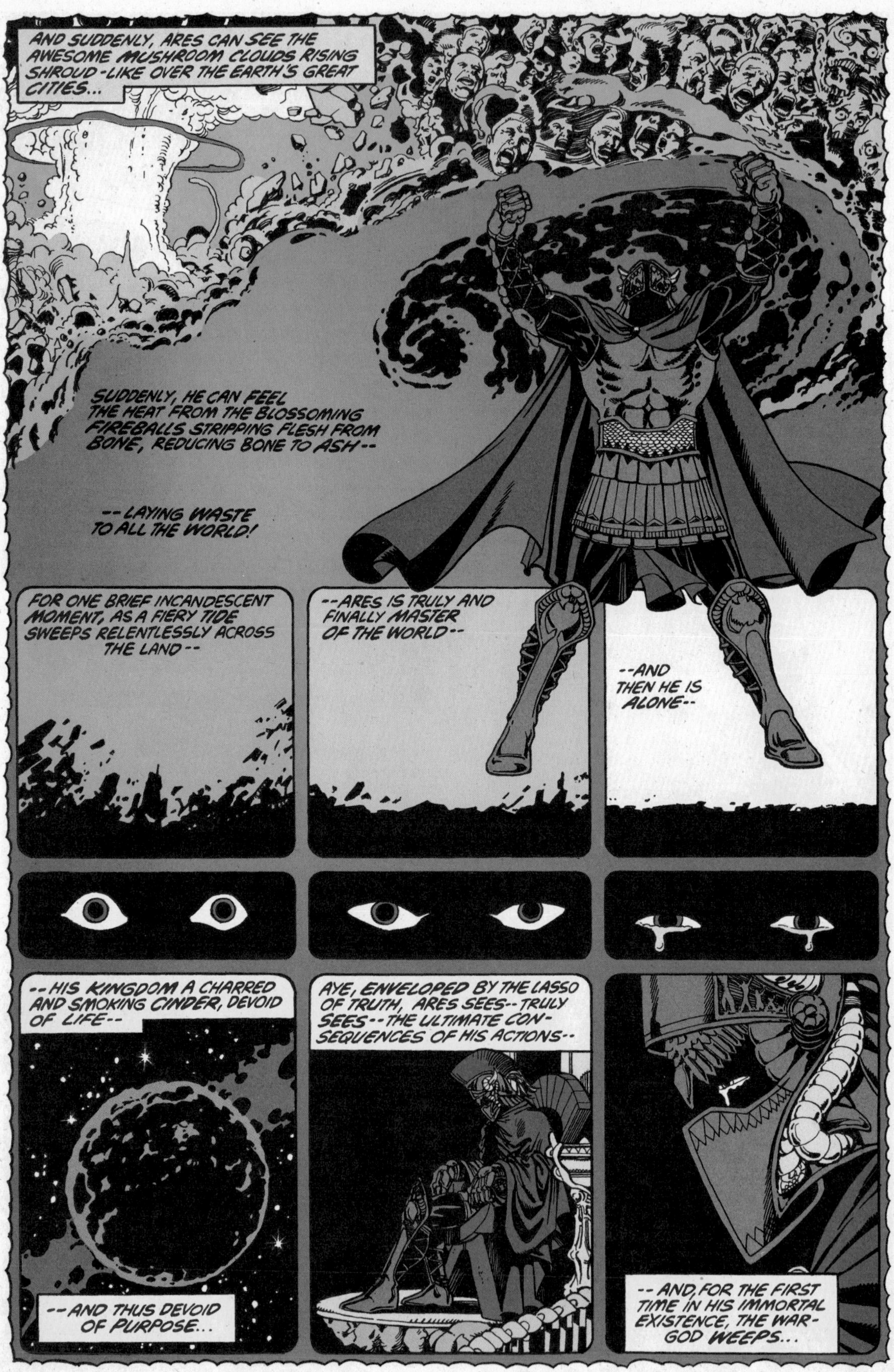
AND SUDDENLY, ARES CAN SEE THE AWESOME MUSHROOM CLOUDS RISING SHROUD-LIKE OVER THE EARTH'S GREAT CITIES...
SUDDENLY, HE CAN FEEL THE HEAT FROM THE BLOSSOMING FIREBALLS STRIPPING FLESH FROM BONE, REDUCING BONE TO ASH--
--LAYING WASTE TO ALL THE WORLD!
FOR ONE BRIEF INCANDESCENT MOMENT, AS A FIERY TIDE SWEEPS RELENTLESSLY ACROSS THE LAND--
--ARES IS TRULY AND FINALLY MASTER OF THE WORLD--
--AND THEN HE IS ALONE--
--HIS KINGDOM A CHARRED AND SMOKING CINDER, DEVOID OF LIFE--
--AND THUS DEVOID OF PURPOSE...
AYE, ENVELOPED BY THE LASSO OF TRUTH, ARES SEES--TRULY SEES--THE ULTIMATE CONSEQUENCES OF HIS ACTIONS--
--AND, FOR THE FIRST TIME IN HIS IMMORTAL EXISTENCE, THE WAR-GOD WEEPS...

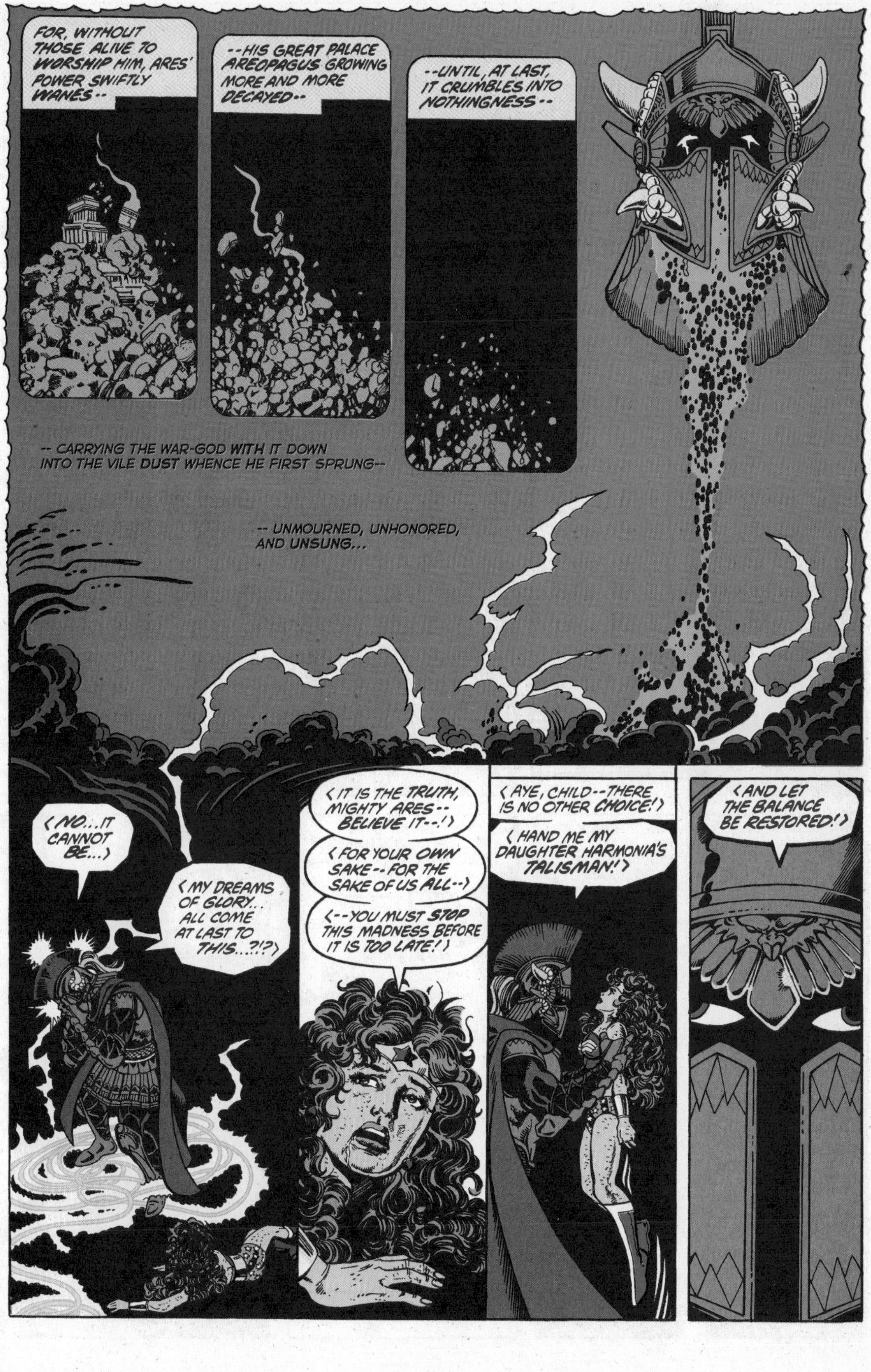
FOR, WITHOUT THOSE ALIVE TO WORSHIP HIM, ARES' POWER SWIFTLY WANES--
--HIS GREAT PALACE AREOPAGUS GROWING MORE AND MORE DECAYED--
--UNTIL, AT LAST, IT CRUMBLES INTO NOTHINGNESS--
-- CARRYING THE WAR-GOD WITH IT DOWN INTO THE VILE DUST WHENCE HE FIRST SPRUNG--
-- UNMOURNED, UNHONORED, AND UNSUNG...
⟨NO...IT CANNOT BE...⟩
⟨MY DREAMS OF GLORY... ALL COME AT LAST TO THIS...?!?⟩
⟨IT IS THE TRUTH, MIGHTY ARES-- BELIEVE IT--!⟩
⟨FOR YOUR OWN SAKE--FOR THE SAKE OF US ALL--⟩
⟨--YOU MUST STOP THIS MADNESS BEFORE IT IS TOO LATE!⟩
⟨AYE, CHILD--THERE IS NO OTHER CHOICE!⟩
⟨HAND ME MY DAUGHTER HARMONIA'S TALISMAN!⟩
⟨AND LET THE BALANCE BE RESTORED!⟩

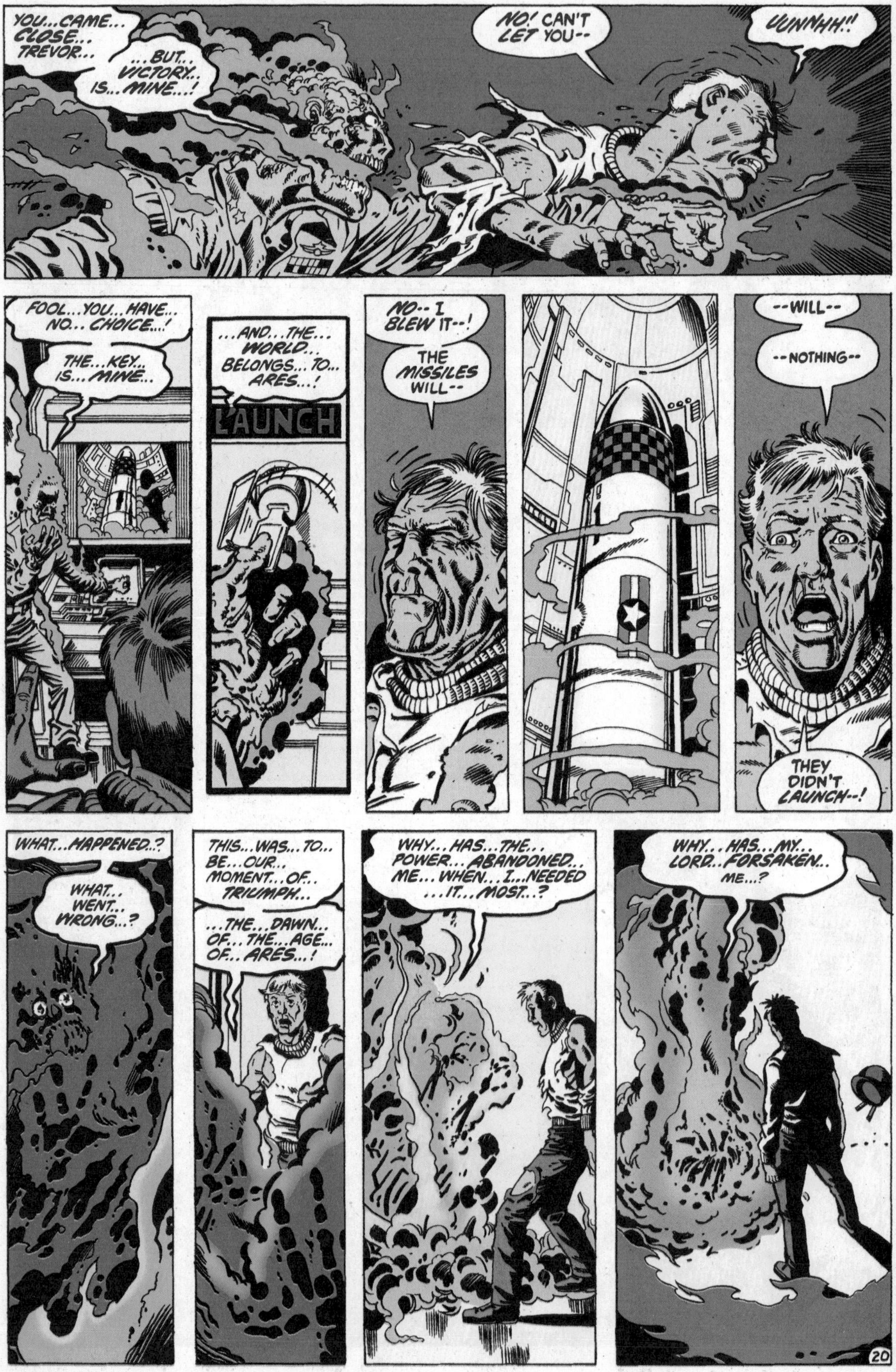
YOU...CAME... CLOSE... TREVOR...
...BUT... VICTORY... IS...MINE...!
NO! CAN'T LET YOU--
UUNNHH!!
FOOL...YOU...HAVE... NO... CHOICE...!
THE...KEY... IS...MINE...
...AND...THE... WORLD... BELONGS...TO... ARES...!
LAUNCH
NO-- I BLEW IT--!
THE MISSILES WILL--
--WILL--
--NOTHING--
THEY DIDN'T LAUNCH--!
WHAT...HAPPENED...?
WHAT... WENT... WRONG...?
THIS...WAS...TO... BE...OUR... MOMENT...OF... TRIUMPH...
...THE...DAWN... OF...THE...AGE... OF...ARES...!
WHY...HAS...THE... POWER...ABANDONED... ME...WHEN...I...NEEDED ...IT...MOST...?
WHY...HAS...MY... LORD...FORSAKEN... ME...?
20

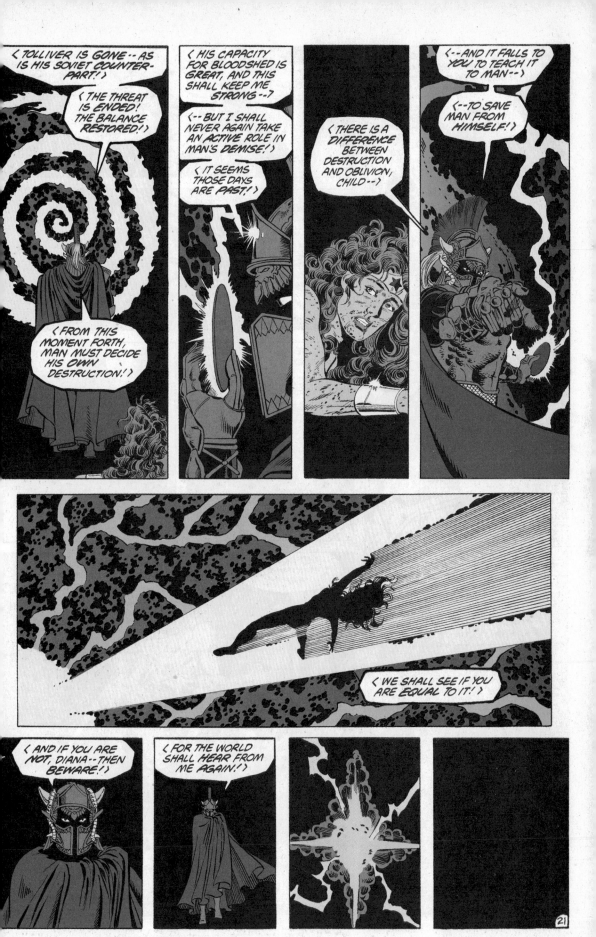

〈TOLLIVER IS GONE-- AS IS HIS SOVIET COUNTER-PART!〉

〈THE THREAT IS ENDED! THE BALANCE RESTORED!〉

〈FROM THIS MOMENT FORTH, MAN MUST DECIDE HIS OWN DESTRUCTION!〉

〈HIS CAPACITY FOR BLOODSHED IS GREAT, AND THIS SHALL KEEP ME STRONG --〉

〈-- BUT I SHALL NEVER AGAIN TAKE AN ACTIVE ROLE IN MAN'S DEMISE!〉

〈IT SEEMS THOSE DAYS ARE PAST!〉

〈THERE IS A DIFFERENCE BETWEEN DESTRUCTION AND OBLIVION, CHILD --〉

〈-- AND IT FALLS TO YOU TO TEACH IT TO MAN --〉

〈--TO SAVE MAN FROM HIMSELF!〉

〈WE SHALL SEE IF YOU ARE EQUAL TO IT!〉

〈AND IF YOU ARE NOT, DIANA--THEN BEWARE!〉

〈FOR THE WORLD SHALL HEAR FROM ME AGAIN!〉

159

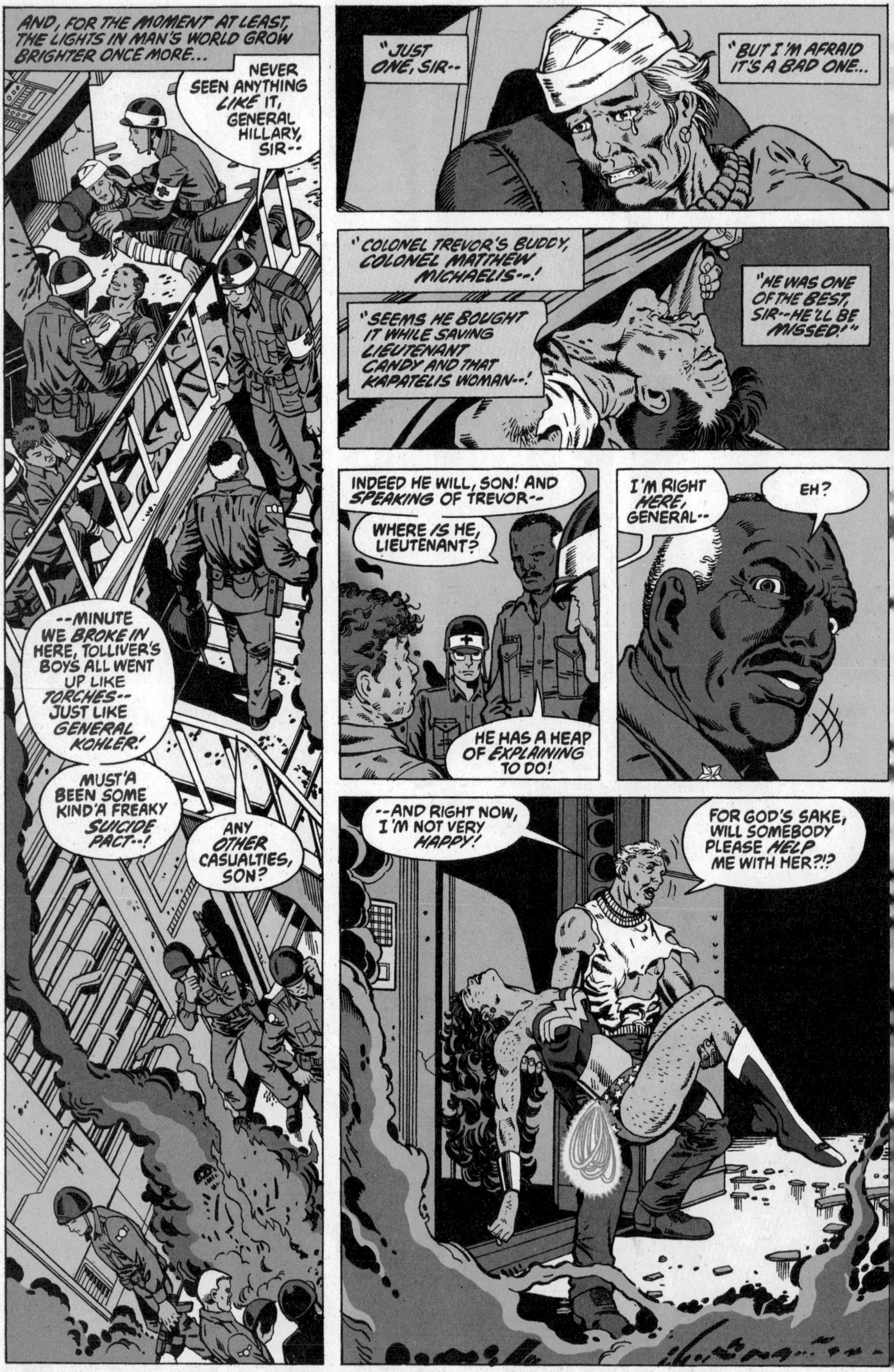
AND, FOR THE MOMENT AT LEAST, THE LIGHTS IN MAN'S WORLD GROW BRIGHTER ONCE MORE...
NEVER SEEN ANYTHING LIKE IT, GENERAL HILLARY, SIR--
--MINUTE WE BROKE IN HERE, TOLLIVER'S BOYS ALL WENT UP LIKE TORCHES--JUST LIKE GENERAL KOHLER!
MUST'A BEEN SOME KIND'A FREAKY SUICIDE PACT--!
ANY OTHER CASUALTIES, SON?
"JUST ONE, SIR--
"BUT I'M AFRAID IT'S A BAD ONE...
"COLONEL TREVOR'S BUDDY, COLONEL MATTHEW MICHAELIS--!
"SEEMS HE BOUGHT IT WHILE SAVING LIEUTENANT CANDY AND THAT KAPATELIS WOMAN--!
"HE WAS ONE OF THE BEST, SIR--HE'LL BE MISSED!"
INDEED HE WILL, SON! AND SPEAKING OF TREVOR--
WHERE IS HE, LIEUTENANT?
HE HAS A HEAP OF EXPLAINING TO DO!
I'M RIGHT HERE, GENERAL--
EH?
--AND RIGHT NOW, I'M NOT VERY HAPPY!
FOR GOD'S SAKE, WILL SOMEBODY PLEASE HELP ME WITH HER?!?

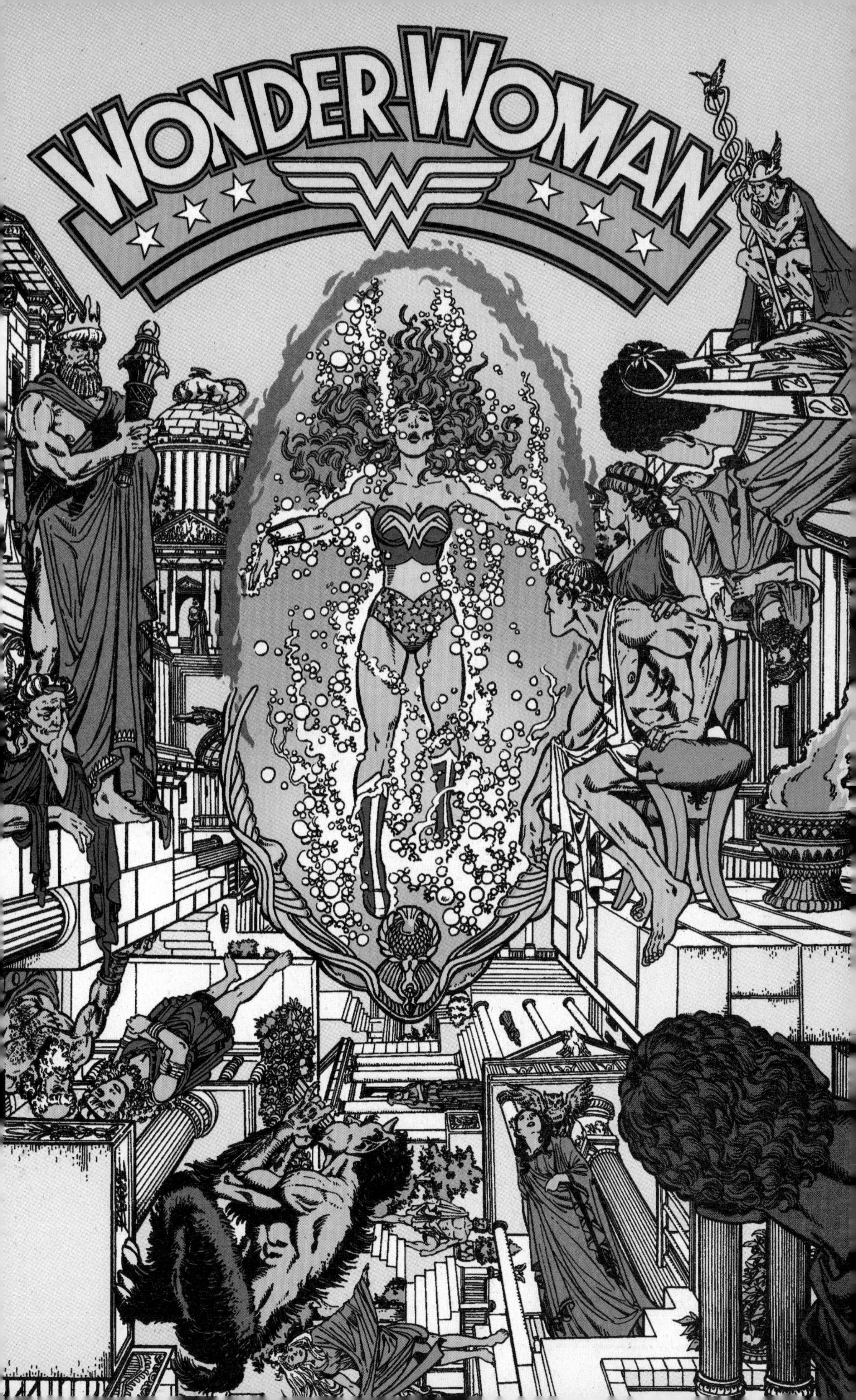
WONDER WOMAN

WONDER WOMAN

CHAPTER SEVEN

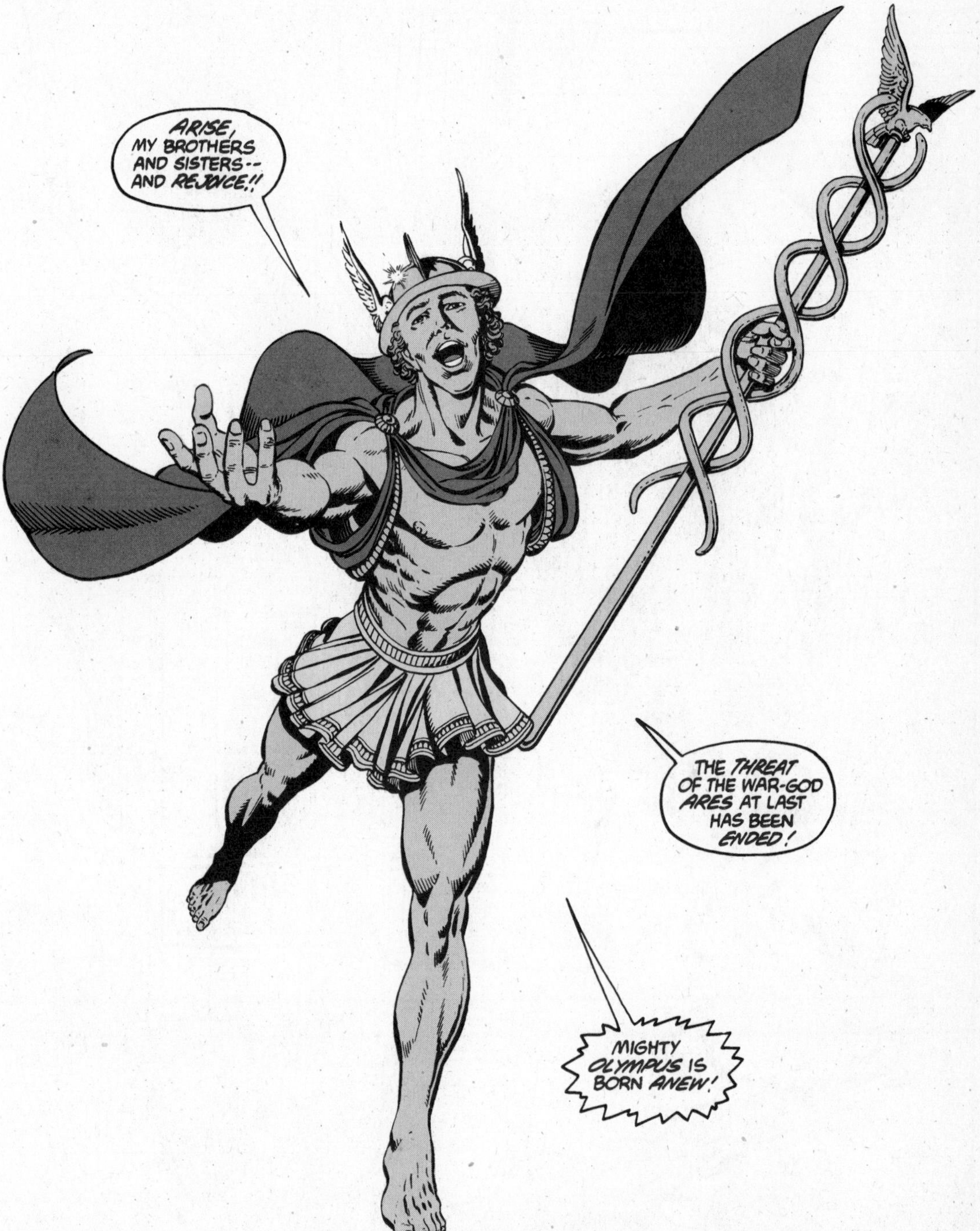
ARISE, MY BROTHERS AND SISTERS-- AND REJOICE!!
THE THREAT OF THE WAR-GOD ARES AT LAST HAS BEEN ENDED!
MIGHTY OLYMPUS IS BORN ANEW!

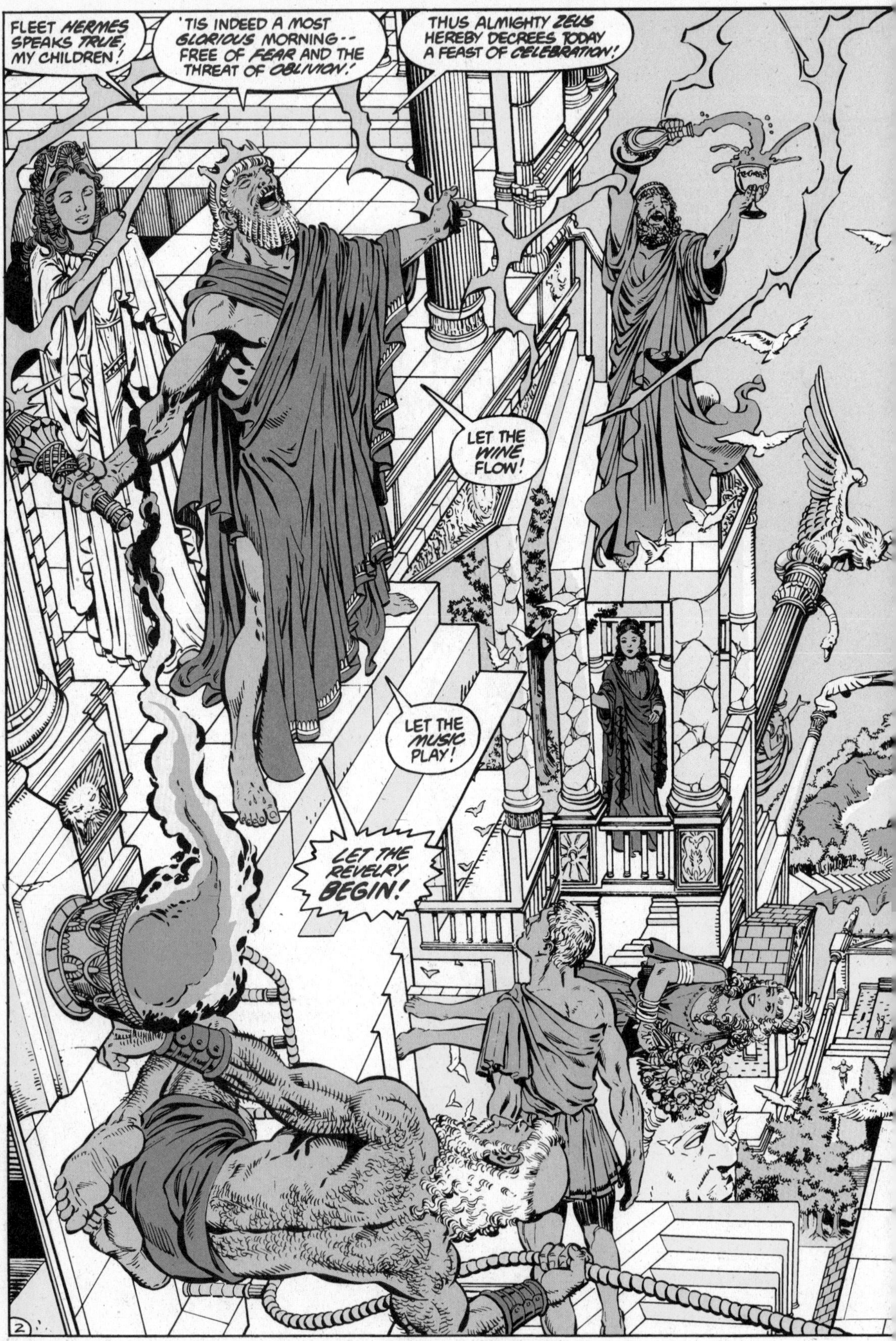
FLEET HERMES SPEAKS TRUE, MY CHILDREN!
'TIS INDEED A MOST GLORIOUS MORNING-- FREE OF FEAR AND THE THREAT OF OBLIVION!
THUS ALMIGHTY ZEUS HEREBY DECREES TODAY A FEAST OF CELEBRATION!
LET THE WINE FLOW!
LET THE MUSIC PLAY!
LET THE REVELRY BEGIN!
2

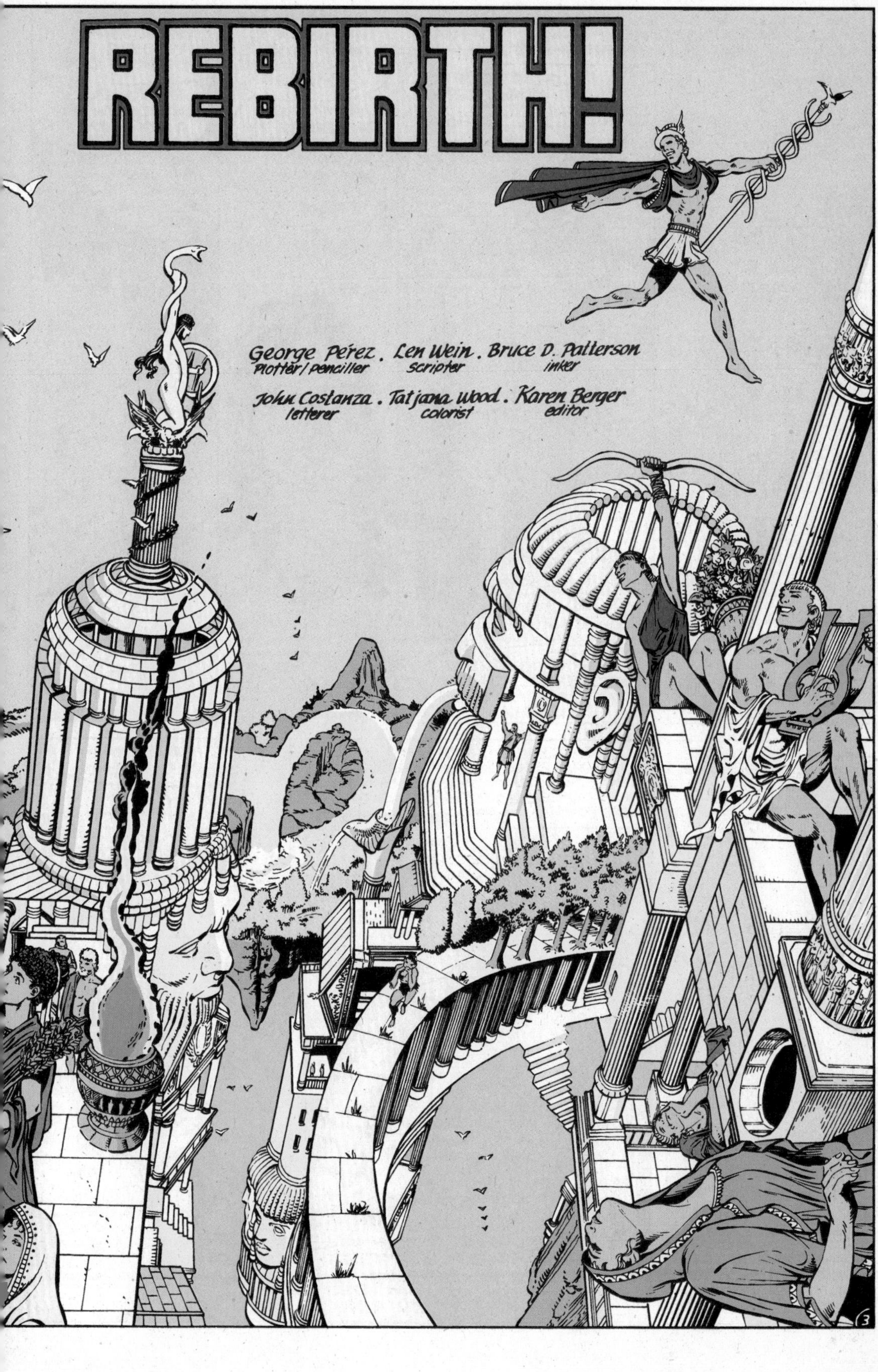

REBIRTH!
George Pérez . Len Wein . Bruce D. Patterson
Plotter/penciller scripter inker
John Costanza . Tatjana Wood . Karen Berger
letterer colorist editor

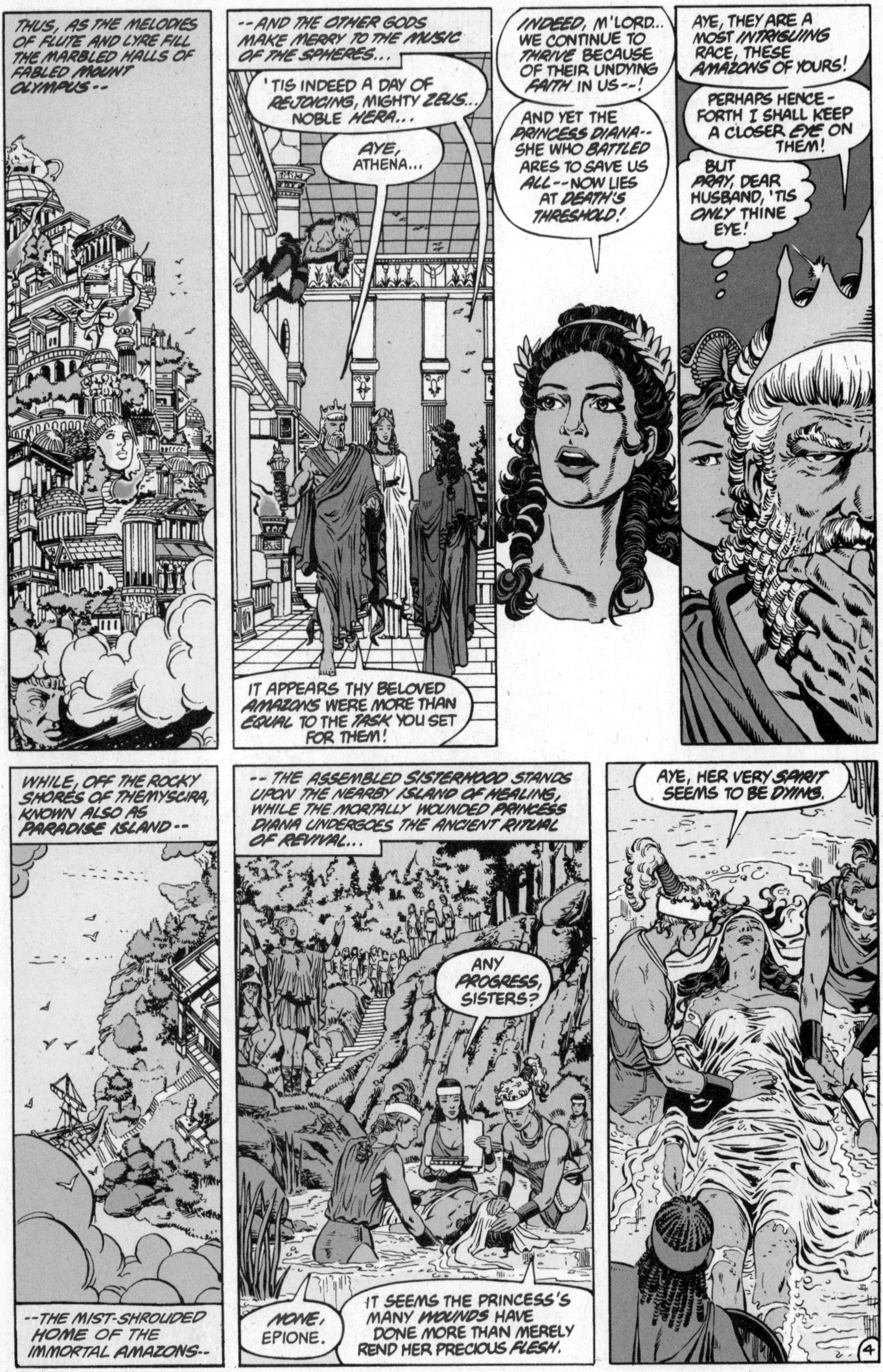
THUS, AS THE MELODIES OF FLUTE AND LYRE FILL THE MARBLED HALLS OF FABLED MOUNT OLYMPUS --
-- AND THE OTHER GODS MAKE MERRY TO THE MUSIC OF THE SPHERES...
'TIS INDEED A DAY OF REJOICING, MIGHTY ZEUS... NOBLE HERA...
AYE, ATHENA...
IT APPEARS THY BELOVED AMAZONS WERE MORE THAN EQUAL TO THE TASK YOU SET FOR THEM!
INDEED, M'LORD... WE CONTINUE TO THRIVE BECAUSE OF THEIR UNDYING FAITH IN US --!
AND YET THE PRINCESS DIANA -- SHE WHO BATTLED ARES TO SAVE US ALL -- NOW LIES AT DEATH'S THRESHOLD!
AYE, THEY ARE A MOST INTRIGUING RACE, THESE AMAZONS OF YOURS!
PERHAPS HENCE-FORTH I SHALL KEEP A CLOSER EYE ON THEM!
BUT PRAY, DEAR HUSBAND, 'TIS ONLY THINE EYE!
WHILE, OFF THE ROCKY SHORES OF THEMYSCIRA, KNOWN ALSO AS PARADISE ISLAND --
-- THE MIST-SHROUDED HOME OF THE IMMORTAL AMAZONS --
-- THE ASSEMBLED SISTERHOOD STANDS UPON THE NEARBY ISLAND OF HEALING, WHILE THE MORTALLY WOUNDED PRINCESS DIANA UNDERGOES THE ANCIENT RITUAL OF REVIVAL...
ANY PROGRESS, SISTERS?
NONE, EPIONE.
IT SEEMS THE PRINCESS'S MANY WOUNDS HAVE DONE MORE THAN MERELY REND HER PRECIOUS FLESH.
AYE, HER VERY SPIRIT SEEMS TO BE DYING.
4

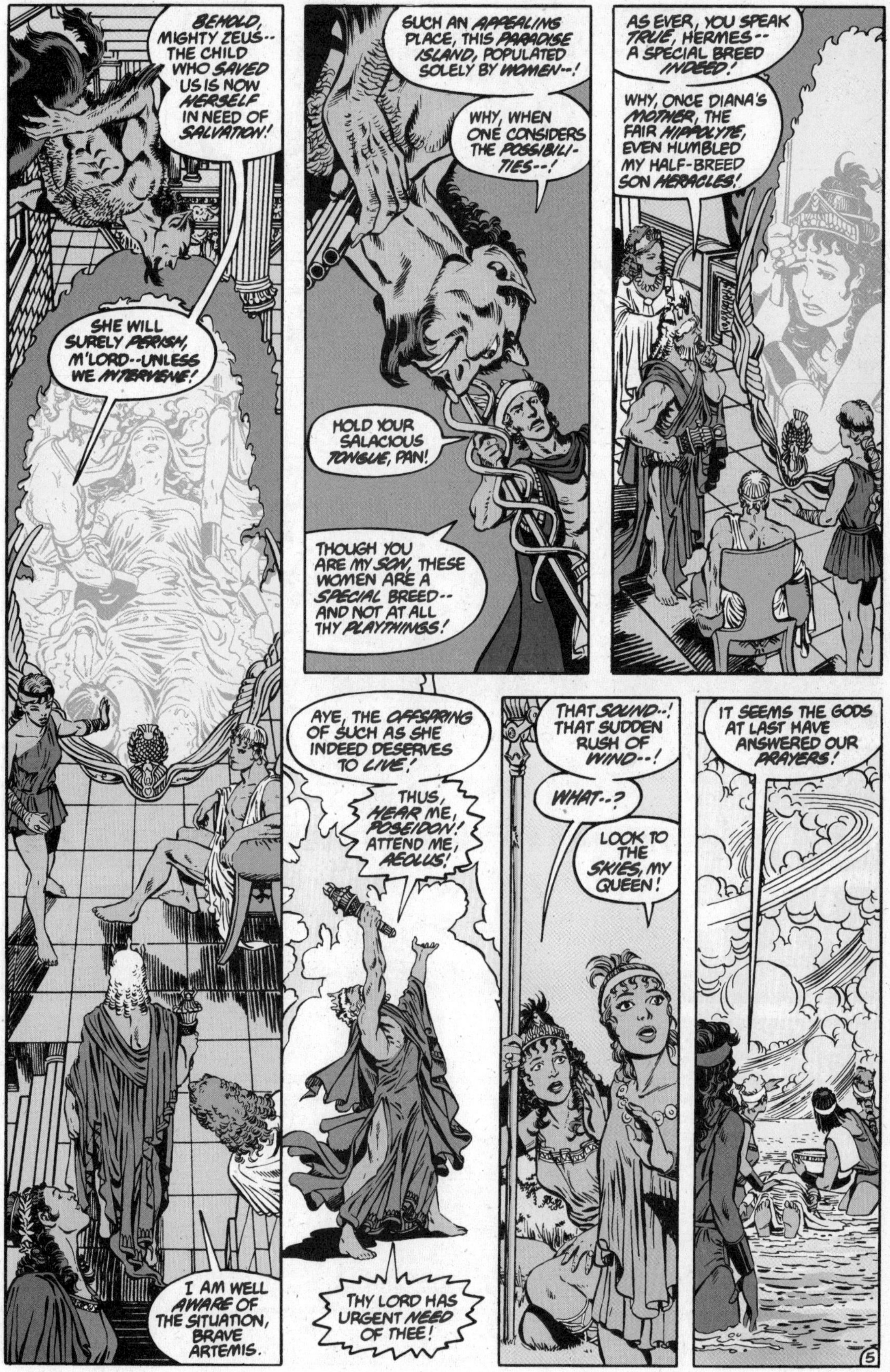
BEHOLD, MIGHTY ZEUS-- THE CHILD WHO SAVED US IS NOW HERSELF IN NEED OF SALVATION!
SHE WILL SURELY PERISH, M'LORD--UNLESS WE INTERVENE!
I AM WELL AWARE OF THE SITUATION, BRAVE ARTEMIS.
SUCH AN APPEALING PLACE, THIS PARADISE ISLAND, POPULATED SOLELY BY WOMEN--!
WHY, WHEN ONE CONSIDERS THE POSSIBILI-TIES--!
HOLD YOUR SALACIOUS TONGUE, PAN!
THOUGH YOU ARE MY SON, THESE WOMEN ARE A SPECIAL BREED-- AND NOT AT ALL THY PLAYTHINGS!
AS EVER, YOU SPEAK TRUE, HERMES-- A SPECIAL BREED INDEED!
WHY, ONCE DIANA'S MOTHER, THE FAIR HIPPOLYTE, EVEN HUMBLED MY HALF-BREED SON HERACLES!
AYE, THE OFFSPRING OF SUCH AS SHE INDEED DESERVES TO LIVE!
THUS, HEAR ME, POSEIDON! ATTEND ME, AEOLUS!
THY LORD HAS URGENT NEED OF THEE!
THAT SOUND--! THAT SUDDEN RUSH OF WIND--!
WHAT--?
LOOK TO THE SKIES, MY QUEEN!
IT SEEMS THE GODS AT LAST HAVE ANSWERED OUR PRAYERS!
5

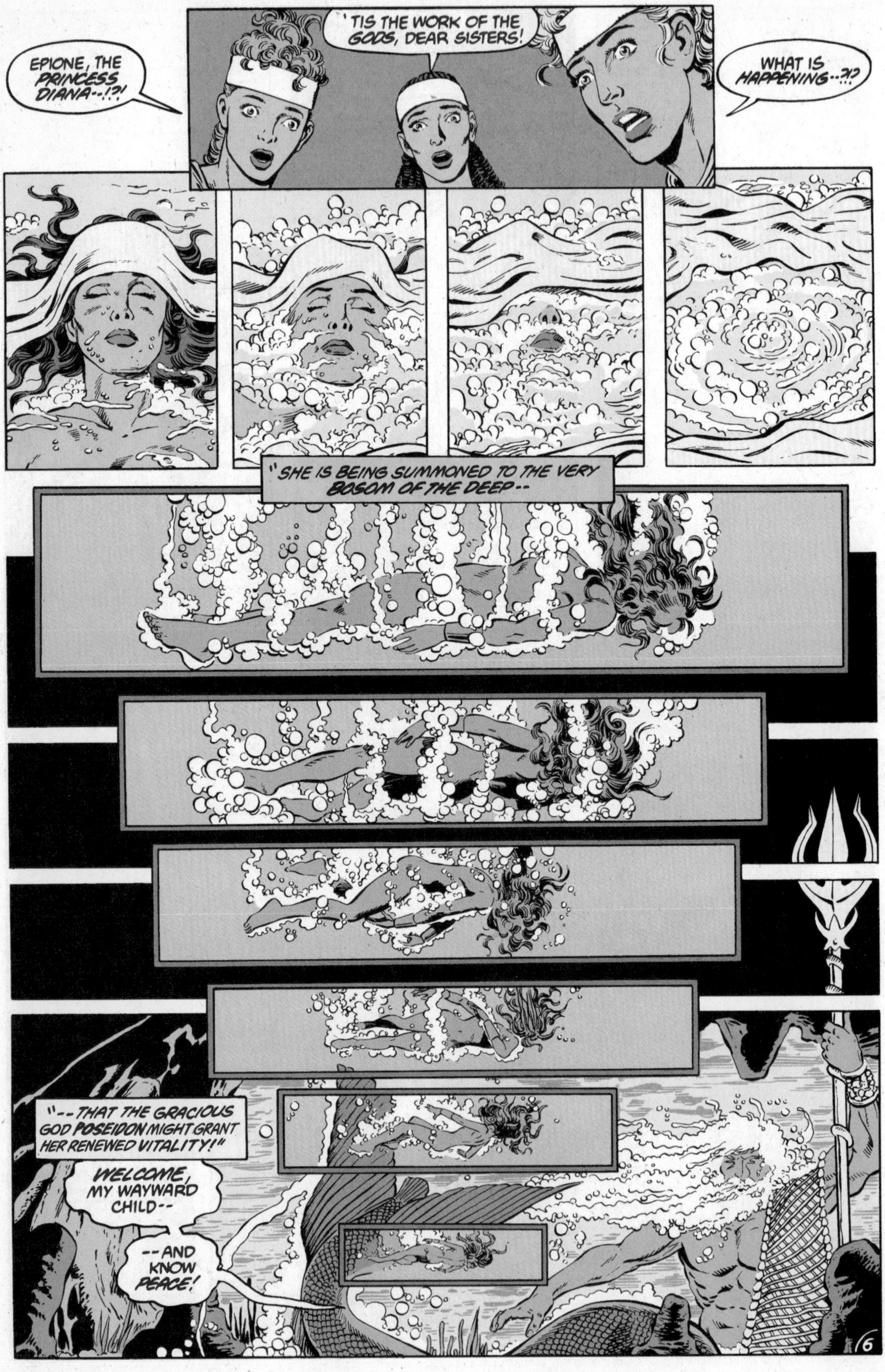
EPIONE, THE PRINCESS DIANA--!?!
'TIS THE WORK OF THE GODS, DEAR SISTERS!
WHAT IS HAPPENING--?!?
"SHE IS BEING SUMMONED TO THE VERY BOSOM OF THE DEEP--
"--THAT THE GRACIOUS GOD POSEIDON MIGHT GRANT HER RENEWED VITALITY!"
WELCOME, MY WAYWARD CHILD--
--AND KNOW PEACE!
16

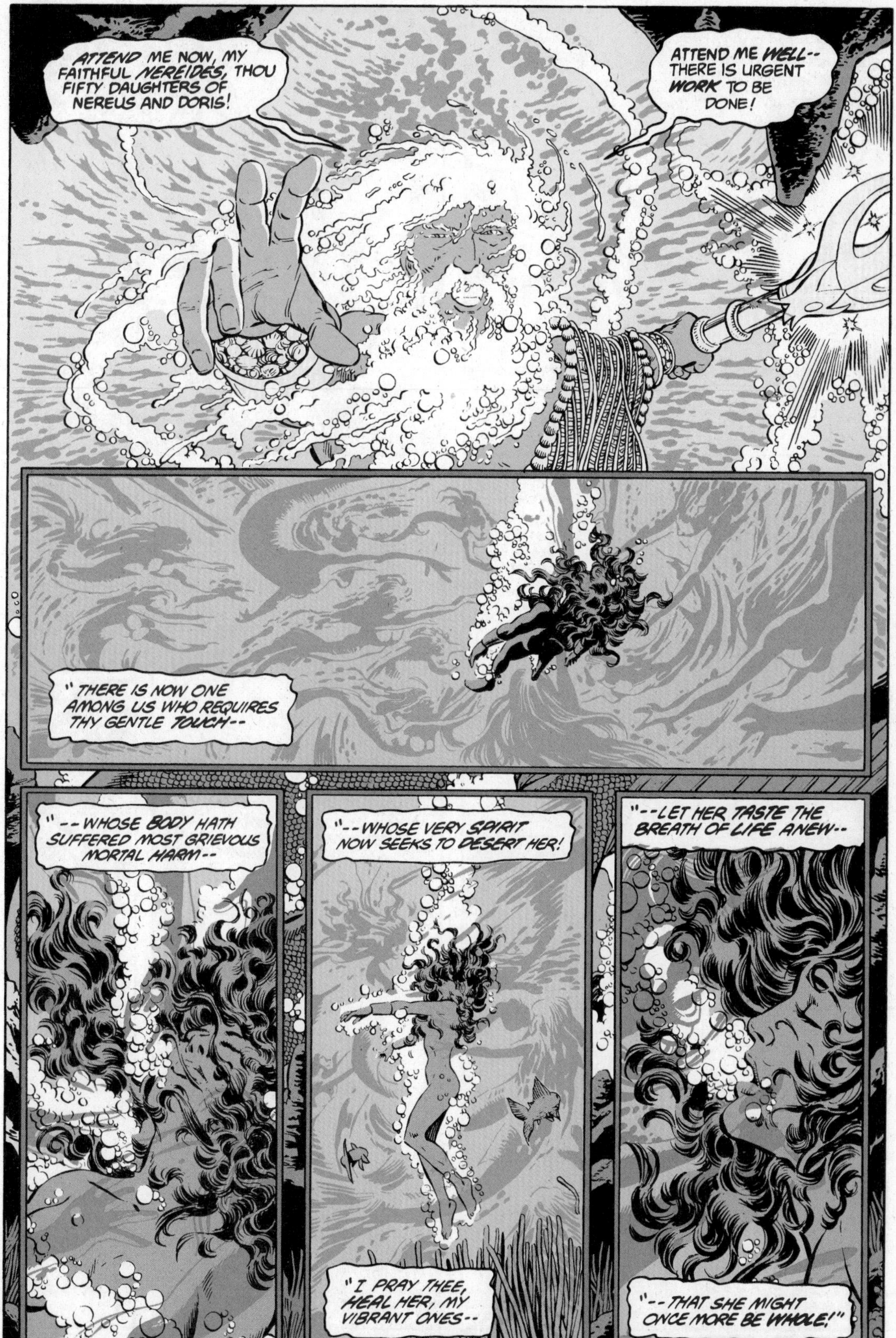
ATTEND ME NOW, MY FAITHFUL NEREIDES, THOU FIFTY DAUGHTERS OF NEREUS AND DORIS!
ATTEND ME WELL-- THERE IS URGENT WORK TO BE DONE!
"THERE IS NOW ONE AMONG US WHO REQUIRES THY GENTLE TOUCH--
"--WHOSE BODY HATH SUFFERED MOST GRIEVOUS MORTAL HARM--
"--WHOSE VERY SPIRIT NOW SEEKS TO DESERT HER!
"I PRAY THEE, HEAL HER, MY VIBRANT ONES--
"--LET HER TASTE THE BREATH OF LIFE ANEW--
"--THAT SHE MIGHT ONCE MORE BE WHOLE!"
7

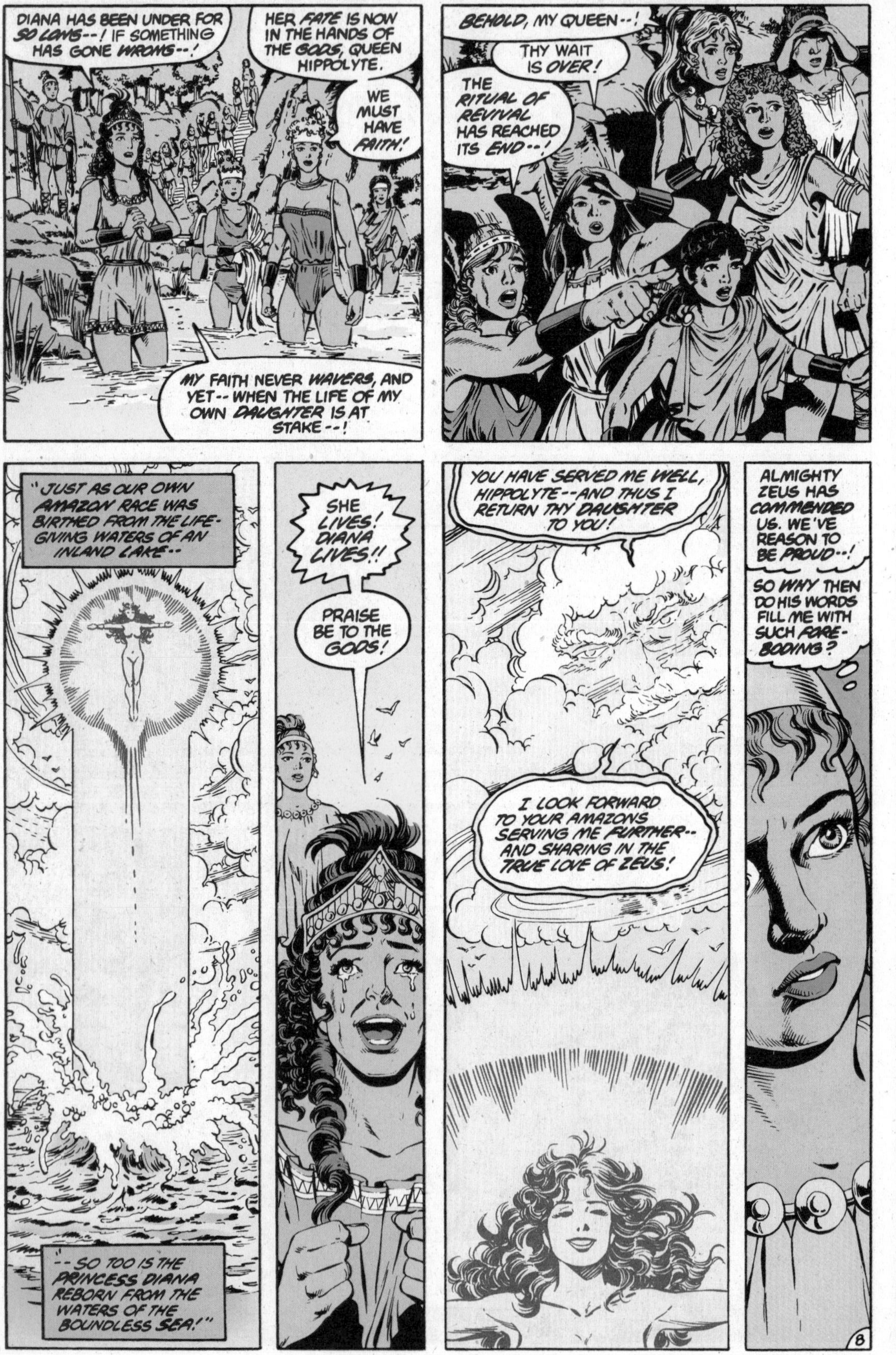
DIANA HAS BEEN UNDER FOR SO LONG--! IF SOMETHING HAS GONE WRONG--!
HER FATE IS NOW IN THE HANDS OF THE GODS, QUEEN HIPPOLYTE.
WE MUST HAVE FAITH!
MY FAITH NEVER WAVERS, AND YET-- WHEN THE LIFE OF MY OWN DAUGHTER IS AT STAKE--!
BEHOLD, MY QUEEN--!
THY WAIT IS OVER!
THE RITUAL OF REVIVAL HAS REACHED ITS END--!
"JUST AS OUR OWN AMAZON RACE WAS BIRTHED FROM THE LIFE-GIVING WATERS OF AN INLAND LAKE--
--SO TOO IS THE PRINCESS DIANA REBORN FROM THE WATERS OF THE BOUNDLESS SEA!"
SHE LIVES! DIANA LIVES!!
PRAISE BE TO THE GODS!
YOU HAVE SERVED ME WELL, HIPPOLYTE--AND THUS I RETURN THY DAUGHTER TO YOU!
I LOOK FORWARD TO YOUR AMAZONS SERVING ME FURTHER--AND SHARING IN THE TRUE LOVE OF ZEUS!
ALMIGHTY ZEUS HAS COMMENDED US. WE'VE REASON TO BE PROUD--!
SO WHY THEN DO HIS WORDS FILL ME WITH SUCH FOREBODING?
8

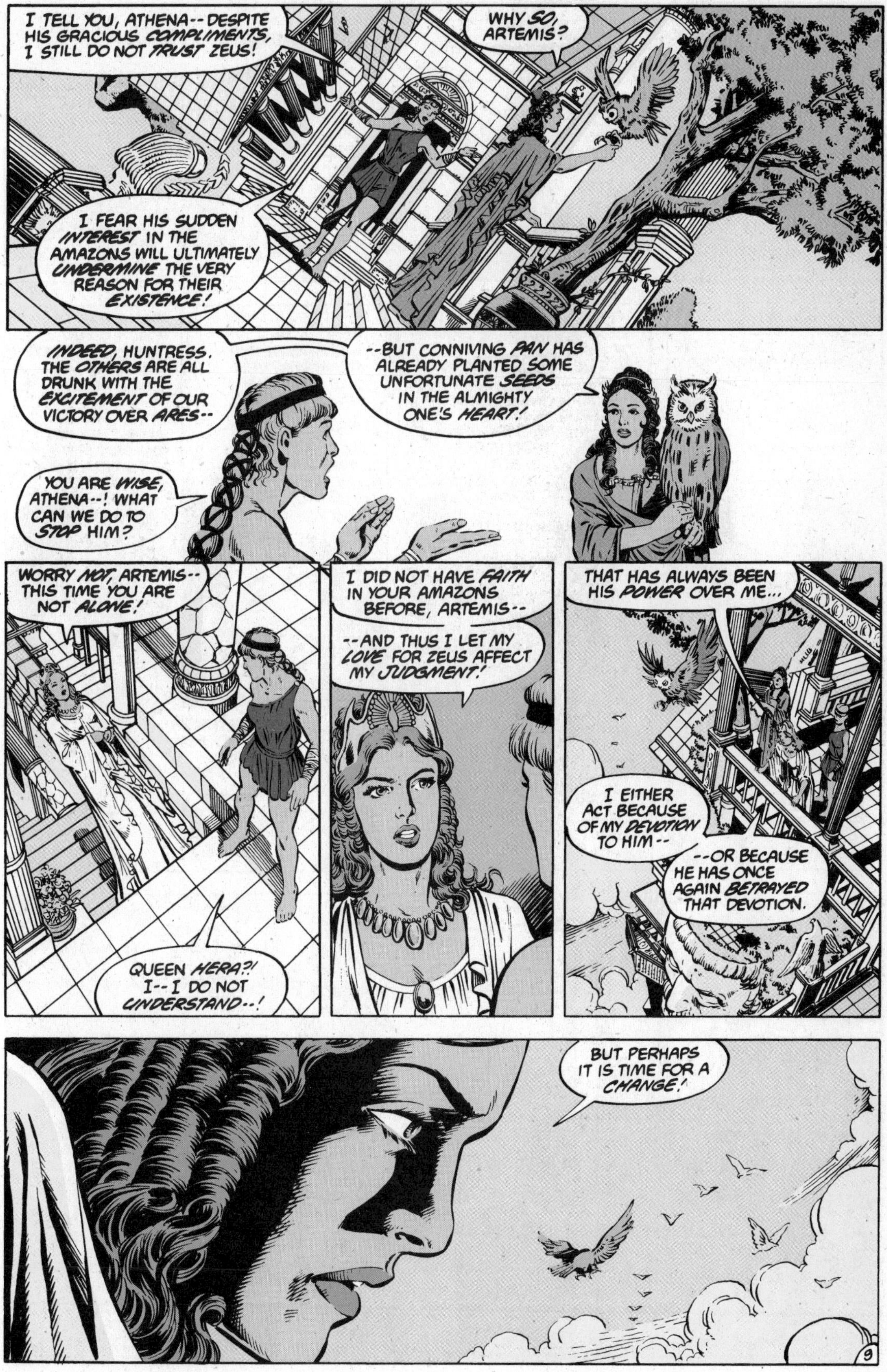
I TELL YOU, ATHENA-- DESPITE HIS GRACIOUS COMPLIMENTS, I STILL DO NOT TRUST ZEUS!
WHY SO, ARTEMIS?
I FEAR HIS SUDDEN INTEREST IN THE AMAZONS WILL ULTIMATELY UNDERMINE THE VERY REASON FOR THEIR EXISTENCE!
INDEED, HUNTRESS. THE OTHERS ARE ALL DRUNK WITH THE EXCITEMENT OF OUR VICTORY OVER ARES--
--BUT CONNIVING PAN HAS ALREADY PLANTED SOME UNFORTUNATE SEEDS IN THE ALMIGHTY ONE'S HEART!
YOU ARE WISE, ATHENA--! WHAT CAN WE DO TO STOP HIM?
WORRY NOT, ARTEMIS-- THIS TIME YOU ARE NOT ALONE!
QUEEN HERA?! I-- I DO NOT UNDERSTAND--!
I DID NOT HAVE FAITH IN YOUR AMAZONS BEFORE, ARTEMIS--
--AND THUS I LET MY LOVE FOR ZEUS AFFECT MY JUDGMENT!
THAT HAS ALWAYS BEEN HIS POWER OVER ME...
I EITHER ACT BECAUSE OF MY DEVOTION TO HIM--
--OR BECAUSE HE HAS ONCE AGAIN BETRAYED THAT DEVOTION.
BUT PERHAPS IT IS TIME FOR A CHANGE!
9

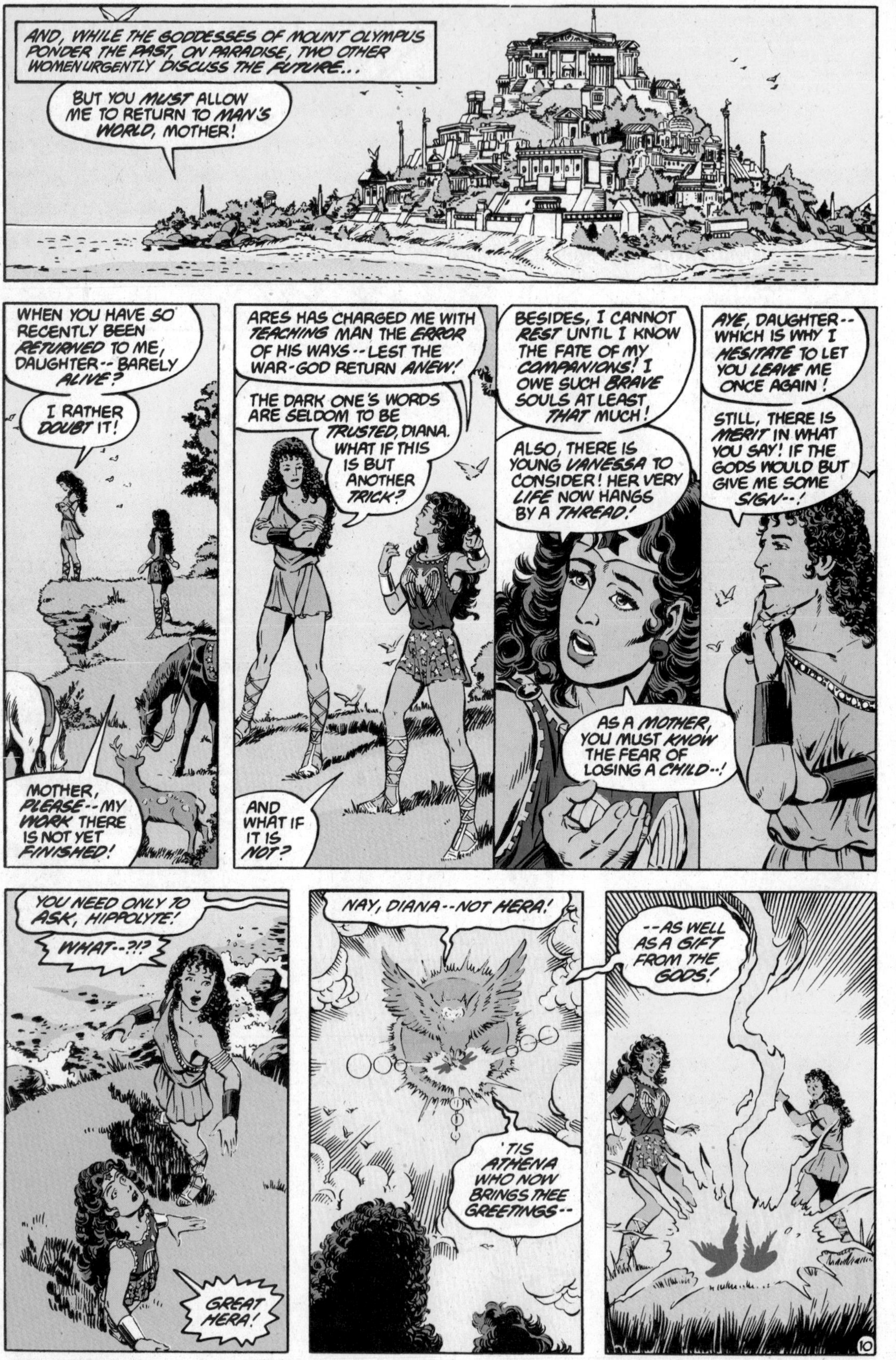

AND, WHILE THE GODDESSES OF MOUNT OLYMPUS PONDER THE PAST, ON PARADISE, TWO OTHER WOMEN URGENTLY DISCUSS THE FUTURE...
BUT YOU MUST ALLOW ME TO RETURN TO MAN'S WORLD, MOTHER!
WHEN YOU HAVE SO RECENTLY BEEN RETURNED TO ME, DAUGHTER-- BARELY ALIVE?
I RATHER DOUBT IT!
MOTHER, PLEASE--MY WORK THERE IS NOT YET FINISHED!
ARES HAS CHARGED ME WITH TEACHING MAN THE ERROR OF HIS WAYS--LEST THE WAR-GOD RETURN ANEW!
THE DARK ONE'S WORDS ARE SELDOM TO BE TRUSTED, DIANA. WHAT IF THIS IS BUT ANOTHER TRICK?
AND WHAT IF IT IS NOT?
BESIDES, I CANNOT REST UNTIL I KNOW THE FATE OF MY COMPANIONS! I OWE SUCH BRAVE SOULS AT LEAST THAT MUCH!
ALSO, THERE IS YOUNG VANESSA TO CONSIDER! HER VERY LIFE NOW HANGS BY A THREAD!
AS A MOTHER, YOU MUST KNOW THE FEAR OF LOSING A CHILD--!
AYE, DAUGHTER--WHICH IS WHY I HESITATE TO LET YOU LEAVE ME ONCE AGAIN!
STILL, THERE IS MERIT IN WHAT YOU SAY! IF THE GODS WOULD BUT GIVE ME SOME SIGN--!
YOU NEED ONLY TO ASK, HIPPOLYTE!
WHAT--?!?
GREAT HERA!
NAY, DIANA--NOT HERA!
'TIS ATHENA WHO NOW BRINGS THEE GREETINGS--
--AS WELL AS A GIFT FROM THE GODS!
10

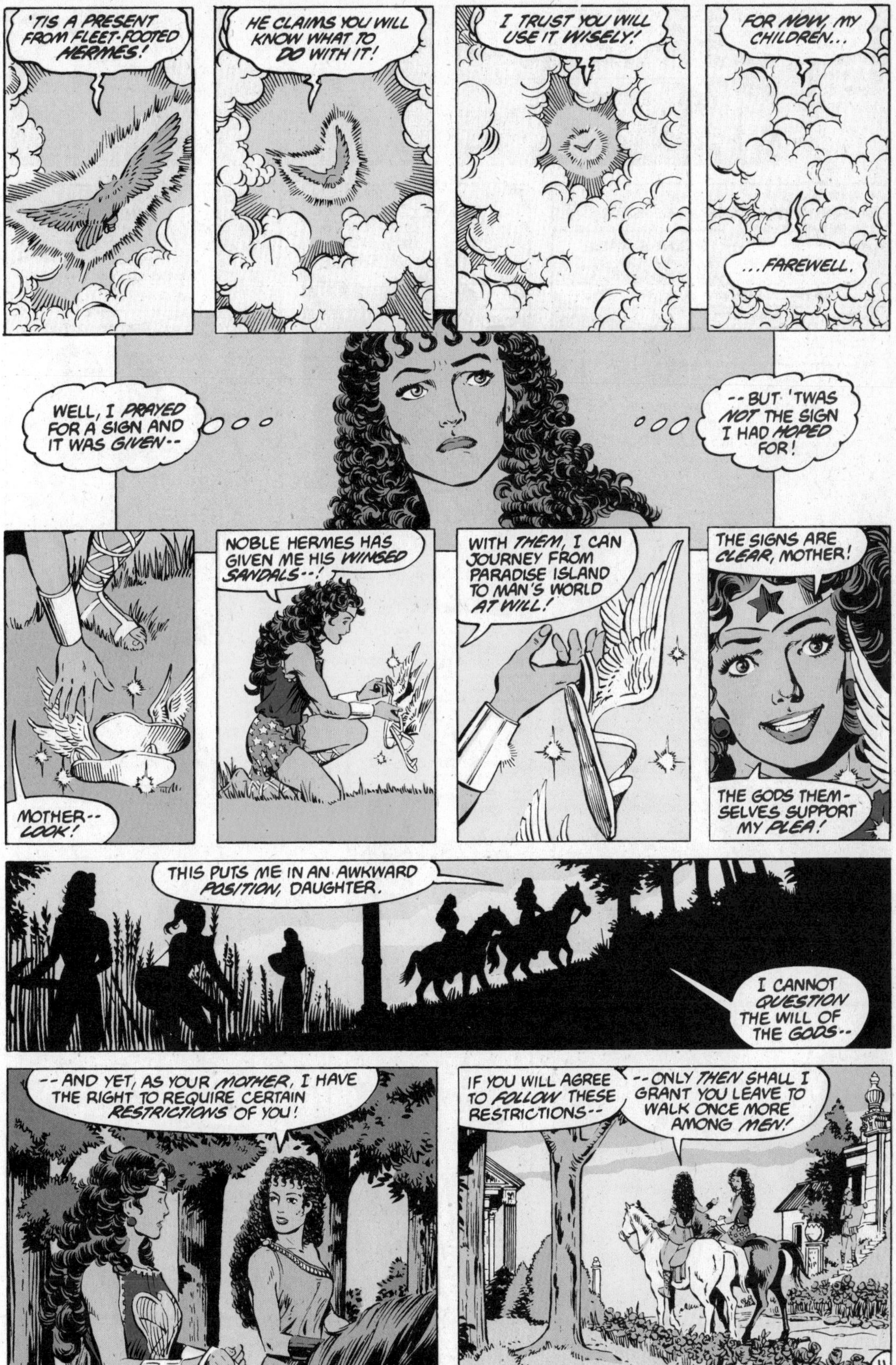
'TIS A PRESENT FROM FLEET-FOOTED HERMES!
HE CLAIMS YOU WILL KNOW WHAT TO DO WITH IT!
I TRUST YOU WILL USE IT WISELY!
FOR NOW, MY CHILDREN...
...FAREWELL.
WELL, I PRAYED FOR A SIGN AND IT WAS GIVEN--
--BUT 'TWAS NOT THE SIGN I HAD HOPED FOR!
MOTHER--LOOK!
NOBLE HERMES HAS GIVEN ME HIS WINGED SANDALS--!
WITH THEM, I CAN JOURNEY FROM PARADISE ISLAND TO MAN'S WORLD AT WILL!
THE SIGNS ARE CLEAR, MOTHER!
THE GODS THEMSELVES SUPPORT MY PLEA!
THIS PUTS ME IN AN AWKWARD POSITION, DAUGHTER.
I CANNOT QUESTION THE WILL OF THE GODS--
--AND YET, AS YOUR MOTHER, I HAVE THE RIGHT TO REQUIRE CERTAIN RESTRICTIONS OF YOU!
IF YOU WILL AGREE TO FOLLOW THESE RESTRICTIONS--
--ONLY THEN SHALL I GRANT YOU LEAVE TO WALK ONCE MORE AMONG MEN!
11

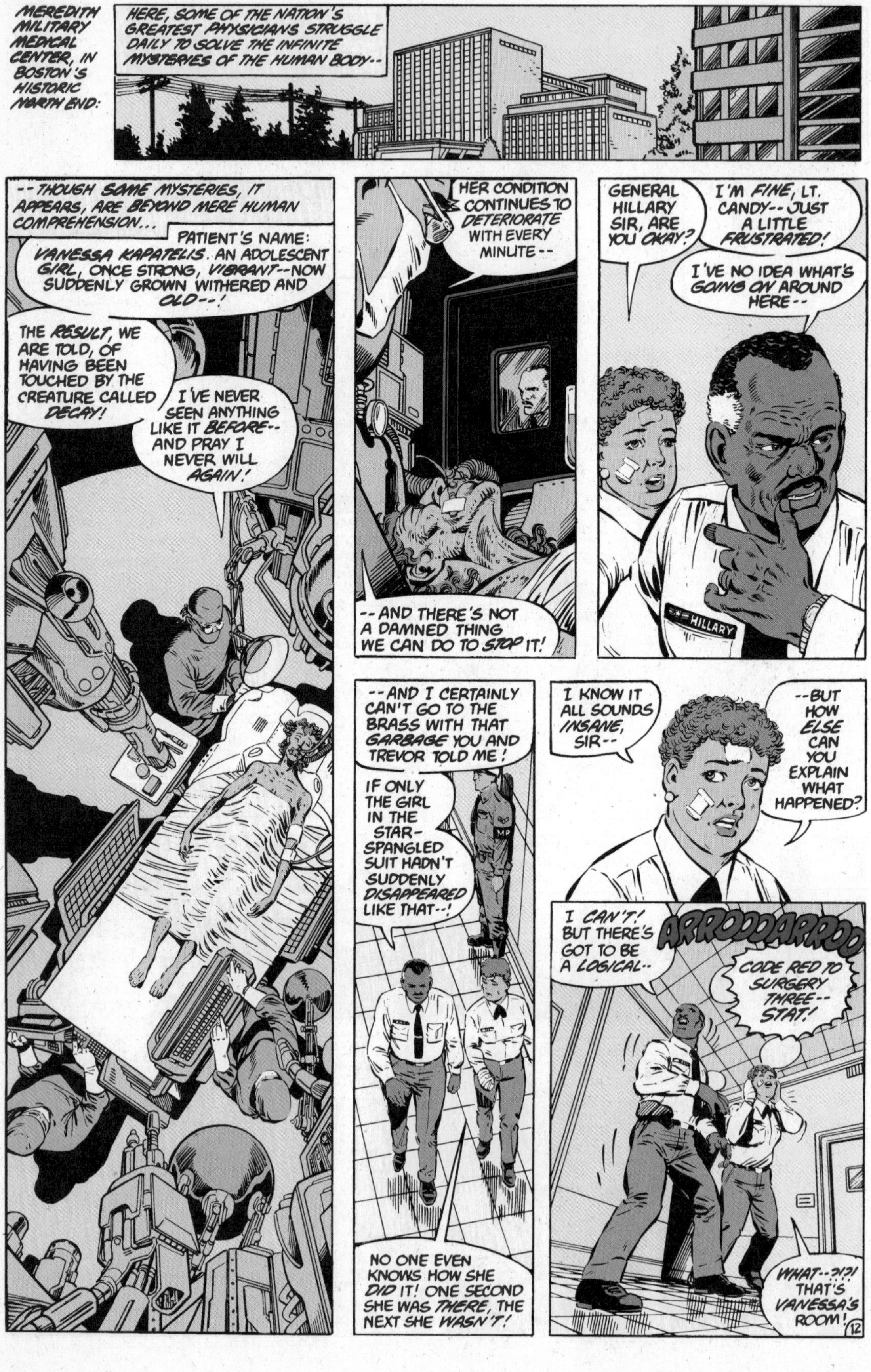

MEREDITH MILITARY MEDICAL CENTER, IN BOSTON'S HISTORIC NORTH END:
HERE, SOME OF THE NATION'S GREATEST PHYSICIANS STRUGGLE DAILY TO SOLVE THE INFINITE MYSTERIES OF THE HUMAN BODY--
--THOUGH SOME MYSTERIES, IT APPEARS, ARE BEYOND MERE HUMAN COMPREHENSION...
PATIENT'S NAME: VANESSA KAPATELIS. AN ADOLESCENT GIRL, ONCE STRONG, VIBRANT--NOW SUDDENLY GROWN WITHERED AND OLD--!
THE RESULT, WE ARE TOLD, OF HAVING BEEN TOUCHED BY THE CREATURE CALLED DECAY!
I'VE NEVER SEEN ANYTHING LIKE IT BEFORE--AND PRAY I NEVER WILL AGAIN!
HER CONDITION CONTINUES TO DETERIORATE WITH EVERY MINUTE--
--AND THERE'S NOT A DAMNED THING WE CAN DO TO STOP IT!
GENERAL HILLARY SIR, ARE YOU OKAY?
I'M FINE, LT. CANDY--JUST A LITTLE FRUSTRATED!
I'VE NO IDEA WHAT'S GOING ON AROUND HERE--
HILLARY
--AND I CERTAINLY CAN'T GO TO THE BRASS WITH THAT GARBAGE YOU AND TREVOR TOLD ME!
IF ONLY THE GIRL IN THE STAR-SPANGLED SUIT HADN'T SUDDENLY DISAPPEARED LIKE THAT--!
MP
NO ONE EVEN KNOWS HOW SHE DID IT! ONE SECOND SHE WAS THERE, THE NEXT SHE WASN'T!
I KNOW IT ALL SOUNDS INSANE, SIR--
--BUT HOW ELSE CAN YOU EXPLAIN WHAT HAPPENED?
I CAN'T! BUT THERE'S GOT TO BE A LOGICAL--
ARROOOARROO
CODE RED TO SURGERY THREE--STAT!
WHAT--?!?! THAT'S VANESSA'S ROOM!
12

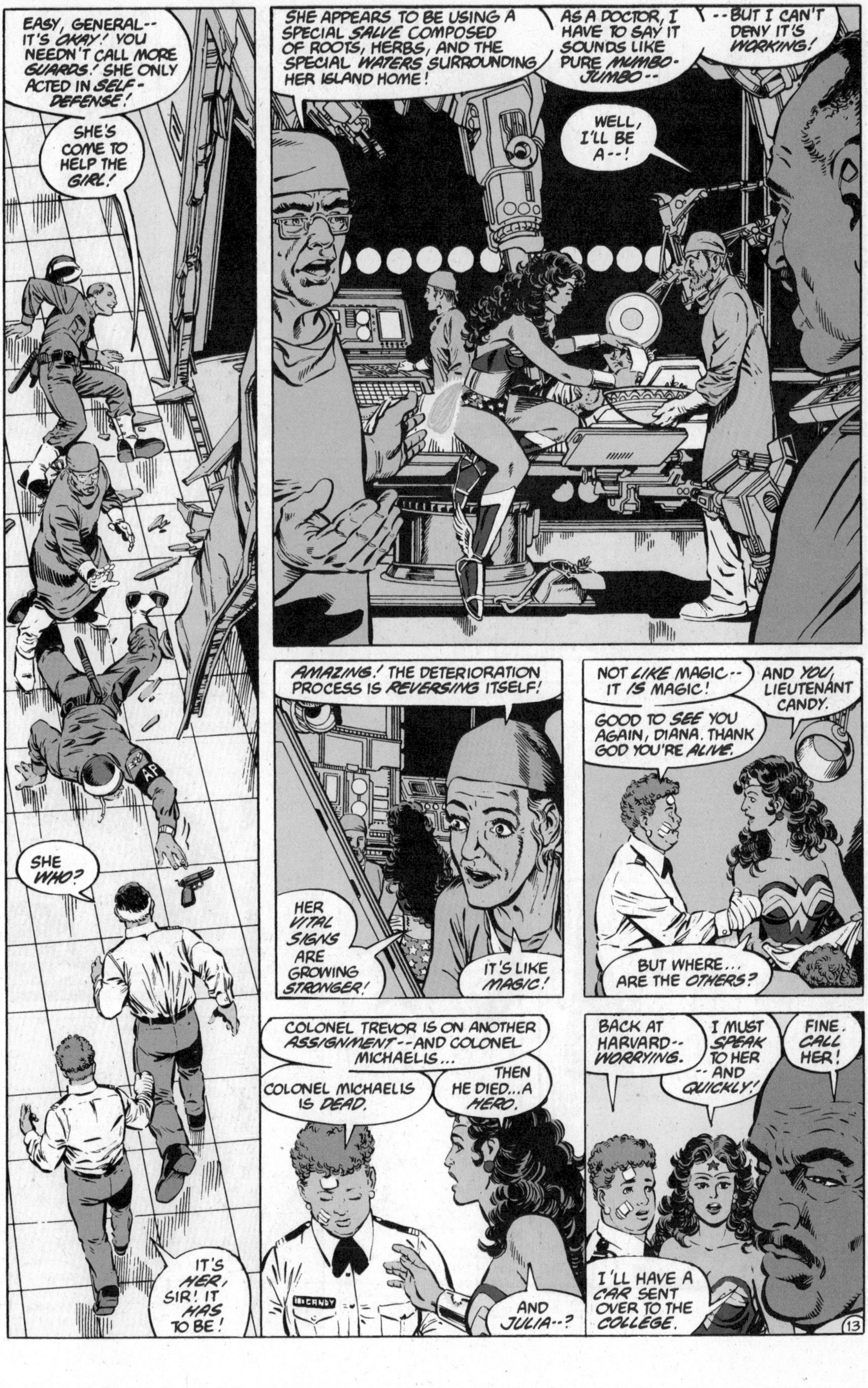

EASY, GENERAL-- IT'S OKAY! YOU NEEDN'T CALL MORE GUARDS! SHE ONLY ACTED IN SELF-DEFENSE!
SHE'S COME TO HELP THE GIRL!
SHE WHO?
IT'S HER, SIR! IT HAS TO BE!
SHE APPEARS TO BE USING A SPECIAL SALVE COMPOSED OF ROOTS, HERBS, AND THE SPECIAL WATERS SURROUNDING HER ISLAND HOME!
AS A DOCTOR, I HAVE TO SAY IT SOUNDS LIKE PURE MUMBO-JUMBO--
--BUT I CAN'T DENY IT'S WORKING!
WELL, I'LL BE A--!
AMAZING! THE DETERIORATION PROCESS IS REVERSING ITSELF!
HER VITAL SIGNS ARE GROWING STRONGER!
IT'S LIKE MAGIC!
NOT LIKE MAGIC-- IT IS MAGIC!
AND YOU, LIEUTENANT CANDY.
GOOD TO SEE YOU AGAIN, DIANA. THANK GOD YOU'RE ALIVE.
BUT WHERE... ARE THE OTHERS?
COLONEL TREVOR IS ON ANOTHER ASSIGNMENT--AND COLONEL MICHAELIS...
COLONEL MICHAELIS IS DEAD.
THEN HE DIED...A HERO.
AND JULIA--?
BACK AT HARVARD-- WORRYING.
I MUST SPEAK TO HER --AND QUICKLY!
FINE. CALL HER!
I'LL HAVE A CAR SENT OVER TO THE COLLEGE.
13

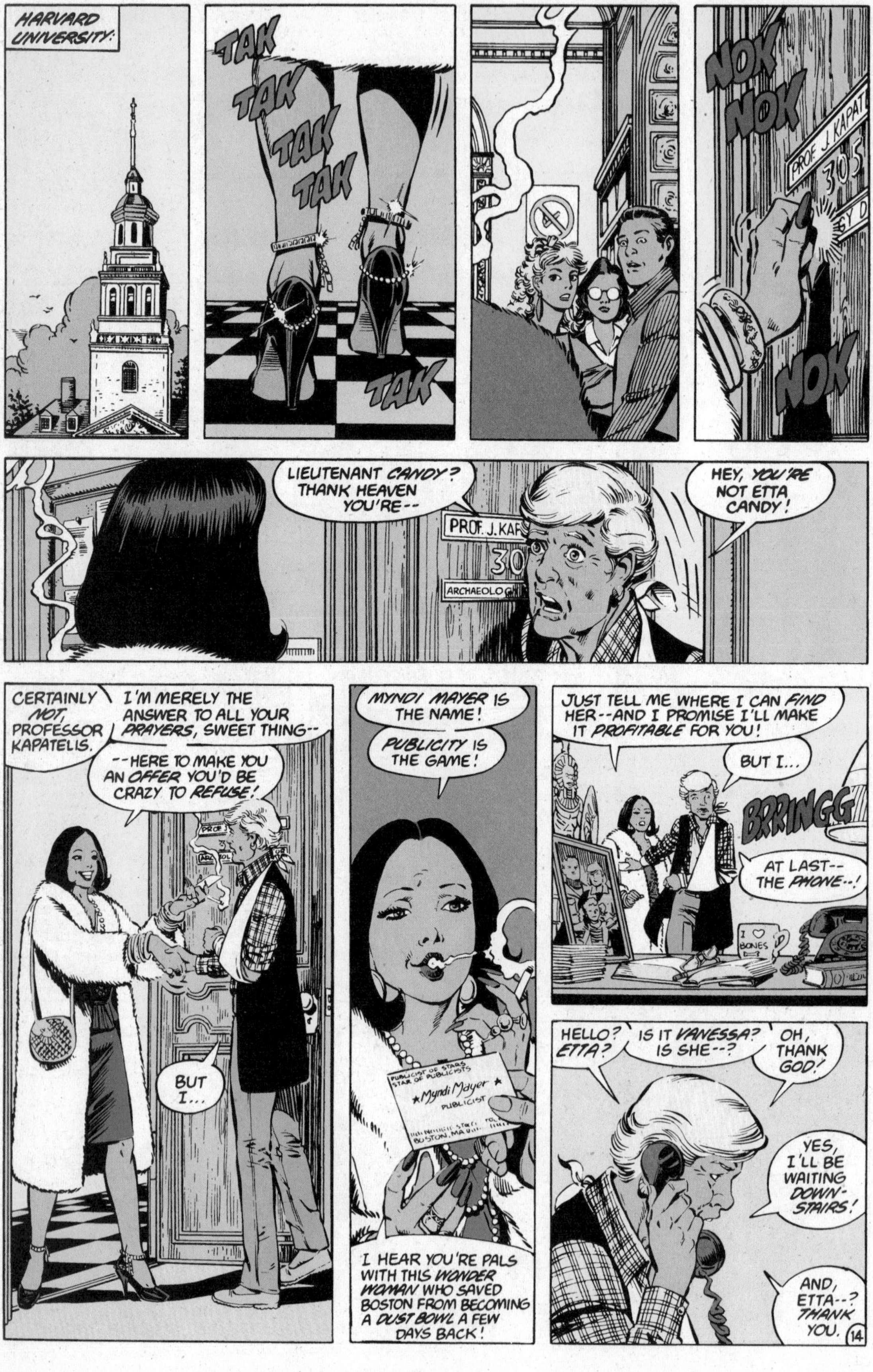
HARVARD UNIVERSITY:
TAK TAK TAK TAK
TAK
NOK NOK
PROF. J. KAPAT
305
NOK
LIEUTENANT CANDY? THANK HEAVEN YOU'RE--
PROF. J. KAP
30
ARCHAEOLOG
HEY, YOU'RE NOT ETTA CANDY!
CERTAINLY NOT, PROFESSOR KAPATELIS.
I'M MERELY THE ANSWER TO ALL YOUR PRAYERS, SWEET THING--
--HERE TO MAKE YOU AN OFFER YOU'D BE CRAZY TO REFUSE!
BUT I...
MYNDI MAYER IS THE NAME!
PUBLICITY IS THE GAME!
PUBLICIST OF STARS STAR OF PUBLICISTS
Myndi Mayer
PUBLICIST
BOSTON, MA
I HEAR YOU'RE PALS WITH THIS WONDER WOMAN WHO SAVED BOSTON FROM BECOMING A DUST BOWL A FEW DAYS BACK!
JUST TELL ME WHERE I CAN FIND HER--AND I PROMISE I'LL MAKE IT PROFITABLE FOR YOU!
BUT I...
BRRINGG
AT LAST-- THE PHONE--!
I ♡ BONES
HELLO? ETTA?
IS IT VANESSA? IS SHE--?
OH, THANK GOD!
YES, I'LL BE WAITING DOWN-STAIRS!
AND, ETTA--? THANK YOU.
14

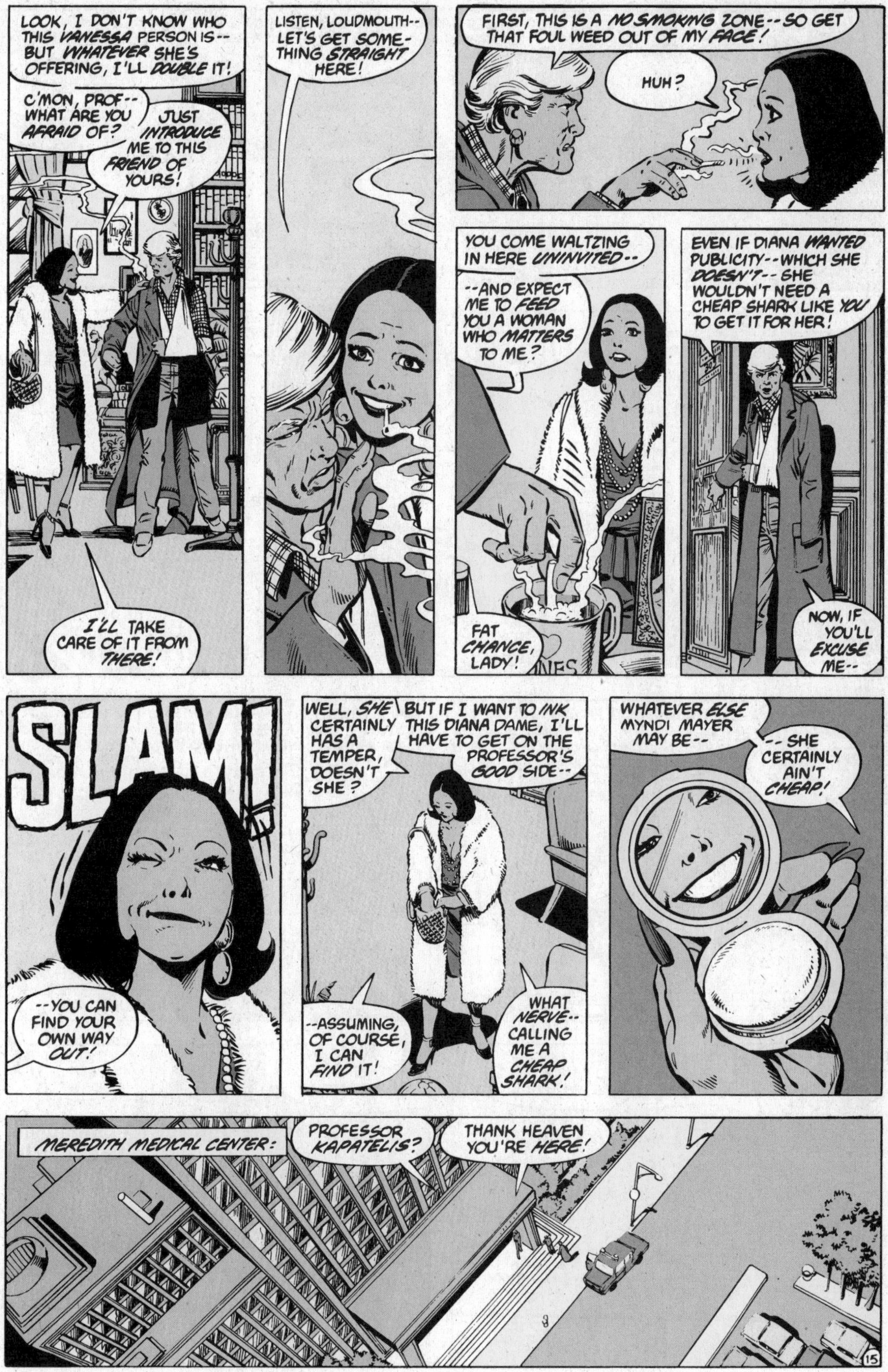

LOOK, I DON'T KNOW WHO THIS VANESSA PERSON IS-- BUT WHATEVER SHE'S OFFERING, I'LL DOUBLE IT!
C'MON, PROF-- WHAT ARE YOU AFRAID OF?
JUST INTRODUCE ME TO THIS FRIEND OF YOURS!
I'LL TAKE CARE OF IT FROM THERE!
LISTEN, LOUDMOUTH-- LET'S GET SOMETHING STRAIGHT HERE!
FIRST, THIS IS A NO SMOKING ZONE-- SO GET THAT FOUL WEED OUT OF MY FACE!
HUH?
YOU COME WALTZING IN HERE UNINVITED--
--AND EXPECT ME TO FEED YOU A WOMAN WHO MATTERS TO ME?
FAT CHANCE, LADY!
EVEN IF DIANA WANTED PUBLICITY--WHICH SHE DOESN'T-- SHE WOULDN'T NEED A CHEAP SHARK LIKE YOU TO GET IT FOR HER!
NOW, IF YOU'LL EXCUSE ME--
SLAM!
--YOU CAN FIND YOUR OWN WAY OUT!
WELL, SHE CERTAINLY HAS A TEMPER, DOESN'T SHE?
BUT IF I WANT TO INK THIS DIANA DAME, I'LL HAVE TO GET ON THE PROFESSOR'S GOOD SIDE--
--ASSUMING, OF COURSE, I CAN FIND IT!
WHAT NERVE-- CALLING ME A CHEAP SHARK!
WHATEVER ELSE MYNDI MAYER MAY BE--
--SHE CERTAINLY AIN'T CHEAP!
MEREDITH MEDICAL CENTER:
PROFESSOR KAPATELIS?
THANK HEAVEN YOU'RE HERE!
15

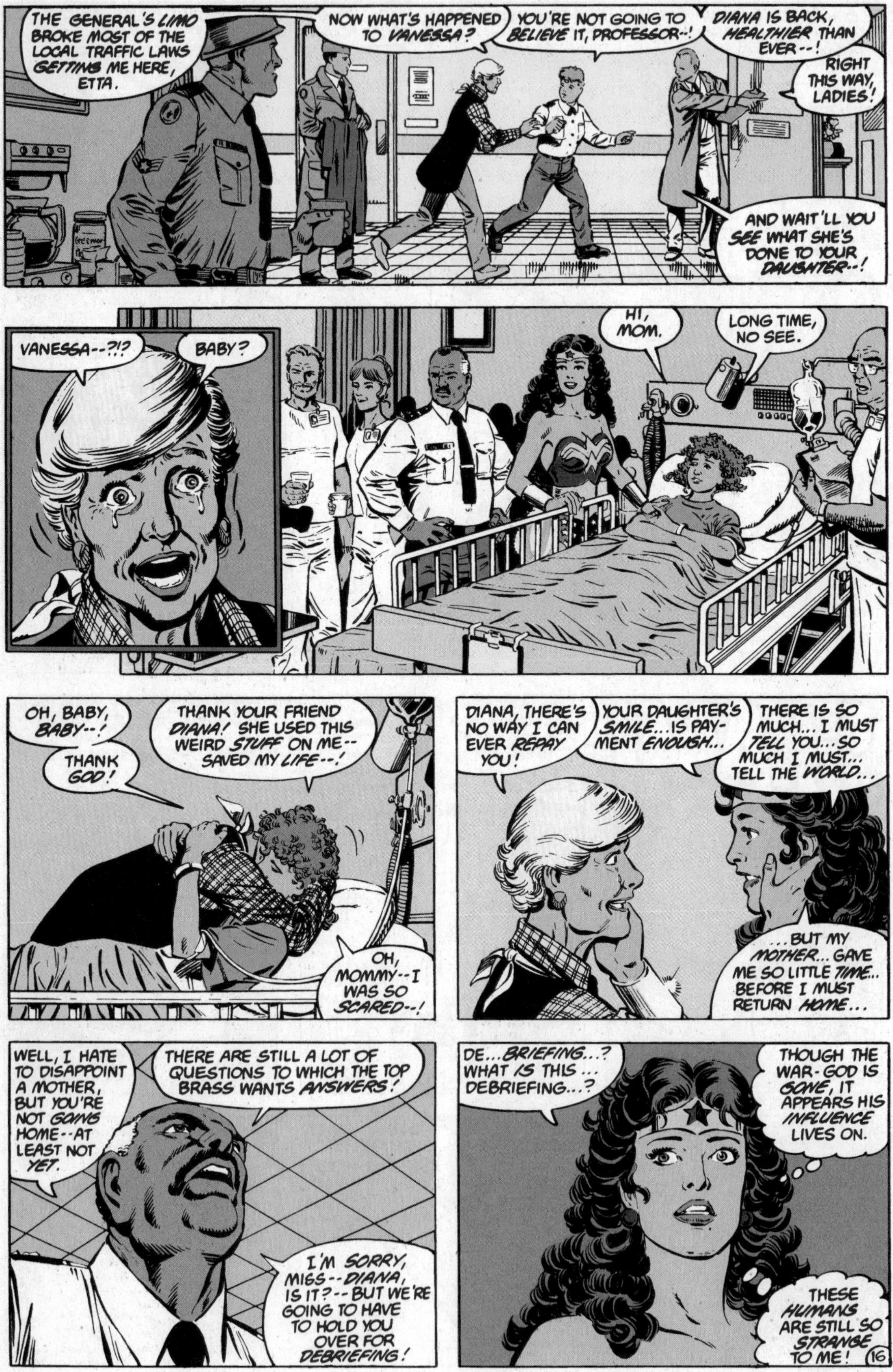
THE GENERAL'S LIMO BROKE MOST OF THE LOCAL TRAFFIC LAWS GETTING ME HERE, ETTA.
NOW WHAT'S HAPPENED TO VANESSA?
YOU'RE NOT GOING TO BELIEVE IT, PROFESSOR--!
DIANA IS BACK, HEALTHIER THAN EVER--!
RIGHT THIS WAY, LADIES!
AND WAIT'LL YOU SEE WHAT SHE'S DONE TO YOUR DAUGHTER--!
VANESSA--?!?
BABY?
HI, MOM.
LONG TIME, NO SEE.
OH, BABY, BABY--!
THANK GOD!
THANK YOUR FRIEND DIANA! SHE USED THIS WEIRD STUFF ON ME-- SAVED MY LIFE--!
OH, MOMMY--I WAS SO SCARED--!
DIANA, THERE'S NO WAY I CAN EVER REPAY YOU!
YOUR DAUGHTER'S SMILE...IS PAYMENT ENOUGH...
THERE IS SO MUCH... I MUST TELL YOU...SO MUCH I MUST... TELL THE WORLD...
...BUT MY MOTHER...GAVE ME SO LITTLE TIME... BEFORE I MUST RETURN HOME...
WELL, I HATE TO DISAPPOINT A MOTHER, BUT YOU'RE NOT GOING HOME--AT LEAST NOT YET.
THERE ARE STILL A LOT OF QUESTIONS TO WHICH THE TOP BRASS WANTS ANSWERS!
I'M SORRY, MISS--DIANA, IS IT?--BUT WE'RE GOING TO HAVE TO HOLD YOU OVER FOR DEBRIEFING!
DE...BRIEFING...? WHAT IS THIS ... DEBRIEFING...?
THOUGH THE WAR-GOD IS GONE, IT APPEARS HIS INFLUENCE LIVES ON.
THESE HUMANS ARE STILL SO STRANGE TO ME!
16

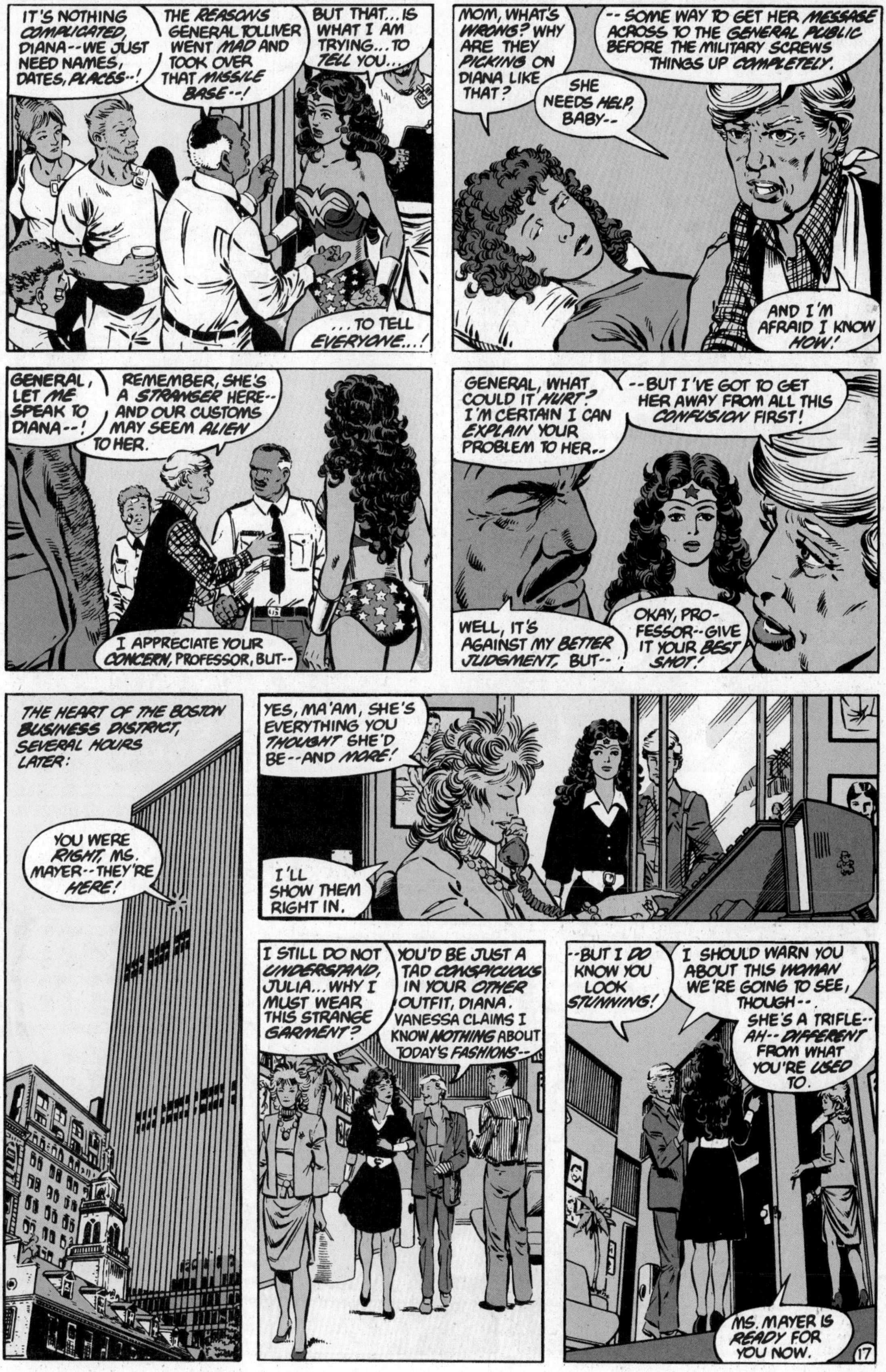

IT'S NOTHING COMPLICATED, DIANA--WE JUST NEED NAMES, DATES, PLACES--!
THE REASONS GENERAL TOLLIVER WENT MAD AND TOOK OVER THAT MISSILE BASE--!
BUT THAT... IS WHAT I AM TRYING... TO TELL YOU...
...TO TELL EVERYONE...!
MOM, WHAT'S WRONG? WHY ARE THEY PICKING ON DIANA LIKE THAT?
SHE NEEDS HELP, BABY--
--SOME WAY TO GET HER MESSAGE ACROSS TO THE GENERAL PUBLIC BEFORE THE MILITARY SCREWS THINGS UP COMPLETELY.
AND I'M AFRAID I KNOW HOW!
GENERAL, LET ME SPEAK TO DIANA--!
REMEMBER, SHE'S A STRANGER HERE--AND OUR CUSTOMS MAY SEEM ALIEN TO HER.
I APPRECIATE YOUR CONCERN, PROFESSOR, BUT--
GENERAL, WHAT COULD IT HURT? I'M CERTAIN I CAN EXPLAIN YOUR PROBLEM TO HER..
--BUT I'VE GOT TO GET HER AWAY FROM ALL THIS CONFUSION FIRST!
WELL, IT'S AGAINST MY BETTER JUDGMENT, BUT--
OKAY, PRO-FESSOR--GIVE IT YOUR BEST SHOT!
THE HEART OF THE BOSTON BUSINESS DISTRICT, SEVERAL HOURS LATER:
YOU WERE RIGHT, MS. MAYER--THEY'RE HERE!
YES, MA'AM, SHE'S EVERYTHING YOU THOUGHT SHE'D BE--AND MORE!
I'LL SHOW THEM RIGHT IN.
I STILL DO NOT UNDERSTAND, JULIA... WHY I MUST WEAR THIS STRANGE GARMENT?
YOU'D BE JUST A TAD CONSPICUOUS IN YOUR OTHER OUTFIT, DIANA. VANESSA CLAIMS I KNOW NOTHING ABOUT TODAY'S FASHIONS--
--BUT I DO KNOW YOU LOOK STUNNING!
I SHOULD WARN YOU ABOUT THIS WOMAN WE'RE GOING TO SEE, THOUGH--.
SHE'S A TRIFLE--AH--DIFFERENT FROM WHAT YOU'RE USED TO.
MS. MAYER IS READY FOR YOU NOW.
17

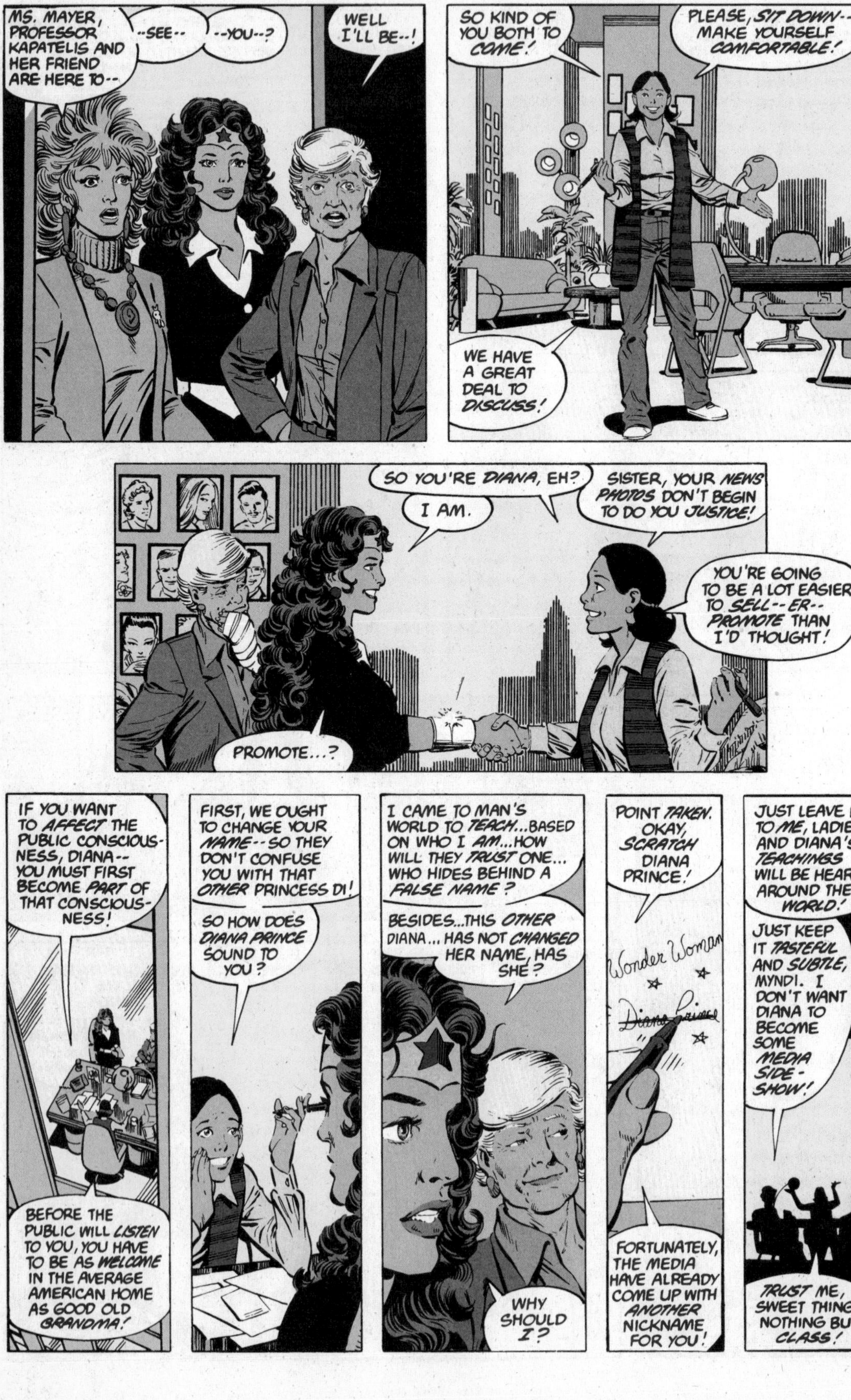
MS. MAYER, PROFESSOR KAPATELIS AND HER FRIEND ARE HERE TO--
--SEE--
--YOU--?
WELL I'LL BE--!
SO KIND OF YOU BOTH TO COME!
PLEASE, SIT DOWN--MAKE YOURSELF COMFORTABLE!
WE HAVE A GREAT DEAL TO DISCUSS!
SO YOU'RE DIANA, EH?
I AM.
SISTER, YOUR NEWS PHOTOS DON'T BEGIN TO DO YOU JUSTICE!
YOU'RE GOING TO BE A LOT EASIER TO SELL--ER--PROMOTE THAN I'D THOUGHT!
PROMOTE...?
IF YOU WANT TO AFFECT THE PUBLIC CONSCIOUSNESS, DIANA--YOU MUST FIRST BECOME PART OF THAT CONSCIOUSNESS!
BEFORE THE PUBLIC WILL LISTEN TO YOU, YOU HAVE TO BE AS WELCOME IN THE AVERAGE AMERICAN HOME AS GOOD OLD GRANDMA!
FIRST, WE OUGHT TO CHANGE YOUR NAME--SO THEY DON'T CONFUSE YOU WITH THAT OTHER PRINCESS DI!
SO HOW DOES DIANA PRINCE SOUND TO YOU?
I CAME TO MAN'S WORLD TO TEACH...BASED ON WHO I AM...HOW WILL THEY TRUST ONE... WHO HIDES BEHIND A FALSE NAME?
BESIDES...THIS OTHER DIANA... HAS NOT CHANGED HER NAME, HAS SHE?
WHY SHOULD I?
POINT TAKEN. OKAY, SCRATCH DIANA PRINCE!
Wonder Woman
Diana Prince
FORTUNATELY, THE MEDIA HAVE ALREADY COME UP WITH ANOTHER NICKNAME FOR YOU!
JUST LEAVE IT TO ME, LADIES--AND DIANA'S TEACHINGS WILL BE HEARD AROUND THE WORLD!
JUST KEEP IT TASTEFUL AND SUBTLE, MYNDI. I DON'T WANT DIANA TO BECOME SOME MEDIA SIDE-SHOW!
TRUST ME, SWEET THING--NOTHING BUT CLASS!
18

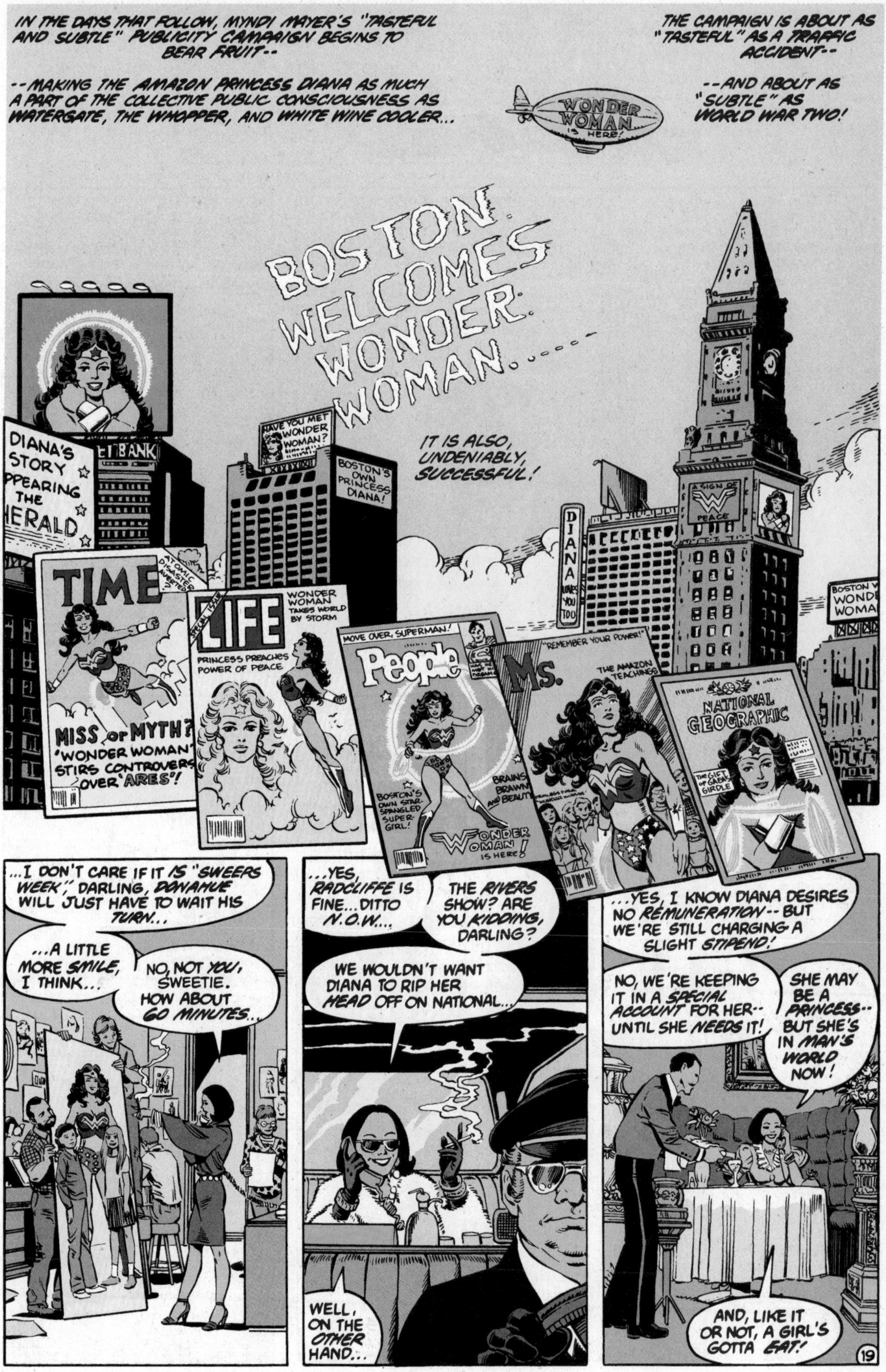
IN THE DAYS THAT FOLLOW, MYNDI MAYER'S "TASTEFUL AND SUBTLE" PUBLICITY CAMPAIGN BEGINS TO BEAR FRUIT--
--MAKING THE AMAZON PRINCESS DIANA AS MUCH A PART OF THE COLLECTIVE PUBLIC CONSCIOUSNESS AS WATERGATE, THE WHOPPER, AND WHITE WINE COOLER...
THE CAMPAIGN IS ABOUT AS "TASTEFUL" AS A TRAFFIC ACCIDENT--
--AND ABOUT AS "SUBTLE" AS WORLD WAR TWO!
WONDER WOMAN IS HERE!
BOSTON WELCOMES WONDER WOMAN
IT IS ALSO, UNDENIABLY, SUCCESSFUL!
DIANA'S STORY APPEARING THE HERALD
HAVE YOU MET WONDER WOMAN?
BOSTON'S OWN PRINCESS DIANA!
DIANA LOVES YOU TOO
SIGN OF PEACE
TIME
MISS or MYTH? 'WONDER WOMAN' STIRS CONTROVERSY OVER 'ARES'!
LIFE
SPECIAL ISSUE
WONDER WOMAN TAKES WORLD BY STORM
PRINCESS PREACHES POWER OF PEACE
MOVE OVER, SUPERMAN!
People
BOSTON'S OWN STAR-SPANGLED SUPER-GIRL!
BRAINS, BRAWN AND BEAUTY
WONDER WOMAN IS HERE!
Ms.
"REMEMBER YOUR POWER!"
THE AMAZON TEACHINGS
NATIONAL GEOGRAPHIC
THE GIFT OF GREAT GIRDLE
...I DON'T CARE IF IT IS "SWEEPS WEEK," DARLING, DONAHUE WILL JUST HAVE TO WAIT HIS TURN...
...A LITTLE MORE SMILE, I THINK...
NO, NOT YOU, SWEETIE. HOW ABOUT 60 MINUTES...
...YES, RADCLIFFE IS FINE... DITTO N.O.W....
THE RIVERS SHOW? ARE YOU KIDDING, DARLING?
WE WOULDN'T WANT DIANA TO RIP HER HEAD OFF ON NATIONAL...
WELL, ON THE OTHER HAND...
...YES, I KNOW DIANA DESIRES NO REMUNERATION -- BUT WE'RE STILL CHARGING A SLIGHT STIPEND!
NO, WE'RE KEEPING IT IN A SPECIAL ACCOUNT FOR HER-- UNTIL SHE NEEDS IT!
SHE MAY BE A PRINCESS-- BUT SHE'S IN MAN'S WORLD NOW!
AND, LIKE IT OR NOT, A GIRL'S GOTTA EAT!
19

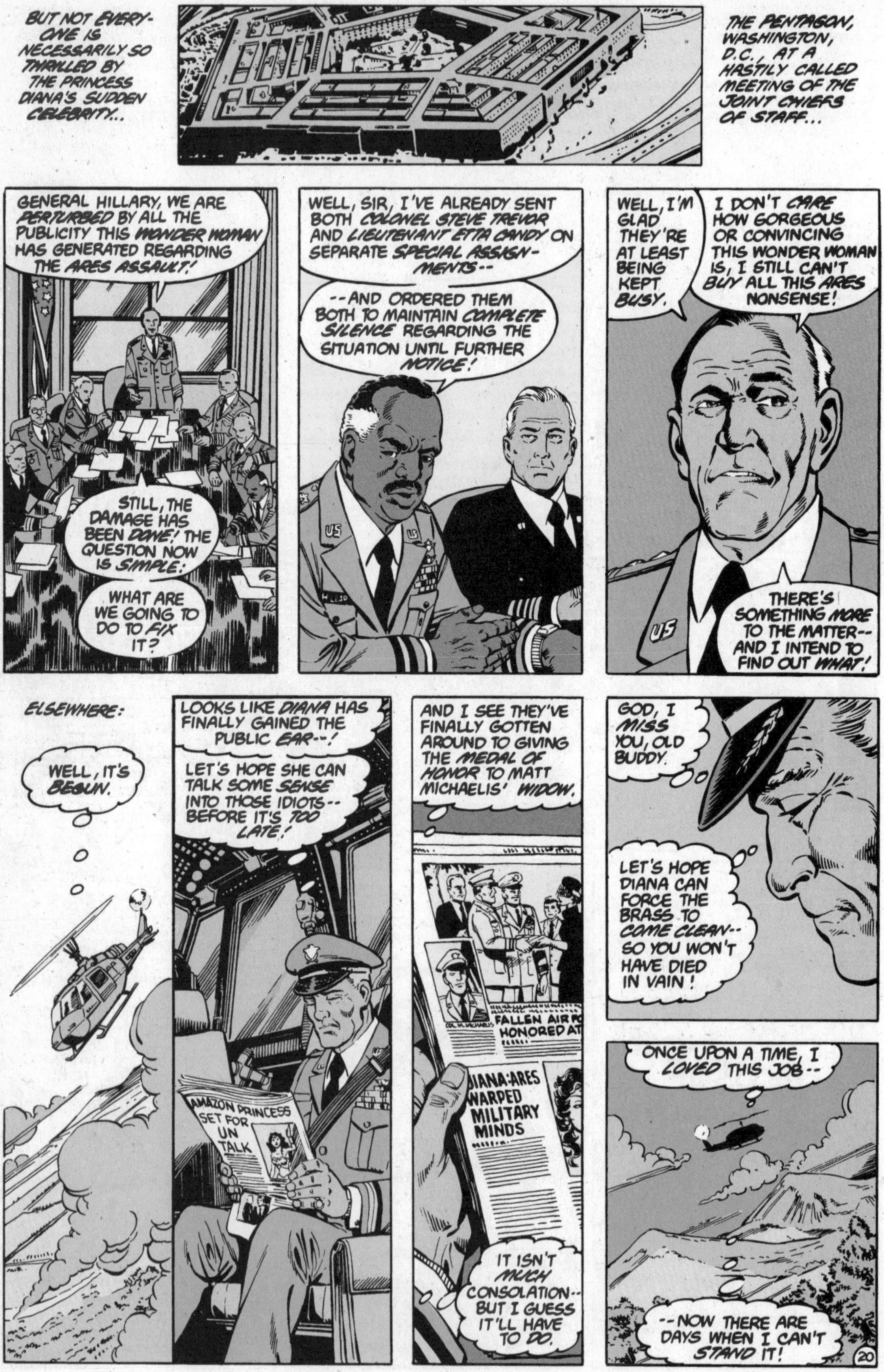
BUT NOT EVERYONE IS NECESSARILY SO THRILLED BY THE PRINCESS DIANA'S SUDDEN CELEBRITY...
THE PENTAGON, WASHINGTON, D.C., AT A HASTILY CALLED MEETING OF THE JOINT CHIEFS OF STAFF...
GENERAL HILLARY, WE ARE PERTURBED BY ALL THE PUBLICITY THIS WONDER WOMAN HAS GENERATED REGARDING THE ARES ASSAULT!
STILL, THE DAMAGE HAS BEEN DONE! THE QUESTION NOW IS SIMPLE:
WHAT ARE WE GOING TO DO TO FIX IT?
WELL, SIR, I'VE ALREADY SENT BOTH COLONEL STEVE TREVOR AND LIEUTENANT ETTA CANDY ON SEPARATE SPECIAL ASSIGNMENTS--
--AND ORDERED THEM BOTH TO MAINTAIN COMPLETE SILENCE REGARDING THE SITUATION UNTIL FURTHER NOTICE!
WELL, I'M GLAD THEY'RE AT LEAST BEING KEPT BUSY.
I DON'T CARE HOW GORGEOUS OR CONVINCING THIS WONDER WOMAN IS, I STILL CAN'T BUY ALL THIS ARES NONSENSE!
THERE'S SOMETHING MORE TO THE MATTER--AND I INTEND TO FIND OUT WHAT!
ELSEWHERE:
WELL, IT'S BEGUN.
LOOKS LIKE DIANA HAS FINALLY GAINED THE PUBLIC EAR--!
LET'S HOPE SHE CAN TALK SOME SENSE INTO THOSE IDIOTS--BEFORE IT'S TOO LATE!
AMAZON PRINCESS SET FOR UN TALK
AND I SEE THEY'VE FINALLY GOTTEN AROUND TO GIVING THE MEDAL OF HONOR TO MATT MICHAELIS' WIDOW.
FALLEN AIR FO HONORED AT
DIANA: ARES WARPED MILITARY MINDS
IT ISN'T MUCH CONSOLATION--BUT I GUESS IT'LL HAVE TO DO.
GOD, I MISS YOU, OLD BUDDY.
LET'S HOPE DIANA CAN FORCE THE BRASS TO COME CLEAN--SO YOU WON'T HAVE DIED IN VAIN!
ONCE UPON A TIME, I LOVED THIS JOB--
--NOW THERE ARE DAYS WHEN I CAN'T STAND IT!
20

NOTTINGHAM, ENGLAND, THE ANCESTRAL HOME OF NOTED ARCHAEOLOGIST BARBARA MINERVA...

MADAM--?

DE DAILY POST HAVE ARRIVED, MA'AM!

IN MY CHAMBERS, CHUMA.

ALL DE ARTICLES YOU WANTED ON DIS NEW WONDER WOMAN--

--THOUGH DE GODS ONLY KNOW WHY YOU WANT DEM!

I HAVE MY REASONS, OLD MAN.

I ALWAYS HAVE MY REASONS.

AYE, MA'AM-- DAT YOU DO!

THIS PRINCESS DIANA IS A MOST FASCINATING SUBJECT, CHUMA--

--SUPPOSEDLY THE HEIR OF A RACE OF AMAZONS!

AND THIS LASSO OF HERS-- ACCORDING TO THIS KAPATELIS WOMAN, IT WAS FORGED FROM THE GOLDEN GIRDLE OF THE EARTH-GODDESS GAEA!

BOSTON HERALD
WONDER WOMA[N] REVEALS 'ARES PROJE[CT]
TOP BRASS SILENT ABOUT C[...]
GODFRE[Y] CAMPAIGN GATHERS MOMENTUM

Gaea's Gift

IF SO, IT IS A PRIZE BEYOND PRICE!

21

183

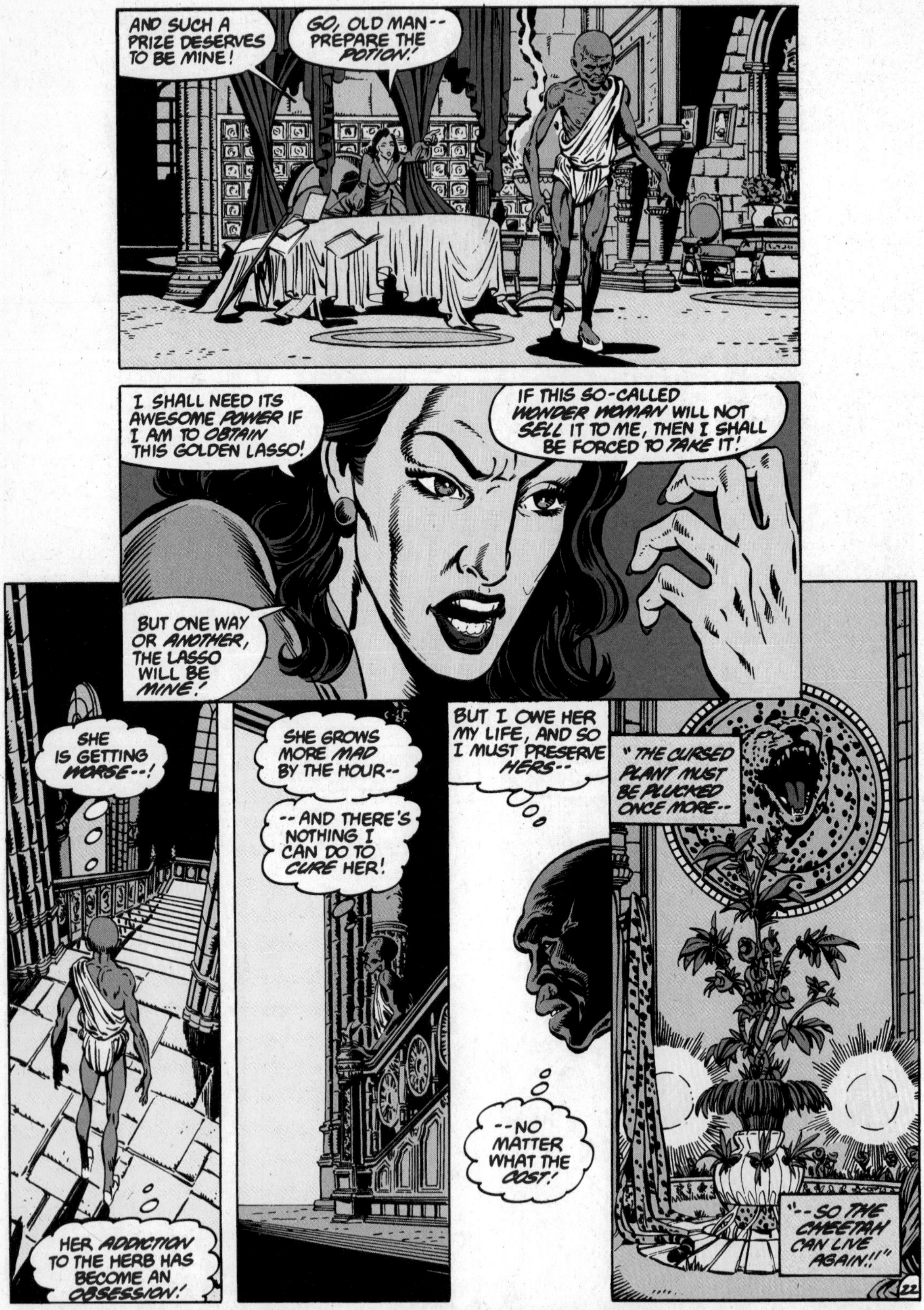
AND SUCH A PRIZE DESERVES TO BE MINE!
GO, OLD MAN-- PREPARE THE POTION!
I SHALL NEED ITS AWESOME POWER IF I AM TO OBTAIN THIS GOLDEN LASSO!
IF THIS SO-CALLED WONDER WOMAN WILL NOT SELL IT TO ME, THEN I SHALL BE FORCED TO TAKE IT!
BUT ONE WAY OR ANOTHER, THE LASSO WILL BE MINE!
SHE IS GETTING WORSE--!
HER ADDICTION TO THE HERB HAS BECOME AN OBSESSION!
SHE GROWS MORE MAD BY THE HOUR--
--AND THERE'S NOTHING I CAN DO TO CURE HER!
BUT I OWE HER MY LIFE, AND SO I MUST PRESERVE HERS--
--NO MATTER WHAT THE COST!
"THE CURSED PLANT MUST BE PLUCKED ONCE MORE--
"--SO THE CHEETAH CAN LIVE AGAIN!!"
22

LOOK FOR THE FURTHER ADVENTURES OF DIANA IN VOLUME TWO--

WONDER WOMAN: CHALLENGE OF THE GODS

VOLUME ONE

WONDER WOMAN GALLERY

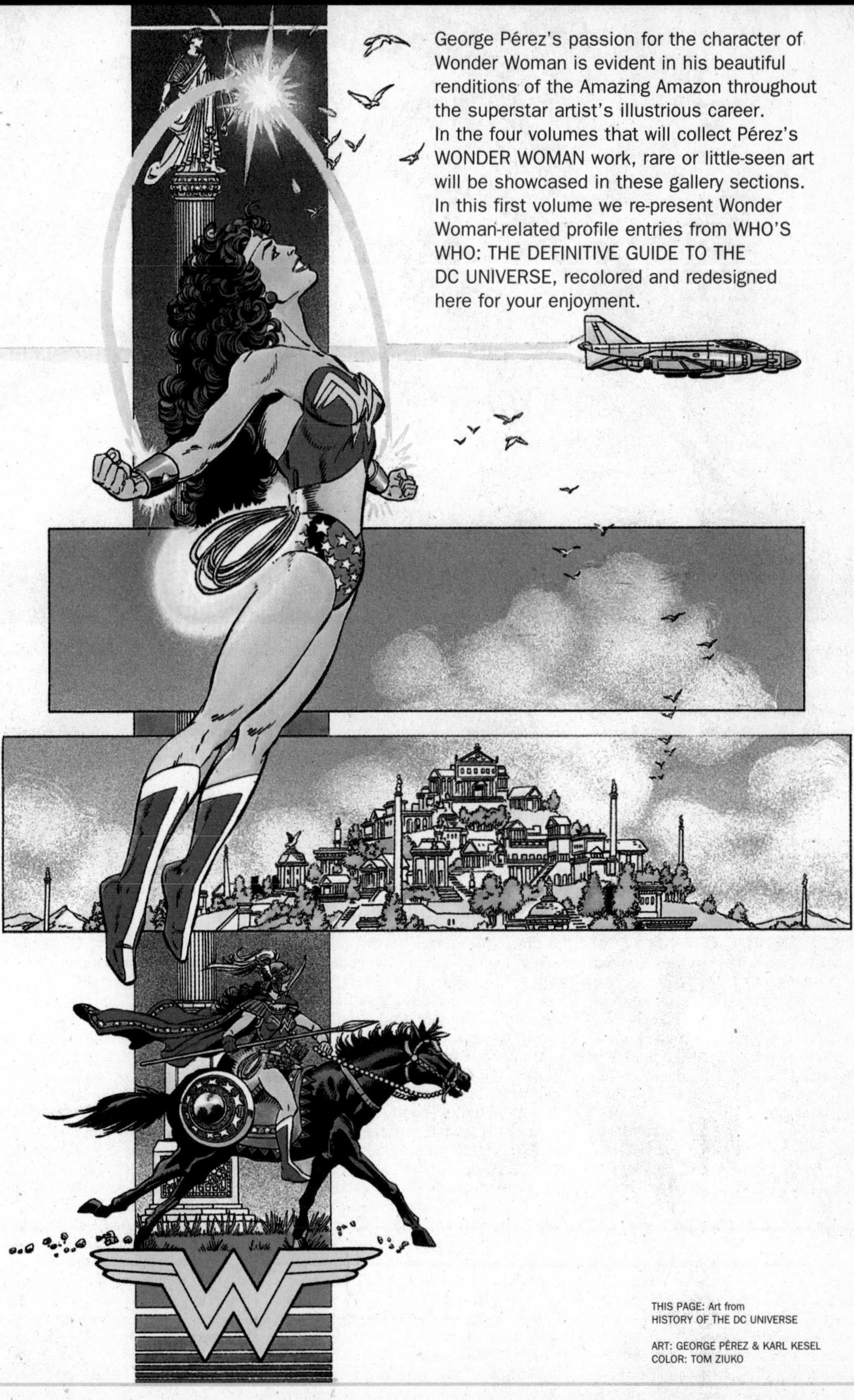

George Pérez's passion for the character of Wonder Woman is evident in his beautiful renditions of the Amazing Amazon throughout the superstar artist's illustrious career.
In the four volumes that will collect Pérez's WONDER WOMAN work, rare or little-seen art will be showcased in these gallery sections.
In this first volume we re-present Wonder Woman-related profile entries from WHO'S WHO: THE DEFINITIVE GUIDE TO THE DC UNIVERSE, recolored and redesigned here for your enjoyment.

THIS PAGE: Art from
HISTORY OF THE DC UNIVERSE

ART: GEORGE PÉREZ & KARL KESEL
COLOR: TOM ZIUKO

W O N D E R W O M A N

ALTER EGO: Princess Diana **OCCUPATION:** Ambassador, Teacher
MARITAL STATUS: Single
KNOWN RELATIVES: Hippolyte (mother), Antiope (aunt)
GROUP AFFILIATION: None
BASE OF OPERATIONS: Paradise Island; Boston, Massachusetts
FIRST APPEARANCE: (historical) ALL STAR COMICS #8, (modern version) WONDER WOMAN
(second series) #1

TEXT: BOB ROZAKIS
ART: GEORGE PÉREZ
COLOR: TOM SMITH

HEIGHT: 5' 11" **WEIGHT:** 135 pounds **EYES:** Blue **HAIR:** Black

HISTORY

In 30,000 B.C. a brutal caveman, made an outcast from his tribe for losing his left hand to a sabertooth tiger, murdered his pregnant wife in a fit of rage. The souls of the woman and her unborn daughter were taken by the Earth goddess Gaea to the Cavern of Souls, which lies within Hades, the realm of the dead known to the people of ancient Greece. Over the following millennia, Gaea brought the souls of other women who died before their designated time.

In 1200 B.C. the goddess Artemis proposed to the Olympian gods that a new race of mortal human beings be created. All of them would be female, and Artemis intended that this new race would set an example to the rest of humanity as to what the proper relationship between men and women should be, one of equality between the sexes. Artemis' proposal was vehemently opposed by the self-proclaimed war god Ares, who sought to reduce humanity to utter submission through force, and ultimately to rule Olympus himself.

Together Artemis, goddess of the hunt; Athena, goddess of wisdom, Aprhodite, goddess of love; Demeter, goddess of fertility; and Hestia, goddess of the hearth were guided by Hermes, messenger of the gods, to Hades itself. There the goddesses went to the Cavern of Souls, where they caused the thousands of souls of the dead women that had been gathering there to be reincarnated on Earth as adult women. The first to be reborn thus became known as Hippolyte and was designated by Artemis as the queen of this new race. Artemis decreed that Hippolyte's sister Antiope rule beside her, and that both sisters always wear Gaea's girdles as symbols of the goddesses' trust in them. Artemis called this new race of women Amazons.

The Amazons founded a city-state called Themyscira, where compassion and justice reigned. But the male rulers of ancient Greece grew jealous of the Amazons, and through false tales alleging that the Amazons committed crimes and atrocities, it caused the Amazons to be regarded as threats

and outcasts.

Ares, feeling the Amazons an obstacle to his quest for absolute power, had a pawn taunt the demigod Heracles (later known as Hercules) with false reports that Hippolyte was besmirching his reputation. Enraged, Heracles led warriors to Themyscira to defeat Hippolyte and her Amazons. But, meeting in single combat, Heracles was himself defeated by Hippolyte instead.

Heracles now professed respect and friendship for the Amazons and, on his suggestion, a celebratory gathering of both his warriors and the Amazons was held. But with the Amazons off-guard, Heracles and his men treacherously attacked, defeated, and enslaved them. Hippolyte was placed in chains and Heracles departed, taking Gaea's girdle from her as a prize.

Hippolyte prayed to the goddesses for forgiveness. Athena appeared to her and said she would be free if she rededicated herself to her ideals. Hippolyte escaped her cell, freed the other Amazons, and led them in defeating their captors. Unlike Hippolyte, Antiope took pleasure in killing their enemies. As a result, once the battle was over, the Amazons divided into two groups: one led by Hippolyte (to whom Antiope gave her girdle of Gaea) and the other led by Antiope, who forsook the Olympian gods.

The goddesses decreed that Hippolyte and her Amazons do penance for failing to lead humanity to establish new ways of justice and equality. Therefore, the goddesses sent Hippolyte's Amazons to a distant island, beneath which lay a source of great evil. As long as Amazons served to keep that evil from menacing humanity, the Amazons would be immortal.

Hippolyte's Amazons established a new city-state on Paradise Island, and the Amazons renewed their sense of purpose and self-discipline as the centuries passed. Various Amazons were killed over the years in carrying out the difficult task of keeping the great evil confined underground. During all this time, the Amazons of Paradise Island had no contact with the outside world.

Hippolyte was the only one of the Amazons who was pregnant when she was killed in her previous incarnation. The soul of Hippolyte's unborn daughter still inhabited the Cavern of Souls.

Recently, on Artemis' instructions, Hippolyte formed the image of a baby from the clay of Paradise Island. The five goddesses who were the Amazons' patrons, along with Hermes, endowed the unborn soul with various gifts, including super-human strength and speed and the power of flight. Then the unborn soul entered into the clay image, which came to life as a real baby. The child was named Diana, after a revered warrior who had died to save the Amazon race.

After Hippolyte's daughter had grown to adulthood, the gods revealed to the Amazons that Ares had gone insane and might destroy all of Earth with a terrible source of power. The gods decreed that the Amazons choose through a tournament a champion who could confront Ares in the world outside Paradise Island.

Diana asked to participate in the tournament but was forbidden to do so by Hippolyte. Nonetheless, urged on by Athena, Diana entered the tournament, concealing her identity, and won. Unable to defy the gods' will, Hippolyte agreed to let Diana be the champion to be sent against Ares. Diana was given a costume bearing the standard of her deceased namesake.

Hermes transported Diana to Boston, Massachusetts, where she met a professor of classical Greek history named Julia Kapatelis, who taught her how to speak English and serves as her guide to contemporary civilization. Diana presented herself as an ambassador from Paradise Island to the rest of society, here to teach the ways of her just and peaceful civilization to a violent world. The media have dubbed her "Wonder Woman." Although she does not actively seek to fight crime, Wonder Woman had already found herself pitted against threats masterminded by Ares.

POWERS & WEAPONS

Wonder Woman possesses super-human strength and the ability to fly. She also has super-human speed and reflexes, and can move swiftly enough to deflect bullets with her silver bracelets. Wonder Woman is another extraordinary hand-to-hand combatant, trained in all the methods of combat of ancient Greece.

She was given the "Lasso of Truth," remolded from the girdle of Gaea by Hephaestus and presented by Hestia. The unbreakable lasso forces anyone within its confines to tell the absolute truth.

HISTORY

One of the three children of the supreme Greek Gods, Zeus and Hera, Ares is the God of War, loving battle for its own sake. Ares never favors one city or party over another, fighting on either side, as inclination prompts him, delighting in the slaughter of men and the sacking of towns.

Ares is hated by all his fellow immortals, from Zeus and Hera downward, except for Eris, and Aphrodite, who nurses a perverse passion for him, ultimately bearing his children, Deimos, Phobos and Harmonia.

Ares opposed the plan of his half-sister Artemis to create a new race of mortals on Earth, a race that would make men worship the gods as never before. Ares was outvoted by the other gods and, through the efforts of Artemis and the other goddesses, the new race was created from the swirling souls of women whose lives had been cut short by man's fear and ignorance. This new race was called the Amazons. From that moment on, Ares became the Amazons' sworn enemy.

Recently, when the Amazon oracle Menalippe sensed a tremendous surge in Ares' power and influence that threatened to consume the very Earth itself, the Amazons were commanded by the other gods to choose a champion to confront Ares in the World of Man. The winner of this tournament was the Princess Diana, daughter of Amazon Queen Hippolyte.

After confronting Decay, an agent of Ares' son Phobos, then Phobos and Deimos themselves, Princess Diana finally confronted the God of War himself, and after battle, defeated him.

At this writing, Ares has withdrawn himself from the affairs of men, to recover from his battle with Wonder Woman and to scheme anew.

POWERS & WEAPONS

As the God of War, Ares is obstinate, hateful, wicked, and untrustworthy. He is the living personification of the savage side of War, an almost unparalleled master of combat, possessed of super-strength and complete command over any weapon.

The vulture and the dog, as scavengers of the battlefield, are his favored pets.

ARES

ALTER EGO: None

OCCUPATION: God of War

MARITAL STATUS: Divorced

KNOWN RELATIVES: Zeus (father), Hera (mother), Hephaestus (brother), Eris (sister), Harmonia (daughter), Deimos (son, deceased?), Phobos (son)

GROUP AFFILIATION: Olympian Gods

BASE OF OPERATIONS: Areopagus, a hill near Mount Olympus

FIRST APPEARANCE: WONDER WOMAN (second series) #1

HEIGHT: 6' 10"   **WEIGHT:** 359 pounds   **EYES:** Red   **HAIR:** Unknown

TEXT: LEN WEIN
ART: GEORGE PÉREZ
COLOR: TOM SMITH

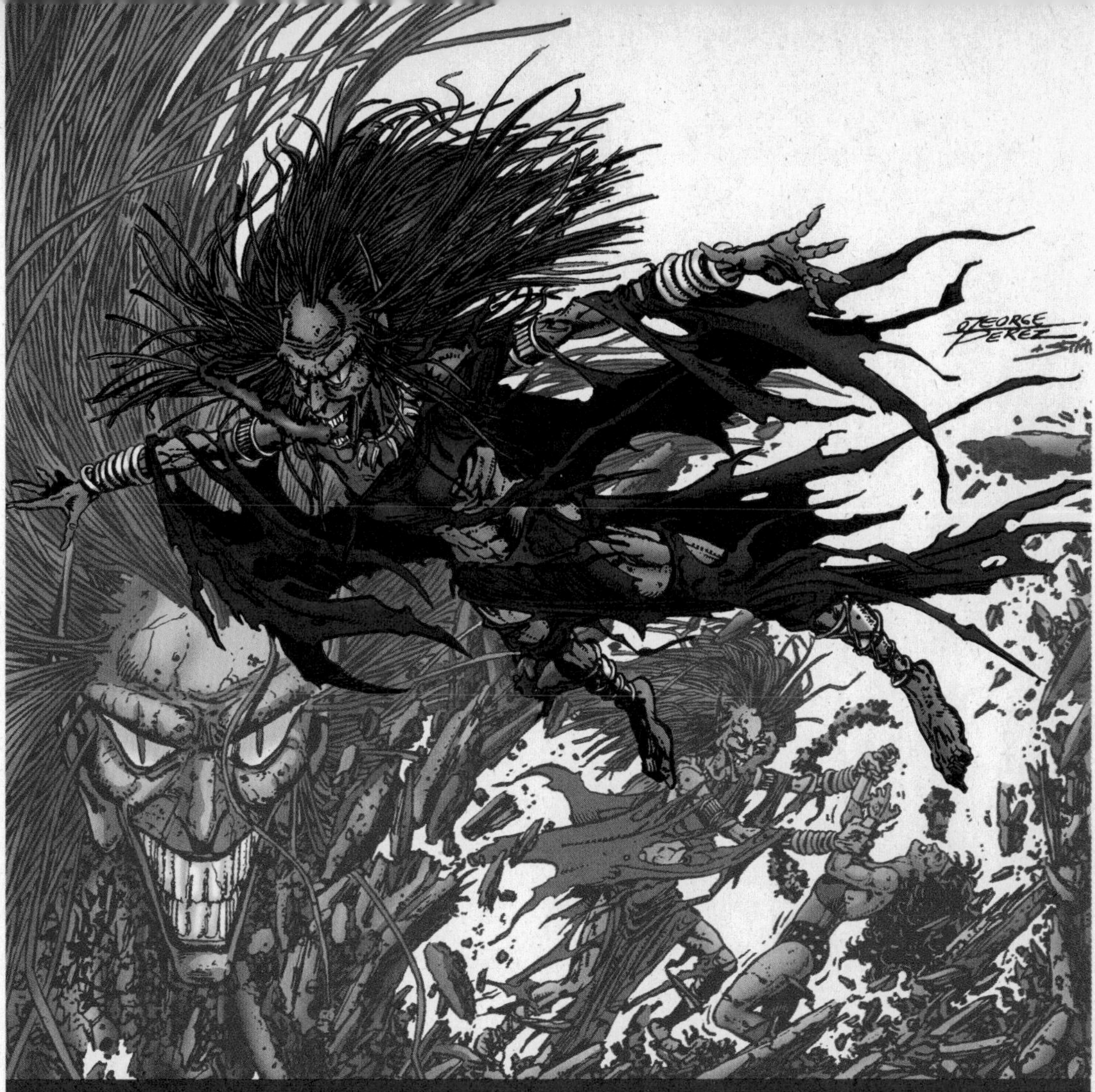

DECAY

TEXT: LEN WEIN
ART: GEORGE PÉREZ
COLOR: TOM SMITH

ALTER EGO: None
OCCUPATION: Demon of Destruction
MARITAL STATUS: Inapplicable
KNOWN RELATIVES: Medusa (mother)
GROUP AFFILIATION: The Gorgons
BASE OF OPERATIONS: Cavern of the Gorgons
FIRST APPEARANCE: WONDER WOMAN (second series) #3
HEIGHT: 6' 2" **WEIGHT:** 95 pounds **EYES:** Red **HAIR:** Violet

HISTORY

When the Princess Diana was sent to Man's World to put an end to the mad schemes of the War-God Ares, the War-God's son Phobos decided to gain favor in his father's eyes by destroying the Amazon Princess. To this end, Phobos journeyed to the Caverns of the Gorgons, where he drove his smoldering hands straight into the mystical matter that was the Gorgon's seething heart. Using his breath to shape the molten material he'd thus extracted, much as the Princess Diana herself had been molded from humble clay, Phobos created a small statuette, the figure of a woman, which he then had delivered to the Boston home of Professor Julia Kapetelis, who had become Diana's mentor in Man's World.

Late that night, as Julia sought to teach Diana the English language, the statuette came to life, assumed full human size, and set about to destroy Julia's home and the Amazon Princess.

The battle between the Princess Diana and the creature who now called herself Decay spread across the entire city of Boston, with Decay leaving a swath of ruin and destruction behind her as they fought. Diana herself almost perished at Decay's hand, until the Amazon finally entangled Decay in the strands of her golden lasso. Since Diana's lasso had been forged from the girdle of the goddess Gaea, she who is mother to all Earth, the lasso possessed the power of constant renewal. Thus, the golden strands continued to pour life into Decay, who was the embodiment of death, until that power consumed her. Screaming in frustrated rage, Decay quite literally exploded from the strain, her lifeless carcass returning once more to the vile dust that had spawned her.

POWERS

Though a superior hand-to-hand combatant, the creature known as Decay rarely had to rely on her abilities since her very touch would immediately age and wither anyone with whom she came into contact, ultimately causing death. Equally deadly was Decay's breath, which would cause whatever it touched to crumble to dust.

Decay also possessed the power of flight and limited invulnerability.

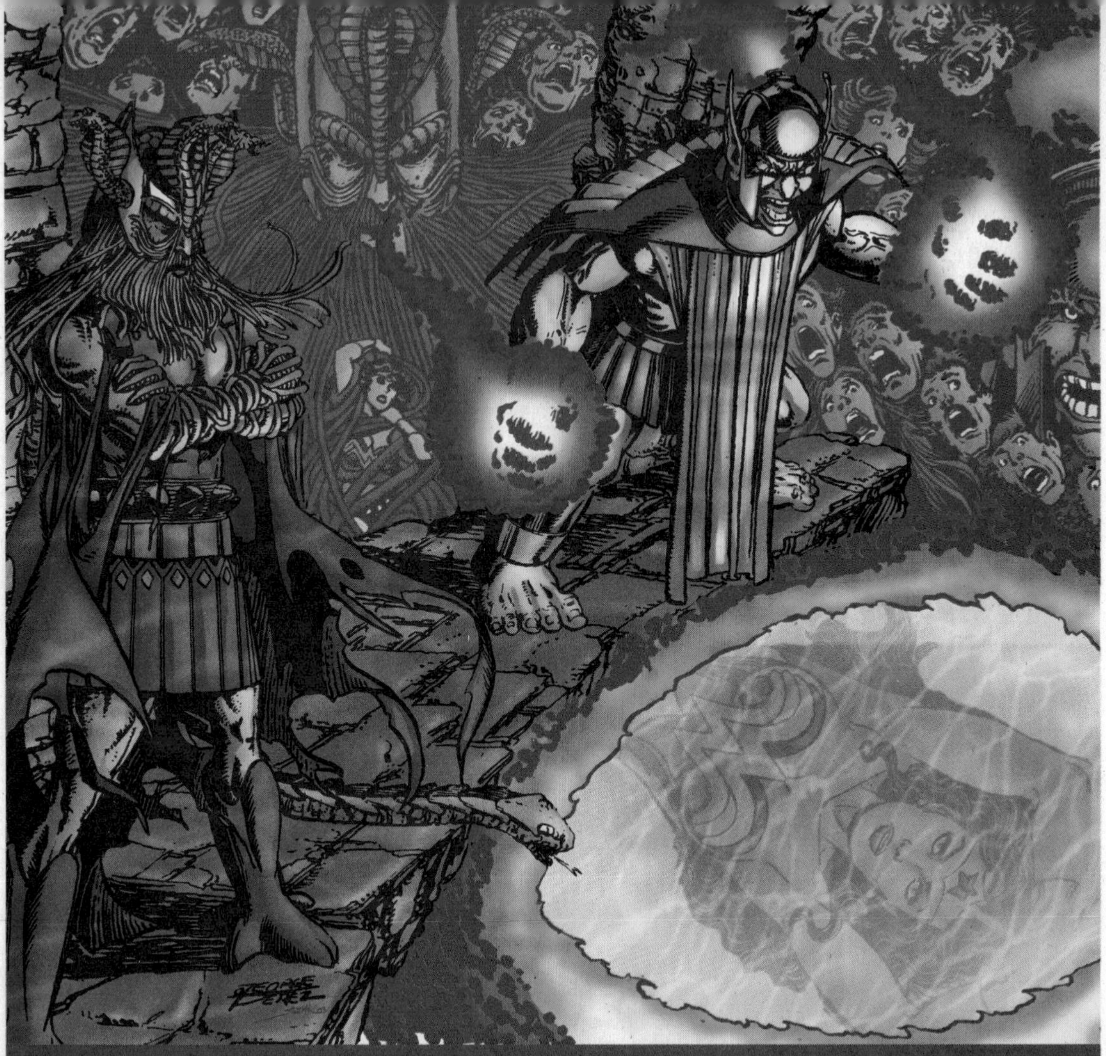

DEIMOS & PHOBOS

TEXT: LEN WEIN
ART: GEORGE PÉREZ
COLOR: TOM SMITH

FULL NAMES: Deimos & Phobos **OCCUPATION:** (Deimos) God of Terror, (Phobos) God of Fear
MARITAL STATUS: Single
KNOWN RELATIVES: Ares (father), Aphrodite (mother), Harmonia (sister), Zeus (grandfather), Hera (grandmother), Hephaestus (uncle). They are brothers.
GROUP AFFILIATION: Olympian Gods **BASE OF OPERATIONS:** the Netherworld
FIRST APPEARANCE: WONDER WOMAN (second series) #2
HEIGHT: (Deimos) 6' 6", (Phobos) 7' 7" **WEIGHT:** (Deimos) 301 pounds, (Phobos) 459 pounds
EYES: Red **HAIR:** (Deimos) Serpentine, (Phobos) Flaming Red

HISTORY

Born of the brief union of the War-God Ares with the goddess Aphrodite, Deimos and Phobos dwelt principally in the Netherworld, from which they intended to aid their father in the destruction of the Earth, and thus of the hated Amazons, as well as the other Olympian Gods.

At first, Phobos attempted to slay the Amazon Princess Diana, who had been chosen by combat and the Gods to oppose Ares' plans, by bringing to life the creature called Decay, but the Amazon Princess destroyed Decay after a savage battle across the city of Boston.

At length, the Princess Diana, accompanied by four humans who had befriended her, brought the battle against Ares to the Netherworld itself. Here she confronted Deimos and Phobos, and a struggle to the death began. During the course of the battle, Deimos attempted to poison the Amazon with the venomous bite of his serpentine hair, venom that would fill the Princess Diana with blind, unreasoning terror.

In the last seconds before she could succumb to the venom, Diana hurled her razor-sharp tiara at the gloating Deimos, and decapitated him. The cowardly Phobos, fearing for his own life, fled into the darkness, swearing vengeance on the Amazon Princess. Phobos' current whereabouts remain unknown.

POWERS

As the God of Terror, Deimos was a master schemer, delighting to plot elaborate plans to destroy his enemies. His serpentine hair was actually alive, each strand an emerald snake whose venom would cause overwhelming terror in its victim.

As the God of Fear, Phobos is capable of manifesting into physical form the darkest fears of those he opposes — manifestations that can slay their victims. He is possessed of such power that his hands and the topknot of his hair are constantly smoldering. Though essentially invulnerable, Phobos is at heart a coward, preferring to flee from mortal combat.

Neither Deimos or Phobos was a particularly skilled hand-to-hand combatant.